For Reference

Not to be taken

from this library

Reference Library of

BLACK

AMERICA

Reference Library of

BLACK AMERICA

VOLUME

I

Edited by

Jessie Carney Smith
Joseph M. Palmisano

Distributed exclusively by:

African American Publications
Proteus Enterprises

Staff

Jessie Carney Smith and Joseph M. Palmisano, *Editors*
Patrick J. Politano, *Assistant Editor*
William Harmer, Ashyia N. Henderson, Brian J. Koski, Gloria Lam, Jeffrey Lehman, Allison McClintic Marion, Mark F. Mikula, David G. Oblender, Rebecca Parks, Shirelle Phelps, Kathleen Romig, *Contributing Staff*
Linda S. Hubbard, *Managing Editor, Multicultural Team*

Maria Franklin, *Permissions Manager*
Margaret Chamberlain, *Permissions Specialist*
Keasha Jack-Lyles and Shalice Shah-Caldwell, *Permissions Associates*

Justine H. Carson, *Manager, Vocabulary Development and Indexer*
Rebecca Abbott Forgette, *Indexing Specialist*

Mary Beth Trimper, *Production Director*
Wendy Blurton, *Senior Buyer*
Cynthia Baldwin, *Product Design Manager*
Gary Popiela, *Graphic Artist*
Barbara J. Yarrow, *Imaging/Multimedia Manager*
Randy Bassett, *Image Database Supervisor*
Pamela A. Reed, *Imaging Coordinator*
Robert Duncan, *Imaging Specialist*
Christine O'Bryan, *Desktop Publisher*

Victoria B. Cariappa, *Research Manager*
Barbara McNeil, *Research Specialists*
Patricia Tsune Ballard, *Research Associate*

Copyright © 2000
Gale Group, Inc.
27500 Drake Road
Farmington Hills, MI 48331-3535

ISBN 0-7876-4363-7 (set)
ISBN 0-7876-4364-5 (volume 1)
ISBN 0-7876-4365-3 (volume 2)
ISBN 0-7876-4366-1 (volume 3)
ISBN 0-7876-4367-X (volume 4)
ISBN 0-7876-4368-8 (volume 5)

Printed in the United States of America

10 9 8 7 6 5 4 3 2 1

Advisory Board

Contributors

Donald F. Amerman, Jr.
Editorial Consultant, A & M Editorial Services

Stephen W. Angell
Associate Professor of Religion, Florida A & M University

Calvert Bean
Associate Editor, *International Dictionary of Black Composers*

Lean'tin Laverne Bracks
Editorial Consultant

Rose M. Brewer
Morse Alumni Distinguished Teaching Professor of Afro-American and African Studies, University of Minnesota-Minneapolis

Christopher A. Brooks
Professor of African American Studies, Virginia Commonwealth University

Paulette Coleman
General Officer, African Methodist Episcopal Church

DeWitt S. Dykes, Jr.
Professor of History, Oakland University

James Gallert
Vice President, Jazz Alliance of Michigan

Joseph Guy
Jazz and Touring Coordinator, Southern Arts Federation

Tracey Desirnaí Hicks
Membership and Volunteer Services Coordinator,
Charles H. Wright Museum of African American History

Phyllis J. Jackson
Assistant Professor of Art and Art History, Pomona College

Kristine Krapp
Editor, *Notable Black American Scientists* and *Black Firsts in Science and Technology*

Kevin C. Kretschmer
Reference Librarian, Blazer Library, Kentucky State University

Bernadette Meier
Editorial Consultant

Hollis F. Price, Jr.
Professor of Economics, Tennessee State University

Guthrie P. Ramsey Jr.
Assistant Professor of Music, University of Pennsylvania

Houston B. Roberson
Assistant Professor of History, University of the South

Gil L. Robertson IV
Founder, The Robertson Treatment

Audrey Y. Williams
Professor of Management, Zicklin School of Business, Baruch College, City University of New York

Raymond A. Winbush
Director, Race Relations Institute, Fisk University
Benjamin Hooks Professor of Social Justice, Fisk University

Michael D. Woodard
President, Woodard & Associates

Linda T. Wynn
Assistant Director of State Programs, Tennessee Historical Commission
Adjunct Professor, Department of History, Fisk University

Contents

Introduction

The *Reference Library of Black America* is based on the eighth edition of *The African American Alamanac*, first published in 1967 as *The Negro Almanac* and subsequently cited by *Library Journal*, in conjunction with the American Library Association, as "Outstanding Reference Source." It offers a comprehensive and accurate survey of black culture in the United States and around the world.

New Features in This Edition

All material was extensively reviewed by the editors and a board of prominent advisors and, where appropriate, updated and/or expanded; in many instances completely new topics were added to the existing essays. As a result, most chapters have been rewritten and focus on issues facing African Americans as we enter a new millenium.

African American women and their significant contributions have been given greater emphasis in the reference work than ever before. Examples of this expanded coverage include: speeches and writings of Sojourner Truth, Ida B. Wells-Barnett, Mary McLeod Bethune, and Barbara Jordan (Chapter 3); genetic evidence of a link between Sally Hemings and Thomas Jefferson (Chapter 6); biographical profiles of historic female activists of the black nationalist and civil rights movements (Chapters 8 and 9); female leadership in African American churches (Chapter 17); prominent women artists in the musical fields of gospel, blues, and jazz (Chapters 23, 24, and 25); and the increasing presence of female athletes in professional sports (Chapter 28).

The tremendous impact of the Internet is also reflected in the content of the *Reference Library of Black America*. Many entry listings in such sections as "National Organizations" (Chapter 9); "Historically and Predominantly African American Colleges and Universities" and "Research Institutions" (Chapter 16); "African American Media in Cyberspace" and "Magazines and Journals" (Chapter 19); "Museums and Galleries Exhibiting African American Art" (Chapter 26); and "Popular African American Internet Sites" (Chapter 27) now include website addresses. In addition, the promising effects of information technology on the African American community are discussed in "Entrepreneurship" (Chapter 14), "Media" (Chapter 19), and "Science and Technology" (Chapter 27).

Important African American towns and settlements are described for the first time in "African American Landmarks" (Chapter 4) and "Population" (Chapter 12). Included are listings of such historic sites as Nicodemus, Kansas; Boley, Oklahoma; the Sea Islands in South Carolina and Georgia; and Eatonville, Florida. In addition, expanded, up-to-date profiles of African and Western Hemisphere nations are offered in "Africa and the Black Diaspora" (Chapter 5).

Two new chapters have been added that significantly enhance the broad coverage of the *Reference Library of Black America*:

- "Film and Television" (Chapter 20) offers an overview of African Americans in the film and television industries, a selected filmography of more than two hundred films and documentaries depicting African American themes and issues, and biographical profiles of actors, filmmakers, and industry executives both current and historical.

- "Sacred Music Traditions" (Chapter 23) provides an essay that thoroughly describes the important periods and styles of African American sacred music, as well as concise biographical profiles of notable sacred music composers, musicians, and singers.

Approximately thirty new statistical charts compiled by the Bureau of the Census for the *Statistical Abstract of the United States* appear in pertinent chapters. Finally, a completely revised name and keyword index provides improved access to the contents of the *Reference Library of Black America.*

Content and Arrangement

Information in this edition of the *Reference Library of Black America* appears in 29 subject chapters. Many chapters open with an essay focusing on historical developments or the contributions of African Americans to the subject area, followed by concise biographical profiles of selected individuals. Although the listees featured here represent only a small portion of the African American community, they embody excellence and diversity in their respective fields of endeavor. Where an individual has made a significant contribution in more than one area, his or her biographical profile appears in the subject area for which he or she is best known.

Nearly seven hundred photographs, illustrations, maps, and statistical charts aid the reader in understanding the topics and people covered in the reference work. An expanded appendix contains the names and contributions of African American recipients of selected awards and honors.

Chronology

1492 • Blacks are among the first explorers to the New World. Pedro Alonzo Niño, identified by some scholars as a black man, arrives with Christopher Columbus.

1501 • The Spanish throne officially approves the use of African slaves in the New World.

1502 • Portugal brings its first shipload of African slaves to the Western Hemisphere, selling them in what is now Latin America.

1513 • Cuba
Spain authorizes the use of African slaves in Cuba. Thirty black men accompany Balboa when he discovers the Pacific Ocean.

1526 • South Carolina
The first group of Africans to set foot on what is now the United States are brought by a Spanish explorer to South Carolina to erect a settlement. However, they soon flee to the interior and settle with Native Americans.

1538 • Estevanico, a black explorer, leads an expedition from Mexico into what is now Arizona and New Mexico.

1562 • Britain enters the slave trade when John Hawkins sells a large cargo of African slaves to Spanish planters.

1600 • Historical records indicate that by the year 1600 over 900,000 slaves have been brought to Latin America. In the next century, 2,750,000 are added to that total. Slave revolts in the sixteenth century are reported in Hispaniola, Puerto Rico, Panama, Cuba, and Mexico.

1618 • Gambia
The Gambian government grants monopolies to a group of companies established for the purpose of slave trading.

1619, August • Jamestown, Virginia
Twenty African indentured servants arrive aboard a Dutch vessel. Most indentured servants are released after serving one term, usually seven years in duration, and are allowed to own property and participate in political affairs. The arrival of these indentured servants is the precursor of active slave trade in the English colonies.

1624 • West Indies
The Dutch, who had entered the slave trade in 1621 with the formation of the Dutch West Indies Company, import Africans to serve on Hudson Valley farms.

1629 • Connecticut
African slaves are imported into Connecticut (1629), Maryland and Massachusetts (1634), and New Amsterdam (1637).

1630 • Massachusetts
A law protecting slaves from abusive owners is enacted.

1639 • Salem, Massachusetts
New England enters the slave trade when Captain William Pierce sails to the West Indies and purchases a group of African slaves.

1640 • West Indies
The increasing use of sugar as a cash crop leads to a rapid rise in the African slave population in the West Indies. However, growth in mainland English colonies remains slow. The African slave population in Barbados, for example, grows from a few hundred in 1640 to 6,000 in 1645. In contrast, there are only three hundred slaves in Virginia in 1649 and only 2,000 by 1671.

1640 • Connecticut
Punitive fugitive laws applying to both indentured ser-

The Portuguese/Dutch fortress "El Mina" is where innumerable captured Africans were gathered for the European slave trade (The Granger Collection Ltd.).

vants and slaves are enacted in Connecticut, Maryland, New Jersey, South Carolina, and Virginia. The Virginia law, passed in 1642, penalizes violators twenty pounds of tobacco for each night of refuge granted to a fugitive slave. Slaves are branded after a second escape attempt.

1641 • Massachusetts
Massachusetts becomes the first colony to legalize slavery, adding a modification that forbids capture by "unjust violence." This provision was subsequently adopted by all of the New England colonies.

1643 • The groundwork is laid for eighteenth and nineteenth century fugitive slave laws in the United States when an intercolonial agreement of the New England Confederation declares that mere certification by a magistrate is sufficient evidence to convict a runaway slave.

1651 • North Hampton, Virginia
Anthony Johnson, a black man, imports five servants and qualifies to receive a 200-acre land grant along the Puwgoteague River in Virginia. Others soon join Johnson and attempt to launch an independent African community. At its height, the settlement has 12 African homesteads with sizable holdings.

1662 • Virginia
The colony passes a law which provides that the status of children, slave or free, be determined by the lineage of the mother.

1663 • Maryland
Settlers pass a law stipulating that all imported Africans are to be given the status of slaves. Free white women who marry black slaves are also considered slaves during the lives of their spouses; children of such unions are also to be classified as slaves. In 1681, a law is passed which stipulates that children born from a union of a white servant woman and an African are free citizens.

1670 • Virginia
Voting rights are denied to recently freed slaves and indentured servants. All non-Christians imported to the territory "by shipping" are to be slaves for life. However, slaves who enter Virginia by land route are to serve until the age of thirty if they are children and for 12

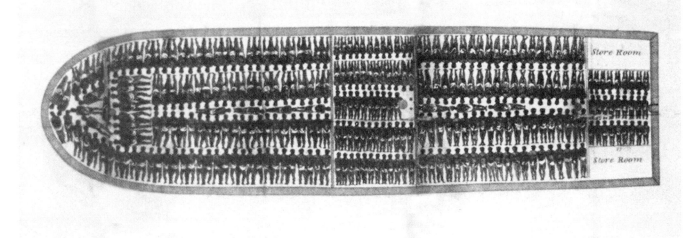

Diagram of the British slave ship *Brookes* illustrating the regulated stowing of African slaves (The Library of Congress).

years if they are adults when their period of servitude commences.

1672 • Virginia
A law is enacted providing for a bounty on the heads of Maroons—black fugitives who form communities in the mountains, swamps, and forests of Southern colonies. Many members of Maroon communities attack towns and plantations.

1685 • French West Indies
The French *code noir* is enacted. The code requires religious instruction for African slaves, permits intermarriage, outlaws working of slaves on Sundays and holidays, but forbids emancipation of mulatto children who have reached the age of 21 if their mothers are still enslaved. However, the code is largely ignored by the French settlers.

1688 • Germantown, Pennsylvania
Mennonites sign an anti-slavery resolution, the first formal protest against slavery in the Western Hemisphere. In 1696, Quakers importing slaves are threatened with expulsion from the society.

1700 • The population of black slaves in the English colonies is estimated at 28,000. Approximately 23,000 of these slaves reside in the South.

1704 • New York City, New York
Elias Neau, a French immigrant, opens a "catechism school" for slaves.

1705 • Virginia
The Virginia assembly declares that "no Negro, mulatto,

or Indian shall presume to take upon him, act in or exercise any office, ecclesiastic, civil or military." African Americans are forbidden to serve as witnesses in court cases and are condemned to lifelong servitude, unless they have been either Christians in their native land or free men in a Christian country.

1711 • Pennsylvania
The colonial legislature, after receiving intense pressure from the Mennonite and Quaker communities, outlaws slavery in the Pennsylvania colony but is overruled by the British Crown.

1712, April 6 • New York City, New York
The Maiden Lane slave revolt claims the lives of nine whites and results in the execution of twenty-one slaves. Six others commit suicide.

1723 • Virginia
The colony of Virginia enacts laws to limit the rights of freed African Americans. Free African Americans are denied the right to vote and forbidden to carry weapons of any sort.

1739 • South Carolina
Three slave revolts occur, resulting in the deaths of 51 whites and many more slaves. One of the insurrections results in the death of 30 whites.

1740 • South Carolina
The South Carolina colony passes a slave code which forbids slaves from raising livestock, provides that any animals owned by slaves be forfeited, and imposes severe penalties on slaves who make "false appeals" to

Africans also participated in the European slave trade by capturing and selling fellow Africans for goods and weapons (The Granger Collection Ltd.).

the governor on the grounds that they have been placed in bondage illegally.

1744 • Virginia

The colony of Virginia amends its 1705 law declaring that African Americans cannot serve as witnesses in court cases; it decides, instead, to admit "any free Negro, mulatto, or Indian being a Christian," as a witness in a criminal or civil suit involving another African American, mulatto, or Indian.

1746 • Deerfield, Massachusetts

Slave poet Lucy Terry writes *Bars Fight*, a commemorative poem recreating the Deerfield Massacre. Terry, generally considered the first African American poet in America, later tries unsuccessfully to convince the board of trustees at Williams College to admit her son to the school.

1747 • South Carolina

The South Carolina assembly commends slaves for demonstrating "great faithfulness and courage in repelling attacks of His Majesty's enemies." It then makes provisions for the utilization of African American recruits in the event of danger or emergency.

1749 • Georgia

Prohibitions on the importation of African slaves are approved in a law which also attempts to protect slaves from cruel treatment and from being hired out.

1750 •

The slave population in the English colonies reaches 236,400, with over 206,000 of the total living south of Pennsylvania. Slaves comprise about twenty percent of the population in the colonies.

1752 • Mount Vernon, Virginia

George Washington acquires his estate at Mount Vernon. Prior to Washington's arrival, there are 18 slaves at Mount Vernon. This number eventually swells to 200. Records indicate that while Washington was concerned for the physical welfare of slaves, he also utilized their services on many occasions and did not advocate their freedom from servitude.

1754 • Philadelphia, Pennsylvania

A Quaker, John Woolman, publishes *Some Considera-*

tions On the Keeping Of Negroes, an exhortation to fellow members of the Society of Friends to consider emancipating their slaves on grounds of morality. Three years later, some Quakers take legal action against members who ignore this plea.

1760 • New York City, New York
Jupiter Hammon, an African American poet, publishes *Salvation By Christ With Penitential Cries*.

1767 • Boston, Massachusetts
Phillis Wheatley, a 14-year-old slave, writes *A Poem by Phillis, A Negro Girl, On the Death of Reverend Whitefield*. It is printed in 1770 by the University of Cambridge in New England.

1769 • Virginia
In the Virginia House of Burgesses, Thomas Jefferson unsuccessfully presses for a bill to emancipate African slaves.

1770, March 5 • Boston, Massachusetts
Crispus Attucks is shot and killed during the Boston Massacre, becoming one of the first casualties of the American Revolution.

1770 • Philadelphia, Pennsylvania
Led by Anthony Benezet, the Quakers open a school for African Americans.

1773 • Savannah, Georgia
George Liele and Andrew Bryan organize the first Baptist Church for African Americans in the state.

1774 • The Continental Congress demands elimination of the trans-Atlantic slave trade and economic embargoes on all countries participating in it. Rhode Island enacts a law prohibiting slavery. However, this law does not apply to slaves brought into Rhode Island before 1774.

1775 • Bunker Hill, Massachusetts
Peter Salem, Salem Poor, and other African Americans fight heroically during the Battle of Bunker Hill.

1775 • Germany
Johann Friedrich Blumenbach publishes the first article refuting the theory that blacks are racially inferior. In *On the Natural Variety of Mankind*, Blumenbach asserts that the skulls and brains of African Americans are the same as those of Europeans. Blumenbach's paper serves as a counter to the views of Voltaire, Hume, and Linne that African Americans are akin to apes.

Thomas Jefferson (The Library of Congress)

1775 • Philadelphia, Pennsylvania
The Continental Congress bars African Americans from serving in the army during the American Revolution.

1775 • Philadelphia, Pennsylvania
The first abolitionist society in the United States is organized.

1775 • Virginia
Lord Dunmore, British governor of Virginia, offers freedom to all male slaves who join the loyalist forces. General George Washington, originally opposed to the enlistment of African Americans, is alarmed by the response to the Dunmore proclamation and orders recruiting officers to accept free African Americans for service.

1776 • Trenton, New Jersey
Two African Americans, Prince Whipple and Oliver Cromwell, cross the Delaware with George Washington en route to an attack on the British and their Hessian mercenaries in Trenton, New Jersey.

1776 • Philadelphia, Pennsylvania
The amended form of the Declaration of Independence,

which omits Thomas Jefferson's proposal denouncing slavery, is adopted.

1776 • Long Island, New York
French general Marquis de Lafayette praises African American soldiers for successfully assisting Washington's retreat to Long Island. African Americans also help assist Washington's retreat at Trenton and Princeton.

1777 • Vermont
Vermont becomes the first state to abolish slavery.

1778
An African American battalion consisting of three hundred former slaves is formed. They are compensated on a par with their white comrades-in-arms and promised freedom after the war. The battalion kills 1,000 Hessians and takes part in a battle at Ponts Bridge in New York.

1779 • New York
Alexander Hamilton endorses the plan of South Carolina's Henry Laurens to use slaves as soldiers in the South. "I have not the least doubt that the Negroes will make very excellent soldiers," says Hamilton, ". . . .for their natural faculties are as good as ours." Hamilton reminds the Continental Congress that the British will make use of African Americans if the Americans do not. In Hamilton's words: "The best way to counteract the temptations they will hold out, will be to offer them ourselves."

1780 • Pennsylvania
The Pennsylvania assembly enacts a law providing for the gradual emancipation of slaves.

1782 • Virginia
Thomas Jefferson's *Notes on the State of Virginia* exhibits a curious mixture of perception and naivete with regard to African Americans. On the one hand, Jefferson believes that "the whole commerce between master and slave is a perpetual exercise of the most boisterous passions," On the other hand, he invents the fantasy that African American "griefs are transient."

1783 • Massachusetts
Slavery in the Commonwealth is abolished by the Massachusetts Supreme Court; African Americans in taxable categories are granted suffrage.

1783
At the end of the American Revolution, some 10,000 African Americans have served in the continental armies—5,000 as regular soldiers.

1787 • New York City, New York
The African Free School is opened by the New York Manumission Society.

1787
Congress passes the Northwest Ordinance which forbids the extension of slavery into this area.

1787 • Philadelphia, Pennsylvania
African American preachers Richard Allen and Absalom Jones organize the Free African Society.

1787
The Constitution of the United States is adopted. In it, importation of slaves cannot be prohibited before 1808, and five slaves are considered the equivalent of three free men in congressional apportionment.

1790
According to the first census, there are 757,000 African Americans in the United States, comprising 19 percent of the total population. Nine percent of African Americans are free.

1790 • Dominican Republic
African Americans comprise seven-eighths of the islands' 529,000 inhabitants. Less than three percent are free. Mulattoes in French Santo Domingo own ten percent of the slaves and land.

1790 • Chicago, Illinois
Jean Baptiste Pointe du Sable, the son of a French mariner and an African slave mother, establishes the first permanent settlement at what is to become the city of Chicago.

1791 • Washington, DC
On the recommendation of Thomas Jefferson, Benjamin Banneker—astronomer, inventor, mathematician, and gazetteer—is appointed to serve as a member of the commission charged with laying out plans for the city of Washington.

1791 • Haiti
Toussaint L'Ouverture, a self-educated slave, leads an unsuccessful uprising.

1791 • Louisiana
Twenty-three slaves are hanged and three white sympathizers deported, following suppression of a slave revolt.

1791 • Philadelphia, Pennsylvania
Congress excludes African Americans and Indians from serving in peacetime militias.

1793 • Mulberry Grove, Georgia
Eli Whitney patents the cotton gin, which strengthens slavery by vastly increasing profits in cotton growing.

Slaves working on a cotton plantation in Beaufort, South Carolina (The Library of Congress).

1793 • Philadelphia, Pennsylvania
Congress passes the Fugitive Slave Act, which makes it a criminal offense to harbor a slave or prevent his or her arrest.

1793 • Virginia
The state of Virginia passes a law which forbids free African Americans from entering the state.

1794 • Philadelphia, Pennsylvania
The First African Church of St. Thomas, the first African American Episcopal Congregation in the United States, is dedicated. This same year, Richard Allen organizes the Bethel Church, an African American Methodist Episcopal Church.

1795 • Louisiana
Several slave uprisings are suppressed with some fifty African Americans killed and executed.

1796 • Tennessee
Tennessee is admitted to the Union as a slave state. The state's constitution, however, does not deny suffrage to free African Americans.

1797 • North Carolina
Congress refuses to accept the first recorded anti-slavery petition seeking redress against a North Carolina law which requires that slaves, although freed by their Quaker masters, be returned to the state and to their former condition.

1798 • Washington, DC
Secretary of the Navy Stoddert forbids the deployment of African American sailors on man-of-war ships, in violation of a nonracial enlistment policy which had been operative in the U.S. Navy for many years. Nevertheless, a few African Americans slip past the ban including William Brown, who serves as a "powder monkey" on the *Constellation* and George Diggs, quartermaster of the schooner *Experiment*.

1799 • Mount Vernon, Virginia
George Washington dies. His last will and testament declares: "It is my will and desire that all the slaves which I hold in my right, shall receive their freedom."

1800 • Richmond, Virginia
Gabriel Prosser, a slave insurrectionist, plans to lead thousands of slaves in an attack on Richmond. The plan

fails and Prosser and 15 of his followers are arrested, tried, and hanged.

1800 • Washington, DC
By a vote of 85–1, Congress rejects a petition by free African Americans in Philadelphia to gradually end slavery in the United States.

1803 • South Carolina
The state legislature, which had been trying to limit importation of slaves, reopens the slave trade with Latin America and the West Indies.

1804 • New Jersey
New Jersey passes an emancipation law. All states north of the Mason-Dixon Line now have laws forbidding slavery or providing for its gradual elimination.

1804 • Ohio
The legislature enacts the first of a group of laws restricting the rights and movements of African Americans. Other western states soon follow suit. Illinois, Indiana, and Oregon later have anti-immigration clauses in their state constitutions.

1807 • New Jersey
The state alters its 1776 constitution by limiting the vote to free white males.

1808, January 1 • Congress bars the importation of any new slaves into the territory of the United States (effective January 1, 1808). The law is widely ignored.

1808 • The 1807 ban on the importation of slaves is scheduled to take effect. There are one million slaves in the country.

1810 • Louisiana
Courts declare in *Adelle v. Beauregard* that an African American is free unless it is otherwise proven.

1811 • Delaware
The state forbids the immigration of free African Americans and declares that any native-born free African American who has lived outside of Delaware for more than six months will be deemed a nonresident.

1811 • Louisiana
U.S. troops suppress a slave uprising in two parishes (counties) of Louisiana, some 35 miles from New Orleans. The revolt is led by Charles Deslands. Some one hundred slaves are killed or executed.

1811 • Westport, Connecticut
Paul Cuffe, son of African American and Indian parents

and later a wealthy shipbuilder, sails with a small group of African Americans to Sierra Leone to underscore his advocacy of an African American return to Africa.

1812 • Louisiana
Louisiana is admitted to the Union as a slave state. State law enables freed men to serve in the state militia.

1815 • Fort Blount, Florida
African Americans and Creek Indians capture Fort Blount from Seminoles and use it as a haven for escaped slaves and a base for attacks on slave owners. An American army detachment eventually recaptures the fort.

1816 • Baltimore, Maryland
Bethel Charity School is founded by Daniel Coker, an African American.

1816 • Louisiana
State laws are enacted which prohibit slaves from testifying against whites and free blacks, except in cases involving slave uprisings.

1816 • New Orleans, Louisiana
James P. Beckwourth, an African American and one of the great explorers of the nineteenth century, signs on as a scout for General William Henry Ashley's Rocky Mountain expedition.

1816 • Philadelphia, Pennsylvania
The African Methodist Episcopal Church is organized.

1816 • Virginia
A slave rebellion led by George Boxley, a white man, fails.

1816 • Washington, DC
The American Colonization Society, which seeks to transport free African Americans to Africa, is organized. Protest meetings are subsequently held by many free African Americans in opposition to the society's efforts.

1817 • Mississippi
Mississippi enters the union as a slave state. New York passes a gradual slavery abolition act.

1818 • Connecticut
African Americans are denied the right to vote in Connecticut.

1818 • Philadelphia, Pennsylvania
Free African Americans form the Pennsylvania Augustine Society "for the education of people of colour."

A group of Africans disembarking from a slave ship in Jamestown, Virginia (The Library of Congress).

1819 • Alabama
Alabama enters the Union as a slave state, although its constitution provides the legislature with the power to abolish slavery and compensate slave owners. Other measures include jury trials for slaves accused of crimes above petty larceny and penalties for malicious killing of slaves.

1820 • Liberia
The *Mayflower of Liberia* sails for the West African nation of Sierra Leone with 86 African Americans aboard.

1820, March 3 • The Missouri Compromise is enacted. It provides for Missouri's entry into the Union as a slave state and Maine's entry as a free state. There are thus 12 slave and 12 free states in the United States. All territory north of latitude 36°30' is declared free; all territory south of that line is open to slavery.

1821 • New York City, New York
The African Methodist Episcopal Zion Church is founded with James Varick as its first bishop.

1821 • New York
The state constitutional convention alters the voting requirements of 1777 by establishing higher property and longer residence requirements for African Americans.

1822 • Charleston, South Carolina
The Denmark Vesey conspiracy, one of the most elaborate slave revolts on record, fails. Vesey, a sailor and carpenter, and 36 collaborators are hanged, an additional 130 blacks and four whites are arrested, and stricter controls are imposed on free African Americans and slaves. Following this insurrection, slave states adopt laws to further restrict the mobility of African Americans.

1822 • Rhode Island
Free African Americans are denied the right to vote in Rhode Island.

1822 • Liberia
Liberia is founded by African Americans with the aid of the American Colonization Society.

1823 • Mississippi
A law is enacted in Mississippi which prohibits the teaching of reading and writing to African Americans and meetings of more than five slaves or free African Americans.

1824 • As the United States moves toward universal male suffrage, more states in the North and West as well as the South move to deny the vote to African Americans. Illinois, Indiana, Iowa, and Michigan require African Americans to post bond in guarantee of good behavior.

1825 • Maryland
Josiah Henson leads a group of slaves to freedom in Kentucky. Henson later crosses the border into Ontario and becomes leader of a community of former slaves.

1826 • Virginia
Thomas Jefferson dies. His will stipulates that only five of his many slaves should be freed. The remainder are bequeathed to his heirs.

1827, March 16 • New York City, New York
Freedom's Journal, the first African American newspaper, begins publication.

1827, July 4 • New York
Slavery is abolished in New York.

1828 • Bennington, Vermont
William Lloyd Garrison, a journalist and reformer, writes his first anti-slavery article in the *National Philanthropist.*

1829 • Boston, Massachusetts
David Walker, a free African American, publishes the anti-slavery pamphlet *An Appeal to the Colored People of the World*, which is distributed throughout the country and arouses a furor among slaveholders.

1829 • Cincinnati, Ohio
After a riot in which whites attack black residents in Cincinnati and loot and burn their homes, 1,200 blacks flee to Canada.

1829 • Philadelphia
The first National Negro Convention convenes.

1830 • North Carolina
Slavemasters, in compliance with a state law, transfer control of more than four hundred slaves to Quaker residents of North Carolina. The Quakers retain theoretical ownership, but allow slaves virtual freedom until they can afford to transport them to free states.

1830 • Philadelphia, Pennsylvania
The first National Negro Convention meets on September 20 at Philadelphia's Bethel Church. The four-day convention launches a church-affiliated program to improve the social status of African Americans.

1830 • In an attempt to counter the increasing strength of the abolitionist movement, a number of states pass laws restricting the education, legal safeguards, and citizenship rights of slaves and free African Americans. Many states require the deportation of free African Americans; slave codes are enforced more strictly and the number of slave emancipations decline.

1830 • The U.S. Census Bureau reports that 3,777 African American heads of families own slaves, mostly in Louisiana, Maryland, Virginia, North Carolina, and South Carolina.

1831, January 1 • Boston, Massachusetts
The Liberator, an abolitionist newspaper, is founded by William Lloyd Garrison.

1831 • Philadelphia, Pennsylvania
The first Annual Convention of the People of Color meets at Wesleyan Church, where delegates from five states resolve to study African American conditions, explore settlement possibilities in Canada, and raise money for an industrial college in New Haven. Delegates oppose the American Colonization Society and recommend annual meetings.

1831, August • Southampton County, Virginia
Nat Turner leads the biggest slave rebellion in history. Some sixty whites are killed and the entire South is thrown into panic. Turner is captured on October 30 and hanged in Jerusalem, Virginia, 12 days later.

1831 • Virginia
Thomas Dew, a legislator, proudly refers to Virginia as a "Negro-raising state" for the nation. Between 1830 and 1860, Virginia exports some 300,000 slaves, and South Carolina exports 179,000. The price of slaves increases sharply due to expanding territory in which slaves are permitted and a booming economy in products harvested and processed by slave labor.

1832 • Boston, Massachusetts
The New England Anti-Slavery Society is established by 12 whites at the African Baptist Church on Boston's Beacon Hill.

1833 • Philadelphia, Pennsylvania
Black and white abolitionists organize the American Anti-Slavery Society.

1834 • South Carolina
South Carolina enacts a law prohibiting the teaching of African American children, either free or slave.

William Lloyd Garrison (The Library of Congress)

1834 • Great Britain
Parliament abolishes slavery in the British Empire; seven hundred thousand slaves are liberated at a cost of twenty million British pounds sterling.

1835 • North Carolina
North Carolina, the last Southern state to deny suffrage to African Americans, repeals a voting rights provision of the state constitution. The state also makes it illegal for whites to teach free blacks.

1835 • Washington, DC
President Andrew Jackson seeks to restrict the mailing of abolitionist literature to the South.

1836 • Washington, DC
The U.S. House of Representatives adopts the "gag rule" which prevents congressional action on anti-slavery resolutions or legislation.

1837 • Alton, Illinois
Elijah P. Lovejoy, an abolitionist, is murdered by a mob in Alton after refusing to stop publishing anti-slavery material.

1837 • Boston, Massachusetts
A series of abolitionist works are published including Reverend Hosea Eaton's *A Treatise on the Intellectual Character and Political Condition of the Colored People of the United States.*

1837 • Canada
African Americans are given the right to vote in Canada.

1839 • Montauk, New York
The slaveship *Amistad* is brought into Montauk by a group of Africans who have revolted against their captors. The young African leader, Joseph Cinque, and his followers are defended before the U.S. Supreme Court by former President John Quincy Adams and awarded their freedom.

1839 • Warsaw, New York
The first anti-slavery political organization, the Liberty Party, is founded. African American abolitionists Samuel R. Ward and Henry Highland Garnet are among its leading supporters. The party urges boycotts of Southern crops and products.

1839 • Washington, DC
The U.S. State Department rejects an African American's application for a passport on the grounds that African Americans are not citizens.

1840 • Massachusetts
Massachusetts repeals a law forbidding intermarriage between whites and blacks, mulattoes, or Indians.

1840 • New York
These states institute a law advocating jury trials for fugitive slaves.

1840 • Pope Gregory XVI declares the Roman Catholic Church's opposition to slavery and the slave trade.

1841 • Massachusetts
Frederick Douglass begins his career as a lecturer with the Massachusetts Anti-Slavery Society.

1841 • Throughout the country, increasingly restrictive segregation statutes are enacted. The New York state legislature grants school districts the right to segregate their educational facilities. South Carolina forbids white and black mill hands from looking out the same window. Whites and blacks in Atlanta are required to swear on different Bibles in court.

A depiction of the execution of Captain Ferrer by the mutinying African slaves aboard the *Amistad* in 1839 (The Library of Congress).

1841 • Hampton, Virginia

Slaves aboard the vessel *Creole* revolt en route from Hampton, Virginia, to New Orleans. The slaves overpower the crew and sail the ship to the Bahamas, where they are granted asylum and freedom.

1842 • Boston, Massachusetts

The capture of George Latimer, an escaped slave, precipitates the first of several famous fugitive slave cases straining North-South relations. Latimer is later purchased from his master by Boston abolitionists.

1842 • Rhode Island

African Americans are granted the right to vote in Rhode Island.

1842 • Washington, DC

In the case *Prigg v. Pennsylvania*, the U.S. Supreme Court finds a Pennsylvania anti-kidnapping law unconstitutional, claiming that the authority to regulate the recapture of fugitive slaves was an exclusive power of Congress. The case arises when Edward Prigg is convicted of kidnapping for his recapture of an escaped slave.

1843 • Buffalo, New York

Henry Highland Garnet calls for a slave revolt and general strike while addressing the National Convention of Colored Men. Garnet, Samuel R. Ward, and Charles Ray participate in the Liberty Party convention, becoming the first African Americans to take part in a national political gathering.

1843 • Massachusetts

The Massachusetts and Vermont state legislatures defy the Fugitive Slave Act and forbid state officials from imprisoning or assisting federal authorities in the recapture of escaped slaves.

1843 • Washington, DC

The Webster-Ashburton Treaty, in which Britain and the United States agree to prevent slave ships from reaching the African coast in order to suppress the slave trade there, is approved. No agreement is reached, however, to restrict slave trade within the Western Hemisphere.

1845 • Washington, DC

The U.S. Congress overturns the gag rule of 1836. Texas is admitted to the Union as a slave state.

1847 • New York
The plan of abolitionist Gerritt Smith to parcel up thousands of acres of his land in New York fails to attract prospective African American farmers. Lack of capital among African Americans and the infertility of the land doom the project.

1847 • Rochester, New York
Frederick Douglass publishes the first issue of his abolitionist newspaper *The North Star.*

1847 • St. Louis, Missouri
Dred Scott files suit for his freedom in the Circuit Court of St. Louis.

1848 • Buffalo, New York
The convention of the Free Soil Party is attended by a number of African American abolitionists.

1848 • Virginia
Postmasters are forced to inform police of the arrival of pro-abolition literature and turn it over to authorities for burning.

1849 • Maryland
Harriet Tubman, soon to be a conductor on the Underground Railroad, escapes from slavery. Tubman later returns to the South no less than 19 times to help transport more than three hundred slaves to freedom. In the same year, the Maryland legislature enacts laws to override restrictions on the importation of slaves.

1849 • Maryland
The Maryland Supreme Court establishes the "separate but equal" doctrine in response to a suit brought by Benjamin Roberts to have his daughter admitted to a white school.

1850 • New York
Samuel R. Ward becomes president of the American League of Colored Laborers, a union of skilled African American workers who train African American craftsmen and encourage African American-owned business.

1850 • Washington, DC
The Compromise of 1850, also known as Clay's Compromise, is enacted, strengthening the 1793 Fugitive Slave Act. Federal officers are now offered a fee for the slaves they apprehend. California is admitted to the union as a free state.

1851 • Virginia
New laws require freed slaves to leave Virginia within a year or be enslaved again.

Harriet Tubman (The Library of Congress)

1852 • Akron, Ohio
Sojourner Truth addresses the National Women's Suffrage Convention.

1852 • Boston, Massachusetts
The first edition of Harriet Beecher Stowe's controversial *Uncle Tom's Cabin* is published.

1853 • London
William Wells Brown publishes *Clotel, or The Presi-*

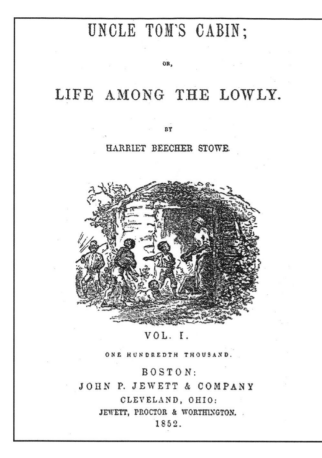

Title page from Harriet Beecher Stowe's *Uncle Tom's Cabin* (The Granger Collection Ltd.).

Anthony Burns (The Library of Congress)

dent's Daughter: A Tale of the Southern States, the first published African American novel.

1853 • Oxford, Pennsylvania
Lincoln University, the first African American college, is founded as Ashmum Institute.

1854 • Boston, Massachusetts
Anthony Burns, a fugitive slave, is arrested and escorted through the streets of Boston by U.S. troops prior to being returned to his master. His master refuses an offer of $1,200 from Boston abolitionists attempting to purchase his freedom.

1854 • The New England Emigration Society is founded to help settle former slaves in Kansas.

1854 • Under the Kansas-Nebraska Act, the territories of Kansas and Nebraska are admitted to the Union without slavery restrictions, in direct contradiction to the provisions of the Missouri Compromise of 1820.

1855 • Maine and Massachusetts
The slavery issue is further polarized by enactment in these states of laws forbidding state officials from aiding the federal government in enforcement of the fugitive slave laws. The Massachusetts legislature abolishes school segregation and integration proceeds without incident.

1855 • New York
The Liberty Party nominates Frederick Douglass for secretary of the U.S. State Department.

1856 • Kansas
Pro-slavery forces sack the town of Lawrence, noted for its abolitionist, free-soil sentiment.

1857 • Maine
Maine, in defiance of the fugitive slave laws, grants freedom and citizenship to people of African descent.

1857, March 6 • Washington, DC
In the *Dred Scott v. Sandford* decision, the U.S. Supreme Court, by a 6–3 vote, opens federal territory to slavery, denies citizenship rights to African Americans, and decrees that slaves do not become free when taken into free territory. The *Dred Scott* decision is followed by a

This advertisement served to encourage African Americans to migrate to the Nicodemus, Kansas settlement (The Library of Congress).

Dred Scott (The Library of Congress)

ruling that African Americans are not entitled to land grants.

1858 • Vicksburg, Mississippi
The Southern Commercial Convention calls for reestablishment of the slave trade, despite opposition from Tennessee and Florida delegations.

1859 • Baltimore, Maryland
Businessmen attending a slaveholders convention complain that free African American laborers and entrepreneurs monopolize some service industries. However, a resolution to expel free African Americans from the state fails.

1859, October 16 • Harpers Ferry, West Virginia
John Brown and his followers seize the U.S. Armory. Two African Americans are killed, two are captured, one escapes. Brown is captured and hanged at Charles Town, West Virginia.

1859 • Washington, DC
In the case of *Ableman v. Booth*, the U.S. Supreme Court upholds the Fugitive Slave Act of 1850. The case arises when Sherman Booth rescues a fugitive slave from a Wisconsin jail and is charged by federal marshals with violating federal law.

1860 • As the Civil War approaches, the United States is sharply divided between pro- and anti-slavery forces. In Virginia, a law stipulates that free African Americans can be sold into slavery for committing imprisonable offenses. Maryland forbids emancipation of slaves. President James Buchanan advocates a constitutional amendment confirming the Fugitive Slave Acts. The Democratic party platform supports the *Dred Scott v. Sandford* decision. The Republican platform opposes the expansion of slavery into the western territories, and Abraham Lincoln, still a moderate on the subject of abolition, is elected president. On December 17, South Carolina secedes from the Union.

1861 • Fort Sumter, South Carolina
Confederate forces attack Fort Sumter, South Carolina, marking the beginning of Civil War. Jefferson Davis is elected president of the Confederate States of America and defends slavery as necessary to "self-preservation."

Abraham Lincoln (Corbis Corporation [Bellevue])

The Confederates conscript slaves for military support jobs. Some Confederate states use free African Americans in their armed forces.

1861 • Washington, DC

The secretary of the U.S. Navy solicits enlistment of African Americans into the Union Army, but most African American offers to help militarily are rejected. Federal policy toward liberated slaves is erratic, depending mostly on the viewpoint of individual commanders. Lincoln moves warily, counter-manding General Freemont's order that slaves of masters who fight against the Union are to be "declared free men."

1862 • New York

The National Freedmen's Relief Association, one of many groups dedicated to assist slaves in making the transition to freedom, is formed. Groups in Philadelphia, Cincinnati, and Chicago are eventually consolidated as the American Freedmen's Aid Commission.

1862 • Washington, DC

The U.S. Congress authorizes the enlistment of African Americans for military service in the Union Army.

1862 • Washington, DC

President Abraham Lincoln proposes a plan for the gradual, compensated emancipation of slaves. Included is a provision to subsidize emigration to Haiti or Liberia. Lincoln's cautious policies are clarified in a letter to Horace Greeley in which he states his paramount objective as saving the Union "not either to save or destroy slavery." However, Lincoln does sign bills abolishing slavery in the territories and freeing slaves of masters disloyal to the United States. Military commanders are forbidden from returning fugitive slaves to owners and, in September, Lincoln issues an ultimatum giving hostile areas until January 1 to cease fighting or lose their slaves.

1863 • Cow Island, Haiti

Lincoln sends a ship to bring back five hundred African American settlers after a colonization attempt in Haiti fails.

1863 • New York

In anti-draft riots, twelve hundred people, mostly African Americans, are killed. The riot is spurred in part by the provision that exemption from military service can be bought for $300, a provision bitterly resented by poor white immigrants who vent their frustrations on blacks.

1863, January 1 • Washington, DC

Lincoln issues the Emancipation Proclamation, declaring freedom for all slaves in rebellious areas.

1864 • Louisiana

The Louisiana legislature, elected under auspices of occupying Union forces, votes to abolish slavery. However, it denies suffrage to African Americans.

1864 • Virginia

Fourteen African American soldiers are awarded the Medal of Honor by President Lincoln.

1865 • Montgomery, Alabama

Jefferson Davis authorizes the enlistment of African Americans into the Confederate Army. However, Davis stipulates that the number of African American troops cannot exceed 25 percent of the able-bodied slave population.

1865 • Appomattox, Virginia

The Confederacy surrenders. Of the 179,000 African Americans who served in the Union Army, 3,000 were killed in battle, 26,000 died from disease, and 14,700

Following the arrival of Union troops, African American slaves flee Richmond, Virginia, by means of barges (The Library of Congress).

deserted. African Americans represented nine to ten percent of the Union's armed forces.

1865 • Tennessee

The Ku Klux Klan is formed with the purpose of reasserting white supremacy in the South.

1865 •

All-white legislatures in many states enact black codes. These codes impose heavy penalties for "vagrancy," "insulting gestures," "curfew violations," and "seditious speeches." South Carolina requires African Americans entering the state to post a $1,000 bond in guarantee of good behavior and entitles employers to whip African American employees.

1865 • Wisconsin

Wisconsin, Connecticut, and Minnesota deny suffrage to African Americans.

1865 • Washington, DC

Abraham Lincoln is assassinated. The new president, Andrew Johnson, calls for ratification of the Thirteenth Amendment, but opposes African American suffrage. The Thirteenth Amendment, abolishing slavery and involuntary servitude in all of the United States, is ratified December 16, 1865.

1865, December 6 • Washington, DC

Congress establishes the Freedmen's Bureau and passes the Thirteenth Amendment to the Constitution which abolishes slavery.

1866 • Memphis, Tennessee

In a race riot in Memphis, 48 blacks and 2 white sympathizers are killed. Also, 35 blacks are killed in a riot in New Orleans.

1866 • Washington, DC

Congress passes civil rights legislation despite President Johnson's veto. The act is intended to nullify the black codes. In the District of Columbia, a referendum is held on African American suffrage. Over 6,500 vote against extension of the franchise to African Americans; only 35 favor it. The Fourteenth Amendment passes the House and Senate despite opposition from Johnson.

Recently freed African Americans searching for employment opportunities.

1867 • Iowa
Iowa and the Dakota Territory grant suffrage to African Americans.

1868 • Hampton, Virginia
Samuel Chapman Armstrong, a former Union officer, founds Hampton Institute.

1868 • Nine states grant suffrage to African Americans, but two deny it. The Republican party platform omits demand for African American suffrage in Northern states.

1868 • Many states are readmitted to the Union. The Alabama legislature votes to racially segregate all state schools.

1868 • Louisiana
Oscar Dunn, a former slave and captain in the Union Army, is elected lieutenant governor of Louisiana. Blacks outnumber whites 87 to 40 in the South Carolina legislature, but whites maintain a majority in the state Senate.

1868 • South Carolina
The South Carolina House is the first state legislature to have a majority of African Americans.

1868 • Washington, DC
The Fourteenth Amendment is ratified, establishing the concept of "equal protection" for all citizens under the U.S. Constitution. President Johnson's veto of the bill granting vote to African Americans in the District of Columbia is overridden by Congress.

1869 • Washington, DC
The Colored National Labor Union is organized and advocates purchase and distribution of land.

1870 • Washington, DC
Recruitment of African Americans for the U.S. Cavalry intensifies. By 1890, 14 African American cavalrymen had received Medals of Honor for bravery in campaigns in the West.

1870 • Washington, DC
The Fifteenth Amendment to the Constitution, guaranteeing all citizens the right to vote, is ratified.

1871 • Washington, DC
Congress enacts the Ku Klux Klan Act to enforce the provisions of the Fourteenth Amendment.

1874 • Washington, DC
Reverend Patrick F. Healy is named president of Georgetown, the oldest Catholic university in the United States.

1875 • Kentucky
Oliver Lewis, an African American jockey, rides the horse Aristides to victory in the first Kentucky Derby.

1875 • Washington, DC
Congress passes civil rights legislation prohibiting discrimination in such public accommodations as hotels, theaters, and amusement parks.

1876 • Hamburg, South Carolina
Federal troops are sent by President Ulysses S. Grant to restore order after five African Americans are killed.

1876 • Washington, DC
In *United States v. Cruikshank*, the Supreme Court declares that the Fourteenth Amendment provides African Americans with equal protection under the law but does not add anything "to the rights which one citizen has under the Constitution against another." The Court rules that "the right of suffrage is not a necessary attribute of national citizenship."

1878 • Washington, DC
In the case *Hall v. DeCuir*, the U.S. Supreme Court rules that states cannot prohibit segregation on public transportation.

1878 • Washington, DC
The U.S. attorney general reveals widespread intimidation of African Americans attempting to vote and stuffing of ballot boxes in several Southern states.

1879 • Frustrated by poverty and discrimination, large numbers of African Americans start to emigrate north and west. A leader of the emigration movement is Benjamin "Pap" Singleton, a former slave who had earlier escaped to Canada and favors separate African American communities. Emigration is vigorously opposed by many whites, some of whom prevent ships from transporting blacks on the Mississippi River.

1879 • Washington, DC
Upon hearing the case of *Strauder v. West Virginia*, the U.S. Supreme Court rules that the Fourteenth Amendment ensures blacks all rights that, under law, are enjoyed by whites. In a separate case, the Court rules that one of the purposes of both the Thirteenth and Fourteenth Amendments is to raise the condition of blacks to one of perfect equality with whites.

1881 • Tennessee passes a "Jim Crow" railroad law

which sets a trend soon taken up by Florida (1887), Mississippi (1888), Texas (1889), Louisiana (1890), and a host of other Southern and border states.

1881 • Tuskegee, Alabama
Booker T. Washington opens Tuskegee Institute with a $2,000 appropriation from the Alabama legislature.

1883 • Washington, DC
Upon hearing a set of cases challenging the Civil Rights Act of 1875, the U.S. Supreme Court declares the act unconstitutional.

1884 • New York
The first issue of the *New York Age* is published by T. Thomas Fortune.

1884 • Washington, DC
Former Reconstruction Representative John Roy Lynch is elected temporary chairman of the Republican convention—the first African American to preside over a national political gathering.

1884 • Memphis, Tennessee
Fiery journalist Ida Wells-Barnett is successful in her suit against the Chesapeake, Ohio, and Southwestern Railroad Company for racial segregation on a trip from Memphis to Woodstock. The Tennessee Supreme Court reverses the decision on April 5, 1887.

1888 • Richmond, Virginia
Two African American banks are founded—the Savings Bank of the Grand Fountain United Order of True Reformers in Virginia and the Capital Savings Bank in Washington, DC.

1889 • Washington, DC
Frederick Douglass is appointed U.S. Minister to Haiti.

1890 • Mississippi
The Mississippi constitutional convention begins the systematic exclusion of African Americans from the political arena by adopting literacy and other complex "understanding" tests as prerequisites to voting. Seven other Southern states follow suit.

1890 • Washington, DC
In the *In re Green* decision, the U.S. Supreme Court sanctions control of elections by state officials, thus weakening federal protection for Southern black voters. In the case *Louisville, New Orleans and Texas Railway v. Mississippi*, the Court permits states to segregate public transportation facilities.

1891 • Baffin Bay, Greenland
Matthew Henson accompanies Admiral Robert E. Peary in his exploration of the Arctic.

1891 • Chicago, Illinois
Daniel Hale Williams, physician and surgeon, founds Provident Hospital with the first training school for African American nurses in the United States.

1895 • Atlanta, Georgia
Booker T. Washington delivers his famous "Atlanta Compromise" speech at the Cotton States International Exposition.

1896 • Cambridge, Massachusetts
W. E. B. Du Bois publishes *Suppression of the African Slave Trade*, the first of some twenty annual sociological studies of African Americans in the United States.

1896 • Washington, DC
The National Association of Colored Women, a politically active self-help group, is formed.

1896 • Washington, DC
The U.S. Supreme Court in the *Plessy v. Ferguson* decision upholds the doctrine of "separate but equal," paving the way for segregation of African Americans in all aspects of life.

1898 • Louisiana
The addition of a "grandfather clause" to the state constitution enables poor whites to qualify for the franchise while curtailing black voter registration. In 1896, there were over 130,000 African American voters on the Louisiana rolls. Four years later, that number has been reduced to roughly five thousand.

1898 • Santiago, Cuba
Four African American regiments in the U.S. Army compile an outstanding combat record in and around Santiago during the Spanish-American War. Five African Americans receive Medals of Honor. At the close of the war, over one hundred African Americans are promoted to officer status.

1900 • Boston, Massachusetts
Booker T. Washington organizes the National Negro Business League.

1900 • London, England
W. E. B. Du Bois attends the conference of the African and New World Intellectuals, where he delivers an address incorporating his famous dictum: "The problem of the twentieth century is the problem of the color line." Du Bois also attends the first Pan-African Congress, an international body of concerned African nations protesting Western imperialism and promoting the concept of self-government among colonized peoples.

1902 • Richmond, Virginia
Virginia joins other Southern states in adopting the "grandfather clause" as a means of denying African Americans access to the polls.

1903 • Georgia
Whites attack blacks in riots, which are spurred by charges that blacks have murdered whites.

1903 • Washington, DC
Upon hearing the case *Giles v. Harris*, the U.S. Supreme Court rules that it cannot remedy discrimination in voter registration.

1904 • Atlanta, Georgia
Financier Andrew Carnegie brings together a group of prominent African American leaders, including Booker T. Washington and W. E. B. Du Bois, who discuss "the interests of the Negro race." The personal and ideological differences between Washington and Du Bois are evident at the meeting, though there is agreement that the group should press for "absolute civil, political, and public equality." The group shows little fire in advancing familiar proposals for African American self-help.

1905 • Fort Erie, New York
Twenty-nine militant African American intellectuals from 14 states organize the Niagara Movement, a forerunner of the National Association for the Advancement of Colored People (NAACP).

1906 • Atlanta, Georgia
An extended riot, in which respected African American citizens are killed, brings the city to a standstill for several days. After the riot, interracial groups are formed which attempt to improve conditions for African Americans. Despite the efforts of these groups, many African Americans decide to leave Georgia.

1906 • Brownsville, Texas
Several African American soldiers of the 25th Infantry Division are involved in a riot with Brownsville police and merchants. Following the incident, President Theodore Roosevelt dishonorably discharges three companies of African American troops. These dishonorable discharges are finally reversed by the U.S. Army in 1972. The lone survivor from these companies is awarded $25,000 by the U.S. Army in 1973.

1907 • Washington, DC
The U.S. Supreme Court upholds the right of railroads to

segregate passengers traveling between states, even when this runs counter to the laws of states in which the train is traveling.

1908 • Washington, DC
The U.S. Supreme Court, in the case *Berea College v. Kentucky,* upholds a state statute requiring segregation in private institutions.

1909 • New York City, New York
The NAACP is founded in New York. The signers of the original charter of incorporation include Jane Addams, John Dewey, W. E. B. Du Bois, William Dean Howells, and Lincoln Steffens. Ida Wells-Barnett is placed on the executive committee.

1909 • Matthew Henson places the flag of the United States at the North Pole. Henson, an African American, was part of Admiral Robert E. Peary's expedition.

1910 • On separate lecture tours of Great Britain, W. E. B. Du Bois and Booker T. Washington paint contrasting pictures of the African American condition in the United States. Washington tells the British that blacks are making progress; Du Bois underscores injustices and accuses Washington of acquiescing to powerful white interests.

1910 • New York City, New York
The first edition of *Crisis* magazine, edited by W. E. B. Du Bois, is published. Only 1,000 copies are in print, but before the end of the decade circulation of the magazine increases one hundred-fold.

1910 • New York City, New York
The National Urban League is founded. The new organization stresses employment and industrial opportunities for African Americans. Eugene Kinckle Jones serves as the first executive secretary.

1911 • Jamaica
Marcus Garvey forms the Universal Negro Improvement Association.

1912 • New York City, New York
James Weldon Johnson's *The Autobiography of an Ex-Colored Man* is published, spurring white recognition of black culture and the advent of the Harlem Renaissance.

1913 • Washington, DC
President Woodrow Wilson refuses to appoint a National Race Commission to study the social and economic status of African Americans.

W.E.B. Du Bois (The Library of Congress)

1915 • Spurred by boll weevil devastation of cotton crops, the great migration of African Americans to the North begins. Carter G. Woodson establishes the Association for the Study of Negro Life and History.

1915 • New York City, New York
The NAACP establishes the Spingarn Medal to recognize annually "the highest achievement of an American Negro."

1915 • Washington, DC
The U.S. Supreme Court in *Guinn v. United States* declares the Oklahoma "grandfather clause" unconstitutional.

1917 • East St. Louis, Illinois
A riot erupts after African Americans are hired at a local factory. Forty African Americans are killed.

1917, July 28 • New York City, New York
Over ten thousand African Americans parade down Fifth Avenue in New York, New York, to protest lynchings and the East St. Louis riot. Marchers in the Silent Protest Parade include W. E. B. Du Bois and James Weldon

James Weldon Johnson (Fisk University Library)

Johnson. Women and children protesters dress in white and men wear black arm bands.

1917 • The United States enters World War I. Joel Spingarn presses the War Department to establish an officers' training camp for African Americans. Spingarn's proposal alienates many of his NAACP colleagues who feel that such a camp would only perpetuate segregation and validate theories of African American inferiority. Others concede that the move is prudent, since it is the only way for African American officers to be trained. The NAACP ultimately approves of separate training camps. In October, over six hundred African Americans are commissioned officers, and seven hundred thousand African Americans register for the draft.

1917 • Washington, DC
In the case of *Buchanan v. Warley*, the U.S. Supreme Court declares that a Louisville "block" segregation ordinance is unconstitutional.

1918 • France
Two African American infantry battalions are awarded the Croix de Guerre and two African American officers

win the French Legion of Honor. African Americans are in the forefront of fighting from 1917 until the defeat of Germany in 1918.

1919 • Membership in the NAACP approaches one hundred thousand despite attempts in some areas to make it illegal.

1919 • Washington, DC
The U.S. Supreme Court rules in the case *Strauder v. West Virginia* that African Americans should be admitted to juries.

1920 • New York City, New York
James Weldon Johnson becomes the first African American secretary of the NAACP and campaigns for the withdrawal of U.S. troops occupying Haiti.

1921 • Tulsa, Oklahoma
Twenty-one blacks and ten whites are killed in a riot.

1922 • Washington, DC
Republicans in the Senate vote to abandon the Dyer Anti-Lynching Bill, which imposed severe penalties and fines on "any state or municipal officer convicted of negligence in affording protection to individuals in custody who are attacked by a mob bent on lynching, torture, or physical intimidation." The bill, which was approved by the House of Representatives, had also provided for compensation to the families of victims.

1923 • New York City, New York
Marcus Garvey is sentenced to a five-year term for mail fraud.

1924 • Washington, DC
Congress passes the Immigration Act which excludes people of African descent from entering the country.

1924 • Washington, DC
New York Representative Emanuel Cellar introduces legislation to provide for the formation of a blue-ribbon panel to study racial issues. The idea is met with disdain from the African American press, particularly the *Chicago Defender*, which editorializes: "We have been commissioned to death. . . . We have too many studies and reports already." *The Defender* asserts that African Americans need only to look after their own interests through the creation of a strong party vehicle and potent political leadership in the halls of Congress.

1925 • A. Philip Randolph founds the Brotherhood of Sleeping Car Porters.

African American soldiers leaving by train to serve in World War I (National Archives and Records Administration).

1926 • New York City, New York
Controversy rages among the African American intelligentsia after publication of *Nigger Heaven* by white writer Carl van Vechten. The book glamorizes the free-wheeling style of Harlem life amid the general contention that African Americans are less ashamed of sex and more morally honest than whites. W. E. B. Du Bois finds the assumptions deplorable; James Weldon Johnson, on the other hand, believes the book is neither scandalous nor insulting.

1926 • New York City, New York
Langston Hughes, writing in *The Nation* magazine, urges black artists to write from their experience and to stop imitating white writers.

1926 • Washington, DC
Negro History Week is introduced by Carter G. Woodson and the Association for the Study of Negro Life and History.

1926 • Washington, DC
President Coolidge tells Congress that the country must provide "for the amelioration of race prejudice and the extension to all of the elements of equal opportunity and equal protection under the laws, which are guaranteed by the Constitution." Twenty-three African Americans are reported lynched during 1926.

1927 • Atlanta, Georgia
Marcus Garvey is released from prison and deported to the British West Indies.

1927 • Chicago, Illinois
The National Urban League organizes a boycott of stores that do not hire African Americans. In 1929, boycotts are started in several other Midwest cities.

1927 • Washington, DC
In the case of *Nixon v. Herndon*, the U.S. Supreme Court strikes down a Texas law which bars African Americans from voting in party primaries. Texas goes on to enact a law allowing local committees to determine voter qualifications.

1928 • Illinois
Oscar DePriest, a Republican, is elected as the first African American Representative from a Northern state.

Oscar DePriest (Fisk University Library)

1930 • Detroit, Michigan
W. D. Fard founds the Temple of Islam, later to become the Nation of Islam.

1930 • Washington, DC
A NAACP campaign helps prevent confirmation of U.S. Supreme Court nominee John H. Parker, a one-time, self-admitted opponent of the franchise for African Americans. The NAACP also helps unseat three of the senators who voted for him in later congressional elections.

1931 • Alabama
The first trial of the Scottsboro Boys results in a battle between the NAACP and the International Labor Defense, a Communist-controlled group, for the right to represent the young defendants who are charged with rape. The case, which becomes a worldwide *cause celebre* and important propaganda weapon for Communists, drags on for twenty years despite the recanting of a charge by one of the two plaintiffs and medical testimony that rape was not committed.

1932 • Washington, DC
Following the Supreme Court's 1927 ruling in *Nix-*

on v. Herndon the state of Texas passes a statute authorizing the state Democratic party to set up its own rules regarding primary elections. As a result, the state of Texas adopts a resolution that denies African Americans the right to vote in Democratic Party primaries. However, the Supreme Court's ruling in rules that such legislation violates provisions of the Fourteenth Amendment.

1934 • Chicago, Illinois
The headquarters of the Nation of Islam are established with Elijah Muhammad as leader.

1934 • Washington, DC
A bill that prohibits lynching fails, as President Roosevelt refuses to support it.

1935 • New York City, New York
Mary McLeod Bethune founds the National Council of Negro Women.

1935 • St. Louis, Missouri
The NAACP bitterly criticizes President Franklin Delano Roosevelt for his failure to present or support civil rights legislation.

1935 • Washington, DC
In the case of *Grovey v. Townsend*, the U.S. Supreme Court upholds a Texas law that prevents African Americans from voting in the Texas Democratic primary. The decision is a setback to the NAACP, which has waged several effective legal battles to equalize the ballot potential of the African American voter.

1936 • Berlin, Germany
Jesse Owens wins four gold medals in the 1936 Olympics, but is snubbed by the Chancellor of Germany, Adolf Hitler.

1936 • Washington, DC
In the case of *Gibbs v. Montgomery County*, the U.S. Supreme Court requires Maryland University to admit an African American student, Donald Murray, to its graduate law school.

1937 • New York City, New York
Richard Wright becomes editor of *Challenge*, changes the title to *New Challenge*, and urges African Americans to write with greater "social realism."

1937 • Pennsylvania
A new Pennsylvania state law denies many state services to unions discriminating against African Americans.

The "Scottsboro Boys" being held in detention (Corbis Corporation [Bellevue]).

1937 • Spain
Between 60 to 80 of the 3,200 Americans who fight for the Republican side in the Spanish Civil War are African American. Oliver Law, an African American from Chicago, commands the Lincoln Battalion.

1938 • Boxer Joe Louis defends his heavyweight title against Max Schmeling.

1938 • New York City, New York
Adam Clayton Powell, Jr. and other black leaders convince white merchants in Harlem to hire blacks and to promise equal promotion opportunities.

1938 • Pennsylvania
Crystal Bird Fauset of Philadelphia, the first African American woman state legislator, is elected to the Pennsylvania House of Representatives.

1939 • Miami, Florida
Intimidation and cross-burning by the Ku Klux Klan in the black ghetto of Miami fail to discourage over one thousand of the city's registered African American voters from appearing at the polls. The Klan parades with effigies of African Americans who will allegedly be slain for daring to vote.

1939 • New York City, New York
Jane Bolin is appointed Judge of the Court of Domestic Relations in New York, New York, by Mayor Fiorello LaGuardia, becoming the first African American woman judge in the United States.

1939 • Washington, DC
Marian Anderson, denied the use of Constitution Hall by the Daughters of the American Revolution, sings on Easter Sunday before 75,000 people assembled at the Lincoln Memorial.

1940 • New York
In a mass meeting, West Indians oppose the transfer of West Indian islands to the United States.

1940 • Eighty thousand African Americans vote in eight Southern states. Five percent of voting-age African Americans are registered.

1940 • The 1940 census places life expectancy for

Marian Anderson singing before the Lincoln Memorial in Washington, DC (Corbis Corporation [Bellevue]).

blacks at 51 years, compared with 62 years for whites. Nearly one-fourth of blacks live in the North and West.

1940 • Virginia
The Virginia legislature chooses "Carry Me Back to Ole Virginia," written by African American composer James A. Bland, as the official state song.

1940 • Washington, DC
Benjamin O. Davis, Sr. is appointed as the first African American general in the history of the U.S. armed forces. Responding to NAACP pressure, President Franklin Roosevelt announces that African American strength in the armed forces will be proportionate to African American population totals. Several branches of the military service and several occupational specialties are to be opened to African Americans. However, Roosevelt rules out troop integration because it will be "destructive to morale and detrimental to . . . preparation for national defense." At the start of Selective Service, less than 5,000 of 230,000 men in the U.S. Army are African American and there are only two African American combat officers. Approximately 888,000 African American men and 4,000 African American women are to

serve in the armed forces during World War II. African Americans are mostly confined to service units.

1940 • Washington, DC
The U.S. Supreme Court rules that black teachers cannot be denied wage parity with white teachers.

1941, December 07 • Pearl Harbor, Hawaii
Dorie Miller, messman aboard the *USS Arizona*, mans a machine gun during the Pearl Harbor attack, downs four enemy planes, and is awarded the Navy Cross.

1941 • Washington, DC
Charles R. Drew, an African American physician, sets up the first blood bank.

1941 • Washington, DC
Robert Weaver is appointed director of the government office charged with integrating African Americans into the national defense program.

1941 • Washington, DC
The threat by African Americans to stage a massive protest march on the nation's capital results in the issuance of Executive Order No. 8802, prohibiting discrimination in the defense establishment.

1941 • Washington, DC
In the case of *Mitchell v. United States*, the U.S. Supreme Court rules that separate facilities in railroad travel must be substantially equal. The case is brought before the Supreme Court by African American congressman Arthur Mitchell.

1942 • Chicago, Illinois
The Congress of Racial Equality (CORE), a civil rights group dedicated to a direct-action, nonviolent program, is founded. In 1943, CORE stages its first "sit-in" in a Chicago restaurant.

1942 • Washington, DC
The Justice Department threatens to file suit against a number of African American newspapers which it believes are guilty of sedition because of their strong criticism of the government's racial policies in the armed services. The NAACP steps in to suggest guidelines which will satisfy the Justice Department.

1944 • The United Negro Fund is founded.

1944 • The NAACP secures the release of servicemen detained for protesting discrimination in the armed forces.

1944 • The European Theater of War
The African American 99th Pursuit Squadron flies its five hundredth mission in the Mediterranean Theater. Another African American unit, the 92nd Division, enters combat in Italy. On June 6,500 African Americans land on Omaha Beach as part of the D-Day invasion of northern France. Among them is the 761st Tank Battalion which spends 183 days in action and is cited for conspicuous courage. Also cited in January of 1945 is the 969th Field Artillery Battalion for their support in the defense of Bastogne.

1944 • The restriction of African American seamen to shore duty ends, as is the exclusion of African Americans from the coast guard and marine corps. The War Department officially ends segregation in all army posts, but the order is widely ignored.

1944 • Washington, DC
In the case of *Smith v. Allwright*, the U.S. Supreme Court rules that "white primaries" violate the provisions of the Fifteenth Amendment.

1945 • Italy
African American troops are at the forefront of victorious assaults in Germany and northern Italy. However, the use of African American troops in World War II is more limited than in World War I or the Spanish-American War. Despite efforts by some enlightened naval officers, over ninety percent of African Americans in the U.S. Navy are still messmen when the war ends.

1945 • New York
The first state Fair Employment Practices Commission is established in New York as a result of the Ives-Quinn Bill.

1945 • Washington, DC
Congress denies funds to the federal Fair Employment Practices Commission, which was established during the war to enforce fair employment policies.

1946 • Washington, DC
The U.S. Supreme Court rules in *Morgan v. Virginia* that segregation on interstate buses is unconstitutional.

1947 • Jackie Robinson becomes the first African American to play major league baseball, breaking the national pastime's color barrier.

1947 • Atlanta, Georgia
The Southern Regional Council releases figures that demonstrate that only 12 percent of the African Americans in the Deep South (nearly 600,000) meet voting qualifications. In the states of Louisiana, Alabama, and

Mississippi, the figure is approximately 3 percent. In Tennessee, more than 25 percent of adult African Americans meet the state voting requirements.

1947 • CORE's first "freedom ride" travels through Southern states to press for the integration of transportation facilities.

1947 • Tuskegee, Alabama
Statistics indicate that 3,426 African Americans have been lynched in the United States in the period 1882–1947. Of these, 1,217 were lynched in the decade 1890–1900. From 1947 to 1962, 12 African Americans were lynched.

1947 • Washington, DC
The Truman Committee on Civil Rights formally condemns racial injustice in America in the widely-quoted report *To Secure These Rights*.

1948 • California
The California Supreme Court declares the state statute banning racial intermarriage unconstitutional.

1948 • New York City, New York
Ralph Bunche is confirmed by the United Nations Security Council as acting U.N. mediator in Palestine.

1948 • Washington, DC
The U.S. Supreme Court in *Shelley v. Kraemer* rules that federal and state courts may not enforce restrictive covenants. However, the Court does not declare such covenants illegal. In a separate case, *Sipuel v. University of Oklahoma*, the Court holds that states are required to provide blacks with the same educational opportunities as whites. President Truman issues Executive Order No. 9981 directing "equality of treatment and opportunity" in the armed forces and creates the Fair Practices Board of the Civil Service Commission to deal with complaints of discrimination in government employment.

1949 • Connecticut
Connecticut becomes the first state in the Union to extend the jurisdiction of the Civil Rights Commission into the domain of public housing.

1949 • Washington, DC
Representative William L. Dawson becomes the first African American to head a Congressional committee when he is named chairman of the House Committee on Government Operations.

1950 • Yech'on, Republic of Korea
The African American 24th Infantry Regiment recaptures

the city of Yech'on, the first American victory in the Korean War.

1950 • New York City, New York
Edith Sampson is appointed an alternate delegate to the United Nations.

1950 • Oslo, Norway
Ralph Bunche wins the Nobel Peace Prize.

1950 • The 1950 census places the net ten-year African American emigration from the South at 1.6 million.

1950 • Washington, DC
Several U.S. Supreme Court decisions open university facilities to African Americans. In the case of *Henderson v. United States*, the Court rules that segregated tables on dining cars violate the provisions of the Interstate Commerce Act. A special committee reports to President Harry S. Truman that African American servicemen are still barred from many military specialties and training programs, but that the armed forces has largely been desegregated.

1952 • In a series of legal maneuvers, the NAACP and other African American groups succeed in desegregating a number of colleges and high schools in Southern and border areas. In addition, public housing projects are opened to African Americans in some Northern and Midwestern cities and desegregation is achieved in several businesses and unions. A public swimming pool is integrated in Kansas City, a golf course in Louisville, and Ford's Theater in Baltimore.

1952 • Tuskegee, Alabama
A Tuskegee report indicates that, for the first time in its 71 years of tabulation, no lynchings have occurred in the United States.

1953 • Washington, DC
District of Columbia Commissioners order the abolition of segregation in several district agencies. The fire department is among those which escape the mandate. The Defense Department orders an end to segregation in schools on military bases and in veterans hospitals.

1953 • New York City, New York
Hulan Jack is sworn in as borough president of Manhattan.

1953 • Washington, DC
The U.S. Supreme Court asks to re-hear five school segregation cases first argued in 1942. Sensing a major opportunity, the NAACP puts one hundred lawyers, scholars, and researchers to work in preparation. The

NAACP also files a complaint with the Interstate Commerce Commission to execute earlier Supreme Court desegregation orders in transportation facilities.

1954, March 4 • Washington, DC
President Dwight D. Eisenhower appoints an African American, J. Ernest Wilkins, as undersecretary of labor.

1954, May 17 • Washington, DC
By a unanimous vote, the U.S. Supreme Court in the case of *Brown v. Board of Education, Topeka* declares that "separate but equal" educational facilities are "inherently unequal" and that segregation is therefore unconstitutional. The decision overturns the "separate but equal" doctrine that has legalized segregation since 1896. In the case of *Hawkins v. Board of Control*, the Court rules that the University of Florida must admit African Americans regardless of any "public mischief" it might cause.

1954, September • In the autumn following the *Brown* decision, 150 formerly segregated school districts in eight states and the District of Columbia integrate. However, a number of groups opposing integration emerge in the South. Most prominent among these are white citizens councils that soon claim eighty thousand members and propose constitutional amendments reinstating segregation.

1954, October 1 • Baltimore, Maryland
White parents and students protest the admission of black students to Baltimore's Southern High School. Anti-desegregation demonstrations are also staged in nearby Washington, DC.

1954, October 1 • Florida
State Attorney General Richard Ervin files a brief with the U.S. Supreme Court warning that violent resistance would result from any effort to force desegregation in Florida schools.

1954, October 30 • Washington, DC
The Department of Defense reports the end of "all-Negro" units in the U.S. Army. However, some bases still refuse to integrate. The Veteran's Administration announces their hospitals have been desegregated, but the Department of Health, Education and Welfare declares it will continue to give funds to segregated hospitals.

1954, November 13 • Boca Raton, Florida
Governors attending the Southern Governors Conference pledge to uphold state control over schools and warn that forced school desegregation will create unrest which they claim does not currently exist in their states.

George Hayes (left), Thurgood Marshall (center), and James M. Nabrit (right) celebrate the *Brown v. Board of Education, Topeka* landmark decision (The Library of Congress).

1955, May 31 • Washington, DC
The U.S. Supreme Court orders school boards to draw up desegregation procedures. The Court asserts that school authorities have the responsibility of assessing and solving desegregation problems and must do so "with all deliberate speed." The decision reenforces the Court's ruling in *Brown v. Board of Education*. Reactions to this ruling in the South are mixed. Kansas, Missouri, Oklahoma, and Texas desegregate their school systems with minimal disruption. Georgia's Board of Education adopts a resolution revoking the license of any teacher who teaches integrated classes. Mississippi repeals its compulsory school attendance law and establishes a branch of government for the sole purpose of maintaining segregation. White citizens councils in Mississippi initiate economic pressures against blacks who try to register to vote, while more extreme groups resort to direct terror.

1955, July 14 • Richmond, Virginia
The U.S. Circuit Court of Appeals rules that segregation on city buses is illegal. The court claims that the same principle which outlawed segregation in public schools should be applied.

1955, August 31 • Greenwood, Mississippi
Two white men are arrested in Greenwood on charges of kidnapping, beating, and shooting 15-year-old Emmett Till. Till, who allegedly whistled at and insulted a white woman, was found dead in the Tallahatchie River. Jurors acquit the defendants on grounds that the body could not be positively identified.

1955, November 25 • Washington, DC
In accordance with U.S. Supreme Court edicts, the Interstate Commerce Commission outlaws segregated buses and waiting rooms for interstate passengers. However, many communities ignore the order.

1955, December 1 • Montgomery, Alabama
Rosa Parks takes a seat in the front of a city bus, refuses to surrender it to a white man, and is arrested. Four days later, the Reverend Martin Luther King, Jr. urges the city's African American community to boycott the buses. This marks the beginning of the Montgomery bus boycott, which leads to the desegregation of Montgomery's city bus system the following year.

1956 • Washington, DC
In the case of *Flemming v. South Carolina Electric*, the U.S. Supreme Court strikes down a state statute requiring segregation on public transportation.

1956, February 3 • Tuscaloosa, Alabama
Autherine Lucy is admitted to the University of Alabama by court order, but riots ensue and she is expelled on a technicality.

1956, March 11 • Washington, DC
Southern members of the Senate, led by Harry Byrd of Virginia, launch a fight against school integration. Byrd obtains the signatures of one hundred congressmen on a "Southern Manifesto", attacking the rulings of the U.S. Supreme Court.

1956, July 13 • Washington, DC
Southern members of the House of Representatives unite in opposition to an Eisenhower administration-sponsored civil rights bill. The bill would provide for the investigation of civil rights complaints and permit action by the U.S. attorney general in federal courts.

1956, September • By September of 1956, approximately eight hundred school districts containing 320,000 African American children are desegregated in compliance with the U.S. Supreme Court's 1954 decision. However, nearly 2.5 million African American children remain in segregated schools and there are still no desegregated districts in Virginia, North and South Carolina, Georgia, Florida, Mississippi, Alabama, and Louisiana.

1956, November 13 • Washington, DC
The U.S. Supreme Court rules that the segregation of city buses is unconstitutional.

Rosa Parks is arrested and fingerprinted following her refusal to move to the back of a segregated Birmingham, Alabama bus (AP/Wide World Photos, Inc.).

1957, February 14 • New Orleans, Louisiana
The Southern Christian Leadership Conference (SCLC) is formed by Martin Luther King, Jr. and others to coordinate the activities of nonviolent groups devoted to integration and citizenship for African Americans.

1957, February 26 • Little Rock, Arkansas
Governor Orval Faubus signs four segregation bills enabling parents to refuse to send their children to desegregated schools, authorizing the use of school district funds to pay legal expenses incurred in integration suits, creating a committee to make anti-integration studies, and requiring organizations such as the NAACP to publish membership rosters.

1957, April 9 • Madison, Wisconsin
The state Supreme Court rules that African Americans can be refused membership in trade unions, since such organizations are voluntary associations.

1957, September 4 • Little Rock, Arkansas
Nine black students are turned away from Central High School by a white mob and the Arkansas National Guard when they arrive for classes. The National Guard, which

was called to Little Rock by Governor Orval Faubus, is forced by court order to withdraw on September 20. As mobs of angry whites assemble outside of the school and the threat of mob violence escalates, President Dwight Eisenhower issues a proclamation on September 23 ordering an end to any obstruction to court-ordered integration. On September 24, the president issues Executive Order No. 10730 authorizing the use of federal troops to assist in the integration of Central High School.

1957, September 9 • Washington, DC
President Dwight D. Eisenhower signs a civil rights bill. The bill provides for the creation of a commission on civil rights to investigate allegations of civil rights and voting rights violations.

1958, February 19 • New Orleans, Louisiana
The U.S. Court of Appeals rules that segregation on buses and streetcars in New Orleans is illegal. The Louisiana state assembly later passes a bill which stipulates that the first person seated in a bus's double seat can decide whether a rider of a different race may sit in the adjoining seat. The bill is vetoed by Governor Earl

Governor Orval Faubus argues for the continued segregation of Arkansas public schools (The Library of Congress).

Long because it would require a white rider to request permission to sit next to a black rider.

1958, April 14 • Jackson, Mississippi
Governor J. P. Coleman asserts that African Americans in Mississippi are not ready to vote and vetoes a bill which would have given control of voter registration to a court-appointed registrar.

1958, July 16 • Baton Rouge, Louisiana
Governor Earl Long signs a bill requiring that blood plasma be labeled according to the race of donor.

1960, February 1 • Greensboro, North Carolina
Four African American students refuse to leave a segregated lunch counter, marking the beginning of "sit-in" protests throughout the South.

1960, April • Atlanta, Georgia
The Student Non-Violent Coordinating Committee (SNCC) is formed to organize student protest activities. Church "kneel-ins" and beach "wade-ins" soon join lunch counter and bus station "sit-ins" as effective means of protesting segregation.

1960, April 24 • Biloxi, Mississippi
Rioting erupts when a group of African Americans attempt to swim at the city's 26-mile whites-only beach. A curfew is ordered by the mayor and riot police patrol the city. On April 27, the state legislature passes a law authorizing prison terms for anyone convicted of inciting a riot.

1960, May 6 • Washington, DC
President Eisenhower signs the Civil Rights Act of 1960. This act authorizes judges to appoint referees who can help African Americans register to vote in federal elections. The act also prohibits intimidation of African American voters through bombing and mob violence.

1960, July 31 • New York City, New York
Black Muslim leader, Elijah Muhammad, calls for the creation of a black state either in America or in Africa.

**1960, August • As of August 1, "sit-ins" have led to the successful desegregation of lunch counters in 15 American cities.

1960, September 8 • New York City, New York
New York Governor Nelson Rockefeller, in an address at the National Urban League Conference, declares that the "sit-ins" are "an inspiration to the nation."

**1960, October 3 • The SCLC organizes voter "stand-ins" in several American cities to protest against the remaining barriers to African American voter registration.

1960, November 10 • New Orleans, Louisiana
The city approves a plan to admit black students to an all-white school. Meeting in a special session, the state legislature votes to take control of the city's school system and to have the schools closed on the day the African American students are scheduled to arrive. On November 14, U.S. marshals escort four black students to the selected schools. On November 15, 11 whites are arrested in disturbances; on November 17 the city experiences severe rioting.

1960, November 14 • Washington, DC
In the case of *Gomillion v. Lightfoot*, the U.S. Supreme Court rules that a law designed to redraw the city boundaries of Tuskegee, Alabama, is unconstitutional. The case was brought before the Court after the city of Tuskegee redrew its borders, which excluded all but four or five of the city's four hundred African American residents. The Court asserted that such legislation was in violation of the Fifteenth Amendment.

1960, November 23 • Baton Rouge, Louisiana
At its annual convention, the Louisiana Teachers Association vows to resist all attempts to integrate the state's public schools.

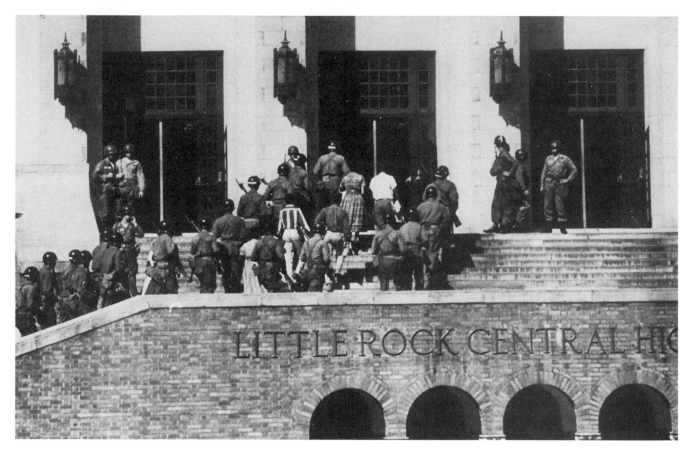

Federal troops escorting nine black students into Little Rock Central High School following violent disturbances by white demonstrators (Corbis Corporation [Bellevue]).

1961, May 4 • Washington, DC
Several busloads of "freedom riders," organized by the Congress of Racial Equality (CORE), embark on a journey through the South to test the compliance of bus stations with the Interstate Commerce Commission's desegregation order. Many of the "freedom riders" are arrested or encounter angry mobs as they travel throughout the South.

1961, May 20 • Montgomery, Alabama
A bus carrying "freedom riders" is attacked by a mob and set on fire. U.S. Attorney General Robert Kennedy orders federal marshals into Montgomery to maintain order. On May 21, a mob forms outside of the First Baptist Church, where Martin Luther King, Jr. and Ralph Abernathy, pastor of the church, are conducting a meeting. The situation in Montgomery becomes so volatile that Governor John Patterson is forced to deploy the Alabama National Guard and declares martial law in the city.

1961, May 22 • Washington, DC
Upon hearing the case *Louisiana ex rel. Gremillion v. NAACP*, the U.S. Supreme Court unanimously rules that two Louisiana laws designed to harass the National Association for the Advancement of Colored People are unconstitutional. The laws required that organizations disclose members' names and attest that its officers are not affiliated with subversive activities.

1961, June 2 • Montgomery, Alabama
Federal Judge Frank Johnson, Jr. issues a restraining order to prevent "freedom riders" from traveling through the state.

1961, September 29 • Atlanta, Georgia
The Southern Regional Council reports that business establishments in more than one hundred cities have been desegregated as a result of "sit-ins."

1961, December 11 • Washington, DC
Ruling on its first cases pertaining to student "sit-ins", the U.S. Supreme Court decides unanimously to reverse the conviction of 16 African American students. The cases *Briscoe v. Louisiana, Garner v. Louisiana*, and *Hoston v. Louisiana* result from a Baton Rouge lunch counter "sit-in" staged in March of 1960. The students, who had not been asked to leave by the proprietor, had

Sit-in demonstrations were a highly effective means of protesting segregation in public places (Magnum Photos, Inc.).

refused a police order to leave and were charged with "disturbing the peace."

1962, February 26 • Washington, DC
The U.S. Supreme Court rules on a suit challenging Mississippi laws that require segregation in intrastate transportation. The case *Bailey v. Patterson* is remanded to district court since, as the Court contends, the issue is no longer litigable; no state may require racial segregation in either inter- or intrastate transportation.

1962, March 24 • Columbia, South Carolina
The NAACP files suit in district court to prohibit the Orangeburg Regional Hospital from operating segregated facilities.

1962, May 2 • Biloxi, Mississippi
A U.S. district court finds nine Mississippi laws requiring segregated travel accommodations unconstitutional.

1962, September 30 • Jackson, Mississippi
Riots erupt on the campus of the University of Mississippi when James Meredith, a 29-year-old African American veteran, is admitted to the university by court order. Federal troops are sent to restore order.

1962, November 20 • Washington, DC
The Kennedy administration issues orders banning segregation in federally-financed housing.

1963, April 3 • Birmingham, Alabama
Martin Luther King, Jr. targets Birmingham for a drive against discrimination. The protesters are driven back by police armed with water hoses and attack dogs. The confrontation, which has been captured on film, awakens public opinion across the country.

1963, June 12 • Jackson, Mississippi
Civil rights leader Medgar Evers is assassinated in the doorway of his home. Thousands attend a march mourning the death of Evers on June 15.

1963, August 28 • Washington, DC
Some 250,000 people gather at the Lincoln Memorial to demonstrate on behalf of the civil rights bill pending in Congress. The march has been organized by several civil rights organizations including the National Association for the Advancement of Colored People, SCLC, CORE, the Urban League, and the Negro American Labor Council. Martin Luther King, Jr., one of many scheduled

Freedom riders viewing demonstrators and law enforcement officers from their bus windows (Magnum Photos, Inc.).

speakers, gives what will become his most famous speech "I Have a Dream."

1963, September • The South
Less than ten percent of African American public school students attend integrated classes in the fall term. Governor George Wallace of Alabama declares: "I draw the line in the dust and toss the gauntlet before the feet of tyranny and I say "segregation now, segregation tomorrow, segregation forever."

1963, September 15 • Birmingham, Alabama
Four African American children are killed in the bombing of the 16th Street Baptist Church.

1963, November 22 • Dallas, Texas
President John F. Kennedy, a major advocate of civil rights, is assassinated in Dallas, Texas. Kennedy's successor, Vice President Lyndon B. Johnson, promises to continue support for civil rights legislation.

1964, January 23 • The Twenty-fourth Amendment to the Constitution is ratified, prohibiting the use of poll taxes in federal elections.

1964, March 8 • New York City, New York
Malcolm X leaves the Black Muslim organization, Nation of Islam, to form the Organization for Afro-American Unity—an organization emphasizing black nationalism and social action.

1964, June 2 • Washington, DC
A major civil rights bill, forbidding discrimination in public accommodations and employment, is signed into law by President Johnson.

1964, June 25 • St. Augustine, Florida
A mob attacks marchers protesting the city's pro-segregation policies. State police watch as some fifty African Americans are prevented from using the city beach.

1964, July–August • New York and New Jersey
On July 18 riots erupt in the Harlem section of New York City. One person is killed, 140 injured, and 500 arrested. This is the first of many large riots to strike urban African American neighborhoods during the 1960s. Shortly after the Harlem disturbances, riots erupt in Brooklyn, New York; Rochester, New York; Jersey City, New Jersey; and Paterson, New Jersey.

Police officers using trained dogs to disrupt a 1963 civil rights demonstration in Birmingham, Alabama (AP/Wide World Photos, Inc.).

1964, August 4 • Philadelphia, Mississippi
Three young civil rights volunteers—James Chaney, Michael Schwerner, and Andrew Goodman—are murdered. A number of arrests on federal charges less severe than murder follow. Among the 19 suspects are the sheriff and a deputy sheriff of Neshoba County. No convictions are obtained and charges are dismissed in December.

1964, December 10 • Oslo, Norway
Martin Luther King, Jr. is awarded the Nobel Peace Prize.

1965, January 2 • Selma, Alabama
Reverend Martin Luther King, Jr. announces his intention to call for demonstrations if African Americans in Alabama are not permitted to register to vote in appropriate numbers. Twelve African Americans, including King himself, book rooms on January 18 at Selma's Hotel Albert, becoming the first blacks accepted at this formerly all-white hotel. While signing the guest register, King is accosted by a white segregationist who is later fined $100 and given a 60-day jail sentence. On

January 19, Sheriff James G. Clark arrests 62 African Americans in Selma after they refuse to enter the Dallas County courthouse through an alley door. Clark and his deputies arrest 150 other African American voter registration applicants the next day. A federal district court order issued on January 23 bars law enforcement officials from interfering with voter registration and warns that violence against African American voters will not be tolerated.

1965, January 15 • Philadelphia, Mississippi
A federal grand jury hands down indictments for the June 1964 slaying of three civil rights workers—James Chaney, Andrew Goodman, and Michael Schwerner—in Philadelphia, Mississippi. The following day 18 men, including two law enforcement officers, are arrested. On February 25, U.S. District Court Judge W. Harold Cox dismisses a federal indictment against 17 of the accused.

1965, January 18 • Washington, DC
Ruling on the case *Cox v. Louisiana*, the U.S. Supreme Court reverses the conviction of protesters charged with disturbing the peace.

1965, February 1 • Selma, Alabama
Reverend Martin Luther King, Jr. and some 770 African Americans are arrested during protest demonstrations. King remains in jail for four days before posting bond. During this time, more than 3,000 persons are arrested. On February 4, a federal district court bars the county board of registrars from administering a literacy test to voter applicants or from rejecting their application on petty technicalities.

1965, February 21 • New York City, New York
Malcolm X, a 39-year-old black nationalist leader and former member of the Black Muslim sect, is shot to death in the Audubon Ballroom as he is about to deliver an address before a rally of several hundred followers. Following the murder, Black Muslim headquarters in New York and San Francisco are burned, and most Muslim leaders are placed under heavy police guard. Three African Americans—Talmadge Hayer, Norman 3X Butler, and Thomas 15X Johnson—are later taken into custody and charged with first-degree murder. The trio is convicted and sentenced to life imprisonment on March 10, 1966.

1965, March 26 • Washington, DC
President Lyndon B. Johnson announces the arrest of four Ku Klux Klan members in connection with the murder of Viola Gregg Liuzzo. Liuzzo, a 39-year-old white civil rights worker from Detroit, was slain on a Lowndes County highway during the Selma-to-Mont-

Nearly 250,000 people from across the nation gather in Washington, DC, in 1963, protesting for increased civil rights (Magnum Photos, Inc.).

gomery Freedom March. The president declares war on the Klan, calling it a "hooded society of bigots." Robert M. Shelton, Jr., Imperial Wizard of the United Klans of America, Inc., answers the president's charges by branding him "a damn liar." On March 30, the House Un-American Activities Committee votes to open a full investigation of the activities of the Klan. The committee chairman, a Louisiana Democrat, asserts that the Klan is committing "shocking crimes."

1965, July 13 • Washington, DC
Thurgood Marshall is nominated as Solicitor General of the United States, the first African American person to hold this office.

1965, August 6 • Washington, DC
President Johnson signs the 1965 Voting Rights Act, providing for the registration by federal examiners of those black voters turned away by state officials.

1965, August 11 • Los Angeles, California
The arrest and alleged mistreatment of a black youth by white policemen sparks an orgy of looting, burning, and rioting in the predominantly African American section of Watts. Thousands of National Guardsmen and state police rush to quell the violence. The rioting which lasts six days claims the lives of 35 people and causes nearly 46 million dollars in property damage. On August 20, President Johnson denounces the Los Angeles rioters, comparing them to Ku Klux Klan extremists. He declares that the existence of legitimate grievances in Watts is no justification for lawlessness. "We cannot . . . in one breath demand laws to protect the rights of all our citizens, and then turn our back . . . and . . . allow laws to be broken that protect the safety of our citizens."

1966 • Oakland, California
Huey P. Newton and Bobby Seale found the Black Panther party.

1966, January 13 • Washington, DC
President Lyndon B. Johnson names Robert Weaver as head of the Department of Housing and Urban Development. Weaver is the first African American appointed to serve in a presidential cabinet in U.S. history. Lisle Carter, also African American, is named as an assistant secretary in the Department of Health, Education and Welfare. Constance Baker Motley, former NAACP law-

Martin Luther King, Jr. holding the Noble Peace Prize medal in 1964 (AP/Wide World Photos, Inc.).

yer and borough president of Manhattan, becomes the first African American woman to be named to a federal judgeship.

1966, February 7 • Lowndes County, Alabama
A federal court finds Lowndes County, Alabama, guilty of "gross, systematic exclusion of members of the African American race from jury duty." County officials are ordered to prepare a new jury list. Lowndes County is also ordered to desegregate its school system within two years, to close 24 "blacks only" schools, and to introduce remedial programs designed to close the educational gap between white and black students.

1966, February 23 • Washington, DC
In the case of *Brown v. Louisiana*, the U.S. Supreme Court reverses the convictions of five blacks charged with disturbing the peace when they refused to leave a whites-only reading room in a public library.

1966, March 25 • Washington, DC
In the case of *Harper v. Virginia State Board of Elections*, the U.S. Supreme Court outlaws the use of poll taxes in state elections. The ruling upholds the Twenty-

Fourth Amendment which bars the use of such taxes in federal elections.

1966, June 6 • Tennessee
James Meredith is shot shortly after beginning a 220-mile voting rights pilgrimage from Memphis, Tennessee to Jackson, Mississippi. Aubrey James Norvell, 40, is arrested at the scene and taken to jail where, according to authorities, he admits to the shooting. Meredith suffers multiple injuries, but recovers.

1966, June 26 • Jackson, Mississippi
The march begun by James Meredith ends with a rally in front of the state capitol in Jackson. Addresses are delivered by Meredith, Martin Luther King, Jr., and Stokely Carmichael, who urges the 15,000 African Americans in attendance to "build a power base . . . so strong that we will bring them [whites] to their knees every time they mess with us." The march results in the registration of about 4,000 African American voters.

1966, July 10 • Chicago, Illinois
Martin Luther King, Jr. addresses a predominantly African American crowd of 30,000 to 45,000 at Soldier Field and launches a drive to make Chicago an "open city." The rally is sponsored by the Coordinating Council of Committee Organizations, a coalition consisting of some 45 local civil rights groups. From July 12 to 15, violence erupts on Chicago's west side in protest of a decision by Chicago police to shut off a fire hydrant which had been opened illegally to give African American children relief from the stifling heat. Two African Americans are killed, scores of police and civilians wounded, and 372 persons are arrested.

1966, July 18 • Cleveland, Ohio
Shootings, fire-bombings, and looting spread throughout Cleveland's east side. Four people are killed and fifty are injured. Most of the 164 persons arrested are charged with looting. The riot results in widespread property damage.

1967, January • Washington, DC
Representative Adam Clayton Powell, Jr. of New York is stripped of his chairmanship of the House Committee on Education and Labor and barred from assuming his seat in the Ninetieth Congress. A congressional committee investigating the case later proposes public censure, loss of seniority, and a $40,000 fine. Powell and his lawyers indicate their intention to challenge the constitutionality of this decision in federal court.

1967, February 15 • Washington, DC
President Lyndon B. Johnson asks Congress to pass new civil rights legislation pertaining to the sale and

Voting registration demonstrators being harassed by Alabama state troopers during a march from Selma to Montgomery in 1965 (AP/Wide World Photos, Inc.).

rental of housing. In a special address to Congress, Johnson outlines the scope of the proposed bill. The bill, Johnson states, is designed to end discrimination in jury selection, permit the Equal Employment Opportunity Commission to issue cease-and-desist orders, extend the life of the Commission on Civil Rights, and authorize $2.7 dollars in appropriations for the Community Relations Service. The bill would enable individuals to file damage suits in housing discrimination cases. Violators of the bill would be subject to court orders and fines issued by the secretary of the Department of Housing and Urban Development.

1967, March 1 • Washington, DC
By a vote of 307–116, the U.S. House of Representatives bars Adam Clayton Powell, Jr. from the Ninetieth Congress. Powell immediately files suit in U.S. district court to combat his ouster, asserting that he has met all citizenship, age, and residency requirements for House membership. The congressman also charges that his constituency is left without representation and, therefore, vulnerable to discrimination.

1967, March 29 • The Fifth Circuit Court of Appeals

upholds the legality of revised federal school desegregation guidelines. The court, in an 8–4 ruling, calls for the desegregation of all students, teachers, school transportation facilities, and school-related activities in six Southern states. The guidelines establish rough percentage goals to be used in determining compliance with the Civil Rights Act of 1964.

1967, May 3 • Montgomery, Alabama
A federal district court overturns an Alabama statute designed to prevent school desegregation. The court rules that no state may nullify the action of "a federal department or agency without initiating Court action" which only the U.S. Supreme Court can review.

1967, May 10 • Jackson, Mississippi
An African American delivery man, Benjamin Brown, is shot and killed during riots on the campus of Jackson State College. Within full view of police, Brown is left at the scene unattended until he is taken to the University Hospital by African American bystanders. The police, unable to contain the demonstrators, are reinforced by more than one thousand National Guardsmen.

Civil rights workers Michael Schwerner, James Earl Chaney, and Andrew Goodman were murdered in Mississippi in 1965 (Corbis Corporation [Bellevue]).

1967, June 2 • Boston, Massachusetts
Rioting erupts in Boston's predominantly African American section of Roxbury. The disturbance occurs in the wake of an attempt by welfare mothers to barricade themselves inside a building as a protest against police brutality. The rioting results in the arrest of nearly one hundred people, while scores of others are severely injured.

1967, June 12 • Newark, New Jersey
The "long hot summer" begins in earnest in Newark, New Jersey, scene of the most devastating riot to sweep an urban center since the 1965 Watts uprising.

1967, June 13 • Washington, DC
Thurgood Marshall is appointed an associate justice of the U.S. Supreme Court, the first African American so designated.

1967, June 19 • Washington, DC
U.S. District Court Judge J. Skelly Wright rules that *de facto* segregation of African Americans in the District of Columbia is unconstitutional and orders the complete desegregation of the district's schools by the fall.

1967, June 27 • Buffalo, New York
Three days of rioting result in more than 85 injuries, 205 arrests, and property damage estimated at $100,000.

1967, July 19 • Washington, DC
The U.S. House of Representatives passes legislation which states that it is a federal crime to cross state lines or to use interstate facilities for the purpose of inciting a riot. The bill is aimed at alleged professional agitators who travel from city to city to inflame the people. New York's Emanuel Celler finds the bill "neither preventive nor curative" and fears it will only arouse African American hostility even further.

1967, July 20 • Newark, New Jersey
Despite objections by New Jersey Governor Hughes, a four-day conclave of African American leaders, many of them Black Power advocates, convenes in Newark. Militancy and a call for separate nationhood dominate the meeting. One participant at the conference, Alfred Black of the Newark Human Relations Commission, states that "the black today is either a radical or an Uncle Tom. There is no middle ground."

1967, July 22 • Detroit, Michigan
Rioting erupts in the morning hours of July 22. By July 29, over 7,000 persons are arrested and 43 persons killed.

1967, July 27 • Washington, DC
President Lyndon B. Johnson appoints a blue-ribbon panel to "investigate the origins of the recent disorders in our cities." The president instructs the commission to set aside political considerations and concern itself solely with the health and safety of American society and its citizens. On August 10, the National Advisory Commission on Civil Disorders urges President Johnson to increase the number of African Americans in the army and air national guard. The panel also recommends increased riot-control training for the guard, as well as a review of promotion procedures. The recommendations, delivered in a letter to President John-

Betty Shabazz leaves the morgue at Bellevue Hospital in New York in 1965 after identifying the body of her husband, Malcolm X (Corbis Corporation [Bellevue]).

son, are forwarded to U.S. Defense Secretary Robert McNamara.

1967, August 14 • Dorchester County, Maryland

H. Rap Brown is indicted *in absentia* by a grand jury on charges of inciting to riot, arson, and other related actions which threaten the public peace. Brown is arrested in New York on August 19 and charged with carrying a gun across state lines while under indictment. After strenuous objections are voiced by his white lawyer, William Kunstler, Brown's bail is reduced to $15,000. On August 22, he is released from jail in time to address a crowd of one hundred blacks on the steps of the Foley Square courthouse. Pointing to whites nearby, Brown says: "That's your enemy out there. And you better not forget, because I ain't going to."

1967, August 19 • New Haven, Connecticut

Nearly 450 persons are arrested during five days of looting, arson, and vandalism. No serious injuries are reported, and no shots are fired by police despite frequent curfew violations.

1967, October 20 • Philadelphia, Mississippi

An all-white federal jury of five men and seven women returns a guilty verdict in a retrial for the 1964 murder of three civil rights workers near Philadelphia, Mississippi. Seven men are convicted of conspiracy. However, eight defendants are acquitted, and three are declared victims of a mistrial. Among the guilty are Chief Deputy Sheriff Cecil Price and Sam Bowers, Imperial Wizard of the Ku Klux Klan.

1968, February 5 • Orangeburg, South Carolina

Three African American youths are shot to death and more than thirty people are wounded in a racial outburst involving police and students at South Carolina State College. The violence is the culmination of student protests against the segregation of a local bowling alley. On February 7, the campus is sealed off and classes are suspended in the wake of rock and bottle-throwing incidents. On February 8, three students are fired on by police who mistakenly believe one of their troopers has been shot. In reality, the trooper was knocked down by a piece of lumber thrown by a demonstrator. On February 9, Governor McNair orders a curfew and attributes the violence to "Black Power" advocates. On February 11, local blacks call for the removal of the National Guard and announce plans for a boycott of white businesses. The city leaders counter by establishing a Human Relations Commission which resolves to prevent further outbreaks of violence. On February 24, the Southern Regional Council issues a report analyzing the Orangeburg upheaval. The report blames the outbreak of violence on the emotional appeal of black power to young blacks, overreaction by white citizens and police, feelings of hopelessness among blacks, and the expectations by whites that police power and military force must be utilized to cope with all forms of public demonstrations.

1968, February 29 • Washington, DC

President Lyndon B. Johnson's National Advisory Commission on Civil Disorders issues an exhaustive report on the causes of the civil disorders that disrupted the nation in 1967. The commission identifies the major cause of the rioting as the existence of two separate bodies in America—"one black, one white, separate and unequal." It charges that white racism, more than anything else, was the chief catalyst in the already explosive mixture of discrimination, poverty, and frustration that ignited so many urban ghettos in the tragic summer of 1967. It reminds white America how deeply it is implicated in the existence of the ghetto. "White institutions created it, white institutions maintain it, and white society condones it." To overcome this terrible and crushing legacy, the commission implores the nation to initiate a massive and sustained commitment to action

The first major race riot of the 1960s occurred in the Watts section of Los Angeles, where an estimated 10,000 rioters participated (Corbis Corporation [Bellevue]).

and reform, and it appeals for unprecedented levels of "funding and performance" in housing, education, employment, welfare, law enforcement, and the mass media.

1968, March 11 • Washington, DC

The U.S. Senate passes the Civil Rights Bill of 1968. Among its major provisions are sweeping housing and anti-riot measures which go far beyond the federal protection offered to civil rights workers in the 1967 House version of the bill.

1968, March 29 • Memphis, Tennessee

A teenage African American youth is slain after a protest march led by Martin Luther King, Jr. deteriorates into violence and looting. The march marks the culmination of six weeks of labor strike activity involving the sanitation workers of the city—ninety percent of whom are African American. Civil rights leaders and African American ministers call for a boycott of downtown businesses and urge massive civil disobedience to express support for the strikers. Such action broadens the focus of the strike and transforms it into a general civil rights action. On the day of the march, disturbances begin almost

immediately. Some African American students who have been refused the right to leave school and participate in the march begin pelting police with bricks; others smash department store windows along Beale Street. Most of the 6,000 to 20,000 marchers demonstrate peacefully. City and county police join the National Guard in quelling the disturbances. After King is spirited away to safety at the nearby Lorraine Motel, tear gas is fired at the crowds. More than 150 people are arrested, 40 of them on looting charges.

1968, April 4 • Memphis, Tennessee

The world is shocked by the assassination of Martin Luther King, Jr. Felled by a single bullet, King is pronounced dead at St. Joseph's Hospital at 7:05 P.M. CST, barely one hour after the shooting. Attorney General Ramsey Clark, on hand to conduct the preliminary investigation in person, declares that the early evidence points to the crime as being the work of a single assassin. Witnesses report seeing a white man running from the doorway of a rooming house at 420 South Main Street minutes after the shooting. The killing triggers a wave of violence in over one hundred cities including such urban centers as Baltimore, Chicago, Kansas City,

Adam Clayton Powell Jr. delivers a speech before the Lincoln Memorial in Washington, DC (Magnum Photos, Inc.).

Missouri, and Washington, DC. Some 70,000 federal troops and National Guardsmen are dispatched to restore order. Official figures report 46 dead: 41 blacks, five whites. Thousands are injured and arrested. On April 5, Reverend Ralph Abernathy is named to succeed King and discloses that SCLC's first public gesture will be to lead the march King himself was planning. Three days later, Coretta Scott King takes her place in the front ranks of the marchers, locking arms with two of the 42,000 people on hand for the demonstration. King's body is put on public view at Ebenezer Baptist Church in Atlanta, Georgia, on April 6. He is buried at South View Cemetery on April 9 after funeral services are held at the church and a general memorial service is conducted at Morehouse College, his alma mater.

1968, April 10 • Washington, DC

The assassination of Martin Luther King, Jr. moves the U.S. House of Representatives to submit to President Johnson a Senate-passed civil rights bill prohibiting racial discrimination in the sale or rental of eighty percent of the nation's housing. Johnson signs the measure on April 11 and counsels the nation to stay on the road to progress by recognizing "the process of law."

1968, May 11 • Washington, DC

Caravans of people representing the Poor People's Campaign begin arriving in Washington, DC. The Defense Department alerts "selected troop units" to help District of Columbia police in the event of violence. On Mother's Day, May 12, Coretta Scott King leads a march of welfare mothers from twenty cities and declares at a subsequent rally that she will try to enlist the support of all the nation's women "in a campaign of conscience." The next day Ralph Abernathy, clad in blue denims and using carpenter's tools, presides at the christening of Resurrection City, the plywood shanty town erected within walking distance of the White House and the Capitol. Abernathy is able to report, as the campaign draws to a close, that certain gains have been recorded. The Department of Agriculture, for instance, agrees to "provide food to the neediest counties in this country." The U.S. Senate approves a bill to increase low-income housing construction and the Office of Economic Opportunity (OEO) allocates $25 million for expanded programs including one encouraging participation from poor people.

1968, June 5 • Los Angeles, California

Senator Robert Kennedy, a champion of civil rights, is

Thurgood Marshall (center) holding discussions with Jacob Javits and Robert Kennedy (Corbis Corporation [Bellevue]).

shot and killed moments after leaving a rally celebrating his victory over Eugene McCarthy in the California Democratic primary.

1968, June 8 • London
James Earl Ray, alleged assassin of Martin Luther King, Jr. is arrested.

1968, July 23 • Cleveland, Ohio
Racial violence erupts in Cleveland's Glenville district, resulting in the deaths of eleven persons, eight of them black, and three white policemen. Mayor Carl Stokes helps to restore order after a night of burning and looting which results in over a million dollars worth of property damage. Over three thousand National Guardsmen are on the scene, but they are not widely utilized. Ahmed (Fred) Evans, a 37-year-old anti-poverty worker and head of the Black Nationalists of New Libya, is blamed for starting the disturbances. On June 26, Ahmed Evans is arraigned on three charges of first-degree murder.

1968, July 27 • Washington, DC
The Kerner Commission releases preliminary findings that indicate a sharp rise in the number of African

Americans who accept urban riots as a justifiable or inevitable response to conditions prevailing in the nation's ghettos.

1968, August 7 • Miami, Florida
Two days of looting, fire bombing, and shooting in the black section of Miami culminate in Florida Governor Claude Kirk's decision to summon the National Guard to quell the disorders. Despite Ralph Abernathy's plea for an end to the violence, crowds of African Americans battle police over an eight-block area. On August 8, three African Americans are killed in gun battles with law enforcement officials. Although Dade County Mayor Chuck Hall accuses outsiders of instigating the trouble, the ten percent unemployment rate among African Americans in the 16–22 age bracket is cited as a major factor contributing to the violence.

1968, September 8 • California
Black Panther Huey P. Newton is tried and convicted of manslaughter in the October 28, 1967, shooting death of a white policeman. Nearly three weeks later, Newton is sentenced to 2–15 years imprisonment. The trial and the conviction introduce the nation at large to a new and formidable Black Panther Party.

President Lyndon B. Johnson signing the 1968 Civil Rights Act. In attendance are Senator Edward W. Brooke (left of middle) and Supreme Court Justice Thurgood Marshall (far right) (AP/Wide World Photos, Inc.).

1968, October 8 • Washington, DC
Some 250 African Americans protest the fatal shooting of an African American pedestrian by a policeman. Demonstrators set fires and block traffic until police reinforcements disperse them with tear gas. The policeman is eventually exonerated of all charges by a federal grand jury.

1968, December 1 • New Jersey
Three members of the Black Panthers are arrested on charges of carrying out a machine gun attack on a Jersey City police station on November 29. A Black Panther spokesman claims that a December 1 bombing of party headquarters in Newark is in response to the Jersey City attack. A police sergeant cites the arrest of seven Newark Panthers on November 28 as the cause of the precinct attack.

1969, January 3 • Washington, DC
After a long and bitter debate concerning his qualifications and conduct, the House of Representatives votes to seat Adam Clayton Powell, Jr. The House, however, fines him $25,000 for alleged misuse of payroll funds and travel allowances and demotes him to freshman status by stripping him of his seniority rank.

1969, February 6 • Washington, DC
President Nixon appoints James Farmer as an assistant secretary of the Department of Health, Education and Welfare; Arthur Fletcher as an assistant secretary of the Department of Labor; and William Brown III, as chairman of the Equal Employment Opportunity Commission.

1969, June 6 • Houston, Texas
Testimony released in a federal court indicates that the telephones of Martin Luther King, Jr. and Elijah Muhammad were tapped by the FBI, despite the fact that President Lyndon B. Johnson had ordered a halt to all wiretaps in 1965.

1969, June 16 • Washington, DC
The U.S. Supreme Court rules that the suspension of Representative Adam Clayton Powell, Jr. by the House of Representatives is unconstitutional.

1969, July 6 • New York City, New York
James Forman of the National Black Economic Devel-

Coretta Scott King and her children leading the funeral procession of slain civil rights leader Dr. Martin Luther King, Jr. (AP/Wide World Photos, Inc.).

opment Conference receives a check for $15,000 from the Washington Square United Methodist Church. The church is the first predominantly white organization to support Forman's demand that American churches pay $500 million in reparations for helping to perpetuate slavery.

1969, August 1 • Washington, DC
The U.S. Justice Department files suit against the state of Georgia to end segregation in its schools. Governor Lester G. Maddox condemns the action as criminal and declares the state will "win the war against these tyrants."

1969, August 19 • California
Black Panther leader Bobby Seale is arrested for the May 19 murder of alleged Panther informer Alex Rackley in New Haven, Connecticut. Bobby Seale's defense attorney accuses the Justice Department of initiating a national campaign to intimidate and harass the Black Panther Party. Seale is later extradited to Connecticut.

1969, August 25 • Pittsburgh, Pennsylvania
Five construction sites are closed by several hundred black construction workers and members of the Black

Construction Coalition to protest "discriminatory hiring practices." Four hundred angry white workers stage counter demonstrations on August 28 and 29 to protest the work stoppage.

1969, September 2 • Hartford, Connecticut
After a relatively quiet summer, the nation is stunned when Hartford becomes the scene of widespread civil disorders including fire bombings and sniping. Scores of people are placed under arrest, and a dusk-to-dawn curfew is imposed.

1969, September 23 • Washington, DC
Secretary of Labor George P. Schultz orders federally-assisted construction projects in Philadelphia to follow the guidelines for minority hiring suggested in the so-called "Philadelphia Plan."

1969, October 29 • Washington, DC
Ruling in the case of *Alexander v. Holmes Board of Education*, the U.S. Supreme Court orders an end to all school segregation. The decision replaces the Warren Court's doctrine of "all deliberate speed," and is regarded as a setback for the Nixon administration.

1970, January 2 • Washington, DC

FBI director J. Edgar Hoover claims that, in 1969, there were over one hundred attacks on police by "hate-type" African American groups such as Black Panthers.

1970, January 3 • Mississippi

Governor John Bell Williams announces his intention to submit to the state legislature a proposal to authorize income tax credits of up to $500 a year for contributors to "private" educational institutions. The plan is designed to create a "workable alternative" to school desegregation. That same day, the Department of Health, Education and Welfare reports that a comprehensive survey indicates that 61 percent of the nation's black students and 65.6 percent of its white students attended segregated schools in 1968. On January 5, black children are enrolled in three formerly all-white Mississippi districts under the watchful eyes of federal marshals and Justice Department officials. Scores of white parents picket the schools, while others keep their children home or send them to private schools.

1970, January 10 • Georgia

Four Southern governors, Maddox of Georgia, Brewer of Alabama, McKeithen of Louisiana, and Kirk of Florida, promise to reject all busing plans designed for their states by the federal government or the courts. Maddox asks the state legislature to abolish compulsory attendance; McKeithen reveals no plan, but describes himself as "drawing the line in the dust;" Brewer denies that the courts have the constitutional authority to order busing as a device to achieve racial balance and promises to use his full executive powers to prevent it; Kirk vows to issue an executive order to block further desegregation of Florida schools.

1970, January 12 • Washington, DC

The U.S. Supreme Court refuses to review the ruling of an Ohio state court which upholds an equal employment plan comparable to the Nixon administration's "Philadelphia Plan." The plan requires state contractors to give assurances that they will employ a specified number of African American workers in projects constructed with federal funds or sponsored completely by the federal government. The Ohio contractor who brought suit in the case had refused to provide such assurances.

1970, January 15 • Though it is not yet a national holiday, the birthday of Martin Luther King, Jr. is celebrated with impressive ceremonies, eulogies, and church services in many parts of the country. Public schools are closed in many cities; in others, they are kept open for formal study of King's life and work. In Atlanta, Coretta Scott King dedicates the Martin Luther King, Jr. Memorial Center, which includes his home, the Ebenezer Baptist Church, and the crypt housing his remains.

1970, January 19 • Washington, DC

G. Harrold Carswell's nomination to the U.S. Supreme Court draws the immediate fire of civil rights advocates. On January 21, the NAACP condemns Carswell's "pro-segregation record." Two days later, the SCLC's Ralph Abernathy sends a telegram to Senate leaders pleading for "reassurance to the black community that there is. . . understanding and support. . . for our needs." AFL-CIO President George Meany calls the appointment "a slap in the face to the nation's black citizens." Testifying before the Senate Judiciary Committee on January 27, Carswell states: "I am not a racist. I have no notions, secretive or otherwise, of racial superiority." This statement contrasts sharply with a 1948 remark that Carswell would yield to no man "in the firm, vigorous belief in the principles of white supremacy."

1970, February 6 • Denver, Colorado

Approximately one-third of Denver school buses are destroyed by bombs in an attempt by segregationists to disrupt the city's school integration plans.

1970, February 16 • Washington, DC

President Richard M. Nixon establishes a Cabinet-level task force to assist and counsel local school districts which have been ordered to desegregate their school immediately. The objective is to spare the public school system undue disruption while, at the same time, insuring compliance with the law. On February 18 the Senate passes, by a 56–36 vote, an amendment to deny federal funds to school districts whose racial imbalance is the result of residential segregation. On February 19, Southerners in the House and Senate incorporate riders into two appropriation bills designed to restore "freedom-of-choice" school plans and to prevent the federal government from resorting to busing as a vehicle to promote racial balance.

1970, February 21 • Texas

Texas Governor Preston Smith recommends a state-wide referendum to give voters the opportunity to approve or reject integrated public school busing. Governors Maddox of Georgia and McKeithen of Louisiana sign bills prohibiting busing and student/teacher transfers to achieve racial balance. Governor Brewer calls a special session of the legislature to sponsor a similar bill for Alabama.

1970, February 28 • Washington, DC

A memo written by Daniel Patrick Moynihan to President Richard M. Nixon is revealed. In the memo, Moynihan, domestic advisor to the president, counseled him that "the time may have come when the issue of race could benefit from a period of benign neglect." Moynihan later claims that the memo was intended to suggest ways that the "extraordinary black progress" in the last decade could be "consolidated." However, African American leaders, including Bayard Rustin and Representative John Conyers, charge that the memo is "symptomatic of a calculated, aggressive, systematic effort of the Nixon administration to wipe out civil rights progress of the past twenty years."

1970, March 6 • Mississippi
The state Senate approves a tax relief bill designed to grant financial support to white parents who intend to enroll their children in private academies.

1970, March 9 • Washington, DC
The U.S. Supreme Court orders the Memphis school system to end racial segregation and remands the case to a lower court where it issues instructions to develop an effective desegregation plan.

1970, April 7 • Detroit, Michigan
The school board approves a busing plan for some 3,000 high school students and announces the initiation of a decentralization plan aimed at dispersing white students among the city's secondary schools. In Detroit, 63 percent of the system's 294,000 students are non-white, as are 42 percent of the teachers.

1970, May 12 • Augusta, Georgia
Six African Americans are shot and twenty other people are wounded during a night of violence punctuated by looting, burning, and sniper activity. The immediate cause of the violence is said to be the killing of an African American youth in a county jail a few days earlier. Autopsies of African Americans slain during the protests indicate that they were shot in the back. The *New York Times* later reports that at least three of the dead were unarmed bystanders.

1970, May 14 • Jackson, Mississippi
Two African American students are shot and killed after a night of violence outside a women's dormitory at Jackson State College. Witnesses charge that police simply moved in and indiscriminately blasted the residence hall with shotguns. President Richard M. Nixon dispatches Justice Department officials to search out the facts, but contradictory explanations make it impossible to assemble a wholly-coherent story. On May 17, the Mississippi United Front vows to provide students and other groups with independent protection.

1970, May 23 • Atlanta, Georgia
A five-day, 100-mile march against repression ends in downtown Atlanta with a rally by the Southern Christian Leadership Conference and the NAACP. Speakers at the rally include Ralph Abernathy, Coretta Scott King, and Senator George McGovern. The speakers condemn racism, the Vietnam War, student killings at Kent State and Jackson State, and alleged police brutality in Augusta.

1970, July 10 • Washington, DC
The Internal Revenue Service announces its intention to tax private academies practicing racial discrimination in their admissions policies. The greatest impact of the policy is expected to be felt in the South. The new policy promises these schools sufficient flexibility to avoid immediate revocation of their tax-exempt status.

1970, August 7 • San Rafael, California
A dramatic shootout results in the death of Superior Court Judge Harold Haley and three African Americans on trial. Later investigation traces the sale of the weapons used in the shootout to Angela Davis, controversial UCLA professor and self-admitted Communist. Davis flees the state following the trial and is placed on the FBI's ten most wanted list.

1970, September • Some 300,000 African American children are integrated in over two hundred Southern school districts. However, parental boycotts and delaying tactics by states and cities slow the pace of desegregation. Whites who are opposed to desegregation are encouraged by the Nixon administration's "Southern policy," which has delayed enforcement of integration orders. Nevertheless, the Internal Revenue Service continues to revoke the tax-exempt status of all-white private academies that refuse to admit black students.

1970, October 13 • New York City, New York
Angela Davis is arrested and arraigned in federal court on charges of unlawful flight to avoid prosecution for her alleged role in the August 7 killing of Superior Court Judge Harold Haley.

1970, November 5 • Henderson, North Carolina
Violence erupts when African Americans protest the reopening of a segregated school. The National Guard is called out to restore order and over one hundred arrests are made.

1970, December 30 • Philadelphia, Pennsylvania
The U.S. Court of Appeals for the Third Circuit rules that the Department of Housing and Urban Development must promote fair housing when it considers applications for mortgage insurance and rent supplements.

1971, February 4 • Washington, DC
Eight African American federal employees file suit in

federal court claiming that the Federal Service Entrance Examination, the principal test for qualifying college graduates for civil service posts is "culturally and racially discriminatory."

1971, March 8 • Media, Pennsylvania

Files are stolen from a Federal Bureau of Investigation (FBI) office and released to the press reveal that in November of 1970, J. Edgar Hoover ordered an investigation of all groups "organized to project the demands of black [college] students, because they posed a threat to the nation's stability and security."

1971, March 29 • Washington, DC

President Richard M. Nixon meets with the Congressional Black Caucus, which had been trying to schedule a meeting with him for several months. The African American members of Congress request increased attention to welfare services, desegregation, housing, and social justice programs. President Nixon reportedly promises stronger enforcement of civil rights laws.

1971, May 5 • Brooklyn, New York

A riot erupts in the Brooklyn's Brownsville section after thousands of residents take to the streets to protest cuts in state welfare, Medicaid, food stamps, and educational programs. One policeman is shot, 12 are injured.

1971, May 17 • Washington, DC

Senator George McGovern of South Dakota urges the government to divert $31 billion of current federal spending in an effort to end racial discrimination by the end of the century. Milton Eisenhower, former chairman of President Lyndon B. Johnson's Commission on Causes and Preventions of Violence, warns that the United States faces a racial war if it does not remedy the social injustice, inequitable law enforcement, and the availability of firearms in American society.

1971, June 1 • Washington, DC

By a vote of 5–4, the U.S. Supreme Court declares unconstitutional a Cincinnati city ordinance making it unlawful for small groups of people to loiter in an annoying manner in public places. Many African Americans claimed that such ordinances had been used by police to harass them.

1971, June 4 • Washington, DC

The Department of Labor announces that it is removing support from the voluntary "Chicago Plan," which was to hire four thousand African Americans and Spanish-speaking Americans for construction jobs on federal projects. After 18 months, less than nine hundred African Americans had been accepted in training programs

and only a few had been admitted to Chicago construction unions.

1971, June 28 • Washington, DC

By an 8–0 vote, with Justice Thurgood Marshall abstaining, the U.S. Supreme Court overturns draft evasion charges against Muhammad Ali. In its decision, the Court agreed that Ali, a Muslim, was objecting to military service on religious grounds, rather than on a political basis, as the Department of Justice had charged.

1971, July 24 • Columbus, Georgia

Fifteen African Americans are arrested and several hospitalized during racial disturbances following the dismissal of eight African American policemen. Fire bombings and sniping are reported. State troopers are summoned to maintain order.

1971, August 7 • Georgia

State Representative Julian Bond tours the state to spark the political interests of African Americans who remain unregistered six years after the passage of the Voting Rights Act. Bond notes that due to a blend of apathy and activism, many African Americans do not perceive the ballot as an effective political weapon that can be used to bring change in their lives. Bond cites as an example the failure of African Americans in 1970 to elect African American officials in a district where they represented a majority of the registered voters. Nevertheless, leaders of the SCLC announce that their goal of electing a Southern black to Congress is feasible in view of the redistricting in a number of Southern states.

1971, August 18 • Jackson, Mississippi

Eleven members of the Republic of New Africa, a black separatist organization, are charged with murder and assault of federal officers after the death of Lieutenant I. Skinner, a Mississippi policeman. Skinner was shot when police and FBI agents raided the organization's headquarters in order to serve fugitive warrants on three members. The county district attorney requests that a special grand jury charge the separatists with treason and that the Justice Department allow these charges to take precedence over any federal prosecution.

1971, August 21 • San Quentin, California

George Jackson, author of *Soledad Brothers* and a folk hero to many black and white radicals, is killed during a prison break. Some supporters of Jackson claim he was "set-up" for assassination, while others feel the official version of Jackson's death is essentially correct.

1971, October • Chicago, Illinois

"Black Expo," a four-day cultural and business exposition, attracts some eight hundred thousand people. The exposition is conducted by Jesse Jackson and a number of African American businessmen.

1972, January 10 • Richmond, Virginia
A federal judge orders the consolidation of Richmond's predominantly black school system with two all-white suburban systems. Judge Robert Mehirge bases his decision on the failure of state officials to take positive action to reverse *de facto* segregation.

1972, January 10 • Baton Rouge, Louisiana
Two Black Muslims and two white police officers are killed in a shootout. Disturbances following the shootings injure 31 people and the National Guard is called in to restore order.

1972, March • Gary, Indiana
Some eight thousand African Americans representing a wide spectrum of political views attend the first National Black Political Convention. The convention is chaired by Imamu Amiri Baraka with Mayor Richard Hatcher of Gary, Indiana, as the keynote speaker. The group approves a political platform, the "Black Agenda" that demands reparations, proportional congressional representation for African Americans, an increase in federal spending to combat crime and drug trafficking, reduction of the military budget, and a guaranteed annual income of $6,500 for a family of four.

1972, March 16 • Washington, DC
President Nixon proposes a moratorium on all court-ordered busing until July of 1973. African American members of Congress charge that the president is suggesting a return to "separate but equal" schools.

1972, June 4 • San Jose, California
After 13 hours of deliberation, a jury of eleven whites and one Mexican-American acquits Angela Davis of murder and other charges in connection with a 1970 courthouse shootout in San Rafael, California.

1972, June 6 • Richmond, Virginia
A U.S. Appeals Court, by a 5–1 vote, overturns a plan which would have required the busing of school children between Richmond and two nearly all-white suburbs.

1972, July 12 • Miami Beach, Florida
Senator George McGovern of South Dakota wins the presidential nomination at the Democratic party's national convention. African American delegates make up approximately 15 percent of the total delegates in attendance. New York Representative Shirley Chisholm,

Shirley Chisholm (AP/Wide World Photos, Inc.)

the first African American woman to seek a presidential nomination, receives 151 votes.

1972, August • Washington, DC
Attorney General Richard Kleindienst files suit against the cities of Los Angeles, California, and Montgomery, Alabama, for discrimination in hiring for public service jobs.

1972, November • Cincinnati, Ohio
The Association for the Study of Black Life History, meeting for its fifty-seventh annual convention, changes its name to the Association for the Study of African American History. The change is based on a mail ballot of the Association's membership, some two-thirds of whom opt to substitute "African-American" for "black" in the title. Prominent speakers at the convention include: Andrew F. Brimmer, a governor of the Federal Reserve Board; Representative Louis Stokes of Cleveland; John Hope Franklin, professor of history at Duke University; and Rayford W. Logan, professor of history at Howard University.

**1972, November • Richard M. Nixon is reelected president in a landslide victory over Senator George McGovern, despite the fact that some 86 percent of the African American vote went to McGovern. However, African Americans achieve a number of electoral successes as the number of African Americans in Congress increases from 12 to 15; Barbara Jordan of Houston, Texas, and Andrew Young of Atlanta become the first

Southern African Americans elected to Congress since Reconstruction. Senator Edward Brooke, an African American Republican from Massachusetts, wins reelection and African American representation in state legislatures increases dramatically.

1972, November 16 • Baton Rouge, Louisiana
Two young African American men, Denver A. Smith and Leonard Douglas Brown, are killed on the campus of Southern University during a confrontation between students and police. The students had been pressing for the resignation of the university's president G. Leon Netterville, whom they charged with arbitrarily dismissing teachers he regarded as militant and for being unreceptive to student demands for better living and academic facilities. Following the shootings, Louisiana Governor Edwin W. Edwards closes the school and sends the National Guard to the Baton Rouge campus.

1972, December 14 • Washington, DC
In the case of *Banks v. Perks*, the U.S. Supreme Court rules unanimously that residents of racially-segregated housing projects can sue to have them integrated. In its opinion, the Court states that white residents living in segregated housing projects suffer the same social and economic injuries as those denied access to these facilities.

1973, April 28 • Washington, DC
A government panel releases its final report determining whether the Tuskegee Syphilis Study, conducted between 1932 and 1972 by the Public Health Service, was justified. The study involved observing the effects of untreated syphilis on 430 African American men living in rural Macon County, Alabama. The panel found no evidence that participants in the study had been given any type of informed consent. The panel concluded that the study was unjustified on both scientific and humanitarian grounds and that all policies regarding research on humans be reformed.

1973, May 29 • Los Angeles, California
Thomas Bradley is elected mayor of Los Angeles after defeating the incumbent Sam Yorty by one hundred thousand votes. Yorty had defeated Bradley in the 1969 mayoral election.

1973, June • Washington, DC
The Joint Center for Political Studies reports that as of April of 1973, 2,621 African Americans held elective offices in the United States at every level from school boards to the Congress. When the first list was compiled, in 1969, the total was only 1,185.

1974 • Henry Aaron breaks Babe Ruth's long-standing record and hits his 715th home run.

1974, March • Washington, DC
The Department of Justice releases memos revealing that in the 1960s and early 1970s, the FBI had waged a campaign designed to disrupt, discredit, and neutralize black nationalist groups including the Black Panther party. A major objective of the effort, according to the memo, was to prevent the emergence of an African American leader capable of uniting disparate factions and inspiring violence. Jesse Jackson remarks that the documents implicate the FBI in the deaths of Martin Luther King, Jr., Malcolm X, and Fred Hampton.

1974, March 15 • Little Rock, Arkansas
The second Black National Political Convention is held. Mayor Richard B. Hatcher of Gary, Indiana, and Imamu Amiri Baraka are among the speakers. Delegates to the convention approve several resolutions including the establishment of a fund to provide money for civil rights causes and a resolution voicing support for African liberation movements.

1974, June • Washington, DC
A draft report from the Senate committee investigating the "Watergate" scandal indicates that the Nixon administration tried to gain the support or neutrality of prominent African Americans during the 1972 presidential campaign by withholding federal funds for government programs. Among those contacted by the Nixon administration were Jesse Jackson, head of Operation PUSH, and James Farmer, an administration official during Nixon's first term.

1974, July 25 • Washington, DC
In the case of *Milliken v. Bradley*, the U.S. Supreme Court nullifies an attempt to implement the "metropolitan integration" of predominantly African American schools in Detroit with those of nearby white suburbs. Chief Justice Warren Burger, writing for the majority, declares that segregation in a city's schools does not justify its combination with schools in its suburbs. Justice Thurgood Marshall calls the Court's decision "an emasculation of the constitutional guarantee of equal opportunity."

1974, November • The number of African American elected officials increases at the federal, state, and local levels. African American members of Congress are reelected and one new member, Harold Ford of Memphis, Tennessee, is added. African Americans are also elected to the post of lieutenant governor in California and Colorado.

1974, December 11 • Boston, Massachusetts
Violence erupts between supporters and opponents of public school integration.

1975, January 16 • Washington, DC
William T. Coleman is named secretary of transportation by President Ford, becoming the second African American in the nation's history to hold a Cabinet post.

1975, January 25 • The *New York Times* reports that the FBI had wiretapped conversations of civil rights leaders including Martin Luther King, Jr.

1975, May 3 • Department of Labor figures report the national unemployment rate at nine percent, the African American rate at 15 percent. Vernon L. Jordan, Jr. of the National Urban League reports that the African American rate is actually 26 percent.

1975, August 18 • Washington, DC
District of Columbia Appellate Court Judge Julia Cooper is confirmed by the Senate, becoming the highest-ranking African American woman in the federal courts.

1975, August 20 • Washington, DC
Senator Edward Brooke calls for a $10 billion federal employment program to end the economic "depression" in black America by creating one million public service jobs.

1975, August 29 • Washington, DC
General Daniel James, Jr. becomes commander-in-chief of the North American Air Defense Command (NORAD). On the same day, he is promoted and becomes the first African American four-star general in U.S. history.

1975, September 27 • Washington, DC
The Congressional Black Caucus holds its fifth annual dinner. The major theme of the affair is "From Changing Structures to Using Structure—1879–1976." Panelists recommend the federal takeover of the welfare system and poverty assistance, that the states assume more fiscal responsibility for education, and that Caucus-directed programs develop a national African American position on matters of policy.

1975, December • Washington, DC
U.S. Attorney General Edward Levy opens an official review of the Martin Luther King, Jr. assassination. Although James Earl Ray was convicted of the crime, many facts point to a conspiracy and suggest that those really responsible for the murder are still at large.

1976, April 26 • New York City, New York
The Metropolitan Applied Research Center, a major African American research organization founded to serve as an advocate for the urban poor, announces that it must close due to declining funds.

1976, August 31 • Mississippi
A chancellery court orders the NAACP to pay the sum of $1,250,058 to 12 white Port Gibson merchants. The money is compensation for the financial hardships inflicted on the merchants due to the NAACP's successful boycott of white businesses in 1966.

1976, November 2 • African American voters play a vital role in Jimmy Carter's victory over President Gerald Ford in the presidential election. Carter received about 94 percent of some 6.6 million African American votes.

1976, November 14 • Plains, Georgia
The congregation of President-elect Jimmy Carter's Baptist church votes to drop its 11-year ban on attendance by African Americans.

1976, December 16 • Washington, DC
President-elect Jimmy Carter appoints Andrew Young as chief delegate to the United Nations and Patricia Roberts Harris as secretary of the Department of Housing and Urban Development.

1977, January 20 • Washington, DC
Clifford Alexander, Jr. is sworn in as the first African American secretary of the U.S. Army. President Carter appoints 19 African Americans to his Cabinet, while 37 other African Americans obtain executive positions within the Carter administration.

1977, April 19 • New York City, New York
Author Alex Haley receives a Pulitzer Prize for his book *Roots*.

1977, July 29 • St. Louis, Missouri
Roy Wilkins, a 42-year veteran of the NAACP, announces his retirement during the organization's 68th annual convention.

1977, September 4 • New York City, New York
At a meeting of the National Urban League, 15 African American members agree to form a loose coalition to combat perceived anti-African American sentiment within the nation and seek greater job opportunities for African Americans.

1978, January 17 • Major Guion S. Bluford, Jr., Major Frederick D. Gregory, and Ronald E. McNair join the space program and begin training as astronauts for future space missions.

1978, May 29 • Washington, DC
Files made public by the FBI reveal that an unidentified African American leader worked with the agency during the 1960s in an effort to remove Martin Luther King, Jr. from national prominence in the Civil Rights movement. The information released is from the files of the late J. Edgar Hoover.

1978, June 28 • Washington, DC
Hearing the case *University of California v. Bakke*, the U.S. Supreme Court, in a 5–4 decision, orders that white student Allan P. Bakke be admitted to the medical school at the University of California, Davis. The Court rules that the refusal to admit Bakke is tantamount to reverse discrimination and that the use of racial or ethnic quotas is an improper means of achieving racial balance. The Court also holds that the college's affirmative action program is invalid since it had the effect of discriminating against qualified white applicants, although the court perceived the goal of attaining a diverse student body as constitutional and permissible.

1978, December 3 • The U.S. Census Bureau reports that from 1960 to 1977, the number of African Americans living in suburban areas increased from 2.4 million to 4.6 million, and that 55 percent of the 24.5 million African Americans in the United States live in central cities, indicating a decline from the 1970 figure of 59 percent.

1979, February 27 • Washington, DC
The Department of Housing and Urban Development announces that it will foreclose on the financially-troubled Soul City, a new town in rural North Carolina that was to have been controlled by African Americans but open to members of all races. Since 1969, when Floyd B. McKissick announced the idea for the city, $27 million had been spent by federal, state, and local sources. McKissick vows to continue efforts to keep the project alive.

1979, May 2 • Washington, DC
The Congressional Black Caucus and delegates from 11 Southern states set up an "action alert communications network." This network is designed to exert pressure on at least one hundred white congressional representatives from predominantly black districts to vote with the caucus on important issues.

1979, June 19 • The U.S. Census Bureau announces a study indicating that although blacks have made enormous advances in employment, income, health, housing, political power, and other measures of social well-being, they remain far behind white Americans.

1979, June 25 • Washington, DC
Amalya L. Kearse becomes the first woman to receive an appointment to the U.S. Court of Appeals.

1979, June 29 • Washington, DC
In the case of *United States Steel v. Brian Weber*, the U.S. Supreme Court rules that private employers can legally give special preference to black workers to eliminate "manifest racial imbalance" in traditionally white jobs.

1979, August 1 • Washington, DC
The U.S. House of Representatives votes 408–1 to place a bust of the late Martin Luther King, Jr. in the Capitol. The bust is the first work of art in the Capitol honoring an African American.

1979, August 16 • New York City, New York
Andrew Young resigns as the chief U.S. delegate to the United Nations after being publicly criticized for conducting unauthorized talks with the Palestine Liberation Organization in New York. The resignation sets off a storm of controversy and animosity between segments of the Jewish and African American communities.

1979, December 22 • Washington, DC
The Joint Center for Political Studies reveals that between 1978 and 1979, the number of African Americans elected to public office increased by 104. This two percent increase is considered meager, especially because such officials were elected in states with substantial African American populations.

1980, February 6 • Washington, DC
The Congressional Black Caucus criticizes President Carter's fiscal 1981 budget proposals because they increase the amount of military spending while reducing the funding for social programs. Caucus members promise to initiate legislation to reduce military spending increases and pronounce the budget "an unmitigated disaster for the poor, the unemployed and minorities."

1980, April 22 • Washington, DC
Hearing the case *City of Mobile v. Bolden*, the U.S. Supreme Court, in a 6–3 decision, overturns a lower court ruling that an at-large city electoral system is

Demonstrators protesting the Supreme Court's decision in the case of *University of California v. Bakke* (AP/Wide World Photos, Inc.).

unconstitutional because it dilutes the voting strength of African Americans.

1980, May 11 • Washington, DC

Early primary results reveal that the African American community is supporting President Carter's second-term bid despite criticism of his record by national African American leaders, according to reports. The "resounding" victories won by Carter in the Southern primaries are interpreted as African Americans lacking faith in their ability to enact a "Great Society-style social renewal" agenda as proposed by Senator Edward M. Kennedy.

1980, May 14 • Birmingham, Alabama

J. B. Stoner, a white supremacist, is convicted for the 1958 bombing of an African American church in Birmingham, Alabama.

1980, May 18 • Miami, Florida

The African American Liberty City area and predominantly African American Coconut Grove section of Miami erupt into riotous violence, ending with nine dead and 163 injured, following the acquittal of four white Dade County police officers in the beating death of a black man. In the night-long unrest, stores are looted, property burned, and whites fatally beaten. During the violence, African Americans are heard screaming the name "McDuffie" (Arthur), the African American insurance executive beaten to death following a high-speed chase with Dade County police officers for a traffic violation. Dade County officials impose an 8 p.m. to 6 a.m. curfew; 350 National Guard troops set up headquarters in an armory with 450 more enroute from Orlando.

1980, May 29 • Fort Wayne, Indiana

Vernon E. Jordan, Jr., president of the National Urban League, is shot and seriously wounded by an unknown assailant. Stating that the shooting evidenced "an element of premeditation," director of the FBI William H. Webster says, "the shooting was not accidental, and was in furtherance of an apparent conspiracy to deprive Vernon Jordan of his civil rights." The shooting occurred just outside Jordan's motel room.

1980, July 3 • Washington, DC

A ruling authorizing Congress to impose racial quotas to

remedy past discrimination against minority contractors in federal jobs programs is upheld by the U.S. Supreme Court in a 6–3 vote. It validates the ten percent minority set-aside of federal public works contracts, challenged by white contractors in *Fullilove V. Klutznick.*

1980, July 3 • Cincinnati, Ohio

In a consent decree with the Justice Department, the city of Cincinnati agrees to hire and promote more African Americans and women within the police department. The decree permanently enjoins the city from engaging in any employment discrimination. Over a five-year period, 34 percent of new police officer vacancies will be filled by African Americans and 23 percent by women. The fire department of the city of Chicago, in a similar action (April 2, 1980), was permanently prohibited from discrimination against any candidate for promotion on the basis of race or national origin. The settlement of this discrimination action was filed in federal district court and resulted from a suit charging violations of the Civil Rights Act of 1964 and the Federal Sharing Act of 1972. In New York City, the U.S. Court of Appeals (August 1, 1980) overturned a lower court ruling that 50 percent of all new police officer hires be African American or Hispanic. The appeals court, however, ruled that the written test used for hiring had "significant disparate racial impact" in violation of the Civil Rights Act of 1964. It concluded that until a new test was implemented, one-third of all newly hired police must be African American or Hispanic.

1980, September 3 • St. Louis, Missouri

St. Louis schools are desegregated peacefully after eight years of struggle. Over sixteen thousand students are bused on the first day of classes under court orders. No violence is reported.

1980, September 26 • Detroit, Michigan

Federal district judge Horace W. Gilmore invalidates the 1980 census on the grounds that it undercounts African Americans and Hispanics, thus violating the one-person, one-vote principle. The action was precipitated by a suit initiated by the city of Detroit with support from dozens of other cities. The census was later upheld in higher courts.

1980, September 26 • Washington, DC

The Congressional Black Caucus marks its tenth anniversary with its annual legislative weekend. The group of bipartisan representatives cite as their major achievements the Humphrey-Hawkins Full Employment Bill and the ten percent "minority-set-aside" law established to ensure minority firms a nearly representative share of federal contracts. The caucus identifies its current concern as the potential reapportionment of congressional districts affected by the outcome of the 1980 census.

1980, September 29 • New York City, New York

The Schomburg Center for Research in Black Culture opens a new $3.8 million building in Harlem.

1980, September 30 • Washington, DC

The first annual Black College Day is attended by eighteen thousand African American students. Speeches on the preservation of African American colleges and universities are given by African American officials and student leaders. The march is organized by African American journalist Tony Brown in an effort to draw public attention to the impact of integration and merging of African American private and public colleges and universities. Brown contends seven out of ten blacks attending predominantly white colleges do not graduate.

1980, November 23 • Philadelphia, Pennsylvania

About 1,000 people from 25 states attend a convention and form the National Black Independent Party. The idea grows out of a National Black Political Assembly in Gary, Indiana, in 1972.

1980, December 12 • Washington, DC

African American leaders of the nation's major civil rights organizations meet with President-elect Ronald Reagan who says he will defend the civil rights of minorities. The leaders urge him to appoint an African American to a Cabinet position in his administration. Present at the meeting are Vernon E. Jordan, Jr., president of the National Urban League; Benjamin Hooks, executive director, NAACP; and Dorothy I. Height, president of the National Council of Negro Women.

1980, December 18 • San Antonio, Texas

A federal grand jury acquits Charles Veverka of four counts of violating the civil rights of Arthur McDuffie, an African American who was beaten to death while in police custody. The jury deliberates for 16 hours, finally breaking an 11–1 deadlock that threatened a mistrial. Veverka was indicted following violent riots in Miami resulting from the acquittal of four white police officers accused of executing the fatal beating.

1980, December 23 • Washington, DC

Samuel R. Pierce, Jr. is named by President-elect Ronald Reagan to the Cabinet post of secretary of the Department of Housing and Urban Development. As such, Pierce is the highest-ranking African American appointee of the new administration. According to reports, Pierce is a life-long Republican, widely respected in legal, financial, and civil rights circles.

Members of the Congressional Black Caucus speaking to the press outside the U.S. Capitol in 1980: William Gray, Charles Rangel, Cardiss Collins, Walter Fauntroy, and Bennett Stewart (AP/Wide World Photos, Inc.).

1981, February 7 • Miami, Florida

Three Miami youths are convicted of murder in connection with the beating deaths of three whites during the Liberty City riots in May of 1980. A fourth youth who was tried with the others is acquitted. Attorneys for the defendants announce plans to appeal the verdicts.

1981, May 7 • Washington, DC

Representative Robert S. Walker, a Republican from Pennsylvania, introduces a bill which prohibits the use of numerical quotas devised to increase the hiring or school enrollment of minorities and women. Entitled the "Equal Employment Opportunity Act," it seeks to amend the Civil Rights Act of 1964 and prevents the federal government from imposing rules on employers or schools to hire workers or to admit students on the basis of race, sex, or national origin. In effect, the proposal no longer requires companies and educational institutions to make up for past discrimination by taking on a set number of minorities and women within a specified time frame.

1981, May 13 • Washington, DC

The Labor Department proposes revisions of Executive Order No. 11246 (prohibiting employment discrimination by federal contractors based on race, sex, color, national origin, or religion) in its continuing effort to ease job-discrimination rules for federal contractors. The contents of an internal memorandum reveal the effort seems targeted toward reducing the record-keeping and affirmative action requirements for small contractors and eliminating "unnecessary confrontations" with all contractors. Timothy Ryan, Labor Department solicitor, says that the revisions make the program more manageable and cut the number of companies covered by two-thirds for certain requirements. Secretary Raymond Donovan maintains that a final decision on revisions within the Office of Federal Contracts Compliance Programs has not been made. Administration officials plan to alter the proposal before its effective date of June 29.

1981, May 23 • Washington, DC

Calling them "ineffective" and unfair remedies to discrimination, Attorney General William French Smith announces that the Justice Department will no longer continue its vigorous pursuit of mandatory busing and the use of racial quotas in employment-discrimination

Benjamin Hooks (AP/Wide World Photos, Inc.)

Samuel R. Pierce (Corbis Corporation [Bellevue])

cases. It also considers amendments which would make "reverse discrimination" illegal under the Civil Rights Act of 1964.

1981, June 10 • Washington, DC

The House once again approves an anti-busing provision by a vote of 265 to 122, forbidding the Justice Department from taking any direct or indirect action to require the busing of students to schools other than those closest to where they live with the exception of cases involving special education needs. The provision is known as an "anti-busing rider" because of its attachment to the department's $2.3 billion authorized bill.

1981, June 16 • Washington, DC

The Reagan administration, in a letter to Attorney General William French Smith, requires the Justice Department to determine whether the political rights of minority Americans are best served by the Voting Rights Act of 1965. Stating that the act marks the nation's commitment to full equality for all Americans, the administration says that what must be answered is whether the act continues to be the most appropriate means of guaranteeing their rights. The completed report is due October 1.

1981, September 9 • New York City, New York

Roy Wilkins, former head of the NAACP and one of the key players in the Civil Rights movement of the 1960s, dies at New York University Medical Center at the age of eighty.

1981, September 10 • New York City, New York

Vernon Jordan announces his plans to resign as executive director of the National Urban League to join the Dallas-based law firm of Akin, Grump, Hauer, and Field. Jordan's office will be in Washington, DC.

1981, October 7 • Washington, DC

A House vote, 389–24, in favor of extending the Voting Rights Act of 1965, seems to ensure the likelihood of an equally strong measure in the Senate, according to Capitol Hill analysts. The House version makes the preclearance provisions of the act permanent (requiring six Southern states and Alaska to submit proposed changes in election laws to the Justice Department before implementation), but also features the so-called bailout provision that exempts jurisdictions from the requirement if they can prove a clean ten-year voting rights record and efforts to encourage minority voting.

1981, November 28 • Washington, DC
The nomination of Clarence M. Pendleton, president of the Urban League of San Diego, to head the U.S. Commission on Civil Rights results in divided opinion over his suitability for the post. Pendleton's selection is controversial because of his promotion of private industry as a cure-all for African American economic problems and because of his opposition to other positions taken traditionally by the Civil Rights movement on issues such as busing and affirmative action.

1981, December 8 • Washington, DC
William Bradford Reynolds, assistant attorney general of the Justice Department's civil rights division, announces plans to seek a ruling by the Supreme Court which would find it unconstitutional to give minorities and women preference in hiring and promotion. Reynolds wants a reversal of the High Court's decision in *Weber v. Kaiser Aluminum and Chemical Corp.*, which upheld the legality of affirmative action hiring and promotion practices negotiated by the company and the United Steel Workers of America. Reynolds contends the *Weber* decision was "wrongly decided" and that different sets of rules for the public sector and the private sector should not exist. Under his direction, the Justice Department has ceased such hiring preferences; the action sought by Reynolds would prohibit individuals, the Labor Department, or the Equal Employment Opportunity Commission from seeking such preferences.

1982, January 2 • Los Angeles, California
Los Angeles Mayor Tom Bradley opens his campaign to become the first African American governor of California. The 64-year-old former policeman has been elected to the mayoralty three times.

1982, January 20 • Alabama
Two African American civil rights workers, Julia Wilder and Maggie Bozeman, are charged with vote fraud.

1982, February 1 • New York City, New York
Representative Shirley Chisholm, a Democrat from New York and the first African American woman to win a seat in Congress, announces that she will not seek another term. She has served the Brooklyn communities of Bedford-Stuyvesant and Bushwick since 1968.

1982, February 1 • Washington, DC
The Justice Department proposes that the city of Chicago be allowed to try to desegregate its schools following a plan that would rely mainly on voluntary student transfers rather than mandatory busing.

1982, February 6 • Alabama
A small band of Southern civil rights workers, followed by three hundred sympathizers, start a 140-mile march in support of the Federal Voting Rights Act and in protest against the vote fraud conviction of two African American political activists. The marchers travel from Carrollton, Alabama, through Selma to the state capitol, Montgomery, a route made famous in early civil rights marches.

1982, February 14 • Alabama
Hundreds of voting rights marchers going from Carrollton to Montgomery march peacefully across the Edmund Pettis Bridge.

1982, April 4 • Washington, DC
The Bureau of Census reports that the 1980 census missed counting 1.3 million African Americans and that the undercount represented 4.8 percent of the nation's 28 million African Americans. The bureau says that in 1970 the census missed 1.9 million out of 24.4 million African Americans.

1983 • Washington, DC
A test case of the Justice Department to eliminate court-ordered busing to desegregate public schools is rejected by the U.S. Supreme Court. It was the contention of the Justice Department that a desegregation plan in Nashville, Tennessee, was contributing to "white flight" from the city.

1983 • Louisiana
Louisiana repeals the United States' last racial classification law.

1983, January 12 • Washington, DC
A majority of the U.S. Civil Rights Commission charges that the Reagan administration's Justice Department has been moving in the direction of getting judicial approval to end affirmative action. The two-and-a-half-page text issued by the majority asserts that cases in several cities, given the current position of the Justice Department, could result in continued discrimination. The committee's assertion is opposed by the chairman of the committee, Clarence Pendleton, an African American Reagan appointee.

1983, April 13 • Chicago, Illinois
Harold Washington becomes the first African American mayor of Chicago. Washington received 656,727 votes (51 percent), while his opponent, Bernard Epton, received 617,159 votes (48 percent). The voting followed racial lines with 90 percent of the votes in black areas going to Washington, as well as some 44 percent of the vote in the city's white liberal areas.

Harold Washington (Corbis Corporation [Bellevue])

1983, April 22 • Greensboro, North Carolina
After 29 months of investigation, a federal grand jury indicts six Ku Klux Klansmen and three members of the American Nazi Party in the deaths of five members of the Communist Workers Party who participated in a "Death-to-the-Klan" rally in Greensboro, North Carolina, in 1979.

1983, May 18 • New York City, New York
Benjamin L. Hooks, executive director of the NAACP, is suspended indefinitely by the association's chairman, Margaret Bush Wilson. The controversy was said to have begun with Wilson's criticism of some internal aspects as to how well the organization was doing.

1983, May 25 • Washington, DC
In an 8–1 decision the Supreme Court rules that private schools which discriminate on the basis of race are not eligible for tax exemptions. The ruling in *Bob Jones University v. IRS* rejects the Reagan administration's contention that because there is nothing in the Internal Revenue Service code banning such exemptions, they are permissible. The opinion, rendered by Chief Justice Warren E. Burger, stated that racial discrimination in education violates widely accepted views of elementary justice and "that to grant tax exempt status to racially discriminatory educational entities would be incompatible with the concepts of tax exemption."

1983, May 26 • Washington, DC
President Ronald Reagan presents three nominees to replace three current members of the U.S. Commission on Civil Rights. If confirmed, the administration would have a majority of its appointees on the six-member commission. A storm of protest and controversy arises from civil rights groups and members of Congress accusing the president of efforts to pack the commission. The three nominees are John H. Bunzel, Morris B. Abram, and Robert A. Destro. The commissioners to be replaced are Mary Frances Berry, Rabbi Murray Saltzman, and Blandina Cardenas Ramirez. However, lawyers from various private and governmental agencies indicated that the president probably does not have the legal authority to dismiss personnel who in effect are members of an independent bipartisan deliberative body with no powers. Jack Greenberg of the NAACP Legal Defense and Educational Fund stated that it was illegal for the president to do what he proposes and that the Fund would represent the commissioners if they decided to mount a challenge.

1983, May 28 • New York City, New York
The NAACP's executive director Benjamin L. Hooks is reinstated to his post after an eight-day suspension by board chairman Margaret Bush Wilson. Wilson states that the objective of the action has been achieved and its continuance no longer serves a useful purpose.

1983, August • Washington, DC
Surveys in the state of Mississippi indicate a probability that enforcement of the Voting Rights Act will be extremely difficult in many counties. As a result, Assistant Attorney General William Bradford Reynolds announces that he will send three hundred federal observers into the state to see that the act is enforced. Many civil rights leaders believe the response to be totally inadequate and Jesse Jackson believes that the planned observers are untrained and will be unable to see or understand many violations.

1983, October 20 • Washington, DC
By a vote of 78–22, action is completed in the Senate and the president signs into law a bill making the third Monday of each January a day honoring the memory of slain civil rights leader Martin Luther King, Jr. Initially opposed by President Ronald Reagan, many prominent Republican senators urged and got the president's support of the bill, thus insuring passage in the Senate. The bill had previously passed in the house by a margin of 338–90. Senator Jesse Helms (Republican, North Carolina) leads an effort to defeat the bill. Helms accuses King of "Marxist" ways. Helms also attempts to have controversial FBI tapes on King opened and made public in the hope that such disclosure would create public scandal. Senator Edward Kennedy (Democrat, Massachusetts) is

outraged by Helms and asks for a renunciation of the senator in the nation and in his home state.

1983, October 25 • Washington, DC
In a surprise move President Ronald Reagan fires three members from the U.S. Commission on Civil Rights because their views are critical of many aspects of the administration's policies in this area. Those fired were Mary Frances Berry, a professor of history and law at Howard University; Blandina Cardenas Ramirez of San Antonio; and Rabbi Murray Saltzman of Baltimore—all highly regarded as effective spokespersons for minorities.

1983, November 10 • In general elections throughout the nation, African Americans make some significant gains. Wilson Goode is elected mayor of Philadelphia, becoming that city's first African American to serve in such capacity and making his city the fourth of the nation's six largest cities to have an African American as chief executive. Other African American winners are Democrat Harvey Gantt who becomes the first African American elected mayor of Charlotte, North Carolina; James A. Sharp, Jr., the first elected African American mayor of Flint, Michigan; Thirman Milner who wins a second term in Hartford, Connecticut; and Richard Hatcher who wins a fifth term in Gary, Indiana.

1983, December 1 • Washington, DC
In a supposed compromise bill President Ronald Reagan signs into law a newly reorganized U.S. Commission on Civil Rights comprised of four presidential and four congressional appointees. As the first of his appointments, Reagan reappoints Clarence M. Pendleton, Jr. as chairman of the new commission.

1984 • The Centers for Disease Control releases figures on the homicide rate for young African American males. Between 1984 and 1988, the homicide rate among African American males ages 15 to 24 had risen 68 percent.

1984, June 6 • Washington, DC
Margaret Bush Wilson, former chairperson of the NAACP, loses the battle to get herself reinstated as a member of the association's governing board. Wilson was the first African American woman chairperson of the NAACP and had been a member of the national board of directors since 1963.

1984, June 13 • Washington, DC
In a 6–3 decision the U.S. Supreme Court invalidated a U.S. district court decision that allowed the layoff of three white firefighters who had seniority over three black firefighters. The Supreme Court decided that

Margaret Bush Wilson (AP/Wide World Photos, Inc.)

affirmative action employment gains are not preferential when jobs must be decreased and that "legitimate" seniority systems are protected from court intervention. However, a dissenting opinion by Justices Blackmun, Brennan, and Marshall argued that under Title 7 of the Civil Rights Act of 1964, race-related preferential practice was an acceptable application. As a result of the Court's decision, the Justice Department announces that it will reexamine all federal anti-discrimination settlements and will advise government agencies to not continue the practice of using racial employment quotas when negotiating affirmative action plans.

1984, July 6 • Washington, DC
Secret tapes of President John F. Kennedy are made public and demonstrate a sincere effort by Kennedy to get mayors, governors, and congressmen to accept integration and support his civil rights programs. The recordings made during the Kennedy presidency also reveal a dramatic conversation with Martin Luther King, Jr. in which King, after a bombing in Birmingham, Alabama, that killed four children at an African American church, calls upon the president to send federal troops into the city to protect the African American community and to prevent riots. In a conversation with

mayor Allen Thompson of Jackson, Mississippi, the president urges him to hire African American police officers. After the mayor assures the president that he will hire African Americans, he said to Kennedy "don't get your feelings hurt" about public statements he may have to make about the president, to which Kennedy replies "well, listen I give you full permission to denounce me in public as long as you don't do it in private."

1984, November 14 • Washington, DC
The Supreme Court rules that redistricting plans and election laws that have discriminatory results are affirmed to be illegal under a provision of the 1982 Voting Rights Act. The ruling came as a result of a Mississippi redistricting plan.

1984, November 12 • Atlanta, Georgia
The Reverend Martin Luther King, Sr. dies of a heart ailment at the age of 82. For 44 years he had been pastor of the Ebenezer Baptist Church and was one of the South's most influential African American clergymen.

1985, January 5 • South Africa
Senator Edward Kennedy visits South Africa at the invitation of Noble Peace Prize-recipient Bishop Desmond Tutu. Kennedy also visits Winnie Mandela, the wife of jailed black nationalist Nelson Mandela, but his request to meet with the imprisoned leader is refused by the government.

1985, February 21 • New York City, New York
As a cost-savings measure the NAACP will move from its headquarters in New York City to Baltimore, Maryland, by 1986. The association is negotiating the purchase of a suitable building for $2 million in Baltimore after being unable to find a suitable and economically-sound location in New York City.

1985, February 26 • Washington, DC
The U.S. Commission on Civil Rights gives enthusiastic support to a Supreme Court decision giving existing seniority systems preference over affirmative action programs even though the African Americans were hired to remedy previously contended discriminatory hiring practices. U.S. Civil Rights Commissioners Mary Frances Berry and Blandina Cardenas Ramirez, in heated disagreement with the Supreme Court and the Civil Rights Commission's report, state that civil rights laws are designed to protect blacks, minorities, and women, not white men. The statement creates new controversy as to the meaning of the existence of the Civil Rights Commission.

1985, March 7 • Washington, DC
Charging that the U.S. Commission on Civil Rights had already decided to oppose such measures as timetables and quotas, national civil rights groups boycott hearings on the use of such goals to achieve racial balance or to remedy discriminatory hiring practices.

1985, March 13 • Washington, DC
Clarence Pendleton, chairman of the U.S. Commission on Civil Rights, estimates that after the issue of preferential treatment is settled, the Civil Rights Commission should be abolished. Responsibility for civil rights, says Pendelton, should be in the hands of the Justice Department and the Equal Employment Opportunity Commission.

1985, May 1 • Washington, DC
A statue of Martin Luther King, Jr. is dedicated at the Washington Cathedral as a memorial to his comprehensive contributions and celebrated leadership in the struggle for civil rights.

1985, May 6 • Washington, DC
The federal government and the state of Maryland reach tentative agreement on a plan to desegregate the state's public colleges and universities. White enrollment at traditionally black colleges will be increased to 19 percent and black enrollment at predominantly white schools will reach 15 percent from 11 percent. The implementation of this plan is to take five years.

1985, August 2 • Washington, DC
Because of the policy of apartheid in South Africa, the U.S. House of Representatives gives final approval to a bill imposing economic sanctions against the South African government by a vote of 380–48. The Reagan administration remains opposed to the legislation.

1985, December 6 • Yonkers, New York
Stating that "discriminatory housing practices" on the part of Yonkers, New York, were responsible for the segregation of blacks from whites in the city's schools, U.S. District Court Judge Leonard B. Sand indicated for the first time in school desegregation cases that a city's housing policies are inextricably linked to school segregation. Judge Sand held that since 1949 Yonkers public housing had been deliberately built in low-income neighborhoods which had the effect of confining students to "inferior and racially unmixed schools." The Justice Department in 1980 charged the city of Yonkers with bias in housing and schools and received from the city a tentative plan in 1984 to build public housing in predominantly white East Yonkers. The case could have

landmark implications since busing had been the primary means for cities to comply with desegregation rulings.

1985, December 23 • Birmingham, Alabama
Federal District Judge Sam Pointer, Jr. dismisses a reverse discrimination suit instituted on behalf of 14 white firefighters in Birmingham, Alabama. It was claimed that the 14 whites were denied advancement because of a city hiring and promotion plan favoring less-qualified blacks. Judge Pointer ruled that the city accepted the consent decree along with the Justice Department in 1981, and therefore the decree is valid; he also ruled that the firefighters failed to prove that the plan violated that agreement.

1986, January 11 • Richmond, Virginia
L. Douglas Wilder becomes the first African American lieutenant governor of the state of Virginia. Wilder, the grandson of a slave, was a Bronze Star recipient in the Korean War and a former member of the state senate.

1986, January 20 • Martin Luther King, Jr.'s birthday is observed for the first time as a federal holiday.

1986, March 19 • Washington, DC
The Supreme Court in *Wygant v. Jackson Board of Education*, the first of three major affirmative action decisions, rules 5–4 that broad affirmative action plans including hiring goals are permissible if they are carefully tailored to remedy past discrimination. In a ruling involving teachers laid off in Jackson, Michigan, the Court sends a mixed signal by deciding that public employers cannot give affirmative action plans as a substitute for seniority when reducing their work forces.

1986, June 16 • Norfolk, Virginia
The U.S. Supreme Court denies an injunction sought by African American parents that would prevent the Norfolk, Virginia, school board from ending school busing to stem "white flight" from the city's public schools. According to the petition, the change would result in "a general resegregation of the public schools of the South."

1986, July 2 • Cleveland, Ohio
The U.S. Supreme Court ruling on an action regarding Cleveland printers and New York sheet metal workers upholds the use of affirmative action plans designed to remedy past discrimination. The decision in *Sheet Metal Workers International v. EEOC* rejects the Reagan administration's argument that only specific victims of discrimination are entitled to such relief.

1986, August 5 • Washington, DC
African American leaders representing major African American organizations meet to urge the passage of legislation that would impose more stringent economic sanctions on South Africa.

1986, September 11 • South Africa
Coretta Scott King visits South Africa, meets with Archbishop Desmond Tutu, cancels a meeting with the prime minister, and later visits Winnie Mandela, wife of the imprisoned South African anti-apartheid leader.

1986, October 3 • Washington, DC
In an effort to win Senate support for his veto of a sanctions bill against South Africa for their apartheid policies, Ronald Reagan appoints an African American career diplomat, Edward J. Perkins, to be the new American ambassador to that country. The bill had been overridden by a wide majority (313–83) in the House. The Senate, despite the appointment, votes with the House by a vote of 78–21 to override the veto.

1986, October 7 • Washington, DC
The 32-year-old case of *Brown v. Board of Education of Topeka* is reopened by the original plaintiff and others who maintain that the school district has failed to integrate fully its schools or to eradicate the remaining elements that permitted racial separation in the past. Richard Jones, the lawyer for the plaintiffs, says he will show that the school board approved boundaries that perpetuate racially-separate schools and allowed white parents to avoid compliance with desegregation efforts by offering school attendance alternatives.

1986, October 20 • Baltimore, Maryland
Four days of dedication ceremonies commence as the NAACP opens its new headquarters. The NAACP was founded in New York in 1909 and maintained its headquarters there until this move. There is official indication that the organization will begin new and diverse programs including business development, in addition to its more fundamental activities such as voter registration and protest demonstrations in its general goal of social and economic justice.

1986, November 4 • Norfolk, Virginia
The Supreme Court declines to review two school desegregation cases, one which allows the city of Norfolk to end its busing plan, and another that attempts to sanction the authority of the Oklahoma City School Board to end busing for students in grades one through four. It is speculated that some high court justices want to leave the lower courts with the means of interpreting law on a local and regional basis. In the Norfolk case, African American parents had claimed that the lower

San Francisco middle school students honoring the inaugural Martin Luther King, Jr. Day in 1986 (AP/Wide World Photos, Inc.).

court ruling ending busing would have the effect of reinstating school segregation.

1986, December 21 • Queens, New York
Michael Griffith, a 23-year-old black male, is struck by a car and killed while seeking safety from a white mob beating him with bats and fists. The incident occurred in the white community of Howard Beach, Queens. The whites were reported shouting, "Niggers, you don't belong here!" Griffith and two companions were in the neighborhood looking for a tow for their disabled car.

1987, January 7 • Washington, DC
New regulations are issued to strengthen the federal government's authority to reject changes in local election laws that have a discriminatory result. No longer does the legal process have to prove that the intent of the local law was to discriminate, it need only demonstrate that it could have a discriminatory result.

1987, February 11 • Queens, New York
In Howard Beach, three white teenagers who participated in a racial attack against three black youths are charged with murder as a result of the death of one of

the black youths who was killed by a car along an adjacent parkway as he attempted to escape from his white attackers.

1987, April 5 • Washington, DC
Representative Charles Rangel (Democrat, New York) introduces two measures in Congress to have the late revolutionary civil rights leader Marcus Garvey exonerated of mail fraud charges of which he was convicted in 1924. The move by Rangel came after Robert Hill, editor of the Marcus Garvey papers project at the University of California at Los Angeles, discovered new evidence which could indicate that Garvey's conviction may have been politically-motivated. In 1927 Garvey's sentence was commuted by President Calvin Coolidge after which he was deported to Jamaica, his place of birth.

1987, April 7 • Chicago, Illinois
Mayor Harold Washington wins reelection to a second four-year term and his supporters win control of the city council for the first time. Voting was along strong racial lines with Washington receiving 97 percent of the black vote cast, and his white opponent Edward R. Vrdolyak receiving 74 percent of the white vote. Hispanics cast 57 percent of their vote for Washington.

Leon Sullivan, Coretta Scott King, Randall Robinson, and U.S. Representatives Walter Fauntroy and William Gray meet to advocate for South African sanctions legislation (AP/Wide World Photos, Inc.).

1987, April 18 • Los Angeles, California
Al Campanis, vice president of personnel for the Los Angeles Dodgers, is pressured to resign from his job after stating that African Americans might not be qualified to be managers or hold executive positions in baseball. The remarks were made by Campanis on the ABC News program "Nightline."

1987, April 25 • Fort Smith, Arkansas
A federal grand jury indicts ten white supremacists on charges of conspiring to assassinate federal officials, including a judge, and to kill members of ethnic groups through bombings. Richard Girnt Butler, the leader of the Aryan Nations Church, was named in the indictment, along with nine others affiliated with the church and other white supremacist groups such as the Order and the Ku Klux Klan.

1987, May 3 • Washington, DC
Japanese Prime Minister Yasuhiro Nakasone meets with the Congressional Black Caucus and other African American leaders after being accused of making racial slurs in a speech angering African Americans and other ethnic groups. Following the meeting Nakasone agreed to pursue Japanese investments in minority-owned American banks, to set up exchange programs between Japanese colleges and African American colleges, and to locate Japanese companies in predominantly African American areas.

1987, July 1 • Phoenix, Arizona
As a result of his decision to rescind state observance of Martin Luther King, Jr.'s birthday, Governor Evan Mecham (Republican) faces a citizens' effort to recall him as the governor of the state. The plan has strong state support from both parties and many Republicans wear "Recall Mecham" buttons.

1987, July 28 • Montgomery, Alabama
After 15 years a tentative settlement is reached between the Alabama State Police Department and the Justice Department. Accordingly there will be an increase in the number of African Americans at various ranks on the force to as high as 25 percent over a three-year period. The department will promote 15 African Americans to the rank of corporal in a month and will eventually have African Americans comprise 20 percent of its sergeants, 15 percent of its lieutenants, and 10 percent of its

captains. Federal District Judge Myron Thompson, who originally ordered the police department to hire one black officer for every white officer hired, has to approve the suggested settlement.

1988 • Jesse Jackson receives 1,218 delegate votes at the Democratic National Convention.

1988, August 15 • Dallas, Texas
The predominantly African American Bishop College, at one time the largest African American college in the West, closes its doors, unable to pay creditors $20 million. Founded in 1881 in Marshall, Texas, Bishop moved to Dallas in 1961. In 1967, Bishop had an enrollment of 1,500; in 1987 its enrollment had dwindled to 300.

1988, August 26 • Boston, Massachusetts
In an effort to prevent a housing settlement between the city of Boston and the U.S. Department of Housing from being implemented, the NAACP files suit to have the agreement blocked, stating that a housing settlement, among other things, should include monetary compensation for people previously denied public housing because of their race and therefore forced to pay higher rent. The Housing Authority of the city of Boston was the largest housing authority in the country to enter into a fair housing voluntary compliance agreement with the federal government.

1988, October 4 • Washington, DC
The General Accounting Office of the federal government makes public a report charging that the Equal Employment Opportunity Commission failed to properly investigate as many as 82 percent of the claims made regarding job discrimination filed with the commission during a three-month period.

1988, November 26 • Chicago, Illinois
As tensions increase between Jews and African Americans, the Reverend Jesse Jackson meets with Jewish leaders in an effort to reduce the anger and heal the wounds. The Congregation Hakafa turns out to overflow capacity to hear Reverend Jackson deliver the evening sermon and say, "The sons and daughters of the Holocaust, and the sons and daughters of slavery, must find common ground again." The tension between Jews and African Americans reached a zenith in May when Mayor Sawyer of Chicago was severely criticized for taking a week to condemn the anti-Semitic remarks made by Steve Cokley, an aide to the mayor. Underlying the problem is the political struggle for power in Chicago. In 1983, Jews gave Harold Washington almost fifty percent of their votes and helped give Chicago its first African American mayor; in that race Washington defeated the white Republican candidate, Bernard Epton, who was Jewish.

1988, December 1 • Washington, DC
Lieutenant General Colin Powell, President Reagan's national security advisor and the top African American official in the administration, is nominated to become one of ten four-star generals in the U.S. Army. Along with the rank goes the assignment to command all U.S. troops in the continental borders of the country and to be responsible for mainland defense. The new rank also puts General Powell in a strong position to become chief of staff as early as 1991 when the post becomes vacant with the retirement of General Carl E. Vuono. General Powell is credited with helping President Reagan's summit meetings in Moscow and Washington, DC, to become diplomatic successes.

1989, January 16 • Miami, Florida
Rioting erupts on the evening of January 16 in the predominantly African American neighborhood of Overtown, following the killing of Anthony Lloyd, a 23-year-old African American, by an Hispanic police officer. On January 18, Miami Mayor Xavier Suarez announces that an independent panel would be appointed to investigate the killing.

1989, January 23 • Decatur, Alabama
Six members of the Ku Klux Klan receive jail sentences and fines for their part in harassing African Americans in a civil rights march conducted ten years earlier in Decatur, Alabama. The May 1979 march had been to protest the jailing of Tommy Lee Hines, a retarded black man convicted of raping three white women. Hines' thirty-year jail sentence was overturned in 1980 and he was committed to a Montgomery mental hospital.

1989, January 23 • Washington, DC
Hearing the case *City of Richmond v. J.A. Croson Co.*, the Supreme Court strikes down a law in Richmond, Virginia, which required thirty percent of public works funds to be channeled to minority-owned construction companies. The landmark decision was decried by minority leaders, hailed by anti-quota officials, and predicted to have national impact on affirmative action and set-aside programs. The "Richmond decision," which was written by Associate Justice Sandra Day O'Connor and carried by a 6–3 majority, said set-aside programs were only justified if they redressed "identified discrimination." O'Connor specifically suggested that "rigid numerical quotas" be avoided, in order to avoid racially-motivated hirings of any kind. The ruling only pertains to the disposition of federal, state, and local government contracts and does not affect affirmative action programs in private industry.

Jesse Jackson greeting African American voters during the 1988 presidential campaign (Courtesy of Jesse Jackson).

1989, January 26 • Richmond, Virginia
Lieutenant Governor L. Douglas Wilder announces his candidacy for governor of Virginia. If successful, he would become the nation's first African American elected to a governorship.

1989, February 7 • The American Council on Education reports that the number of African American men attending college is declining. In 1976, 470,000 African American males were enrolled in college. Ten years later, that number dropped to 436,000. Meanwhile the number of African American female students grew during the same period, from 563,000 in 1976 to 645,000 in 1986. Reasons for the decline of African American male collegians were military enrollment, prohibitive college costs, "school phobia," and the seduction of crime or drugs.

1989, February 10 • Washington, DC
Washington lawyer Ronald H. Brown, who held high-level positions in the presidential campaigns of Senator Ted Kennedy and Reverend Jesse Jackson, is elected

General Colin Powell visiting American troops in Saudi Arabia during the 1990 Persian Gulf War (AP/Wide World Photos, Inc.).

chairman of the Democratic National Committee. The election of Brown marks the first time an African American has been chosen to lead a major American political party.

1989, February 10 • Washington, DC
FBI Director William Sessions orders sweeping changes in the bureau's affirmative action program after finding that the bureau had discriminated against minority employees. African American and Hispanic agents were immediately placed on lists for promotions. Sessions then ordered that FBI employees receive training in racial sensitivity and that the equal employment office budget be increased. Ironically, the FBI is the agency charged with enforcing the nation's civil rights laws.

1989, February 10 • Washington, DC
Louis W. Sullivan, on sabbatical leave as president of Morehouse School of Medicine in Georgia, becomes secretary of the Department of Health and Human Services. He is the only African American selected in the first round of Cabinet posts in the Bush administration.

1989, March • Washington, DC
Statistics show that the nation's capital has already

taken the lead for having the highest homicide rate in the country. Local police figures show the homicide rate as 55.1 percent higher than the same time in 1988. Figures from the District of Columbia Office of Criminal Justice said 80 percent of the time, the motive for the murders was related to drug activity.

1989, April • Los Angeles, California
Mayor Tom Bradley wins reelection to a fifth term by a total of 157,000 votes.

1989, April 21 • New Orleans, Louisiana
The nation's first nonpartisan African American summit convenes April 21–23. Its purpose is to discuss "an African American agenda for the next four years and onto the year 2000," said general chairman and Democratic party leader Richard Hatcher. More than four thousand delegates from the United States, the District of Columbia, and the Virgin Islands were invited.

1989, March 6 • Washington, DC
The U.S. Supreme Court declares a second affirmative action plan unconstitutional in the case *Milliken v. Michigan Road Builders Association*. The Michigan

law required that seven percent of state contracts be awarded to minority-owned businesses.

1989, March 7 • Washington, DC
A student "sit-in" at Howard University results in the resignation of Republican National Committee Chairman Lee Atwater from the university's board of trustees four days following his appointment. The students claim that Atwater's stand on civil rights is the cause for the protest.

1989, June 5 • Washington, DC
In the case *Wards Cove Packing Company v. Antonio*, the U.S. Supreme Court toughens the requirements for proof of discriminatory impact in job discrimination suits. The Court also declares in such cases that an employer might justify policies which have a discriminatory impact by providing a reasonable business explanation.

1989, June 12 • Washington, DC
In *Martin v. Wilks*, the Supreme Court rules by a 5–4 majority that white workers claiming unfair treatment due to affirmative action settlements can seek compensation under civil rights legislation. The case involved white fire fighters in Birmingham, Alabama, who claimed that affirmative action had deprived them of promotions. Civil rights leaders call the decisions a civil rights setback.

1989, July 2 • Washington, DC
The Reverend George A. Stallings, Jr. conducts the first Mass of the Imani Temple African American Catholic Congregation.

1989, August 6 • Washington, DC
The National Urban League holds its annual conference. Addressing the conference, President George Bush remarks that he will not strive for stronger affirmative action legislation. He claims that the 1990s will see a surplus of available jobs and a shrinking worker pool.

1989, August 23 • Brooklyn, New York
Yusuf K. Hawkins, black youth, is fatally shot by five white youths in Brooklyn's predominantly white Bensonhurst section igniting racial tension throughout the New York City area. The attack is regarded as the most serious racial incident in the city since 1986. On August 31, marches are held protesting the killing. On September 2, blacks protesting in Bensonhurst are confronted by white residents. Of the five youths charged with the killing of Hawkins, only one is convicted.

1989, October 12 • The publication of Ralph Abernathy's book *And the Walls Came Tumbling Down* is greeted with outrage. The book claims that Martin Luther King, Jr. spent the night before his murder with two women. Twenty-seven African American leaders issue a statement denouncing Abernathy's book.

1989, November 5 • Montgomery, Alabama
The first memorial dedicated to the Civil Rights movement is unveiled. The memorial is commissioned by the Southern Poverty Law Center and designed by Maya Lin, who also created the Vietnam War Memorial in Washington, DC.

1989, November 7 • New York City, New York
African American candidates do well in elections. In Virginia, L. Douglas Wilder becomes the first elected African American governor in U.S. history. In New York City, David N. Dinkins is elected the city's first African American mayor. In Detroit, Coleman A. Young is reelected to a fifth consecutive term as mayor. Michael R. White is elected as mayor of Cleveland. African American mayors are also elected in Seattle, Washington; New Haven, Connecticut; and Durham, North Carolina, for the first time in history.

1990, January 9 • The United States
The Quality Education for Minorities Project releases its report and recommendations aimed at making schools more responsive to the needs of minority students. The project concludes that minority students are taught in "separate and decidedly unequal" schools resulting in a "gap between minority and non-minority educational achievements."

1990, January 18 • Washington, DC
Mayor Marion S. Barry, Jr. is arrested after being videotaped purchasing and smoking crack cocaine. Following a split verdict, Barry is sentenced to six months in prison. The arrest generates speculation that Jesse Jackson will enter the 1990 Washington, DC, mayoral race.

1990, February 8 • Selma, Alabama
African American students stage a "sit-in" following the firing of the city's first African American school superintendent, Norward Roussell, on February 5. The firing is viewed as a battle to control the city's school board—white school board members outnumber black members six to five, while seventy percent of Selma's student population is African American. The conflict ends after six days of protest. The board amends its position to permit Roussell to stay on as superintendent until the end of his contract.

1990, February 23 • Dallas, Texas
Bishop College, founded in 1881 by a group of freed slaves and once the largest African American college in

the western United States, is sold at a bankruptcy auction.

1990, March 6 • Washington, DC
Clarence Thomas, chairman of the Equal Employment Opportunity Commission, is appointed judge on the U.S. Circuit Court of Appeals for the District of Columbia.

1990, April 18 • Washington, DC
By a 5–4 majority, the U.S. Supreme Court upholds the authority of federal judges to order local governments to increase taxes to finance school desegregation in the case *Missouri v. Jenkins*. The case arose when U.S. District Court Judge Russell G. Clark adopted a desegregation plan which would create magnet schools to lure whites back into the inner city. To support this plan, Clark ordered that 75 percent of the costs be paid by the state and 25 percent by the district.

1990, June 27 • Washington, DC
The U.S. Supreme Court, by a 5–4 majority, upholds federal affirmative action policies created to increase the number of broadcast licenses held by minorities and women in the case *Metro Broadcasting v. FCC*.

1990, August 9 • Georgia
The state's runoff primary system is challenged by the Justice Department. The Justice Department claims that the system is biased against black candidates who often win a plurality of the vote in multi-candidate primaries, but lose when matched with a single white candidate in a runoff election. While seven Southern states have similar primary systems, Georgia is targeted in the lawsuit because, statistically, African Americans make up 26 percent of the population but hold only 10 percent of all elected positions.

1990, August 11 • Chicago, Illinois
Operation PUSH (People United to Save Humanity) calls for a boycott of Nike products. The organization reveals that African American consumers purchase approximately thirty percent of all Nike products, but are not represented on Nike's board of directors or in upper management. Nike is one of the country's largest manufacturers of athletic gear.

1990, August 21 • Washington, DC
Paul R. Philip, the FBI's highest-ranking African American agent, is chosen to investigate racial discrimination within the bureau. The investigation centers around charges made by a black agent against several white agents in the Chicago and Omaha offices.

1990, September 26 • The U.S. Census Bureau releases its annual report on household income. The bureau reports that the average household income of blacks is $18,083; Hispanics, $21,921; whites, $30,406; and Asians, $36,102. Ten percent of whites live in poverty, while 26.2 percent of Hispanics and 30.7 percent of blacks live in poverty. Fifty percent of African American children below age six are classified as poor.

1990, September 27 • Washington, DC
At its annual conference, members of the Congressional Black Caucus charge law enforcement officials with targeting African American politicians for harassment and investigation. The prosecution of Washington, DC, mayor Marion Berry is cited as an example.

1990, October 12 • Cook County, Illinois
The Illinois Supreme Court validates a lower court decision to bar the Harold Washington Party from the ballot. The court cited an inadequate number of nominating signatures as the reason for its decision. The party, a mostly African American third party slate of candidates, is named for the late mayor of Chicago. Cook County Democrats had expressed concern that the Harold Washington party would take votes from their candidates and guarantee the election of Republicans.

1990, October 22 • Washington, DC
President George Bush vetoes the Civil Rights Act of 1990. On October 16, the Senate passed the bill by a vote of 62–34; the House of Representatives passed the bill on October 17 by a 273–154 vote. The legislation was designed to reverse the Court's 1989 decision in the case *Wards Cove Packing Co. v. Antonio*, which made it more difficult for minorities and women to prove job discrimination. Bush cites his fear of the introduction of quotas in the workplace as his reason for rejecting the act. On October 24, an attempt to override the veto in the Senate falls one vote short of the two-thirds majority needed.

1990, November 6 • Arizona
Voters in Arizona defeat two initiatives to reestablish a Martin Luther King, Jr. holiday. The holiday had been a source of conflict since the Democratic governor, Bruce Babbitt, marked the day in 1986 by an executive order only to see it rescinded in 1987 by his successor, Republican Evan Mecham.

1990, December 12 • The Department of Education announces that it will bar colleges and universities that receive federal funds from awarding minority scholarships. The department claims that race-specific scholarships are discriminatory and violate federal civil rights laws. On December 18, the department revises the policy, allowing schools that receive federal funds to award minority scholarships if the money comes from private sources or federal programs designed to aid minority students. On March 20, 1991, the policy is reversed completely.

1990, December 18 • Mississippi
Byron de la Beckwith is charged for the third time with the 1963 murder of civil rights leader Medgar Evers. Beckwith was tried twice in 1964 with both trials ending in a deadlock.

1991, January 8 • Results from a nationwide survey sponsored by the National Science Foundation reveals that white Americans continue to hold negative stereotypes of blacks and Hispanics. Three-quarters of the whites surveyed felt that blacks and Hispanics are more likely to prefer welfare to work. A Census Bureau report shows the household worth of whites with families to average eight times that of Hispanic households and ten times that of black households.

1991, January 15 • Washington, DC
In a 5–3 decision, the U.S. Supreme Court puts an end to court-ordered busing in the Oklahoma City school district. Ruling in the case *Oklahoma City v. Dowell*, the Court declares that the reemergence of single-race schools, resulting from shifting housing patterns, does justify continued court-ordered busing. The decision overturns an appeals court ruling refusing to turn the once-segregated school district over to local control.

1991, January 20 • A *New York Times*/CBS poll of public support for military action in the Persian Gulf reveals that only 47 percent of blacks polled compared to 80 percent of whites favored intervention. One theory on the difference in support points to the disproportionate number of blacks to whites serving in the armed forces. While accounting for only 12 percent of the total U.S. population, African Americans represent 24.6 percent of the U.S. troops in the Gulf. Many African Americans point to the problems of drugs and crime as good places to direct government resources.

1991, February 26 • Detroit, Michigan
By a 9–1 majority, the Detroit Board of Education approves the creation of an all-male school for kindergarten through grade eight. The school's goal would be to provide African American male students with an improved learning environment by focusing on the unique problems facing the African American male. Critics of the school label the program discriminatory. The American Civil Liberties Union and the National Organization

for Women Legal Defense Fund both file suit in federal district court. On August 15, the court rules that such a school must also be open to girls.

1991, March 3 • Los Angeles, California
Black motorist Rodney King is severely beaten by several white police officers after being stopped for a speeding violation. The incident is videotaped by a witness watching from his apartment balcony.

1991, May 6 • Washington, DC
The creation of a National African American Museum within the Smithsonian Institution is approved by the institution's board of regents. The museum will include print and broadcast images of African Americans, along with African American art and artifacts.

1991, May 12 • Hampton, Virginia
Students at Hampton University hold a silent protest while President George Bush gives the commencement address. The students point to the administration's policies regarding civil rights as a reason for the demonstration.

1991, May 14 • The Washington-based Urban Institute releases its study on job discrimination. The study, conducted in Washington, DC, and Chicago, Illinois, reveals that whites seeking entry-level positions were three times more likely to receive favorable treatment than equally qualified blacks.

1991, June 3 • Washington, DC
In the case of *Edmonson v. Leesville Concrete Co.*, the U.S. Supreme Court rules that potential jurors cannot be excluded from civil cases on the basis of race. The Court had, in two earlier cases, ruled that jurors could not be excluded because of race in criminal cases.

1991, June 4 • Washington, DC
After defeating two other civil rights bills, the U.S. House of Representatives passes a civil rights bill by a vote of 273–158. The bill is an effort by Congress to reverse the Supreme Court's 1989 ruling in *Wards Cove Packing Co. v. Antonio* and make it easier for victims of job discrimination to sue for damages. President Bush opposes such legislation, claiming that it will force employers to set quotas for hiring minorities in order to protect themselves from possible discrimination suits.

1991, June 20 • Washington, DC
The U.S. Supreme Court, hearing in two separate cases *Chison v. Roemer* and *Houston Lawyers v. Texas*, rules

Rodney King being severely beaten by Los Angeles police officers in 1991 (AP/Wide World Photos, Inc.).

that the Voting Rights Act of 1965 is applicable to judicial elections. The cases arose from lower court rulings in Louisiana and Texas which claimed that judges were not representatives and, therefore, the election of such was not covered by the act.

1991, June 27 • Washington, DC
U.S. Supreme Court Justice Thurgood Marshall, citing his poor health and advancing age, announces his plans to retire from the bench. Marshall, appointed to the Court by President Lyndon B. Johnson in 1967, was the first African American to serve on the nation's highest court.

1991, July • Washington, DC
President George Bush nominates African American Court of Appeals Judge Clarence Thomas to replace the retiring Justice Thurgood Marshall. Thomas, a conservative and former chairman of the Equal Employment Opportunity Commission, was appointed by Bush in 1990 to the federal appeals court. Stating that while chairman of the EEOC, Thomas failed to display sensitivity regarding affirmative action, major national organizations including the NAACP, the NAACP Legal Defense Fund, the Leadership Conference on Civil Rights,

and the Congressional Black Caucus voice opposition to the Thomas nomination.

1991, July 4 • Memphis, Tennessee
The National Civil Rights Museum, housed in the former Lorraine Motel, is dedicated. Martin Luther King, Jr. was shot at the Lorraine Motel on April 4, 1968.

1991, August 19 • Brooklyn, New York
Tensions between African Americans and Jews in Brooklyn's Crown Heights section increase, when seven-year-old Gavin Cato is struck and killed by a car driven by a Jewish driver. Rioting erupts, and a Jewish rabbinical student is stabbed to death.

1991, September 13 • Richmond, Virginia
Governor L. Douglas Wilder announces his plans to run for the 1992 Democratic presidential nomination. However, by January of 1992, Wilder withdraws from the race. In 1989, Wilder became the first African American elected governor in U.S. history.

1991, September 29 • The Department of Justice releases its report on death row inmates. The report reveals that 40 percent of the inmates awaiting execution in the United States are African American, whereas African Americans constitute only 12.1 percent of the general population.

1991, October 11 • Los Angeles, California
Korean grocer Soon Ja Du is convicted of voluntary manslaughter for the death of Latasha Harlins. The shooting exacerbates racial tension between African Americans and Koreans.

1991, October 30 • Washington, DC
The U.S. Senate approves a new civil rights bill.

1991, November 1 • Washington, DC
In a public ceremony, Judge Clarence Thomas is formally seated as the 106th associate justice of the U.S. Supreme Court.

1991, November 2 • Washington, DC
Jesse L. Jackson announces he will not seek the 1992 Democratic presidential nomination.

1991, November 5 • Washington, DC
In the case *Hafer v. Melo*, the U.S. Supreme Court rules in a unanimous vote that state officials can be sued as individuals acting in an official status and be held personally liable in civil rights suits.

1991, November 7 • Washington, DC
The House of Representatives passes Senate Bill 1745, which was passed by the Senate on October 30. President Bush signs the bill into law on November 21. However, the signing ceremony for the long-anticipated law is dominated by controversy over a proposed presidential directive that tried to impose a conservative interpretation on the new legislation. Immediately after circulation of the draft, civil rights leaders, senators, and Cabinet members condemn it as an attack on all civil rights progress.

1991, December 30 • Alabama
U.S. District Court Judge Harold L. Murphy orders the Alabama state university system to rectify racial discrimination in its hiring, admissions, and financing practices. It is ruled that Alabama's higher education system, divided into predominantly white and predominantly black schools, fosters inferior funding for the predominantly African American universities. Judge Murphy states he will retain jurisdiction over the case for ten years to ensure his orders are carried out.

1992, January 2 • Washington, DC
A lawsuit filed by the National Treasury Employees Union challenges the Equal Employment Opportunity Commission's policy which states that the 1991 Civil Rights Act does not apply to job discrimination lawsuits filed prior to the law's enactment in November of 1991.

1992, January 17 • Atlanta, Georgia
President George Bush visits the Martin Luther King, Jr. Center for Nonviolent Social Change to sign a proclamation officially declaring Martin Luther King, Jr.'s birthday as a national holiday.

1992, January 19 • The American Council on Education releases their tenth annual report confirming the number of minority students attending college increased during the 1980s. The report shows 33 percent of black, 29 percent of Hispanic, and 39.4 percent of white high school graduates were attending college in 1990, up respectively from 21.6 percent, 26.1 percent and 34.4 percent in 1985.

1992, January 20 • Denver, Colorado
The seventh commemoration of Martin Luther King, Jr.'s birthday as a national holiday triggers violence in Denver between civil rights supporters and members of the Ku Klux Klan following a Klan rally. Civil rights supporters throw bricks and bottles at a bus carrying Klan members away from the rally.

1992, February 10 • Seattle, Washington
Alex Haley, the Pulitzer Prize-winning author of *Roots* and *The Autobiography of Malcolm X*, dies of heart failure.

1992, February 15 • Baltimore, Maryland
The NAACP's Benjamin L. Hooks announces his plans to resign from his position as the organization's director. The announcement is made after Hazel Dukes, the national president, and several other prominent board members are denied reelection.

1992, March 31 • Washington, DC
In the case of *Freeman v. Pitts*, the U.S. Supreme Court rules unanimously that school districts operating under court-supervised desegregation orders can slowly be released from court supervision to local control as they achieve racial equality. Reaction to the ruling by educators and civil rights experts is mixed, with general uncertainty as to how the decision will be applied by district courts reviewing individual desegregation orders.

1992, April 29 • Los Angeles, California
Riots erupt in Los Angeles following the acquittal of four white police officers in the beating of black motorist Rodney King. The suburban Simi Valley jury that acquitted the police officers had no African American members. The videotaped beating was broadcast around the

world and provoked outrage condemning police brutality. With the announcement of the verdict, looting and violence break out across the South Central section of Los Angeles. By the end of the first day, 12 people are dead and more than one hundred arson fires engulf the area. Mayor Tom Bradley declares a local state of emergency and Governor Pete Wilson orders the National Guard to assist local police in controlling the increasing violence. President George Bush orders the deployment of 1,500 Marines and 3,000 U.S. Army troops to Los Angeles. Many of the shops targeted for looting are those owned by Korean immigrants. Tension between Los Angeles African Americans and Koreans had been rising since the 1991 fatal shooting of a young African American girl, Latasha Harlins, by a Korean grocer. The Bush administration blames the riots on urban decay, crime, and welfare dependency that it claims grew out of the social welfare programs passed by Congress in the 1960s and 1970s.

1992, June 13 • Washington, DC
Governor Bill Clinton speaks at the Rainbow Coalition convention and criticizes questionable statements made by rap singer Sister Souljah (Lisa Williamson) in reference to the Los Angeles riots. The Reverend Jesse Jackson, founder of the Rainbow Coalition, says he thinks Clinton's comments were intended to embarrass and provoke him.

1992, June 26 • Washington, DC
In the case of *United States v. Fordice*, the U.S. Supreme Court rules 8–1 that the state of Mississippi has not sufficiently desegregated its public universities. Despite "race-neutral" admissions standards, certain policies are targeted as causing informal segregation. Examples include wording of mission statements and higher admissions standards at the predominantly white colleges.

1992, July 23 • Washington, DC
The 1990 U.S. Census shows black median household incomes at $19,758 compared to $31,435 for whites and $30,056 for the national median average. The statistics show that blacks earn 63 percent of the median white income, only slightly better than the 62 percent earned by blacks ten years prior.

1992, August 29 • Washington, DC
The FBI's Uniform Crime Reports gives the rate of violent offenses by juveniles (ages 10 to 17) as 430 out of 100,000 in 1990. Black arrests are 1,429 out of 100,000, five times the amount of whites arrested.

1992, September 3 • Washington, DC
A 1991 U.S. Census Bureau report finds that the number of Americans below the poverty level is the highest number since 1964. In 1991, 14.2 percent of Americans were in poverty compared to 13.5 percent in 1990. In 1991, 32.7 percent of African Americans were in poverty compared to 31.9 percent in 1990.

1992, September 16 • Washington, DC
The U.S. Department of Education's report on high school dropout rates shows a 13.6 percent dropout of black students (ages 16 to 24) in 1991 compared to 21.3 percent in 1972. The dropout rate of Hispanics rose from 34.3 percent to 35.3 percent, whereas the rate for whites dropped from 12.3 percent to 8.9 percent.

1992, September 28 • Berkeley, California
The University of California at Berkeley Law School is found in violation of federal civil rights laws by the U.S. Department of Education Office for Civil Rights. It is discovered that minority applicants to the school receive preferential treatment over other candidates. As a result of this ruling, the school's admission policies are revised.

1992, October 8 • Boston, Massachusetts
A study conducted by the Federal Reserve's regional bank shows evidence of bank discrimination against minorities applying for mortgages. The study measures black, Hispanic, and white rejection rates when all applicants had similar application criteria. The findings show 17 percent rejection of minorities compared to 11 percent rejection of whites. This study is the first to investigate loan application criteria.

1992, November 3 • The presidential election brings 16 new African American members to Congress for a total of 38. Senator Earl F. Hilliard is the first African American Alabaman elected to Congress. The District of Columbia's Marion Barry wins a seat on Washington's city council. Florida's first three African American representatives—Corrine Brown, Carrie Meek, and Alcee Hastings—benefit from court-ordered redistricting. In Georgia, three African Americans join Congress: Senator Nathan Deal, Representative Jackie Barrett, and Representative Cynthia McKinney. McKinney is the first African American woman voted into the Georgia House of Representatives.

1992, November • Detroit, Michigan
Two Detroit policemen are charged with murder and two policemen are charged with lesser criminal charges in the beating death of black motorist Malice Green. Larry Nevers and Walter Budzyn, two white police officers, pulled Green out of his car and beat him on the head with metal flashlights. Sergeant Freddie Douglas, a black policeman, is charged with failing to stop the beating. White policeman Robert Lessnau is charged

with participating in the beating and aggravated assault. Innocent pleas are entered for all four officers.

1992, November 6 • Washington, DC
U.S. Labor Department figures show a decrease in unemployment rates from 7.5 percent in September to 7.4 percent in October. In September, jobless rates drop from 6.7 percent to 6.5 percent for whites, from 11.9 percent to 11.8 percent for Hispanics, and rose to 13.9 percent from 13.7 percent for blacks.

1992, November 7 • An outline for one of Martin Luther King, Jr.'s speeches is purchased at an auction for $35,000 by New Jersey Group, Kaller and Associates. The King estate filed a lawsuit requesting the return of the document plus $5 million in punitive damages from the dealer, Superior Galleries. King rarely made outlines or notes for his speeches, which explains the inflated worth.

1992, November 18 • *Malcolm X*, Spike Lee's motion picture based on Alex Haley's biography of the slain civil rights leader, opens in theaters nationwide.

1992, December 12 • Washington, DC
President Bill Clinton's Cabinet and White House appointments include five African American men and one African American woman. They are Clifton R. Wharton, Jr. as deputy secretary of the Department of State; Hazel R. O'Leary as secretary of the Department of Energy; Mike Espy as head of the Agriculture Department; Ron Brown, the former Democratic National Committee Chairman, as secretary of the Department of Commerce; Jesse Brown as Veterans Affairs secretary; and Joycelyn Elders, as surgeon general.

1993, January 5 • Washington, DC
The House of Representatives passes by 22 votes a rules change that will allow an increase in voting rights to delegates from Washington, DC, and the U.S. territories of American Samoa, Guam, Puerto Rico, and the U.S. Virgin Islands. (The District of Columbia and the Virgin Islands have large black populations.) In the past, the delegates took part in committee actions and votes, but not votes on the House floor, which were restricted to representatives from "the states" because the Constitution stipulated that only "the states" should have legislative authority. Delegates may now participate in all but the final votes affecting legislation.

1993, January 7 • Washington, DC
Senator Carol Moseley Braun is one of two women elected to the Senate Judiciary Committee. Braun claimed she was inspired to run partly as a result of angry feelings over the Anita Hill-Clarence Thomas hearings in

Veterans Affairs Secretary Jesse Brown with President Bill Clinton speaking at a press conference (AP/Wide World Photos, Inc.).

1991. The all-male Judiciary Committee had been admonished by the public for its role in the handling of the hearings.

1993, January 8 • Washington, DC
The unemployment rate for December of 1992 reaches 7.3 percent, according to U.S. Labor Department figures.

1993, January 24 • Bethesda, Maryland
Thurgood Marshall, the first African American Supreme Court justice and lifelong supporter of civil rights, dies of heart failure.

1993, January 18 • New Hampshire renames its January holiday from Civil Rights Day to King Day. This is the first time all fifty states have a holiday for Martin Luther King, Jr.

1993, March 2 • Washington, DC
In the case of *Voinovich v. Quilter*, the U.S. Supreme Court rules that the authority to create voting districts dominated by ethnic minorities is held by individual states. The issue was brought before the Court because

of concern over the reorganization practices of Ohio's state legislative voting districts in 1990.

1993, April 9 • Baltimore, Maryland
Civil rights champion Benjamin F. Chavis, Jr. is elected as executive director of the National Association for the Advancement of Colored People.

1993, April 17 • Los Angeles, California
In a civil suit, two of the four Los Angeles police officers charged in the beating of African American motorist Rodney King are convicted, while the other two are acquitted. Officer Lawrence M. Powell is convicted of violating King's rights to an arrest without "unreasonable force." Powell delivered the majority of hits to King with his baton. Sgt. Stacey C. Koon is convicted of allowing the violation by Powell to occur. Officers Theodore J. Briseno and Timothy E. Wind are found not guilty on all charges. As a result of the riots in 1991, the people of Los Angeles were on edge awaiting the new verdict. Riot training for seven thousand Los Angeles police officers and advance notice of the verdict to the police prepared them for the possibility of further rioting.

1993, May 17 • Washington, DC
The U.S. Supreme Court sends the case of *American Family Mutual Insurance Co. v. National Association for the Advancement of Colored People* back to the lower courts. Until decisions by the lower courts, the federal Fair Housing Act may be interpreted to extend coverage toward homeowner's insurance. The NAACP charged that the insurance company refused to sell to African Americans or charged them exorbitant fees. The practice is also known as "redlining."

1993, May 23 • Washington, DC
The Washington Post begins publishing portions of the late Supreme Court Justice Thurgood Marshall's papers. Immediately following Marshall's death, his papers are made available for use by "researchers or scholars engaged in serious research." These conditions were requested by Marshall when he turned his papers over to the Library of Congress after his retirement. Supreme Court Chief Justice Rehnquist wrote Librarian of Congress James H. Billington a letter admonishing him for lack of judgment in releasing the papers so soon. Marshall's friends, family, and colleagues displayed similar feelings of anger at the papers' speedy release.

1993, June 3 • Washington, DC
President Bill Clinton retracts his nomination of Lani Guinier for the position of head of the civil rights division in the Justice Department. Guinier, an African American law professor, had expressed some controversial ideas relating to race and voting rights in some previous professional writings. Clinton justifies his decision by explaining that the views expressed in the writings clashed with his own opinions on the same topics.

1993, June 7 • Pop star Prince changes his name to a symbol that combines the signs for male and female.

1993, June 26 • Woodland Hills, California
Hall of Fame catcher Roy Campanella, one of the first African Americans to play in the major leagues, dies of a heart attack.

1993, July 23 • Fayetteville, North Carolina
James Jordan, father of Chicago Bulls star Michael Jordan, is shot and killed during a robbery attempt.

1993, July 27 • Waltham, Massachusetts
Boston Celtics guard Reggie Lewis collapses and dies at Brandeis University during a practice.

1993, August 4 • Los Angeles, California
A federal judge sentences Sergeant Stacy Koon and Officer Lawrence Powell to two and a half years in prison for violating the civil rights of motorist Rodney King during a 1991 beating.

1993, August 4 • New York City, New York
Leonard Jeffries, Jr. is reinstated as chairman of City College's black studies department. A judge rules that the decision by college administrators to remove Jeffries following a controversial 1991 speech violated his constitutional right to free speech.

1993, August 23 • Detroit, Michigan
Two white officers, Larry Nevers and Walter Budzyn, are convicted of second-degree murder in the beating death of motorist Malice Green.

1993, September 7 • West Palm Beach, Florida
Two white men are convicted of kidnapping and setting afire a black tourist on January 1, 1993. The men are also convicted of attempted murder and armed robbery. They are sentenced to life imprisonment on October 22.

1993, September 8 • Washington, DC
Joycelyn Elders is sworn in as U.S. surgeon general.

1993, September 14 • Philadelphia, Pennsylvania
The University of Pennsylvania decides not to suspend a group of African American students who seized 14,000 copies of the student newspaper *Daily Pennsylvanian.* The students took the newspapers to protest what they viewed as the *Daily Pennsylvanian*'s conservative and racially-biased views.

Joycelyn Elders (AP/Wide World Photos, Inc.)

1993, September 30 • Fort Myer, Virginia
Colin L. Powell retires as chairman of the Joint Chiefs of Staff.

1993, October 6 • Chicago, Illinois
Chicago Bulls star Michael Jordan announces his retirement from the NBA.

1993, October 8 • New York City, New York
Actor Ted Danson is chastised for appearing onstage in blackface and telling several racist and sexist jokes during a Friars Club roast for actress Whoopi Goldberg.

1993, October 18 • Los Angeles, California
Two African American men are acquitted of attempted murder in the beating of truck driver Reginald Denny during the 1992 riot.

1993, October 20 • Don Cornelius steps down as host of the syndicated television dance show "Soul Train" after 22 years.

1993, November 2 • New York City, New York
Mayor David Dinkins is defeated in a mayoral election by former U.S. attorney Rudolph Giuliani.

1993, November 2 • Detroit, Michigan
Dennis Archer defeats Sharon McPhail to become mayor of Detroit, succeeding Coleman Young.

1994, February 3 • Washington, DC
Nation of Islam leader Louis Farrakhan censures aide Khalid Abdul Muhammad for anti-Semitic remarks made in a November of 1993 speech.

1994, February 5 • Jackson, Mississippi
Byron de la Beckwith, a white supremacist, is convicted of the 1963 murder of civil rights leader Medgar Evers. Beckwith is sentenced to life in prison.

1994, March 1 • Berkeley, California
Former Black Panther leader Eldridge Cleaver is hospitalized after suffering a brain hemorrhage.

1994, March 23 • Los Angeles, California
Earvin "Magic" Johnson is named coach of the Los Angeles Lakers.

1994, April 12 • Washington, DC
Randall Robinson, executive director of TransAfrica, a lobbying group for African and Caribbean issues, begins a liquid fast to protest the U.S. government's "discriminatory policy" on Haiti.

1994, May 24 • Santa Ana, California
Denny's Restaurants agree to pay $54 million to settle lawsuits by African Americans who claim they were discriminated against by the restaurant chain.

1994, May 26 • Dominican Republic
Pop star Michael Jackson and Lisa Marie Presley, daughter of Elvis Presley, are married.

1994, June 20 • Los Angeles, California
Ex-football star O.J. Simpson is arrested and charged with the murder of his wife, Nicole Brown Simpson, and her friend, Ron Goldman.

1994, August 20 • Chicago, Illinois
Benjamin F. Chavis is ousted as executive director of the NAACP by the civil rights organization's board of directors. Earl T. Shinhoster is named interim director.

1994, August 30 • Detroit, Michigan
Civil rights activist Rosa Parks is beaten and robbed in her home.

1994, October 3 • Washington, DC
Mike Espy, secretary of the U.S. Department of Agriculture, resigns following a federal ethics investigation in

which Espy is accused of receiving gifts from businesses regulated by the U.S. Department of Agriculture.

1994, October 21 • Atlanta, Georgia
Dexter Scott King, the youngest son of the late Reverend Martin Luther King, Jr. is named chief executive and chairman of the Martin Luther King, Jr. Center for Nonviolent Social Change.

1994, December 9 • Washington, DC
Joycelyn Elders resigns as U.S. surgeon general after making controversial statements regarding drug use and sex education.

1994, December 10 • New York City, New York
University of Colorado running back Rashaan Salaam wins the Heisman Trophy.

1994, December 14 • Washington, DC
Representative Donald M. Payne, a Democrat from New Jersey, is elected to a two-year term as chairman of the Congressional Black Caucus.

1995, January 12 • Minneapolis, Minnesota
Qubilah Bahiyah Shabazz, daughter of the late black nationalist leader Malcolm X, is arrested and charged with plotting to kill Nation of Islam leader Louis Farrakhan.

1995, March 18 • Chicago, Illinois
Chicago Bulls star Michael Jordan announces his return to the NBA after retiring in 1993.

1995, March 25 • Plainfield, Indiana
Boxer Mike Tyson is released from prison after serving three years for a 1992 rape conviction.

1995, April 21 • Washington, DC
H. Patrick Swygert is named president of Howard University, replacing Franklyn G. Jenifer who resigned on April 22, 1994.

1995, June 21 • Washington, DC
The Senate rejects Dr. Henry Foster, Jr.'s bid to become U.S. surgeon general. Foster, a gynecologist and obstetrician, is rejected due to pressure from anti-abortion groups and Senate Republicans.

1995, June 29 • Washington, DC
The Supreme Court, by a 5–4 vote, rules that electoral districts drawn to ensure fair political representation of African Americans and other minorities are unconstitutional if race is used as the predominant factor in drawing district boundaries.

1995, July 20 • Davis, California
The University of California votes to eliminate affirmative action policies in the admission of students.

1995, October 3 • Los Angeles, California
O. J. Simpson is acquitted of the murder of his former wife Nicole Brown Simpson and her friend, Ron Goldman. The O.J. Simpson trial was televised daily throughout the United States and fueled extensive debate regarding race relations in America.

1995, October 3 • Creve Coeur, Missouri
Eddie Robinson of Grambling State University, Grambling, Louisiana, has 400 wins in 53 seasons to become college football's winningest coach.

1995, October 16 • Washington, DC
The Million Man March, organized by Nation of Islam leader Louis Farrakhan, draws African American men to the nation's capital. The purpose of the march is to offer African American men an opportunity to meet for a day of atonement and to pledge their commitment to themselves, their families, and their communities.

1995, November 8 • Alexandria, Virginia
Former chairman of the Joint Chiefs of Staff, Colin L. Powell, ends months of speculation by announcing that he will not run for the U.S. presidency in 1996.

1995, December 9 • Chicago, Illinois
Kweisi Mfume is unanimously elected as president and chief executive officer of the NAACP.

1995, December 12 • Washington, DC
Jesse Jackson, Jr., son of civil rights activist Rev. Jesse Jackson, is elected as the representative of Illinois's Second Congressional District. He replaced Representative Mel Reynolds who resigned from Congress after being sentenced to five years in prison for sexual misconduct.

1996, January 15 • Five of the largest African American congregations in the United States announce the formulation of Revelation Corporation of America, a for-profit company designed to improve the buying power of African American consumers.

1996, January 17 • Austin, Texas
Barbara Charline Jordan, scholar, educator, and politician, dies in a hospital of pneumonia and complications from leukemia. She had suffered from multiple sclerosis for several years. In 1966, Jordan became the first African American elected state senator in Texas. In 1972, she was elected to the U.S. Congress, becoming

O.J. Simpson stands before the jury wearing the bloody gloves last worn by the assailant of Nicole Brown Simpson and Ron Goldman (Archive Photos, Inc.).

the state's first African American and first woman elected to the position. An excellent orator, Jordan gained national attention in 1974 when she called for the impeachment of President Richard M. Nixon for his involvement in the Watergate scandal. Two years later, she became the first African American woman to give a keynote address at the Democratic National Convention.

1996, January 18 • Los Angeles, California
Lisa Marie Presley files for divorce from her husband, pop singer Michael Jackson.

1996, January 30 • Los Angeles, California
Los Angeles Lakers star Earvin (Magic) announces his return to the NBA after retiring in 1991. He played in 32 of their 40 games remaining. Later that year he was named among the 50 Greatest NBA Players of all time. He retired again and purchased a minority share in the Lakers.

1996, February 20 • Washington, DC
Kweisi Mfume is sworn in as the top executive of the NAACP.

1996, March 11 • Baltimore, Maryland
Political activist C. DeLores Tucker urges churches to boycott stores that sell "gangsta rap" on the grounds that it glorifies the use of violence and drugs and degrades women.

1996, April 3 • Dubrovnik, Croatia
Commerce Secretary Ronald H. Brown and distinguished American business leaders are killed in a plane crash.

1996, April 8 • Cleveland, Ohio
After 17 years of busing, a federal judge lifts a school desegregation order which district officials claim will save $10 million.

1996, May 19 • Jackson, Mississippi
James Meredith, who integrated the University of Mississippi in 1962, is shot at by whites who yell insults from a passing truck.

1996, May 28 • Pensacola, Florida
Donnie Cochran, who in 1994 became the first African American commander of the U.S. Navy's Blue Angels flight demonstration team, resigns. He cites his own shortcomings in flying that could threaten the safety of his pilots and the shows' spectators.

1996, June 13 • Washington, DC
The U.S. Supreme Court declares unconstitutional two congressional districts in North Carolina and three in Texas because the districts—majority African American and majority Hispanic—were illegally drawn.

1996, June 22 • Washington, DC
The Senate approves Vice Admiral J. Paul Reason to become the U.S. Navy's first African American four-star admiral. President Bill Clinton nominated Reason for the promotion on May 13. Reason later assumes command of the U.S. Atlantic Fleet in Norfolk, Virginia.

1996, June 27 • Washington, DC
President Bill Clinton signs the Church Arson Bill affecting racially-motivated burnings. The bill authorizes $10 million to be used to help build churches that are underinsured and increases the sentence for such crimes.

1996, July 1 • Washington, DC
The U.S. Supreme Court confirms the ruling that race cannot be a factor in admitting students to the University of Texas Law School. Previously, separate and lower standards were used to admit African Americans and Hispanics.

1996, August 30 • Tripoli, Libya
Louis Farrakhan receives the Gadhafi International Hu-

Father and son participants in the 1995 Million Man March applauding in response to a speech (AP/Wide World Photos, Inc.).

man Rights Award for organizing the Million Man March. However, U.S. law bars him from accepting gifts from terrorists.

1996, September 13 • Las Vegas, Nevada
Rap artist Tupac Shakur, a victim of a drive-by shooting, dies. His career had been marked by violence and run-ins with law enforcement agents. Shakur was named after an Incan chief and raised by his mother, Afeni Shakur, a Black Panther Party member who was imprisoned while pregnant with her son. Tupac Shakur sold millions of records of "gangsta"-style rap music. In some of his works, he taunted the police and glorified violence and misogyny. He became a target for groups that aimed to clean up rap lyrics.

1996, September 23 • Chicago, Illinois
Talk show host Oprah Winfrey is the highest-paid entertainer, earning $212 million, according to *Forbes* magazine.

1996, October 4 • Washington, DC
Congress passes a bill authorizing the creation of 500,000 black Revolutionary War Patriots commemorative coins. They are to depict the two hundred and seventy-fifth

anniversary of the birth of Revolutionary War hero Crispus Attucks.

1996, October 25 • Tulsa, Oklahoma
J. B. Stradford, who died sixty years earlier, is cleared of charges that he was one of dozens of African Americans accused of inciting the Tulsa riot of May 31, 1921, that ruined 35 city blocks and killed 36 or more people.

1996, November 5 • Atlanta, Georgia
Cynthia McKinney, a Democrat from Georgia, is reelected to the U.S. House of Representatives after district lines are redrawn, making her district predominantly white.

1996, November 15 • White Plains, New York
Texaco Inc., a major oil company headquartered in White Plains, agrees to a $176.1 million settlement of a federal discrimination lawsuit filed in 1994 by African American Texaco employees—the largest race discrimination lawsuit ever filed. The company also agrees to help create an outside task force to oversee a Texaco diversity program. On November 4, the *New York Times* made public the existence of an audiotape containing

Texaco executives' disparaging racial remarks including their reference to African American workers as "black jelly beans." The company has 27,000 employees, more than 1,400 of whom are African American.

1996, November 12 • Washington, DC
President Bill Clinton signs legislation creating the Selma-to-Montgomery National Historic Trail in Alabama, marking the route of the civil rights march that Martin Luther King, Jr. led in 1965.

1996, December 18 • Oakland, California
The school board recognizes black English, or Ebonics, as a separate language rather than slang or dialect. The board subsequently rescinded its decision to make Ebonics a second language.

1997, January 3 • New York City, New York
"Today" show anchor Bryant Gumbel, the longest-serving host in the show's history, resigns after 15 years.

1997, January 13 • Washington, DC
President Bill Clinton awards seven African American soldiers Medals of Honor. Joseph Vernon Baker, 77, the only living recipient in the group, attended the awards ceremony. Baker was a second lieutenant in the U.S. Army's Ninety-second Infantry Division. None of the 433 Medals of Honor awarded to servicemen for acts of gallantry in World War II had been given to African Americans. African American veterans, however, petitioned the Department of the Army to honor African American servicemen as well.

1997, February 13 • Washington, DC
David Satcher is sworn in as U.S. surgeon general and assistant secretary for Health at the Department of Health and Human Services. A physician, educator, and former medical school president, he leaves the position he had held since 1993 as head of the Centers for Disease Control in Atlanta. He was the first African American to head the center. President Bill Clinton nominated Satcher for the surgeon general's post on September 12, 1996.

1997, February 17 • Richmond, Virginia
The Virginia House of Delegates retires the state song "Carry Me Back to Old Virginia" by unanimous vote. African American composer James A. Bland wrote the song in 1875; it was adopted by the state in 1940.

1997, February 26 • Major League Baseball dedicates the season to Jackie Robinson who on April 15, 1947—fifty years ago—broke the league's color barrier.

1997, April 2 • Nashville, Tennessee
Tennessee ratifies the Fifteenth Amendment 127 years after its ratification by Congress. The amendment guarantees the right to vote regardless of "race, color or previous condition of servitude."

1997, April 13 • Augusta, Georgia
Eldrick "Tiger" Woods finishes with the lowest score in tournament history and wins the Sixty-first Masters. He is the first African American and the youngest person to win the Masters.

1997, April 28 • Old Saybrook, Connecticut
Writer Ann Petry, best known for her 1946 novel *The Street*, dies.

1997, May 1 • Washington, DC
The U.S. Senate confirms Alexis M. Herman, assistant to President Bill Clinton, as U.S. secretary of labor.

1997, May 15 • Washington, DC
President Bill Clinton issues an apology to the few remaining survivors and relatives of the African American men who were involved in the federal government's "Tuskegee Experiment" nearly a quarter of a century earlier.

1997, May 28 • Chicago, Illinois
Eighty-four-year-old John H. Stengstacke, owner and editor of the *Chicago Defender*, dies. He founded the Negro Newspaper Publishers Association.

1997, June 13 • Baltimore, Maryland
After conducting a survey of the hotel industry as a part of its Economic Reciprocity Campaign, the NAACP gives failing grades to three major hotel chains for their hiring and promotion practices of African Americans and relations with African American businesses. Receiving the grades were Holiday Inn, Westin, and Best Western.

1997, June 14 • Washington, DC
President Bill Clinton names seven people to the White House Initiative on Race and Reconciliation and appoints historian John Hope Franklin chair. The panel's charge is to lead a year-long national dialogue about race.

1997, June 14 • San Diego, California
President Bill Clinton delivers a speech on race in the United States at the commencement exercises at the University of California, San Diego. He said, "Now we know what we will look like. But what will we be like?

Tiger Woods celebrating at The Masters in 1997 (Archive Photos, Inc.).

Can we be one America, respecting, even celebrating our differences, but embracing even more what we have in common?"

1997, June 23 • New York City, New York
Betty Shabazz, college educator and administrator and widow of slain black nationalist Malcolm X, dies after suffering from extensive burns on June 1. The fires causing her death were apparently set by her grandson, Malcolm Shabazz, a troubled 12-year-old, in her Yonkers, New York, apartment. Betty Shabazz held numerous speaking engagements, often addressing such issues as health and education for disadvantaged youth and black self-determination.

1997, June 28 • Las Vegas, Nevada
In a heavyweight boxing rematch with Evander Holyfield, Mike Tyson is disqualified after three rounds and thrown out for biting Holyfield twice on his ears. Later the Nevada Commission fined Tyson $3 million and revoked his boxing license.

1997, July 10 • Birmingham, Alabama
The FBI reopens investigation into bombings of the 16th Street Baptist Church where four young African American girls were killed on September 15, 1963, while attending Sunday school.

1997, July 24 • Washington, DC
The Army Corps of Engineers agrees to settle a race discrimination suit filed by African American deckhands on the dredge *Hurley* based in Memphis, Tennessee. The Defense Department found that black workers aboard the ship routinely endured racial epithets and jokes from whites and were denied promotions because they were black. The 16 deck-hands each received $62,500 and were given the opportunity to move from part- time to full-time employment.

1997, August 4 • Washington, DC
Robert G. Stanton is sworn into office and becomes the first African American director of the Interior Department's National Park Service. He had worked with the park service from 1962 to January of 1967, then retired from the agency's national capital region.

1997, October • Oakland, California
The Black Panther Legacy Tour begins under the leadership of David Hilliard, former chief of staff for the Panthers. The bus tour winds through the Oakland neighborhood where the Panthers were founded in 1966 and other sites of significance to the Panthers' history.

1997, October 25 • Philadelphia, Pennsyslvania
Over 300,000 African American women arrive for the first Million Woman March. Among the speakers are Maxine Waters, Winnie Mandela, and rapper Sister Souljah.

1997, December 6 • Houston, Texas
Lee P. Brown, Democrat, veteran law enforcement officer, and former "drug czar," is elected mayor, the first African American to hold the post. The city's population of 1.8 million reports a racial mix of one-third white, one-third black, and one-third Hispanic.

1998, January 15 • Atlanta, Georgia
Martin Luther King III succeeds Joseph E. Lowery as head of the SCLC. Lowery held the post for twenty years.

1998, January 16 • Maryland
A county school district in Maryland bans Toni Morrison's novel *Song of Solomon*.

1998, January 23 • Cambridge, Massachusetts
Harvard University announces the appointment of Lani Guinier as a full tenured professor in the Harvard Law

School. She is the first African American woman to receive tenure at the law school and is known for her outspoken stance on issues such as voting rights and affirmative action.

1998, February 2 • Washington, DC
Jane E. Smith becomes president of the National Council of Negro Women, succeeding Dorothy I. Height who held the post for forty years.

1998, February 5 • Washington, DC
Documents from Brown & Williamson Tobacco Company relating to marketing strategies aimed at teenagers and minorities are released during a House judiciary hearing. The documents date back to 1972 and had been used in state lawsuits against the tobacco industry. The Brown & Williamson papers document strategies to attract African Americans, suggesting that a Kool-brand basketball "could become an interesting symbol within the inner city."

1998, February 9 • Baltimore, Maryland
Myrlie Evers-Williams announces that she will not seek a fourth term as chair of the National Association for the Advancement of Colored People's board of directors. She leaves the organization that she has headed since 1995 with what she calls a surplus of over $2 million and with restored credibility and financial integrity.

1998, February 21 • Baltimore, Maryland
Civil rights activist and educator Julian Bond is elected chair of the NAACP's board of directors, succeeding Myrlie Evers-Williams. He announced his aim to continue the organization's progress "on our way to financial health and integrity."

1998, March 21 • Jackson, Mississippi
The state of Mississippi releases documents relating to the now-defunct Mississippi State Sovereignty Commission that used spy tactics and intimidation to preserve racial segregation in the state during the civil rights era. Created in 1956, the commission promoted racial segregation in Mississippi and throughout the country. In 1989, U.S. District Judge William H. Barber ordered the files open. The documents show that previously secret files included information on individual civil rights workers, their religious beliefs, sexual behavior, and other details. License plate numbers were recorded outside civil rights meeting places. Many African American informers were used as spies. Some of the documents discuss the use of violence against the civil rights workers.

1998, March 22 • Africa
President Bill Clinton begins an historic 12-day tour of sub-Saharan Africa in the accompaniment of such notable African Americans as Jesse Jackson, Sr., Congresswoman Maxine Waters, and Camille Cosby.

1998, April 14 • Washington, DC
Franklin D. Raines is named chief executive of the nation's largest mortgage financing company, Fannie Mae.

1998, April 23 • Nashville, Tennessee
James Earl Ray, convicted killer of Martin Luther King, Jr., dies of liver disease.

1998, May 1 • In response to written objections concerning the "n——word," *Merriam-Webster Dictionary* officials announce a plan to revise over two hundred words regarded as offensive.

1998, May 2 • Pomona, California
Eldridge Cleaver, writer, minister, and former leader of the Black Panther party, dies of undisclosed causes.

1998, June 19 • Boston, Massachusetts
Columnist Patricia Smith, on staff since 1990, resigns from the *Boston Globe* after admitting that she fabricated sections of her columns.

1998, July • Atlanta, Georgia
Myrlie Evers, who resigned as board chair of the NAACP, is named chairman emeritus at the organization's annual meeting.

1998, July 19 • New York City, New York
Historian and African history scholar John Henrik Clarke dies of a heart attack in Harlem at age 83.

1998, July 22 • Atlanta, Georgia
A federal judge rules that CBS News is not guilty of copyright infringement for airing film coverage of Martin Luther King, Jr.'s famous "I Have a Dream" speech of 1963, and that the deceased leader's speech is in public domain. CBS used the footage in "The 20th Century with Mike Wallace," shown in 1994. The King family sued CBS for its use of the film.

1998, July 24 • Manning, South Carolina
In the largest award given to the victims of a hate crime, a jury orders the Ku Klux Klan and its grand dragon to pay $37.8 million for the 1995 burning of the Macedonia Baptist Church in Bloomville.

1998, September 7 • Atlanta, Georgia
Hundreds of young people attend the Million Youth March supported by such organizations as the NAACP,

President Bill Clinton acknowledging cheers from students during his visit to Goree Island near the coast of Senegal in 1998 (AP/ Wide World Photos, Inc.).

the Student Christian Leadership Conference, and Operation PUSH (People United to Serve Humanity). A similar march was held earlier in New York City, but without the organizations' support.

1998, September 18 • Washington, DC
The White House Initiative on Race and Reconciliation, after 15 months of examination, releases its report and confirms that racism is still a critical problem in the United States.

1998, September 26 • Langston, Oklahoma
Prairie View Agricultural and Mechanical University in Texas ends its eighty-game losing streak by beating Langston University. This is the longest losing streak in National Collegiate Athletic Association history.

1998, September 21 • Mission Viejo, California
Olympic star Florence Griffith Joyner, the first woman to win four Olympic medals, dies of an epileptic seizure while sleeping.

1998, November 1 • Oxford, England
Genetic evidence, based on blood samples from living descendants of Thomas Jefferson and his slave Sally Hemings, prove it is likely that Jefferson had fathered a son by Hemings. The DNA was analyzed by an Oxford University research team in England and the results published in the November 5 issue of *Nature*.

1998, November 9 • Chicago, Illinois
U.S. Senator Carol Mosely Braun loses her bid for reelection to Republican Peter Fitzgerald.

1998, December 2 • Washington, DC
Mike Espy, former secretary of the U.S. Department of Agriculture, is acquitted of charges involving gifts received from businesses regulated by the department.

1999, January 13 • Chicago, Illinois
Chicago Bulls star Michael Jordan retires from the NBA a second time. He had led the Bulls to their third straight NBA title and their sixth in eight years.

1999, February 2 • Berkeley, California
Five civil rights advocacy groups file suit against the University of California at Berkeley, charging that the school discriminates against minorities in its admis-

sions policies. The groups argue that the elimination of race-based admissions places too much importance on grade point averages (GPA), Scholastic Aptitude Test (SAT) scores, and advanced placement (AP) courses, which they already regard as inherently biased and discriminatory against minorities. The suit follows recent abolition of race-based admissions policies in California's state universities.

1999, February 19 • Washington, DC
Fifty-nine years after his death, President Bill Clinton pardons Henry O. Flipper, the first African American graduate of West Point who was court-martialed in 1881 and dishonorably discharged in 1882. Clinton notes that "This good man now has completely recovered his good name." Flipper was ostracized by his white classmates. Although acquitted of apparently trumped-up charges of embezzling commissary funds, he was found guilty of "conduct unbecoming an officer" for lying to investigators. In 1976, the army formally exonerated Clipper, changed his discharge to honorable, and reburied him with full honors in his hometown, Thomasville, Georgia. An annual award is now given in his name to an outstanding West Point cadet.

1999, February 25 • Jasper, Texas
White supremacist John William King is sentenced to die for the dragging death on June 7, 1998, of James Byrd, Jr., behind a truck. Trials for two other men accused in the murder, Lawrence Russell Brewer and Shawn Allen Berry, are pending.

1999, March 16 • Miami, Florida
Henry Lyons, convicted earlier this month of racketeering and grand theft, resigns as president of the National Baptist Convention USA—a position he had held since 1994. He had survived earlier attempts of his church denomination to oust him from the convention's presidency and retained the support of his parishioners at Bethel Metropolitan Baptist Church—the church he pastored in St. Petersburg, Florida. Lyons was convicted of pocketing $240,000 in donations earmarked to African American churches burned by arson and for swindling over $4 million from corporations seeking business transactions with the convention.

1999, March 28 • San Jose, California
Carolyn Peck, women's head basketball coach at Purdue University and Big 10 Conference Coach of the Year and Associated Press Coach of the Year, ignites the number one-ranked Boilermakers to beat the Duke University Blue Devils 62–45 and win its first NCAA women's championship title. She is the first African American to win the national championship in women's basketball. Peck is scheduled to leave Purdue after this season to become head coach and general manager of the WNBA's Orlando Miracle.

1999, April • Trenton, North Carolina
The Trenton Town Council unanimously selects its first black and first woman mayor. Sylvia Willis succeeded white mayor Joffree Legett who resigned under pressure after denouncing blacks as unfit to govern and claiming that blacks would rather be led by whites. Earlier the town of about two hundred residents, fifty of them African American, refused to annex three African American neighborhoods with about one hundred residents. Intervention by the NAACP and an African American boycott of Trenton's white-owned businesses persuaded the town to annex the neighborhoods.

1999, April 12 • New York, New York
Legendary band leader and composer Edward Kennedy "Duke" Ellington (1899–1974) is awarded a Pulitzer Prize posthumously on the centennial of his birth. The special music citation was given "in recognition of his musical genius, which evoked aesthetically the principles of democracy through the medium of jazz and thus made an indelible contribution to art and culture."

1999, April 14 • Washington, DC
Federal District Court Judge Paul L. Friedman approves a settlement that could provide $2 billion for thousands of African American farmers who sued two years ago because their access to government loans and subsidies had been denied. Over 18,000 farmers have signed up for the settlement. Farmers with less documented evidence of discrimination in loan approvals may take a $50,000 settlement, $12,500 for taxes, and have their federal debts forgiven. Those with more evidence may appear before an independent arbitrator to petition for larger amounts in damages.

1999, April 20 • San Francisco, California
U.S. District Judge William Orrick orders an end to 16 years of race-based enrollment in the public schools of San Francisco and approves a lawsuit by Chinese Americans denied admission to preferred campuses in the city. Although African Americans and Hispanics protest his decision, Orrick rules that racial admissions violate Chinese Americans' constitutional rights to equal treatment in a school of their choice. The agreement repeals a limit of 45 percent of racial or ethnic enrollment in a single school and 40 percent in magnet schools.

1999, May 1 • Belgrade, Yugoslavia
Jesse Jackson wins the release of the three U.S. soldiers—staff sergeants Andrew Ramirez and Christopher Stone and specialist Steven Gonzales—who Yugoslav authorities had held as prisoners of war since their

Venus Williams (Archive Photos, Inc.)

capture on March 31 near the Yugoslavia-Macedonia border.

1999, June 6 • Paris, France
Venus Williams, 18, and her sister, Serena Williams, 17, win the French Open women's doubles title against Martina Hingis and Anna Kournikova 6–3, 6–7, 8–6.

1999, June 15 • Washington, DC
Under legislation approved by the U.S. Congress on May 3, Rosa Parks receives the Congressional Gold Medal. Congressman John Lewis said that "one, simple, defining act" by Parks, who in 1955 stood up "for what is right and just," stoked the Civil Rights movement nationwide and led to the end of legalized segregation.

1999, June 15 • Hattiesburg, Mississippi
A mistrial is declared in the reopened case against Sam Bowers for the 1966 slaying of NAACP member Vernon Dahmer.

1999, June 23 • Springfield, Massachusetts
Former Georgetown University coach John Thompson is elected to the NBA Hall of Fame, along with former basketball player and general manager Wayne Embry.

1999, July 10 • Baltimore, Maryland
The U.S. Coast Guard posthumously honored Alex Haley, Pulitzer Prize-winning author of *Roots*, by commissioning a cutter in his name. Haley spent twenty years in the Coast Guard, rising from ship's steward to become the first head of the Guard's public affairs office.

1999, August 4 • Phoenix, Arizona
Isiah Thomas, all-time Detroit Pistons basketball great and current NBC-TV analyst, announced that he had purchased majority ownership of the Continental Basketball Association (CBA). Thomas acquired the nine teams that comprise the CBA for approximately $10 million. Organized as an association with approximately forty owners, Thomas said he planned to reorganize the CBA into a single entity league.

2

African American Firsts

While not comprehensive, the following list of firsts covers a wide spectrum of pioneering events and people in history. Many of the individuals and events described hold considerable intrinsic significance—such as the first publication of a novel by an African American author in 1853—while other events listed are merely interesting. Nevertheless, all are trendsetters in African American history.

1619 • At Jamestown colony, the first twenty Africans arrive in English North America from the Caribbean as indentured servants.

1623 • The first African American child in the colonies to be baptized a Christian becomes a member of the Anglican Church in Jamestown. The child's name is William, son of Isabel and William.

1624 • Jamestown, Virginia
William Tucker, who is believed to have been the first African American child born in the American colonies, is born in Jamestown, Virginia.

1752 • Benjamin Banneker builds the first grandfather clock.

1758 • Born in 1702 to free parents in Jamaica, Frances Williams graduates from Cambridge University and becomes the first black college graduate in the Western Hemisphere.

1770 • While leading fellow patriots in protest against British soldiers, Crispus Attucks is killed, thus becoming the first American to die during the Revolutionary Period. This event is later memorialized as the Boston Massacre.

1783 • James Derham, born a slave in Philadelphia in 1762, becomes the first African American physician in the United States. Having served as an assistant to his master (a doctor by profession), Derham purchases his freedom in 1783 and goes on to develop a thriving practice with both black and white clientele.

1785, May 15 • New York
The first African American missionary minister to work with Native Americans is John Morront of New York. He was ordained a Methodist minister in London, England. Among his converts to the Christian faith are a Cherokee chieftain and his daughter.

1786 • Lemuel Haynes, who served during the American Revolution as a Minuteman in Connecticut, becomes the first African American minister with a white congregation.

1787 • Prince Hall organizes the first African American Masonic Lodge in America.

1816 • Richard Allen, founder of the African Methodist Episcopal Church, becomes the first African American bishop.

1827 • The first African American newspaper *Freedom's Journal* is published in New York City.

1829 • The first African American congregation of Catholic nuns, the Oblate Sisters of Providence, is founded in the United States by Mary Rosine Boegues, Mary Frances Balas, Mary Theresa Duchemin, and Elizabeth Lange.

1829 • The first National Negro Convention meets in Philadelphia, Pennsylvania.

1834 • Greenross, Maryland
The first African American believed to have been grant-

ed a patent from the United States Patent Office is Henry Blair of Greenross, Maryland.

1845 • Worcester, Massachusetts
Macon B. Allen becomes the first African American lawyer formally admitted to the bar after he passes the state bar examination in Worcester, Massachusetts.

1847 • David John Peck graduates from Rush Medical College, becoming the first African American to graduate from an American school of medicine.

1853 • The first novel written and published by an African American is a work by William Wells Brown, entitled *Clotel, A Tale of the Southern States. The work is published in England.*

1854 • Brownhelm, Ohio
John Mercer Langston, who is believed to have been the first African American elected to public office, is elected clerk of Brownhelm, Ohio.

1860 • The first African American baseball team to tour various parts of the country is called the Brooklyn Excelsiors.

1861 • Nicholas Biddle becomes one of the first African Americans wounded during the Civil War. An escaped slave, Biddle attaches himself to a troop unit heading for the defense of Washington, but is stoned by an angry mob in Baltimore. He manages to escape death only with the aid of his white comrades-in-arms.

1861 • Boston, Massachusetts
In Boston, Massachusetts, William C. Nell is appointed postal clerk, becoming the first African American to hold a federal civilian post.

1862 • Oberlin, Ohio
Mary Patterson becomes the first African American woman in the United States to earn a Master of Arts degree, awarded by Oberlin College.

1863 • The first African American appointed a chaplain in the United States Army is Henry McNeal Turner.

1864 • Rebecca Lee Crumpler, believed to be the first African American woman physician, graduates from New England Female Medical College.

1865 • Martin R. Delany becomes the first African American to attain the rank of major in the United States Army. A graduate of Howard University Medical School,

John Mercer Langston (The Library of Congress)

Delany served in the Medical Corps. He was also a writer.

1865 • Alexander T. Augusta becomes the first African American to hold a medical commission in the U.S. Army. A surgeon and physician with the rank of major, he then becomes the highest ranking African American officer in the Civil War on March 13, when he is promoted to brevet lieutenant colonel.

1865 • John Rock becomes the first African American lawyer admitted to practice before the United States Supreme Court. His admittance is moved by Senator Charles Sumner of Massachusetts. Chief Justice Salmon P. Chase presides.

1865 • Augusta, Georgia
The first African American newspaper in the South— *The Colored American*—is published in Augusta, Georgia, and edited by J. T. Shutten.

1866 • Massachusetts
Edward G. Walker and Charles L. Mitchell are elected to the Massachusetts House of Representatives, becoming

the first African Americans to serve in a legislative assembly.

1867 • Cambridge, Massachusetts
Robert Tanner Freeman becomes the first African American to graduate from Harvard University's School of Dentistry.

1869 • Ebenezer Don Carlos Bassett, believed to be the first African American to receive an appointment in the diplomatic service, becomes United States Minister to Haiti.

1869 • Harried E. Adams Wilson becomes the first African American to publish a novel in the United States entitled *Our Nig; or, Sketches from the Life of a Free Black, In a Two Story White House North, Showing That Slavery's Shadows Fall Even There.*

1870 • Cambridge, Massachusetts
Richard Greener becomes the first African American to receive a degree from Harvard. Active as a teacher and editor, Greener is admitted to the South Carolina bar in 1876 and becomes dean of Howard University Law School in 1879.

1870 • Mississippi
Hiram R. Revels, of Mississippi, becomes the first African American elected to the United States Senate. Joseph H. Rainey, of South Carolina, and Jefferson F. Long, of Georgia, are the first black elected members of the House of Representatives.

1872 • The first African American midshipman to attend the United States Naval Academy is James Henry Conyers of South Carolina. Conyers did not graduate, however, and left the academy on November 11, 1873.

1872 • Louisiana Lieutenant Governor Pinckney Benton Stewart Pinchback becomes the first African American governor upon impeachment of the incumbent.

1872 • Washington, District of Columbia
The first African American woman lawyer, Charlotte E. Roy, receives her degree from Howard University School of Law in Washington, DC.

1872 • Philadelphia, Pennsylvania
The first African American delegates to the presidential nominating convention of a major party appear at the Republican Convention in Philadelphia.

1873 • Little Rock, Arkansas
The first African American municipal judge, Mifflin W. Gibbs, is elected in Little Rock, Arkansas.

P.B.S. Pinchback (AP/Wide World Photos, Inc.)

1873 • Susan McKinney, believed to be the first African American woman to formally enter the medical profession, is certified as a physician. (Records at the medical college of the New York Infirmary indicate that Rebecca Cole was the first African American woman physician in the United States, having practiced from 1872 to 1881.)

1875 • Reverend James Augustine Healy becomes the first African American Roman Catholic bishop in the United States on June 10.

1875 • Oliver Lewis, an African American riding in the first Kentucky Derby, becomes the race's first winner, on May 17.

1876 • New Haven, Connecticut
Graduating from Yale University, Edward A. Bouchet becomes the first African American to earn a Ph.D. from an American university.

1877 • George Washington Henderson is elected to Phi Beta Kappa, becoming the first African American to gain membership in the honor society.

1877 • Henry O. Flipper becomes the first African

James Augustine Healy

American to graduate from the United States Military Academy at West Point.

1879 • Boston, Massachusetts
In Boston, Mary E. Mahoney becomes the first African American woman to receive a diploma in nursing from New England Hospital for Women and Children, on August 1.

1882 • Illinois
The first daily newspaper owned by an African American, *The Cairo Illinois Gazette*, is published by W. S. Scott.

1884 • John Roy Lynch becomes the first African American to preside over a national political convention, when he is nominated temporary chairman of the Republican Party's national convention.

1884 • Toledo, Ohio
Moses Fleetwood Walker becomes the first African American major league baseball player when he plays for Toledo in the American Association.

1885 • The first African American state legislator elect-

ed to represent a majority white constituency is Bishop Benjamin William Arnett of the African Methodist Episcopal Church.

1885 • New York City, New York
The first African American professional baseball team, The Cuban Giants, is formed in New York City by Frank Thompson from a group of waiters at a Long Island hotel.

1885 • The first African American Protestant Episcopal bishop in the United States, the Reverend Samuel David Ferguson, is elected to the House of Bishops.

1885 • Jonathan Jasper Wright becomes the first African American elected to the State Supreme Court of South Carolina. He is also the first African American to be admitted to the bar in Pennsylvania.

1890 • Louisiana
Thomy Lafon, a real estate speculator and money lender in Louisiana, is believed to have been the first African American millionaire in the United States.

1892 • The first African American college football game is played between Biddle College (now Johnson C. Smith University) and Livingstone College. Biddle wins 4 to 0.

1893 • Dr. Daniel Hale Williams becomes the first surgeon to successfully enter the chest cavity and suture the heart of a living patient.

1893 • E. R. Robinson patents the electric railway trolley on September 19.

1894 • Massachusetts
William Edward Burghardt Du Bois becomes the first African American to be awarded a Ph.D. by Harvard University.

1902 • Paris, France
Off Bloomingdale Asylum, a satirical comedy, is the first film to use African American actors. The film is made in Paris, France.

1903 • Richmond, Virginia
Maggie Lena Walker becomes the first African American woman bank president when she founds the Saint Luke Penny Thrift Savings Bank in Richmond, Virginia.

1906 • Ithaca, New York
The first African American fraternity, Alpha Phi Alpha, is organized at Cornell University.

1907 • Alain Leroy Locke becomes the first African American awarded a Rhodes Scholarship.

1908 • Washington, District of Columbia
The first African American sorority, Alpha Kappa Alpha, is founded at Howard University in Washington, DC.

1908 • John Baxter Taylor, Jr., collegiate champion, sets a world record in the 440-yard relay at the London Olympic Games, becoming the first African American to win a gold medal. Other members of his relay team are Nathaniel Cartmell, Melvin Sheppard, and William Hamilton.

1908 • Jack Johnson wins a bout with Tommy Burns to become the first African American heavyweight champion.

1911 • The Omega Psi Phi Fraternity becomes the first Greek-letter fraternity formed by African Americans on an African American college campus. It was founded on November 17 at Howard University, Washington, DC.

1915 • Carter G. Woodson organized the Association for the Study of Negro Life and History, which sponsored the first Black History Week, the prelude to Black History Month.

1917 • Eugene Jacques Bullard, flying for France, becomes the first African American aviator. A member of the French Air Service, he flew his first mission September 8. Denied a commission three quarters of a century before, the Air Force granted Bullard an Air Force Commission in 1994

1918 • Starring on the Rutgers football team, Paul Robeson becomes the first African American to receive All-American honors.

1918 • Hugh N. Mulzac becomes the first African American in the United States to earn a shipmaster's license and have the right to take command of a ship. Mulzac, however, is unable to find employment as a shipmaster and instead must take jobs at sea as a cook and steward for the next twenty-four years. He finally takes command of a ship in 1942, a Liberty cargo vessel transporting troops and supplies into the war zones.

1919 • Fritz Pollard becomes the first African American to play professional football for a major team, the Akron Indians. In 1916, Pollard had been the first African American to play in the Rose Bowl, for Brown University.

1923 • The first African American basketball team, known as the Renaissance, is organized.

Jack Johnson (The Library of Congress)

1924 • William DeHart Hubbard becomes the first African American in Olympic history to win an individual gold medal in the long jump at the Paris games on July 8.

1926 • Violette Anderson becomes the first African American woman lawyer to practice before the United States Supreme Court.

1926 • Mordecai Wyatt Johnson becomes the first African American president of Howard University on June 20. He retires in 1960.

1931 • Columbia, New York
Estelle Massey Osborne becomes the first African American recipient in the United States of a master's degree in nursing education when she graduates from Columbia Teachers College.

1933 • The first transcontinental flight by African American civilian pilots is made by Charles Alfred Anderson of Bryn Mawr, Pennsylvania, and Albert Ernest Forsythe of Atlantic City, New Jersey.

1936 • The first African American musician to conduct

Fritz Pollard

Jane M. Bolin (Fisk University Library)

a major American symphony orchestra is William Grant Still, who conducts the Los Angeles Philharmonic in the Hollywood Bowl.

1936 • At the Olympic Games in Berlin with German Chancellor Adolph Hitler in attendance, Jesse Owens becomes that first Olympian to win four gold medals, three of which were world record marks.

1937 • Virgin Islands of the United States
William H. Hastie is the first African American appointed to the federal District Court.

1938 • Crystal Bird Fauset becomes the first African American woman elected to a state legislature in the United States, acquiring this distinction when she is named to the Pennsylvania House of Representatives on November 8, 1938.

1939 • The first African American woman judge, Jane Matilda Bolin, is appointed to the Court of Domestic Relations by Mayor Fiorello LaGuardia of New York City.

1940 • Benjamin O. Davis, Sr. is promoted to the rank of

brigadier general, becoming the first African American to hold this post in the United States Army.

1940 • For her role as supporting actress in the movie *Gone with the Wind*, on November 20 Hattie McDaniel becomes the first African American to win an Oscar from the Academy of Motion Picture Arts and Sciences.

1940 • Tuskegee, Alabama
The first postage stamp honoring an African American, the ten-cent Booker T. Washington stamp, goes on sale at Tuskegee Institute. The stamp, which is a part of the Famous American Series, is the culmination of a seven-year campaign sponsored by Major R. R. Wright, president of the Citizens and Southern Bank and Trust Company of Philadelphia. (Some seven years later, a three-cent postage stamp honoring George Washington Carver is issued on the fourth anniversary of the renowned scientist's death.)

1942 • Bernard W. Robinson, a medical student at Harvard, becomes the first African American commissioned an officer in the United States Naval Reserve.

1942 • The U.S. Army lifts its color barrier and admits

African American women into its women's branch, the Women's Army Corps (WACS).

1943 • The first African Americans to crew a warship sail into the North Atlantic on the *USS Mason*. One of the crew is Thomas W. Young, who becomes the first African American war correspondent on a Navy warship.

1943 • New Jersey
The first Liberty ship named for an African American, the *George Washington Carver*, is launched from a New Jersey shipyard to begin its career of carrying war cargo to Europe during World War II. The *USS Harmon* becomes the first fighting ship to be named for an African American. Leonard Roy Harmon won the Navy Cross for his heroism aboard the *USS San Francisco* in a battle with the Japanese near the Solomon Islands. Harmon died of wounds suffered during the engagement.

1943 • William Edward Burghardt Du Bois becomes the first African American admitted to the National Institute of Arts and Letters. At the time of his admittance, Du Bois is head of the Department of Sociology at Atlanta University.

1944 • Harry McAlpin of Atlanta's *Daily World* becomes the first accredited African American White House news correspondent.

1944 • The United States Navy lifts its color band and on October 19 admits African American women into the Women's Reserves (WAVES) .

1945 • New York City, New York
Phyllis Mae Daley becomes the first African American nurse commissioned in the Navy Reserve Corps. Daley, a registered nurse from New York City, is sworn in as an ensign.

1945 • Irving Charles Mollison becomes the first African American appointed judge in the continental United States when President Harry S. Truman names him to the United States Customs Court on October 3.

1945 • Operatic soprano Camilla Williams becomes the first African American to sign a full contract with a major U.S. opera company, the New York City Opera, on May 15. She performed the title role in Madame Butterfly.

1946 • Nashua, New Hampshire
Roy Campanella, a catcher for a Nashua, New Hamp-

shire team, becomes the first African American to manage an organized, integrated, professional baseball team when the regular manager Walt Alston is ejected from the field by the umpire. Nashua wins the game when an African American pitcher, Don Newcombe, hits a pinch hit home run.

1946 • The first coin honoring African Americans is issued. The coin is a fifty-cent piece bearing a relief bust of Booker T. Washington, the founder of Tuskegee Institute.

1947 • Brooklyn, New York
Jackie Robinson joins the National League's Brooklyn Dodgers and becomes the first African American in major league baseball in the twentieth century. He plays his first game as first baseman on April 15 in Brooklyn's Ebbets Field against the Boston Braves.

1947 • Brooklyn, New York
Dan Bankhead of the National League's Brooklyn Dodgers becomes the first African American pitcher in the major leagues. The first African American pitcher in the American League, Leroy Satchel Paige, follows in 1948.

1947 • Larry Doby becomes the first African American baseball player to play in the American League. He made his debut with the Cleveland Indians on July 5.

1947 • Louis Lautier, Washington Bureau Chief of the Negro Newspaper Publishers Association, becomes the first African American issued credentials for both the Senate and the House press galleries. Lautier is admitted to the galleries on March 18 after a Senate Rules Committee overrides the refusal of the Standing Committee of Newspaper Correspondents to grant him the necessary credentials.

1947 • Indianapolis, Indiana
John Lee of Indianapolis, Indiana, becomes the first African American commissioned officer in the United States Navy. His first assignment upon being commissioned is on the *USS Kearsage*.

1948 • Pianist and singer Hazel Scott becomes the first African American to host her own television show.

1948 • Washington, District of Columbia
William Thaddeus Coleman, Jr. becomes the first appointed African American clerk of the United States Supreme Court when named to the post by Supreme Court Justice Felix Frankfurter.

USS Harmon was named in honor of African American naval hero Roy Harmon (AP/Wide World Photos, Inc.).

Roy Campanella (AP/Wide World Photos, Inc.)

1948 • Alice Coachman wins the gold medal in high jump in the Olympic Games held in London, becoming the first African American woman to win gold and the only American woman to win a track event that year.

1948 • Nancy Leftenant-Colon becomes the first African American member of the Regular Army Nurse Corps. She is commission in the Nurse Corps at Lockbourne Air Force Base. She would gain experience as a flight nurse. In 1989–1991 she becomes the only woman to hold the presidency of the Tuskegee Airmen.

1948 • John Earl Rudder becomes the first African American commissioned officer in the United States Marine Corps.

1949 • Jesse Leroy Brown becomes the first African American pilot in the United States Naval Reserve. On December 4, 1950 at Changjin Reservoir in Korea, Brown is the first African American naval pilot killed in action.

1949 • Annapolis, Maryland
Wesley A. Brown becomes the first African American to graduate from the Naval Academy at Annapolis.

1949 • Oklahoma City, Oklahoma
The University of Oklahoma Law School admits its first African American student, Ada Lois Sipuel (Fisher).

1949 • William H. Hastie becomes the first African American judge appointed to the United States Circuit Court of Appeals. Hastie is also the first African American appointed governor of the United States Virgin Islands.

1949 • Jackie Robinson becomes the first African American baseball player to win his league's "Most Valuable Player" award. The first African American to win the award three times is Roy Campanella, who is awarded the title in 1951, 1953, and 1955.

1950 • Gwendolyn Brooks is awarded the Pulitzer Prize for her volume of poetry titled *Annie Allen*. She is the first African American poet to win the award and also the first African American woman elected to the National Institute of Arts and Letters.

1950 • United Nations Undersecretary Ralph Bunche becomes the first African American to receive a Nobel Peace Prize.

1950 • President Dwight D. Eisenhower appoints Archibald T. Carey, Jr. as chair of the Committee on Government Employment Policy. Carey becomes the first African American to hold that position.

1950 • Atlantic City, New Jersey
Arthur Dorrington becomes the first African American professional hockey player when he plays the 1950–1951 season with the Atlantic City Sea Gulls. He made his debut on November 15.

1950 • Charles Cooper signs with the Boston Celtics on April 15 to become the first African American to sign with an NBA team.

1950 • Juanita Hall becomes the first African American to win a Tony Award for her supporting role in the musical *South Pacific*.

1951 • New York City, New York
Janet Collins becomes the first African American to dance for the Metropolitan Opera in New York. Collins, signed by an agent of the company, makes her debut in *Aida*.

1951 • New York City, New York
William L. Rowe becomes the first African American

Gwendolyn Brooks (Courtesy of Gwendolyn Brooks)

Ralph Bunche examines his Noble Peace Prize diploma in 1950 (AP/Wide World Photos, Inc.).

deputy police commissioner. He is appointed to this position in New York by Mayor Vincent Impellitieri.

1952 • Joe Black, Rookie of the Year, leads the Brooklyn Dodgers to a win over the New York Yankees and becomes the first African American pitcher to win a World Series game.

1952 • Frank E. Petersen, Jr. becomes the first African American Marine pilot. He becomes the first African American brigadier general in the marines on February 23, 1979, and retires in 1988 with the rank of lieutenant general.

1953 • Ralph Ellison, author of *The Invisible Man,* becomes the first African American to receive the National Book Award.

1953 • The University of Virginia awards a doctoral degree to Walter Nathaniel Ridley, the first African American to earn a doctoral degree from a traditional Southern white university. Later Ridley was president of Elizabeth City State College (now University)in North Carolina.

1953 • Second baseman Marcenia Lyle "Toni" Stone joins the Negro League's Indianapolis Clowns as the first African American woman to play on a regular big league professional baseball team. She would play one season with the Clowns and another with the Kansas City Monarchs. The five-foot seven-inch St. Paul, Minnesota, native was an experienced player on men's teams, first with the San Francisco Sea Lions and next with the New Orleans Creoles.

1954 • Benjamin Oliver Davis, Jr. becomes the first African American general in the U.S. Air Force on October 27.

1954 • Charles H. Mahoney becomes the first African American appointed a permanent delegate to the United Nations.

1954 • New York City, New York
Dr. James Joshua Thomas becomes the first African American pastor of the Reformed Dutch Church. He is installed as minister of the Mott Haven Reformed Church in the Bronx, New York City.

General Benjamin O. Davis, Sr. (left) discussing military strategy with General George C. Patton.

1954 • New York
The first African American radio network, the National Negro Network, begins programming. The New York outlet is station WOV. The first program of the network, a soap opera titled *The Story of Ruby Valentine*, stars Juanita Hall and is carried on forty stations. The program, sponsored by Phillip Morris and Pet Milk, runs five days a week.

1955 • Conductor and musician Everett Lee directs the New York Opera Company's performance of *La Traviata*

on April 17 and becomes the first African American to conduct a professional grand opera or Broadway show in this country.

1956 • Compton, California
Charles Dumas, a freshman at Compton College, Compton, California, becomes the first athlete to high jump over seven feet.

1957 • Althea Gibson becomes the first African American tennis player to win at Wimbledon.

1957 • Willie O'Ree breaks racial barriers in professional hockey and becomes the first African American to play in the National Hockey League with the Boston Bruins.

1957 • James Plinton, Jr. becomes the first African American named to an executive position by a major airline when Trans World Airlines names him executive assistant to the director of personnel and industrial relations.

1958 • New York City, New York
Gloria Davy sings *Aida* at New York's Metropolitan Opera House and becomes the first African American to sing at this celebrated palace of music.

1958 • Ruth Carol Taylor becomes the first African American flight attendant when she is hired to work for Mohawk Airlines.

1959 • Lorraine Hansberry's play *A Raisin in the Sun* is the first play by an African American to receive the New York Drama Critics' Circle Award for best American play.

1959 • Hal DeWindt becomes the first male model in the Ebony Fashion Fair.

1959 • Cleveland, Ohio
John McLendon becomes the first African American to coach a racially-integrated professional basketball team, the Cleveland Pipers of the National Industrial Basketball League.

1960 • Rome, Italy
Wilma Rudolph, who wore leg braces until she was nine years old, becomes the first African American woman to win three gold medals in track and field in a single Olympic year.

1961 • Ernie Davis becomes the first African American to be awarded college footballs Heisman Memorial Trophy at the Downtown Athletic Club of New York City, Inc.

1961 • On August 9, President John F. Kennedy appoints James Benton Parsons judge of the U.S. Federal District Court. He is the first African American to hold this position and also the first African American to receive a lifetime appointment in that post.

1962 • Jackie Robinson becomes the first African American to be inducted into the Professional Baseball Hall of Fame.

Lorraine Vivian Hansberry being presented the Drama Critics Circle Award in 1959 (Corbis Corporation [Bellevue]).

1962 • Mal Goode becomes the first African American television news correspondent.

1962 • Harvey Russell, Jr. is named vice president of Pepsico and becomes the first African American man named vice president of a major American corporation.

1962 • Lieutenant Commander Samuel L. Gravely, Jr. becomes the first African American to command a United States warship when he assumes command of the *USS Falgout*, a destroyer escort.

1962 • Former civil rights lawyer Thelton Henderson becomes the first African American to join the U.S. Justice Department's Civil Rights Division.

1963 • William "Count" Basie becomes the first African American to win the Grammy Award for record of the year.

1963 • Katherine Dunham becomes the first African American choreographer to work at the Metropolitan Opera House in New York.

1963 • Wendell Scott becomes the first African American to win the NASCAR race, at Speedway Park in Jacksonville, Florida. He is inducted into the International Motorsports Hall of Fame in 1999, the first African American so honored.

1963 • Sidney Poitier becomes the first African American male to win an Oscar for his leading role in *Lilies in the Field*. Poitier is also the first African American to be nominated for an Oscar since Hattie McDaniel in 1939.

1965 • Vivian Malone Jones becomes the first African American graduate of the University of Alabama. Jones and James Hood were among the first African American students enrolled in the university in 1963.

1966 • Bill Cosby becomes the first African American male to be awarded an Emmy for his leading role in the television drama *I Spy*.

1966 • Internationally known graphic artist George Olden is the first African American to design a U.S. postage stamp, the Emancipation Proclamation stamp.

1966 • Emmett Ashford, the first African American umpire in the major leagues, makes his debut in the American League opening day game between the Cleveland Indians and the Washington Senators. Ashford umpired in the Southwestern International League in 1952 and in the Pacific Coast League where he was umpire-in-chief in 1965.

1966 • Constance Baker Motley becomes the first African American to serve as a federal judge.

1966 • Boston, Massachusetts
Bill Russell, star center of the world champion Boston Celtics, becomes the first African American to direct a major league sports team when he is named to succeed Red Auerbach as coach of the Boston basketball franchise, on April 18.

1966 • Washington, District of Columbia
Robert C. Weaver is named as secretary of the newly created Department of Housing and Urban Development, becoming the first African American appointed to serve in a presidential cabinet.

1966 • Edward W. Brooke becomes the first African American elected to the U.S. Senate since Reconstruction. He was seated on January 10, 1967.

1967 • Emlen Tunnell becomes the first African American to be inducted into the Professional Football Hall of Fame.

Judge Constance Baker Motley with President Lyndon B. Johnson (AP/Wide World Photos, Inc.).

1967 • Thurgood Marshall is appointed an associate justice of the United States Supreme Court, becoming the first African American to serve on the nation's highest court. On August 11, 1965, he became the first African American solicitor general and held the position until he joined the Supreme Court.

1967 • Cleveland, Ohio
The first African American elected mayor of a major U.S. city is Carl B. Stokes, on November 13. He became known in the 1960s as a symbol of minority voting strides. Richard G. Hatcher, mayor of Gary, Indiana, was elected in the same year but not sworn in until January 1, 1968, as the city's first African American mayor.

1967 • Washington, District of Columbia
Walter E. Washington is appointed to head the newly reorganized municipal government of Washington, DC, in September.

1968 • Diahann Carroll becomes the first African American actress to star in a network television series, titled *Julia*.

Robert C. Weaver (AP/Wide World Photos, Inc.)

1968 • Arthur Ashe becomes the first African American to win the American Singles Tennis Championship. In 1963 Ashe was the first African American to play on the United States Davis Cup team.

1968 • Martin Briscoe becomes the first African American professional football player.

1968 • Atlanta, Georgia
Xernona Clayton becomes the first African American woman in the South to host a regular television program, in August.

1968 • Newark, New Jersey
Henry Lewis is the first African American director of an American orchestra—the Newark-based New Jersey Symphony.

1968 • Shirley Chisholm of New York becomes the first African American woman elected to the U.S. Congress.

1969 • Gail Fisher becomes the first African American to win an Emmy Award.

1969 • Federal Judge A. Leon Higginbotham, Jr. is

elected a trustee of Yale University, the first African American to be so honored.

1969 • Parks Sausage Company becomes the first African American-owned company to become a publicly traded company, having its stock traded on the National Association of Securities Dealers Automated Quotation (NASDAQ) exchange.

1969 • The first African American male and the first African American photographer to win a Pulitzer Prize is Moneta J. Sleet, Jr. His prize-winning photograph was a portrait of Coretta Scott King and her youngest child, Bernice, taken at the funeral of Martin Luther King, Jr.

1969 • Joseph L. Searles III becomes the first African American proposed for a seat on the New York Stock Exchange. Searles, former aide in the administration of New York City Mayor John Lindsay, resigned to become one of the three floor traders, as well as a general partner, for Newburger, Loeb and Co.

1970 • Chris Dickerson becomes the first African American to win the title "Mr. America," one of fifteen body building titles Dickerson will earn during his career. One of a set of triplets born in Montgomery, Alabama on August 25, 1939, Dickerson proves to be an outstanding athlete throughout his school years. An early interest in a singing career and the desire to improve his voice quality and breath control led him into bodybuilding in the mid–1960s.

1970 • Philadelphia, Pennsylvania
Renard Edwards becomes the first African American musician to play for the Philadelphia Orchestra when he is hired as a violist for the 1970–1971 season. Edwards was formerly with the Symphony of the New World, an integrated orchestra, one-third to one-half of whose members are African Americans.

1971 • Samuel L. Gravely, Jr. becomes the first African American admiral in the history of the United States Navy.

1972 • U.S. Rep. Shirley Chisholm seeks the Democratic nomination for the presidency, thus becoming the first woman to ever to do so.

1972 • Barbara Jordan wins a seat in Congress on November 17, becoming the first woman from Texas elected to Congress.

1973 • Stevie Wonder becomes the first African American to win the Grammy Award for album of the year.

1973, May 29 • Los Angeles, California
Thomas Bradley, of Los Angeles, becomes the first African American elected mayor of a city with population exceeding one million. He defeated the incumbent Sam Yorty by 100,000 votes. Yorty had defeated Bradley in the 1969 mayoral election.

1973 • Detroit, Michigan
Coleman A. Young is elected mayor, the first African American to hold the post in the white-majority city. On the same evening, Maynard H. Jackson is elected mayor of Atlanta.

1974 • Washington, District of Columbia
Barbara Hancock becomes the first African American woman White House Fellow.

1974 • The Thunderbirds, the U.S. Air Force Aerial Demonstration Squadron, has its first African American member in November, when General Lloyd W. "Fig" Newton joins the squad.

1974 • Cicely Tyson becomes the first African American female to be awarded an Emmy for outstanding lead actress in a television comedy or drama special for her performance in *The Autobiography of Miss Jane Pittman.*

1974 • Leo Miles becomes the first African American to officiate a Super Bowl game.

1974 • Joe Gilliam, Jr. becomes a trailblazer for African American quarterbacks in modern times. He is the first African American quarterback to start in a NFL game.

1975 • The United States Navy commissions Donna P. Davis as a lieutenant in the Navy's medical corps, making Davis the first African American woman physician in the corps history.

1975 • General Daniel "Chappie" James, Jr. becomes commander-in-chief of the North American Air Defense Command (NORAD). On the same day, he is promoted in the air force and becomes the first African American four-star general in United States history.

1975 • Cleveland, Ohio
Frank Robinson becomes the first African American to manage a major league baseball team and leads his Cleveland Indians to an opening-day victory over the New York Yankees, hitting a home run.

1975 • Detroit, Michigan
WGPR-TV, in Detroit, goes on the air, becoming the first African American-owned and operated television station in the United States.

1977 • Clifford Alexander, Jr. becomes the first African American to be appointed Secretary of the Army.

1977 • Milwaukee, Wisconsin
Former basketball player Wayne Embry becomes the first African American general manager of an NBA team—the Milwaukee Bucks.

1977 • Oakland, California
Lionel Wilson is elected mayor, the first African American to hold that position. In 1960 he became the first African American Judge in Alameda County.

1977 • Washington, District of Columbia
Karen Farmer becomes the first African American member of the Daughters of the American Revolution (DAR). It was the DAR that refused to allow Marian Anderson to perform in concert in Washington, DC, in 1939.

1977 • Patricia Roberts Harris is appointed Secretary of the Department of Housing and Urban Development, becoming the first African American woman to serve in a Cabinet-level position.

1978 • Washington, DC
Contralto Marian Anderson becomes the first African American to be awarded the Congressional Gold Medal, the highest honor that can be bestowed upon a civilian.

1978 • New York City, New York
Reverend Emerson Moore, Jr. is named the first African American monsignor of the Catholic Church in the United States. Monsignor Moore is pastor of St. Charles Borromeo Church in New York City.

1979 • United States Army Second Lieutenant Marcella A. Hayes, a graduate of the University of Wisconsin and the Army ROTC program, earns her aviator wings and becomes the first African American woman pilot in United States armed services history.

1979 • Birmingham, Alabama
Council Richard Arrington, Jr. is elected major on October 30, the first African American ever elected to the post.

1979 • New Jersey
Audrey Neal becomes the first African American woman (or woman of any ethnic group), longshoreperson. Neal is employed at the Bayonne Military Ocean Terminal in New Jersey.

1980 • Levi Watkins, Jr., an African American surgeon,

Clifford Alexander, Jr. (AP/Wide World Photos, Inc.)

performs the first surgical implantation of the automatic implantable defibrillator in the human heart. The device corrects an ailment known as ventricular fibrillation or arrhythmia, which prevents the heart from pumping blood.

1981 • Charles P. Chapman is the first African American to swim across the English channel

1981 • Isabel Sanford becomes the first African American female to be awarded an Emmy for outstanding lead actress in a television comedy series for her performance in *The Jeffersons.*

1981 • Ithaca, New York
Pamela Johnson is named publisher of the *Ithaca Journal* and becomes the first African American woman to hold that position with a major newspaper in the United States.

1981 • Chicago, Illinois
Ruth Love becomes the first African American to serve as superintendent of the Chicago school system. Prior to her appointment to this post, Love held a similar position in Oakland, California.

1982 • Bryant C. Gumbel becomes the first African American to co-host the "Today" show on NBC Television.

1982 • Alaska
Ralph Bradley becomes the first African American to

complete the Iditarod Sled Dog Race. Though he finishes last in the 1,049-mile race, he wins the Red Lantern prize with a time of 26:13:59:59.

1983 • Louis Gossett, Jr. is the first African American male to be awarded an Oscar for best supporting actor for his role in *An Officer and a Gentleman.*

1983 • Chicago
Harold Washington is sworn in as mayor on April 19, becoming the first African American to hold the position.

1983 • Guion Bluford becomes the first African American to travel in space when he serves as a crew member on the space shuttle Challenger, on August 30. The crew would have a six-day flight on the Challenger.

1983 • Atlantic City, New Jersey
Representing New York, Vanessa Williams becomes the first African American Miss America in the 62-year history of the Atlantic City pageant. The first runner-up is Suzette Charles representing New Jersey, who, coincidentally, is also African American and also the first African American Miss New Jersey. When Williams is forced to surrender her title, Charles is crowned Miss America.

1984 • Methodist Reverend Leontine Turpeau Current Kelly becomes the first African American woman bishop of a major religious denomination.

1984 • Philadelphia, Pennsylvania
W. Wilson Goode takes the oath of office as the first African American mayor of Philadelphia.

1984 • Former Boston Celtics player John Thompson, Jr. becomes the first African American coach to win an NCAA Division I basketball championship. He coached the Georgetown University Hoyas, led by center Patrick Ewing, to victory on April 2.

1984 • Oprah Winfrey becomes the first African American woman to host a nationally syndicated television talk show, on September 8.

1986 • The first national Martin Luther King, Jr. holiday is celebrated on January 20.

1986 • Georg Stanford Brown becomes the first African American to win an Emmy for outstanding directing in a drama series. Brown directed the episode titled "Parting

NASA astronauts Guion Bluford (left), Ronald McNair (seated), and Frederick Gregory (right) (AP/Wide World Photos, Inc.).

Shots" for the highly acclaimed series *Cagney and Lacey.*

1986 • Lieutenant Commander Donnie Cochran becomes the first African American pilot in the United States Navy to fly with the Navy's elite special flying squadron, the Blue Angels. Two years later he becomes the first African American to head the squad. The precision flight team was formed in the 1940s and has performed its highly sophisticated aerobatics in air shows in the United States and Europe ever since.

1986 • Debi Thomas becomes the first African American to win the U.S. Ladies Figure Skating Championship and the World Championship.

1986 • The first African American to win a Professional Bowlers Association title is George Branham, on November 22.

1987 • Dain Blanton, in his third professional season, is the first African American to win a major tournament with the Association of Volleyball Professionals. He is

Miss America Vanessa Williams posing with first runner-up Suzette Charles in 1983 (AP/Wide World Photos, Inc.).

the first and only African American on the AVP tour. Blanton and his partner, Canyon Ceman, won the $300,000 Miller Lite/AVP Hermosa Beach, California, Grand Slam. This is the largest AVP tournament ever held and awards most prize money in the history of the sport.

1988 • Spelman College appoints its first African American woman president, Johnetta B. Cole.

1988 • Atlanta, Georgia
Eugene Antonio Marino becomes the first African American Roman Catholic archbishop in the United States as he is named archbishop of the Atlanta archdiocese. Marino was one of three auxiliary bishops in Washington, DC.

1988 • Doug Williams becomes the first African American to quarterback a Super Bowl team, the Washington Redskins. The Redskins won over the Denver Broncos 42–10 in Super Bowl XXII.

1988 • Seoul, Korea
Florence "Flo Jo" Griffith Joyner becomes the first American woman to win four gold medals in track and field at a single Olympics.

1988 • Juanita Kidd Stoutt is appointed to the supreme court of Pennsylvania and becomes the first African American woman to serve on the highest court of any state.

1987 • The rap duo D. J. Jazzy Jeff and the Fresh Prince win a Grammy Award for the hit *Parents Just Don't Understand* and becomes the first African American rap group to win a Grammy.

1989 • Washington, DC native Colonel Frederick Gregory becomes the first African American astronaut to command a space shuttle.

1989 • Washington, DC lawyer Ronald H. Brown is elected chairman of the Democratic Party's national committee. Brown is the first African American to head a major American political party.

1989 • Seattle, Washington
Norm Rice, who became known as "Mayor Nice," is elected mayor, the city's first African American to hold the position.

1989 • Episcopal Reverend Barbara C. Harris, an African American, becomes the first woman bishop in the worldwide Anglican communion. The Episcopal Church decided in 1976 that women could be ordained priests.

1989 • Vermont
Rodney S. Patterson, an ordained Baptist minister, starts the first African American congregation in Vermont, which a magazine has dubbed "the whitest state in America" because of its small African American population. Patterson, who moved to Burlington to join the staff at the University of Vermont, names the church the New Alpha Missionary Baptist Church.

1989 • Army General Colin L. Powell becomes the first African American to serve as chairman of the Joint Chiefs of Staff and principal military advisor to the President of the United States, the Secretary of Defense, and the National Security Council.

1989 • Former St. Louis Cardinal first baseman Bill White assumes office as president of the National League, becoming the first African American to head a professional sports league.

1990 • New York City, New York
David Dinkins becomes the first African American mayor of New York City.

1990 • Michigan
Carole Gist of Michigan becomes the first African American Miss USA.

1990 • Virginia
In Virginia, L. Douglas Wilder becomes the first African American elected governor of a state.

1990 • Sharon Pratt Dixon is elected mayor of Washington, DC, thus becoming the first African American woman to manage a major U.S. city.

1991 • Corporal Freddie Stowers is posthumously awarded the Medal of Honor for serving in France during World War I. Stowers is the first African American to receive the medal for service in either world war. In 1988, the Secretary of the Army directed the army to conduct a study to determine whether African American soldiers had been overlooked in the recognition process. Research found that Stowers had been recommended for the medal, but for reasons unknown, the recommendation had not been processed.

1991 • Former Roman Catholic nun Rose Vernell is

L. Douglas Wilder being sworn in as governor of Virginia in 1990 (AP/Wide World Photos, Inc.).

ordained a priest of the Imani Temple African American Catholic Congregation by Bishop George A. Stallings, Jr. Vernell is the first woman priest in the church. The congregation was founded in 1989 when Stallings broke with the Roman Catholic Church; this was the first split from the Roman Catholic Church in the United States since 1904.

1991 • Lynn Whitfield becomes the first African American female to be awarded an Emmy for outstanding lead actress in a miniseries or special for her performance in *The Josephine Baker Story*.

1992 • Illinois
Carol Moseley Braun of Illinois is elected to the United States Senate, becoming the first African American woman senator.

1992 • Mae C. Jemison, 35, a physician and chemical engineer, is the first African American woman in space on the United States space shuttle *Endeavor* mission. The crew studies the behavior of living organisms in a weightless atmosphere and looks for ways to cure space sickness.

1992 • Captain William "Bill" Pinckney becomes the first African American to navigate a sailboat singlehandedly around the world. His journey on the boat *Commitment* began in Boston in 1990, covered 32,000 nautical miles, and included several stops.

Carol Moseley Braun waves to the crowd at the 1992 Democratic National Convention (AP/Wide World Photos, Inc.).

1992 • Fulton County, Georgia
Elected on November 3, Jacquelyn H. Barrett becomes the country's first African American woman sheriff.

1993 • Washington, District of Columbia
Joycelyn Elders, Arkansas health director, is named surgeon general of the United States. Elders is the first African American and the second woman to hold this position. She is sworn into office as U.S. surgeon general in a private ceremony. Elders, 59, is the former head of the Arkansas Health Department.

1993 • Atlanta, Georgia
The first African American student from a historically African American college to win a Rhodes Scholarship is Nima Warfield, an English major at Morehouse College. He plans to study at Oxford's School of Modern History and English in fall 1994.

1993 • Eleanor Holmes Norton becomes the first voting delegate in the United States House of Representatives for Washington, DC. Previously, delegates representing the District of Columbia and the United States Trust Territory were not allowed to vote on the House floor

because the Constitution of the United States specifically restricts legislative authority to state representatives.

1993 • Toni Morrison becomes the first African American woman to receive the Nobel Prize for literature, on November 7.

1993 • African American candidates in Selma, Alabama, win a majority of seats on the city council for the first time, despite efforts by white council members to maintain a majority.

1993 • South Carolina's Kimberly Clarice Aiken is crowned Miss America, becoming the first African American woman from the South to win the pageant.

1993 • Sharon Sayles Belton becomes the first woman and first African American mayor of Minneapolis, Minnesota.

1993 • In his 13th year as a National League umpire, Charlie Williams becomes the first African American to call balls and strikes in a World Series game.

1994 • On February 3, Commander Charles Bolden

Mae C. Jemison (NASA)

leads NASA's first American-Russian Space Shuttle Discovery mission.

1994 • William G. Anderson becomes the first African American president of the American Osteopathic Association, a major medical organization in the United States.

1994 • Whoopie Goldberg is the first African American to serve as sole host of the Academy Awards and the first African American Oscar winner to host the show.

1994 • Donnie Cochran, the only African American pilot in the Blue Angels, the precision flying squad, becomes the squad's first African American commander.

1994 • Louis Westerfield is named academic dean at the University of Mississippi, the first African American to hold that position at the university.

1994 • Eighteen year-old Eldrick (Tiger) Woods becomes the youngest player and the first African American to win the U.S. Amateur Golf Championship.

1994 • Forty-four year old Beverly Harvard becomes

the first African American woman to reach the rank of chief of police in a major U.S. city (Atlanta).

1995 • Atlanta Hawks coach Lenny Wilkins becomes the winningest coach in NBA history.

1995 • In June, Lonnie Bristow becomes the first African American president of the 147-year-old American Medical Association.

1995 • Marcelite J. Harris, the Air Force's first African American general in 1990, becomes the first woman of her race to receive the rank of major general.

1995 • A retired U.S. Army major general, John Stanford becomes the first African American school superintendent in Seattle, Washington.

1995 • Ronald Kirk is elected Dallas's first African American mayor and is the first African American to lead a major Texas city.

1995 • Gene C. McKinney becomes the first African American sergeant major, the highest non-commissioned officer in the U.S. Army.

1995 • San Francisco
Former speaker and 31-year-veteran of the California General Assembly, Willie L. Brown, Jr., defeats incumbent Frank Jordan to become San Francisco's first African American mayor.

1995 • Chelsi Smith of Texas is the first African American crowned Miss Universe.

1995 • Bernard A. Harris, Jr., a physician from Houston, Texas, becomes the first African American to walk in space, on February 27. Winston E. Scott became the second African American to make the trek, from a bridge in the cargo bay of space shuttle Endeavour.

1995 • Orlando "Tubby" Smith becomes the first African American head basketball coach at the University of Georgia.

1995 • Carolyn G. Morris becomes the first African American assistant director and the highest ranking African American woman in the history of the FBI.

1995 • Minnesota Vikings quarterback Warren Moon is the first quarterback to eclipse 60,000 yards in passing.

1996 • The first African American to head the Office of

Management and Budget for the United States is Franklin D. Raines. This is the highest executive post ever held by an African American.

1996 • Former U.S. Secret Servicemen Hubert T. Bell, Jr. is confirmed as Inspector General of the Nuclear Regulatory Commission, the first African American to hold that position.

1996 • BET Holdings, a parent company of the Black Entertainment Network, launches the nation's first African American-controlled cable movie premium channel, BET Movies/STARZ!3.

1996 • St. Adolpho A. Birch, Jr. is sworn in as the first African American Chief Justice of the Tennessee Supreme Court. From 1987 until he joined the Supreme Court in 1993, he was the first African American to serve on the Tennessee Court of Appeals.

1996 • **St. Louis, Missouri**
Darlene Green becomes the first woman elected comtroller in St. Louis.

1996 • A member of the Maryland House of Delegates since 1983, Richard N. Dixon is sworn in as Maryland's first African American state treasurer.

1996 • Seventy-three-year old composer George Walker wins the 1996 Pulitzer Prize in music, the first African American to win the prize for music.

1996 • Jacquelyn M. Belcher, former president of Minneapolis Community College in Minneapolis, is inaugurated president of Dekalb College in Georgia. She is the first African American woman president of a University System of Georgia school.

1996 • The U.S. Navy appoints its first African American four-star admiral, Vice Admiral J. Paul Reason.

1996 • The first African American president of the American Association of Retired Persons (AARP) is Margaret A. Dixon.

1996 • Sargeant Heather Lynn Johnson of the 3rd U.S. Infantry becomes the first woman to receive the U.S. Army's tomb guard badge to become a sentinel at the Tomb of the Unknown Soldier in Arlington National Cemetery, Arlington, Virginia.

1996 • The National Council of Negro Women dedicates

its new headquarters office building. The facility is the first African American-owned building on Pennsylvania Avenue between Capitol Hill and the White House.

1996 • The White House unveils Henry Ossawa Tanner's painting *Sand Dunes at Sunset, Atlantic City*, an oil on canvas. The acquisition is the first work by an African American artist to become a part of the White House collection.

1996 • **Hattiesburg, Mississippi**
The University of Southern Mississippi names James Green head basketball coach, making him the first African American to hold the post.

1996 • Detroit Lions running back Barry Sanders becomes the first back in NFL history to rush for 1,000 yards in eight consecutive seasons, with 11,271 total yards.

1996 • Marcus Allen becomes the NFL's all-time leader in rushing touchdowns and breaks the record held by former Chicago Bears star Walter Payton.

1996 • Eighteen-year-old Chantè Lauree Griffin is the first African American to be crowned Miss Teen of America for 1996–1997. She was elected Miss Teen of California in 1995.

1997 • **New York City, New York**
The *Sports Illustrated* swimsuit issue features supermodel Tyra Banks. Banks is the first African American model to be solely featured on the magazine cover in its 34-year history.

1997 • Eldrick (Tiger) Woods becomes the first African American and the youngest player (21 years old) to win the Masters. He also has the largest victory margin and the lowest 72-hole total for a Master's winner.

1997 • **Jackson, Mississippi**
Harvey Johnson is sworn in as mayor, becoming the first African American mayor in the state's capital. The ceremony is held on the steps of city hall, which was built by slaves before the Civil War.

1997 • Wynton Marsalis becomes the first jazz musician to win a Pulitzer Prize for his jazz opera *Blood on the Fields*.

1997 • Moses Ector becomes the highest ranking African American in the Georgia Bureau of Investigation. He is also the first African American to be named bureau chief of staff.

1997 • Conrad L. Mallett, Jr. becomes the first African American Chief Justice of the Michigan Supreme Court.

1997 • Des Moines, Iowa
Councilman Preston Daniels is the first African American to be elected mayor.

1997 • Massachusetts State Appeals Court Justice Roderick Ireland is confirmed as the first African American justice on the state's Supreme Court.

1997 • Robert Stanton is sworn in as director of the National Park Service, the first African American to head the service in its 80-year-old history.

1997 • Knoxville, Tennessee
Profitts Inc. elects Julius "Dr. J." Erving to its board of directors, making him the first African American on the 13-member board

1997 • The U.S. Army commissions West Point's first African American cadet 123 years after the former slave was expelled from the academy for failing an examination. The certificate is given posthumously to James Webster Smith during a ceremony in Orangeburg, South Carolina.

1997 • Alexis Herman is confirmed as U.S. Secretary of Labor, making her the first African American to head that department.

1997 • The first African American woman to serve as chief federal judge of the U.S. District Court for the District of Columbia is Norma Holloway Johnson.

1997 • The first African American head of the Federal Communications Commission is William E. Kinnard, who previously served the commission as general counsel.

1997 • Former Olympian Chris Campbell is named executive director of U.S. Amateur Boxing, Inc., and becomes the first African American to hold the post.

1997 • Thurgood Marshall, Jr. is appointed assistant to

President Bill Clinton and Cabinet secretary, becoming the first African American to serve as Cabinet secretary.

1997 • Selma, Alabama
Earnest L. Tate is appointed to the position of chief of police. He is the first African American to hold the position in Selma, a city once known for its intolerance for beating protest marchers.

1997 • Eric Holder becomes the highest ranking African American law enforcement officer in the nation's history when he is sworn in as deputy U.S. attorney general, the second highest-ranking position in the U.S. Justice Department. He was the first African American U.S. attorney for the District of Columbia since 1993.

1997 • Chicago, Illinois
Dawn Peter becomes the city's first African American mounted police officer. Previously she served as patrol officer and plain clothes officer in the city.

1997 • Washington, District of Columbia
The nation's first known African American sextuplets are born to Jacqueline and Linden Thompson. One daughter was stillborn. The four surviving girls and one boy are born in Georgetown University Medical Center.

1997 • Violet Palmer is named referee in the NBA, becoming the first African American in that position. Palmer and Dee Kanter become the league's first two female officials.

1997 • Chicago, Illinois
The first predominantly defensive player to win football's Heisman Trophy is Charles Woodson, a defensive back for the University of Michigan.

1997 • Chicago, Illinois
Dorothy Walker, 57, becomes the first person in the country to undergo an experimental new laser heart surgery procedure, thorascopic investigational heart surgery, at Northwestern Memorial Hospital.

1997 • The Association of Trial Lawyers of America elects its first African American president, Indianapolis attorney Richard D. Hailey.

1997 • Dallas Mavericks forward A. C. Green breaks the NBA's consecutive game streak when he plays his 907th consecutive game.

University of Kentucky Coach Tubby Smith is carried off the court by his basketball players after their 1998 NCCA Finals victory (AP/Wide World Photos, Inc.).

1997 • After coaching at the University of Georgia for two seasons, Orlando "Tubby" Smith, is the first African American head basketball coach at the University of Kentucky. In 1998, he leads Kentucky to the national championship.

1997 • Nashville, Tennessee
The first African American to win the junior women's title at the U.S. Figure Skating Championship is Andrea Gardiner, a 16-year-old Bay City, Texas, native.

1997 • Nashville, Tennessee
Vivian Fuller is named athletic director at Tennessee State University and becomes the country's first African American woman director of athletics at an NCAA Division I program.

1997 • Ann Dibble Jordan, co-chair of the inaugural activities for President Bill Clinton's for a second term in office, is the first African American woman to serve in the command role.

1997 • Walter G. Sellers of Wilberforce, Ohio, is unani-mously elected president of Kiwanis International and becomes the first African American to serve in that position.

1997 • Washington, DC
The U.S. Senate confirms William E. Kennard as chairman of the Federal Communications on October 29, making him the organization's first African American chairman.

1998 • New York, New York
The first African American Male Empowerment Summit (AAMES) is held and attracts over five hundred men.

1998 • Houston, Texas
The nation's fourth largest city gets its first African American mayor on January 1, when Lee Patrick Brown takes office. Brown also served as police chief of the city from 1982 to 1990.

1998 • Baltimore, Maryland
The first African American-owned securities brokerage

firm to become a publicly-traded company is Chapman Holdings, Inc.

1998 • Ben Ruffin, vice president of R. J. Reynolds Tobacco Company, is elected the first African American chair of the University of North Carolina's board. The board approves policies for the 16 campuses in the system.

1998 • The U.S. Navy selects 32-year career Naval officer Captain James A. Johnson for promotion to rear admiral in the Navy Medical Corps, making him the first African American on active duty to hold that post in the 127-year history of the corps.

1998 • Glenn Ivey is the first African American to head Maryland's five-member Public Service Commission

1998 • The first African American Republican elected to a leadership post in modern times is J.C. Watts, Jr., Oklahoma Congressman from the Fourth District. In November he becomes chairman of the Republican Conference, the number four position in the House. In 1990 he was the first African American in Oklahoma to win statewide elective office, when he captured a seat on the Oklahoma Corporate Commission, which regulates gas and oil utilities. Watts became the first African American to respond to a President's State of the Union Address in 1997, when he followed President Bill Clinton's speech before the nation.

1998 • Seven members of the more than 2,000 African American soldiers who, along with whites, fought in front line battles in 1944 during World War II, are awarded the Bronze Star. White soldiers received their awards soon after the war. Vernon Baker, the only surviving member of the group, is the first and only African American hero from the war to receive the award; the others are awarded posthumously.

1998 • Three-time World Championship Calf Roper Fred Whitfield is the first African American to cross the million-dollar mark in professional rodeo. He is also the fastest cowboy in the history of Professional Rodeo Cowboys Association to cross the mark.

1998 • San Francisco Giants outfielder Barry Bonds becomes the only player in major league baseball to

J.C. Watts (AP/Wide World Photos, Inc.)

have 400 home runs and 400 steals in a career. The record is set at Pro Player Stadium in Miami, Florida.

1998 • *Newsweek* promotes managing editor Mark Whitaker to the position of editor of the weekly news magazine. A Harvard graduate, Whitaker joined the magazine's staff in 1977.

1998 • Cambridge, Massachusetts
Lani Guinier is named Professor of Law in the Harvard University School of Law on January 23, and becomes the first African American woman tenured in the law school.

1998 • Iowa
Drs. Paula Mahone and Karen Drake became the first African American physicians to assist in the delivery of sextuplets—the McCaughey babies—on November 19.

1998 • Washington, DC
Lieutenant General Benjamin O. Davis, Jr., former commander of the Tuskegee Airmen during World War II,

received his fourth star on December 9 in a White House ceremony. Davis, a graduate of West Point Military Academy, is the son of the nation's first African American brigadier general in the army, Benjamin O. Davis, Sr.

1998 • Tampa, Florida
Twenty-two-year old Jonathan Lee Iverson became the first African American and the youngest person ever to serve as ringmaster for Ringling Bros. and Barnum & Bailey.

1999 • New York City, New York
On March 15, chess player Maurice Ashley, a Jamaican immigrant, became the first African American to earn grandmaster status in chess during a tournament sponsored by the Manhattan Chess Club.

1999 • San Jose, California
On March 28, Purdue coach Carolyn Peck leads the Lady Boilermakers to victory over Duke University, becoming the first African American female coach to win a national championship in women's college basketball history.

3

Significant Documents in African American History

◆ The Germantown Mennonite Resolution Against Slavery ◆ The Declaration of Independence
◆ The Omitted Anti–Slavery Clause to the Declaration of Independence
◆ The Constitution of the United States ◆ The Bill of Rights ◆ Fugitive Slave Act (1793)
◆ Benjamin Franklin's Address to the Public ◆ George Washington's Last Will and Testament
◆ Act to Prohibit the Importation of Slaves ◆ Editorial from the First Edition of *Freedom's Journal*
◆ Editorial from the First Edition of *The Liberator*
◆ American Anti–Slavery Society's *American Slavery As It Is* (Excerpt)
◆ Henry Highland Garnet's Address to the Slaves of the United States of America (Excerpt)
◆ Editorial from the First Edition of *The North Star* ◆ Fugitive Slave Act (1850)
◆ Act to Suppress the Slave Trade in the District of Columbia
◆ Narrative of Sojourner Truth, "Book of Life" (Excerpt)
◆ Frederick Douglass's Independence Day Address ◆ *Dred Scott v. Sandford*
◆ The Emancipation Proclamation ◆ Freedman's Bureau Act
◆ Amendment Thirteen to the United States Constitution ◆ Black Codes of Mississippi
◆ Civil Rights Act (1866) ◆ Amendment Fourteen to the United States Constitution
◆ Amendment Fifteen to the United States Constitution ◆ Ku Klux Klan Act
◆ Civil Rights Act (1875) ◆ Frederick Douglass's Speech on Woman Suffrage (Excerpt)
◆ Ida B. Wells–Barnett's Speech on Lynch Law in All Its Phases (Excerpt)
◆ Booker T. Washington's "Atlanta Compromise" Speech ◆ *Plessy v. Ferguson*
◆ "Lift Every Voice and Sing" ◆ Marcus Garvey's Speech at Liberty Hall, New York City
◆ Executive Order No. 8802 ◆ Executive Order No. 9981
◆ *Brown v. Board of Education of Topeka*
◆ *The Souls of Black Folk: Essays and Sketches* by W. E. B. Du Bois (Excerpt)
◆ Mary McLeod Bethune's Last Will and Testament (Excerpt) ◆ Civil Rights Act of 1957
◆ Executive Order No. 10730 ◆ Civil Rights Act of 1960 ◆ Executive Order No. 11053
◆ The Birmingham Manifesto ◆ Dr. Martin Luther King's Speech at the Lincoln Memorial
◆ Amendment Twenty–Four to the United States Constitution ◆ Civil Rights Act of 1964
◆ Executive Order No. 11246 ◆ Voting Rights Act of 1965 ◆ The Black Panther Manifesto
◆ Civil Rights Act of 1968
◆ Barbara Jordan's Speech on the Presidential Impeachment Proceedings (Excerpt)
◆ President George Bush's Message to the Senate Returning without Approval
the Civil Rights Act of 1990 ◆ Civil Rights Act of 1991
◆ The Million Man March/Day of Absence Mission Statement (Excerpt by Dr. Maulana Karenga)
◆ The President's Initiative on Race–The Advisory Board's Report to the President (Excerpt)

The text of proclamations and orders, legislative enactments, speeches, letters, and even poems and songs representing the course of American history display the presence of African Americans in the yesterday of this country and provide a picture of the changing place they have held in the national consciousness. The documents collected here separately capture for a moment in time the African American's role in American society. However, together these documents bear witness to the African American experience.

◆ THE GERMANTOWN MENNONITE RESOLUTION AGAINST SLAVERY (1688)

The Mennonites, a group of Protestant Christians who settled mainly in Pennsylvania and the Northwest Territory, rejected the use of violence, refused to bear arms or take oaths, and advocated the separation of church and state and the separation of their community from society. The Germantown Mennonite resolution against slavery represents one of the earliest protests against slavery in colonial America. It was passed 69 years after the introduction of the first African slaves in America, at a time when the number of slaves in the colonies was comparatively small. It was not until 1775, however, that the Quakers, a religious group similarly opposed to the institution, formed the first anti-slavery society in the colonies.

This is to the monthly meeting held at Richard Worrell's:

These are the reasons why we are against the traffic of men-body, as followeth: Is there any that would be done or handled at this manner? viz., to be sold or made a slave for all the time of his life? How fearful and faint-hearted are many at sea, when they see a strange vessel, being afraid it should be a Turk, and they should be taken, and sold for slaves into Turkey. Now, what is *this* better done, than Turks do? Yea, rather it is worse for them, which say they are Christians; for we hear that the most part of such negers are brought hither against their will and consent, and that many of them are stolen. Now, though they are black, we cannot conceive there is more liberty to have them slaves, as it is to have other white ones. There is a saying, that we should do to all men like as we will be done ourselves; making no difference of what generation, descent, or colour they are. And those who steal or rob men, and those who buy or purchase them, are they not all alike? Here is liberty of conscience, which is right and reasonable; here ought to be likewise liberty of the body, except of evil-doers, which is another case. But to bring men hither, or to rob and sell them against their will, we stand against. In Europe there are many oppressed for conscience-sake;

and here there are those oppressed which are of a black colour. And we who know that men must not commit adultery—some do commit adultery *in* others, separating wives from their husbands, and giving them to others: and some sell the children of these poor creatures to other men. Ah! do consider well this thing, you who do it, if you would be done at this manner—and if it is done according to Christianity! You surpass Holland and Germany in this thing. This makes an ill report in all those countries of Europe, where they hear of [it], that the Quakers do here handel men as they handel there the cattle. And for that reason some have no mind or inclination to come hither. And who shall maintain this your cause, or plead for it? Truly, we cannot do so, except you shall inform us better hereof, viz.: that Christians have liberty to practice these things. Pray, what thing in the world can be done worse towards us, than if men should rob or steal us away, and sell us for slaves to strange countries; separating husbands from their wives and children. Being now this is not done in the manner we would be done at; therefore, we contradict, and are against this traffic of men-body. And we who profess that it is not lawful to steal, must, likewise, avoid to purchase such things as are stolen, but rather help to stop this robbing and stealing, if possible. And such men ought to be delivered out of the hands of the robbers, and set free as in Europe. Then is Pennsylvania to have a good report, instead, it hath now a bad one, for this sake, in other countries; especially whereas the Europeans are desirous to know in what manner *the Quaker* do rule in *their* province; and most of them do look upon us with an envious eye. But if this is done well, what shall we say is done evil?

If once these slaves (which they say are so wicked and stubborn men) should join themselves—fight for their freedom, and handel their masters and mistresses, as they did handel them before; will these masters and mistresses take the sword at hand and war against these poor slaves, like, as we are able to believe, some will not refuse to do? Or, have these poor negers not as much right to fight for their freedom, as you have to keep them slaves?

Now consider well this thing, if it is good or bad. And in case you find it to be good to handel these black in that manner, we desired and require you hereby lovingly, that you may inform us herein, which at this time never was done, viz., that Christians have such a liberty to do so. To the end we shall be satisfied on this point, and satisfy likewise our good friends and acquaintances in our native country, to whom it is a terror, or fearful thing, that men should be handled so in Pennsylvania.

This is from our meeting at Germantown, held ye 18th of the 2nd month, 1688, to be delivered to the monthly meeting at Richard Worrell's.

Garret Henderich,

Derick op de Graeff,

Francis Daniel Pastorius,

Abram op de Graeff.

◆ THE DECLARATION OF INDEPENDENCE (1776)

A concept of particular interest to eighteenth-century men and women was the theory of natural rights, the idea that all individuals possess certain fundamental rights which no government can deny. Using this argument as a justification for revolt, the American colonists, on July 4, 1776, formally announced their intention to separate from Great Britain in a Declaration of Independence.

The responsibility of writing this document was given to Thomas Jefferson. In his original draft, Jefferson included among the colonists' grievances the denial of the "most sacred rights of life and liberty" to African slaves. However, the draft was revised, and the final version of the declaration was accepted by Congress without Jefferson's indictment against slavery.

In Congress, July 4, 1776. The unanimous Declaration of the thirteen United States of America,

When in the Course of human events, it becomes necessary for one people to dissolve the political bands which have connected them with another, and to assume among the Powers of the earth, the separate and equal station to which the Laws of Nature and of Nature's God entitle them, a decent respect to the opinions of mankind requires that they should declare the causes which impel them to the separation.

We hold these truths to be self-evident, that all men are created equal, that they are endowed by their Creator with certain unalienable Rights, that among these are Life, Liberty and the pursuit of Happiness. That to secure these rights, Governments are instituted among Men, deriving their just powers from the consent of the governed, That whenever any Form of Government becomes destructive of these ends, it is the Right of the People to alter or to abolish it, and to institute new Government, laying its foundation on such principles and organizing its powers in such form, as to them shall seem most likely to effect their Safety and Happiness. Prudence, indeed, will dictate that Governments long established should not be changed for light and transient causes; and accordingly all experience hath shown, that mankind are more disposed to suffer, while evils are sufferable, than to right themselves by abolishing the forms to which they are accustomed. But when a long train of abuses and usurpations, pursuing invariably the same Object evinces a design to reduce them

under absolute Despotism, it is their right, it is their duty, to throw off such Government, and to provide new Guards for their future security.—Such has been the patient sufferance of these Colonies; and such is now the necessity which constrains them to alter their former Systems of Government. The history of the present King of Great Britain is a history of repeated injuries and usurpations, all having in direct object the establishment of an absolute Tyranny over these States. To prove this, let Facts be submitted to a candid world.

He has refused his Assent to Laws, the most wholesome and necessary for the public good.

He has forbidden his Governors to pass Laws of immediate and pressing importance, unless suspended in their operation till his Assent should be obtained; and when so suspended, he has utterly neglected to attend to them.

He has refused to pass other Laws for the accommodation of people, unless those people would relinquish the right of Representation in the Legislature, a right inestimable to them and formidable to tyrants only.

He has called together Legislative bodies at places unusual, uncomfortable, and distant from the depository of their Public Records, for the sole purpose of Fatiguing them into compliance with his measures.

He has dissolved Representative Houses repeatedly, for opposing with manly firmness his invasions on the rights of the people.

He has refused for a long time, after such dissolutions, to cause others to be elected; whereby the Legislative Powers, incapable of Annihilation, have returned to the People at large for their exercise; the state remaining in the meantime exposed to all the dangers of invasion from without, and convulsions within.

He has endeavoured to prevent the Population of these States; for that purpose obstructing the Laws of Naturalization of Foreigners; refusing to pass others to encourage their migration hither, and raising the conditions of new Appropriations of Lands.

He has obstructed the Administration of Justice, by refusing his Assent to Laws for establishing Judiciary Powers.

He has made Judges dependent on his Will alone, for the tenure of their offices, and the amount and payment of their salaries.

He has erected a multitude of New Offices, and sent hither swarms of Officers to harass our People, and eat out their substance.

He has kept among us, in times of peace, Standing Armies without the Consent of our legislature.

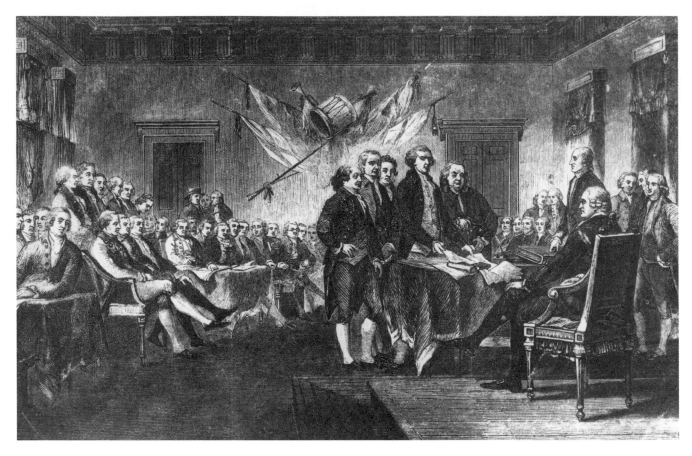

Signing of the Declaration of Independence (AP/Wide World Photos, Inc.).

He has affected to render the Military independent of and superior to the Civil Power.

He has combined with others to subject us to a jurisdiction foreign to our constitution, and unacknowledged by our laws; giving his Assent to their acts of pretended legislation:

For quartering large bodies of armed troops among us:

For protecting them, by a mock Trial, from Punishment for any Murders which they should commit on the Inhabitants of these States:

For cutting off our Trade with all parts of the world:

For imposing taxes on us without our Consent:

For depriving us in many cases, of the benefits of Trial by Jury:

For transporting us beyond Seas to be tried for pretended offenses:

For abolishing the free System of English Laws in a neighboring Province, establishing therein an Arbitrary government, and enlarging its Boundaries so as to render it at once an example and fit instrument for introducing the same absolute rule into these Colonies:

For taking away our Charters, abolishing our most valuable Laws, and altering fundamentally the Forms of our Governments:

For suspending our own Legislature, and declaring themselves invested with Power to legislate for us in all cases whatsoever.

He has abdicated Government here, by declaring us out of his Protection and waging War against us.

He has plundered our seas, ravaged our Coasts, burnt our towns, and destroyed the lives of our people.

He is at this time transporting large armies of foreign mercenaries to complete the works of death, desolation and tyranny, already begun with circumstances of Cruelty and perfidy scarcely paralleled in the most barbarous ages, and totally unworthy of the Head of a civilized nation.

He has constrained our fellow Citizens taken Captive on the high Seas to bear Arms against their Country, to become the executioners of their friends and Brethren, or to fall themselves by their Hands.

He has excited domestic insurrections amongst us, and has endeavoured to bring on the inhabitants of our frontiers, the merciless Indian Savages, whose known rule of warfare, is an undistinguished destruction of all ages, sexes and conditions.

In every stage of these Oppressions We have Petitioned for Redress in the most humble terms: Our repeated Petitions have been answered only by repeated injury. A Prince, whose character is thus marked by every act which may define a Tyrant, is unfit to be the ruler of a free People.

Nor We have been wanting in attention to our British brethren. We have warned them from time to time of attempts by their legislature to extend an unwarrantable jurisdiction over us. We have reminded them of the circumstances of our emigration and settlement here. We have appealed to their native justice and magnanimity, and we have conjured them by the ties of our common kindred to disavow these usurpations, which would inevitably interrupt our connections and correspondence. They too have been deaf to the voice of justice and of consanguinity. We must, therefore, acquiesce in the necessity, which denounces our Separation, and hold them, as we hold the rest of mankind, Enemies in War, in Peace, Friends.

We, therefore, the Representatives of the United States of America, in General Congress, Assembled, appealing to the Supreme Judge of the world for the rectitude of our intentions, do, in the Name, and by Authority of the good People of these Colonies, solemnly publish and declare, That these United Colonies are, and of Right ought to be Free and Independent States; that they are Absolved from all Allegiance to the British Crown, and that all political connection between them and the State of Great Britain, is and ought to be totally dissolved; and that as Free and Independent States, they have full Power to levy War, conclude Peace, contract Alliances, establish Commerce, and to do all other Acts and Things which Independent States may of right do. And for the support of this Declaration, with a firm reliance on the Protection of Divine Providence, we mutually pledge to each other our Lives, our Fortunes and our sacred Honor.

◆ THE OMITTED ANTI-SLAVERY CLAUSE TO THE DECLARATION OF INDEPENDENCE (1776)

Thomas Jefferson's attitudes regarding African slaves wavered during the course of his life. In his early years, Jefferson thought Africans to be biologically inferior. Later, spurred by his conviction that natural rights should be accrued to all men, he decided that slavery had a destructive conditioning effect which stamped Africans with "odious peculiarities."

When Jefferson was assigned the task of drafting a declaration calling for separation from Great Britain,

he included a short, passionate attack on King George III's indulgence of the slave traffic. However, at the request of delegates from South Carolina and Georgia and of Northern delegates whose ports sheltered and profited from slave ships, the clause was omitted from the final version. Many historians and critics have since argued that the elimination of this passage offers adequate proof that Africans in America were never meant to share in the fruits of independence and equality in their adopted homeland.

He [King George III] has waged cruel war against human nature itself, violating its most sacred rights of life and liberty in the persons of a distant people who never offended him, captivating and carrying them into slavery in another hemisphere, or to incur miserable death in their transportation thither. This piratical warfare, the opprobrium of *infidel* powers, is the warfare of the *Christian* king of Great Britain. Determined to keep open a market where MEN should be bought and sold, he has prostituted his negative for suppressing every legislative attempt to prohibit or restrain this execrable commerce.

◆ THE CONSTITUTION OF THE UNITED STATES, ART.1, SECTIONS 2 AND 9, ART. 4, SECTION 2 (1787)

Drawn up in 1787 and ratified a year later, the Constitution of the United States outlines the fundamental principles upon which the American republic is built. In a historical context, the Constitution and its amendments are a manifestation of the issues which have faced Americans and their attempts at resolving these issues.

Among the concepts important to Americans living during the eighteenth century were the ideas that all people are created equal and are endowed with certain unalienable rights, and that a government derives its power from the consent of those it governs. However, despite the fact that almost twenty percent of the population was bound in slavery, the economic and social arguments of the time regarding the status of African slaves overrode the tenets of natural rights. In 1857, Chief Justice Roger Brook Taney, delivering the Court's opinion in the case Dred Scott v. Sandford, *summarized the attitude of the writers of the Constitution toward African slaves.*

. . . They are not included, and were not intended to be included, under the word "citizens" in the constitution, and can therefore claim none of the rights and privileges which that instrument provides and secures. . . .On the contrary, they were at that time considered as a subordinate and inferior class of beings. . . .

Specifically, it is Article I, Sections 2 and 9, and Article IV, Section 2 of the Constitution, which deal directly with the status of Africans in America.

Preamble

We the People of the United States, in order to form a more perfect Union, establish Justice, insure domestic Tranquility, provide for the common defense, promote the general Welfare, and secure the Blessings of Liberty to ourselves and our Posterity, do ordain and establish this Constitution for the United States of America.

Article I

Section 2. . . . Representatives and direct Taxes shall be apportioned among the several States which may be included within this Union, according to their respective Numbers, which shall be determined by adding to the whole Number of free Persons, including those bound to Service for a Term of Years, and excluding Indians not taxed, three-fifths of all other Persons. The actual Enumeration shall be made within three Years after the first Meeting of the Congress of the United States, and within every subsequent Term of Ten Years, in such manner as they shall by Law direct. . . .

Section 9. The Migration or Importation of such Persons as any of the States now existing shall think proper to admit, shall not be prohibited by the Congress prior to the Year one thousand eight hundred and eight, but a Tax or duty may be imposed on such Importation, not exceeding ten dollars for each Person. . . .

Article IV

Section 2. The Citizens of each State shall be entitled to all privileges and Immunities of Citizens in the several States.

A Person charged in any State with Treason, Felony, or other Crime, who shall flee from Justice, and be found in another State, shall on Demand of the executive authority of the State from which he fled, be delivered up, to be removed to the State having Jurisdiction of the Crime.

No Person held to Service or Labour in one State, under the Laws thereof, escaping into another, shall, in Consequence of any Law or Regulation therein, be discharged from such Service or Labour, but shall be delivered up on Claim of the Party to whom such Service or Labour may be due.

◆ THE BILL OF RIGHTS (1791)

Ratified in 1791, the first ten amendments to the Constitution of the United States, commonly referred to as the Bill of Rights, further outline the fundamental rights and freedoms of citizens of the United States. This set of additions to the Constitution was a crucial part of the constitutional ratification process (several states had only ratified the Constitution on the condition that a bill of rights would be added), since eighteenth-century Americans held dearly to the concept of personal freedom. Despite these beliefs, it was not until after ratification of the Fourteenth Amendment to the Constitution and several civil rights laws that the freedoms protected in the Bill of Rights were extended to all United States citizens.

Amendment 1

Congress shall make no law respecting an establishment of religion, or prohibiting the free exercise thereof; or abridging the freedom of speech, or of the press; or the right of the people peaceably to assemble, and to petition the government for a redress of grievances.

Amendment 2

A well regulated Militia, being necessary to the security of a free State, the right of the people to keep and bear Arms, shall not be infringed.

Amendment 3

No Soldier, shall, in time of peace be quartered in any house, without the consent of the Owner, nor in time of war, but in a manner to be prescribed by law.

Amendment 4

The right of the people to be secure in their persons, houses, papers and effects, against unreasonable searches and seizures, shall not be violated and no Warrants shall issue, but upon probable cause, supported by Oath or affirmation, and particularly describing the place to be searched, and the persons or things to be seized.

Amendment 5

No person shall be held to answer for a capital, or otherwise infamous crime, unless on a presentment or indictment of a Grand Jury, except in cases arising in the land or naval forces, or in the Militia, when in actual service in time of War or public danger; nor shall any person be subject for the same offense to be twice put in jeopardy of life or limb; nor shall be compelled in any criminal case to be a witness against himself, nor be deprived of life, liberty, or property, without due process of law; nor shall private property be taken for public use, without just compensation.

Amendment 6

In all criminal prosecutions, the accused shall enjoy the right to a speedy and public trial, by an impartial jury of the State and district wherein the crime shall have been committed, which district shall have been previously ascertained by law, and to be informed of the nature and cause of the accusation; to be confronted with witnesses against him; to have compulsory process for obtaining witnesses in his favor, and to have the Assistance of Counsel for his defence.

Amendment 7

In Suits at common law, where the value in controversy shall exceed twenty dollars, the right of trial by jury shall be preserved, and no fact tried by a jury, shall be otherwise re-examined in any Court of the United States, than according to the rules of the common law.

Amendment 8

Excessive bail shall not be required, nor excessive fines imposed, nor cruel and unusual punishments inflicted.

Amendment 9

The enumeration in the Constitution, of certain rights, shall not be construed to deny or disparage others retained by the people.

Amendment 10

The powers not delegated to the United States by the Constitution, nor prohibited by it to the States, are reserved to the States respectively, or to the people.

◆ FUGITIVE SLAVE ACT CH. 7, STAT. 302 (1793)

The Fugitive Slave Act of 1793 was designed to enforce Article IV, Section 2 of the Constitution and incur penalties against those who aided or abetted attempts of slaves to escape bondage.

Section 1. *Be it enacted by the Senate and House of Representatives of the United States of America in Congress assembled*, That whenever the executive authority of any state in the Union, or of either of the territories northwest or south of the river Ohio, shall demand any person as a fugitive from justice, of the executive authority of any such state or territory to which such person shall have fled, and shall moreover produce the copy of an indictment found, or an affidavit made before a magistrate of any state or territory as aforesaid, charging the person so demanded, with having committed treason, felony or other crime, certified as authentic by the governor or chief magistrate of the state or territory from whence the person so charged fled, it shall be the duty of the executive authority of the state or territory to which such person shall have fled, to

cause him or her to be arrested and secured, and notice of the arrest to be given to the executive authority making such demand, or to the agent of such authority appointed to receive the fugitive, and to cause the fugitive to be delivered to such agent when he shall appear: But if no such agent shall appear within six months from the time of the arrest, the prisoner may be discharged. And all costs or expenses incurred to the state or territory making such demand, shall be paid by such state or territory.

Section 2. *And be it further enacted*, That any agent, appointed as aforesaid, who shall receive the fugitive into his custody, shall be empowered to transport him or her to the state or territory from which he or she shall have fled. And if any person or persons shall by force set at liberty, or rescue the fugitive from such agent while transporting, as aforesaid, the person or persons so offending shall, on conviction, be fined not exceeding five hundred dollars, and be imprisoned not exceeding one year.

Section 3. *And be it also enacted*, That when a person held to labour in any of the United States, or in either of the territories on the northwest or south of the river Ohio, under the laws thereof, shall escape into any other of the said states or territory, the person to whom such labour or service may be due, his agent or attorney, is hereby empowered to seize or arrest such fugitive from labour, and to take him or her before any judge of the circuit or district courts of the United States, residing or being within the state, or before any magistrate of a county, city or town corporate, wherein such seizure or arrest shall be made, and upon proof to the satisfaction of such judge or magistrate, either by oral testimony or affidavit taken before and certified by a magistrate of any such state or territory, that the person so seized or arrested, doth, under the laws of the state or territory from which he or she fled, owe service or labour to the person claiming him or her, it shall be the duty of such judge or magistrate to give a certificate thereof to such claimant, his agent or attorney, which shall be sufficient warrant for removing the said fugitive from labour, to the state or territory from which he or she fled.

Section 4. *And be it further enacted*, That any person who shall knowingly and willing obstruct or hinder such claimant, his agent or attorney in so seizing or arresting such fugitive from labour, or shall rescue such fugitive from such claimant, his agent or attorney when so arrested pursuant to the authority herein given or declared; or shall harbor or conceal such person after notice that he or she was a fugitive from labour, as aforesaid shall, for either of the said offenses, forfeit and pay the sum of five hundred dollars. Which penalty may be recovered by and for the benefit of such claimant, by action of debt, in any court proper to try the same; saving moreover to the person claiming such labour or service, his right of action for or on account of the said injuries or either of them.

◆ BENJAMIN FRANKLIN'S ADDRESS TO THE PUBLIC (1798)

Despite the frames of the Constitution's handling of the slavery issue, influential opponents to slavery attempted to exert pressure on the Congress to enact an anti-slavery amendment to the Constitution. Among such groups was the Pennsylvania Society for Promoting the Abolition of Slavery and the Relief of Free Negroes Unlawfully Held in Bondage. Over the signature of the president of the Society, Benjamin Franklin, the following "Address to the Public," urging abolition, was made on November 9, 1789.

It is with peculiar satisfaction we assure the friends of humanity that, in prosecuting the design of our association, our endeavors have proved successful, far beyond our most sanguine expectations.

Encouraged by this success, and by the daily progress of that luminous and benign spirit of liberty which is diffusing itself throughout the world, and humbly hoping for the continuance of the divine blessing on our labors, we have ventured to make an important addition to our original plan; and do therefore earnestly solicit the support and assistance of all who can feel the tender emotions of sympathy and compassion, or relish the exalted pleasure of beneficence.

Slavery is such an atrocious debasement of human nature, that its very extirpation, if not performed with solicitous care, may sometimes open a source of serious evils.

The unhappy man, who has long been treated as a brute animal, too frequently sinks beneath the common standard of the human species. The galling chains that bind his body do also fetter his intellectual faculties, and impair the social affections of his heart. Accustomed to move like a mere machine, by the will of a master, reflection is suspended; he has not the power of choice; and reason and conscience have but little influence over his conduct, because he is chiefly governed by the passion of fear. He is poor and friendless; perhaps worn out by extreme labor, age, and disease.

Under such circumstances, freedom may often prove a misfortune to himself, and prejudicial to society.

Attention to emancipated black people, it is therefore to be hoped, will become a branch of our national police; but, as far as we contribute to promote this emancipation, so far that attention is evidently a serious

Benjamin Franklin (The Library of Congress)

duty incumbent on us, and which we mean to discharge to the best of our judgment and abilities.

To instruct, to advise, to qualify those who have been restored to freedom, for the exercise and enjoyment of civil liberty; to promote in them habits of industry; to furnish them with employments suited to their age, sex, talents, and other circumstances; and to procure their children an education calculated for their future situation in life—these are the great outlines of the annexed plan, which we have adopted, and which we conceive will essentially promote the public good, and the happiness of these our hitherto too much neglected fellow-creatures.

A plan so extensive cannot be carried into execution without considerable pecuniary resources, beyond the present ordinary funds of the Society. We hope much from the generosity of enlightened and benevolent freemen, and will gratefully receive any donations of subscriptions for this purpose which may be made to our Treasurer, James Starr, or to James Pemberton, Chairman of our Committee of Correspondence.

Signed by order of the Society,

B. FRANKLIN, President

Philadelphia, 9th of November, 1789

◆ GEORGE WASHINGTON'S LAST WILL AND TESTAMENT (1799)

By the eighteenth century, the slavery of Africans had become a firmly entrenched institution of American life, particularly in the South where it was justified as an economic necessity. This argument notwithstanding, it was Washington's decision, at the writing of his last will and testament in 1799, to free all those slaves which he held in his "own right."

In the Name of God Amen

I, George Washington of Mount Vernon—a citizen of the United States,—and lately President of the same, do make, ordain and declare this Instrument; which is written with my own hand and every page thereof subscribed with my name, to be my last Will and Testament, revoking all other. . . .Upon the decease of my wife, it is my Will and desire that all the Slaves which I hold in my *own right*, shall receive their freedom. . . .And whereas among those who will receive freedom according to this devise, there may be some, who from old age or bodily infirmities, and others who on account of their infancy, that will be unable to support themselves; it is my Will and desire that all who come under the first and second description shall be comfortably clothed and fed by my heirs while they live;—and that such of the latter description as have no parents living, or if living are unable, or unwilling to provide for them, shall be bound by the Court until they shall arrive at the age of twenty-five year;—and in cases where no record can be produced, whereby their ages can be ascertained, the judgment of the Court upon its own view of the subject, shall be adequate and final.—The Negros thus bound, are (by their Masters or Mistresses) to be taught to read and write; and to be brought up to some useful occupation, agreeably to the Laws of the Commonwealth of Virginia, providing for the support of Orphan and other poor Children.—And I do hereby expressly forbid the Sale, or transportation out of the said Commonwealth of any Slave I may die possessed of, under any pretence whatsoever.—And I do moreover most pointedly, and most solemnly enjoin it upon my Executors hereafter named, or the Survivors of them, to see that this clause respecting Slaves, and every part thereof be religiously fulfilled at the Epoch at which it is directed to take place; without evasion, neglect or delay, after the Crops which may then be on the ground are harvested, particularly as it respects the aged and infirm;—Seeing that a regular and permanent fund be established for their Support so long as there are subjects requiring it; not trusting to the uncertain provision to be made by individuals.—And to my Mulatto man William (calling himself William Lee) I

U.S. President George Washington (The Library of Congress)

give immediate freedom; or if he should prefer it (on account of the accidents which have befallen him, and which have rendered him incapable of walking or of any active employment) to remain in the situation he now is, it shall be optional in him to do so: In either case however, I allow him an annuity of thirty dollars during his natural life, which shall be independent of the victuals and cloaths he has been accustomed to receive, if he chooses the last alternative; but in full, with his freedom, if he prefers the first;—and this I give him as a testimony of my sense of his attachment to me, and for his faithful services during the Revolutionary War.

◆ ACT TO PROHIBIT THE IMPORTATION OF SLAVES CH. 22, 2 STAT. 426 (1807)

In adherence with the provisions of Article I, Section 9 of the Constitution, Congress passed and President Thomas Jefferson signed into law an act to end the slave trade. The act, however, which went into effect January 1, 1808, was not rigidly enforced. Evidence of this can be found in the fact that, between 1808 and 1860, some 250,000 slaves were illegally imported into the United States.

Slave cell used to hold newly arrived Africans in America (The Library of Congress).

An Act to prohibit the importation of Slaves into any port or place within the jurisdiction of the United States, from and after the first day of January, in the year of our Lord one thousand eight hundred and eight.

Be it enacted, that from and after the first day of January, one thousand eight hundred and eight, it shall not be lawful to import or bring into the United States or the territories thereof from any foreign kingdom, place, or country, any negro, mulatto, or person of colour, as a slave, or to be held to service or labour.

Section 2. That no citizen of the United States, or any other person, shall, from and after the first day of January, in the year of our Lord one thousand eight hundred and eight, for himself, or themselves, or any other person whatsoever, either as master, factor, or owner, build, fit, equip, load or to otherwise prepare any ship or vessel, in any port or place within the jurisdiction of the United States, nor shall cause any ship or vessel to sail from any port or place within the same, for the purpose of procuring any negro, mulatto, or person of colour, from any foreign kingdom, place, or country, to be transported to any port or place whatsoever within the jurisdiction of the United States, to be held, sold, or disposed of as slaves, or to be held to service or labour: and if any ship or vessel shall be so fitted out for the purpose aforesaid, or shall be caused to sail so as aforesaid, every such ship or vessel, her tackle, apparel, and furniture, shall be forfeited to the United States, and shall be liable to be seized, prosecuted, and condemned in any of the circuit courts or district courts, for the district where the said ship or vessel may be found or seized. . . .

Section 4. If any citizen or citizens of the United States, or any person resident within the jurisdiction of the same, shall, from after the first day of January, one thousand eight hundred and eight, take on board, receive or transport from any of the coasts or kingdoms of Africa, or from any other foreign kingdom, place, or country, any negro, mulatto, or person of colour in any ship or vessel, for the purpose of selling them in any port or place within the jurisdiction of the United States as slaves, or be held to service or labour, or shall be in any ways aiding or abetting therein, such citizen or citizens, or person, shall severally forfeit and pay five thousand dollars, one moiety thereof to the use of any person or persons who shall sue for and prosecute the same to effect. . . .

Section 6. That if any person or persons whatsoever, shall, from and after the first day of January, one thousand eight hundred and eight, purchase or sell any negro, mulatto, or person, of colour, for a slave, or to be held to service or labour, who shall have been imported, or brought from any foreign kingdom, place, or country, or from the dominions of any foreign state, immediately adjoining to the United States, after the last day of December, one thousand eight hundred and seven, knowing at the time of such purchase or sale, such negro, mulatto, or person of colour, was so brought within the jurisdiction of the United States, as aforesaid, such purchaser and seller shall severally forfeit and pay for every negro, mulatto, or person of colour, so purchased, or sold as aforesaid, eight hundred dollars. . . .

Section 7. That if any ship or vessel shall be found, from and after the first day of January, one thousand eight hundred and eight, in any river, port, bay, or harbor, or on the high seas, within the jurisdictional limits of the United States, or hovering on the coast thereof, having on board any negro, mulatto, or person of colour, for the purpose of selling them as slaves, or with intent to land the same, in any port or place within the jurisdiction of the United States, contrary to the prohibition of the act, every such ship or vessel, together with her tackle, apparel, and furniture, and the goods or effects which shall be found on board the same, shall be forfeited to the use of the United States, and may be

seized, prosecuted, and condemned, in any court of the United States, having jurisdiction thereof. And it shall be lawful for the President of the United States, and he is hereby authorized, should he deem it expedient, to cause any of the armed vessels of the United States to be manned and employed to cruise on any part of the coast of the United States, or territories thereof, where he may judge attempts will be made to violate the provisions of this act, and to instruct and direct the commanders of armed vessels of the United States, to seize, take, and bring into any port of the United States all such ships or vessels, and moreover to seize, take, or bring into any port of the U.S. all ships or vessels of the U.S. wheresoever found on the high seas, contravening the provisions of this act, to be proceeded against according to law. . . .

◆ EDITORIAL FROM THE FIRST EDITION OF *FREEDOM'S JOURNAL* (1827)

Freedom's Journal, published by Samuel Cornish and John B. Russwurm, was the first African American owned and edited newspaper to be published in the United States. This editorial, printed here in its entirety, illustrates the *Journal*'s aim at bringing an end to slavery and discrimination.

To Our Patrons

In presenting our first number to our Patrons, we feel all the diffidence of persons entering upon a new and untried line of business. But a moment's reflection upon the noble objects, which we have in view by the publication of this Journal; the expediency of its appearance at this time, when so many schemes are in action concerning our people—encourage us to come boldly before an enlightened public. For we believe, that a paper devoted to the dissemination of useful knowledge among our brethren, and to their moral and religious improvement, must meet with the cordial approbation of every friend to humanity.

The peculiarities of this Journal, renders it important that we should advertise to the world our motives by which we are actuated, and the objects which we contemplate.

We wish to plead our own cause. Too long have others spoken for us. Too long has the public been deceived by misrepresentations, in things which concern us dearly, though in the estimation of some mere trifles; for though there are many in society who exercise towards us benevolent feelings; still (with sorrow we confess it) there are others who make it their business to enlarge upon the least trifle, which tends to the discredit of any person of colour; and pronounce anathemas and denounce our whole body for the misconduct of this guilty one. We are aware that there are many instances of vice among us, but we avow that it is because no one has taught its subjects to be virtuous; many instances of poverty, because no sufficient efforts accommodated to minds contracted by slavery, and deprived of early education have been made, to teach them how to husband their hard earnings, and to secure to themselves comfort.

Education being an object of the highest importance to the welfare of society, we shall endeavor to present just and adequate views of it, and to urge upon our brethren the necessity and expediency of training their children, while young, to habits of industry, and thus forming them for becoming useful members of society. It is surely time that we should awake from this lethargy of years, and make a concentrated effort for the education of our youth. We form a spoke in the human wheel, and it is necessary that we should understand our pendency on the different parts, and theirs on us, in order to perform our part with propriety.

Though not desiring of dictating, we shall feel it our incumbent duty to dwell occasionally upon the general principles and rules of economy. The world has grown too enlightened, to estimate any man's character by his personal appearance. Though all men acknowledge the excellency of Franklin's maxims, yet comparatively few practice upon them. We may deplore when it is too late, the neglect of these self-evident truths, but it avails little to mourn. Ours will be the task of admonishing our brethren on these points.

The civil rights of a people being of the greatest value, it shall ever be our duty to vindicate our brethren, when oppressed; and to lay the case before the public. We shall also urge upon our brethren, (who are qualified by the laws of the different states) the expediency of using their elective franchise; and of making an independent use of the same. We wish them not to become the tools of party.

And as much time is frequently lost, and wrong principles instilled, by the perusal of works of trivial importance, we shall consider it a part of our duty to recommend to our young readers, such authors as will not only enlarge their stock of useful knowledge, but such as will also serve to stimulate them to higher attainments in science.

We trust also, that through the columns of the FREEDOM'S JOURNAL, many practical pieces, having for their bases, the improvement of our brethren, will be presented to them, from the pens of many of our respected friends, who have kindly promised their assistance.

It is our earnest wish to make our Journal a medium of intercourse between our brethren in the different states of this great confederacy: that through its columns an expression of our sentiments, on many inter-esting subjects which concern us, may be offered to the public: that plans which apparently are beneficial may be candidly discussed and properly weighed; if worth, receive our cordial approbation; if not, our marked disapprobation.

Useful knowledge of every kind, and everything that relates to Africa, shall find a ready admission into our columns; and as that vast continent becomes daily more known, we trust that many things will come to light, proving that the natives of it are neither so ignorant nor stupid as they have generally been supposed to be.

And while these important subjects shall occupy the columns of the FREEDOM'S JOURNAL, we would not be unmindful of our brethren who are still in the iron fetters of bondage. They are our kindred by all the ties of nature; and though but little can be effected to us, still let our sympathies be poured forth and our prayers in their behalf, ascend to Him who is able to succor them.

From the press and the pulpit we have suffered much by being incorrectly represented. Men whom we equally love and admire have not hesitated to represent us disadvantageously, without becoming personally acquainted with the true state of things, nor discerning between virtue and vice among us. The virtuous part of our people feel themselves sorely aggrieved under the existing state of things—they are not appreciated.

Our vices and our degradation are ever arrayed against us, but our virtues are passed by unnoticed. And what is still more lamentable, our friends, to whom we concede all the principles of humanity and religion, from these very causes seem to have fallen into the current of popular feeling and are imperceptibly floating on the stream—actually living in the practice of prejudice, while they abjure it in theory, and feel it not in their hearts. Is it not very desirable that such should know more of our actual condition; and of our efforts and feelings, that in forming or advocating plans for our amelioration, they may do it more understanding? In the spirit of candor and humility we intend by a simple representation of facts to lay our case before the public, with a view to arrest the progress of prejudice, and to shield ourselves against the consequent evils. We wish to conciliate all and to irritate none, yet we must be firm and unwavering in our principles, and persevering in our efforts.

If ignorance, poverty and degradation have hitherto been our unhappy lot; has the Eternal decree gone forth, that our race alone are to remain in this state, while knowledge and civilization are shedding their enlivening rays over the rest of the human family? The recent travels of Denham and Clapperton in the interior of Africa, and the interesting narrative which they have published; the establishment of the republic of Haiti after years of sanguinary warfare; its subsequent progress in all the arts of civilization; and the advancement of liberal ideas in South America, where despotism has given place to free governments, and where many of our brethren now fill important civil and military stations, prove the contrary.

The interesting fact that there are FIVE HUNDRED THOUSAND free persons of color, one half of whom might peruse, and the whole be benefitted by the publication of the Journal; that no publication, as yet, has been devoted exclusively to their improvement—that many selections from approved standard authors, which are within the reach of few, may occasionally be made—and more important still, that this large body of our citizens have no public channel—all serve to prove the real necessity, at present, for the appearance of the FREEDOM'S JOURNAL.

It shall ever be our desire so to conduct the editorial department of our paper as to give offence to none of our patrons; as nothing is farther from us than to make it the advocate of any partial views, either in politics or religion. What few days we can number, have been devoted to the improvement of our brethren; and it is our earnest wish that the remainder may be spent in the same delightful service.

In conclusion, whatever concerns us as a people, will ever find a ready admission into the FREEDOM'S JOURNAL, interwoven with all the principal news of the day.

And while every thing in our power shall be performed to support the character of our Journal, we would respectfully invite our numerous friends to assist by their communications, and our coloured brethren to strengthen our hands by their subscriptions, as our labour is one of common cause, and worthy of their consideration and support. And we most earnestly solicit the latter, that if at any time we should seem to be zealous, or too pointed in the inculcation of any important lesson, they will remember, that they are equally interested in the cause in which we are engaged, and attribute our zeal to the peculiarities of our situation; and our earnest engagedness in their well-being.

◆ EDITORIAL FROM THE FIRST EDITION OF *THE LIBERATOR* (1831)

The Liberator, *one of the most well-known abolitionist newspapers in the nineteenth century, was published weekly out of Boston, Massachusetts between 1831 and 1865. The paper's founder, William Lloyd Garrison, who was also the founder of the American Anti-Slavery Society, was white. However, most of* The Liberator's *subscribers were black. During 34 years of publication, Garrison worked at shifting the senti-*

ment of the nation away from the notion of gradual emancipation toward that of total abolition—as illustrated in this excerpt from the paper's first editorial.

. . . During my recent tour for the purpose of exciting the minds of the people by a series of discourses on the subject of slavery, every place that I visited gave fresh evidence of the fact, that a greater revolution in public sentiment was to be effected in the free states—and particularly in New England—than at the south. I found contempt more bitter, opposition more active, detraction more relentless, prejudice more stubborn, and apathy more frozen, than among slave owners themselves. Of course, there were individual exceptions to the contrary. This state of things afflicted, but did not dishearten me. I determined, at every hazard, to lift up the standard of emancipation in the eyes of the nation, within sight of Bunker Hill and in the birth place of liberty. That standard is now unfurled; and long may it float, unhurt by the spoliations of time or the missiles of a desperate foe—yea, till every chain be broken, and every bondman set free! Let Southern oppressors tremble—let their secret abettors tremble—let their Northern apologists tremble—let all the enemies of the persecuted blacks tremble.

I am aware that many object to the severity of my language; but is there not cause for severity? I will be as harsh as truth, and as uncompromising as justice. On this subject, I do not wish to think, or speak, or write, with moderation. No! No! Tell a man whose house is on fire to give a moderate alarm; tell the mother to gradually extricate her babe from the fire into which it has fallen;—but urge me not to use moderation in a cause like the present. I am in earnest—I will not equivocate—I will not excuse—I will not retreat a single inch—AND I WILL BE HEARD. . . .

William Lloyd Garrison

◆ THE AMERICAN ANTI-SLAVERY SOCIETY'S AMERICAN SLAVERY AS IT IS (1839) (EXCERPT)

In 1839, The American Anti-Slavery Society compiled a massive portfolio of testimonies entitled American Slavery As It Is, *which sought to document the inhumanities of slavery. The introduction, by Theodore D. Weld of New York, written in the style of a prosecutor addressing a court, stirred abolitionist sentiments in the North and was attacked by pro-slavery forces in the South.*

READER, YOU are empaneled as a juror to try a plain case and bring in an honest verdict. The question at issue is not one of law, but of act—"What is the actual condition of slaves in the United States?"

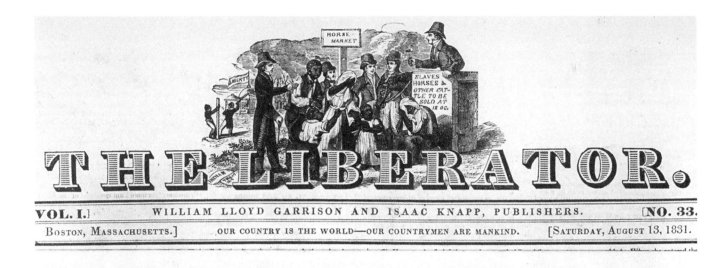

Masthead of William Lloyd Garrison's newspaper *The Liberator* (The Library of Congress).

A plainer case never went to jury. Look at it. TWENTY SEVEN HUNDRED THOUSAND PERSONS in this country, men, women, and children, are in SLAVERY. Is slavery, as a condition for human beings, good, bad, or indifferent?

We submit the question without argument. You have common sense, and conscience, and a human heart— pronounce upon it. You have a wife, or a husband, a child, a father, a mother, a brother or a sister—make the case your own, make it theirs, and bring in your verdict.

The case of Human Rights against Slavery has been adjudicated in the court of conscience times innumerable. The same verdict has always been rendered— "Guilty;" the same sentence has always been pronounced "Let it be accursed;" and human nature, with her million echoes, has rung it round the world in every language under heaven. "Let it be accursed. . . ."

As slaveholders and their apologists are volunteer witnesses in their own cause, and are flooding the world with testimony that their slaves are kindly treated; that they are well fed, well clothed, well housed, well lodged, moderately worked, and bountifully provided with all things needful for their comfort, we propose—first, to disprove their assertions by the testimony of a multitude of impartial witnesses, and then to put slaveholders themselves through a course of cross-questioning which will draw their condemnation out of their own mouths.

We will prove that the slaves in the United States are treated with barbarous inhumanity; that they are overworked, underfed, wretchedly clad and lodged, and have insufficient sleep; that they are often made to wear round their necks iron collars armed with prongs, to drag heavy chains and weights at their feet while working in the field, and to wear yokes and bells, and iron

horns; that they are often kept confined in the stocks day and night for weeks together, made to wear gags in their mouths for hours or days, have some of their front teeth torn out or broken off, that they may be easily detected when they run away; that they are frequently flogged with terrible severity, have red pepper rubbed into their lacerated flesh, and hot brine, spirits of turpentine etc., poured over the gashes to increase the torture; that they are often stripped naked, their backs and limbs cut with knives, bruised and mangled by scores and hundreds of blows with the paddle, and terribly torn by the claws of cats, drawn over them by their tormentors; that they are often hunted with bloodhounds and shot down like beasts, or torn in pieces by dogs; that they are often suspended by the arms and whipped and beaten till they faint, and when revived by restoratives, beaten again till they faint, and sometimes till they die; that their ears are often cut off, their eyes knocked out, their bones broken, their flesh branded with red hot irons; that they are maimed, mutilated and burned to death, over slow fires. All these things, and more, and worse, we shall *prove*. . . .

We shall show, not merely that such deeds are committed, but that they are frequent; not done in corners, but before the sun; not in one of the slave states, but in all of them; not perpetrated by brutal overseers and drivers merely, but by magistrates, by legislators, by professors of religion, by preachers of the gospel, by governors of states, by "gentlemen of property and standing," and by delicate females moving in the "highest circles of society."

We know, full well, the outcry that will be made by multitudes, at these declarations; the multiform cavils, the flat denials, the charges of "exaggeration" and "falsehood" so often bandied, the sneers of affected contempt at the credulity that can believe such things, and the rage and imprecations against those who give them currency. We know, too, the threadbare sophistries by which slaveholders and their apologists seek to evade such testimony. If they admit that such deeds are committed, they tell us that they are exceedingly rare, and therefore furnish no grounds for judging of the general treatment of slaves; that occasionally a brutal wretch in the *free* states barbarously butchers his wife, but that no one thinks of inferring from that, the general treatment of wives at the North and West.

They tell us, also, that the slaveholders of the South are proverbially hospitable, kind, and generous, and it is incredible that they can perpetrate such enormities upon human beings; further, that it is absurd to suppose that they would thus injure their own property, that self-interest would prompt them to treat their slaves with kindness, as none but fools and madmen wantonly destroy their own property; further, that Northern visitors at the South come back testifying to the kind treatment of the slaves, and that slaves themselves corroborate such representations. All these pleas, and scores of others, are build in every corner of the free States; and who that hath eyes to see, has not sickened at the blindness that saw not, at the palsy of heart that felt not, or at the cowardice and sycophancy that dared not expose such shallow fallacies. We are not to be turned from our purpose by such vapid babblings. In their appropriate places, we proposed to consider these objections and various others, and to show their emptiness and folly.

◆ HENRY HIGHLAND GARNET'S ADDRESS TO THE SLAVES OF THE UNITED STATES OF AMERICA (1843) (EXCERPT)

In 1843, Henry Highland Garnet attended the National Convention of Negro Citizens in Buffalo, New York, and on August 16 he delivered a militant oration calling for slave rebellions as the most assured means of ending slavery. It was perhaps the most radical speech by an African American during the period prior to the Civil War. The proposal moved the delegates and failed by a single vote of being adopted. After reading the speech, anti-slavery advocate John Brown had it published at his own expense in 1848.

Garnet's speech is, for all intents and purposes, addressed to an audience not present to receive it. Garnet speaks "to" the enslaved "on behalf of" the assembled conventioneers. Apologizing for the softness and ineffectiveness of abolitionist efforts, Garnet en-

Henry Highland Garnet (The Granger Collection Ltd.)

courages slaves to "Arise! Strike for your lives and liberties." For Garnet's immediate audience, his message is one of anger, exasperation, and a summons for heightened militancy.

Brethren and fellow citizens: Your brethren of the North, East and West have been accustomed to meet together in national conventions, to sympathize with each other, and to weep over your unhappy condition. In these meetings we have addressed all classes of the free, but we have never, until this time, sent a word of consolation and advice to you. We have been contented in sitting still and mourning over your sorrows, earnestly hoping that before this day your sacred liberties would have been restored. But we have hoped in vain. Years have rolled on, and tens of thousands have been borne on streams of blood and tears to the shores of eternity. While you have been oppressed, we have also been partakers with you; nor can we be free while you are enslaved. We, therefore, write to you as being bound with you.

Many of you are bound to us, not only by the ties of a common humanity, but we are connected by the more tender relations of parents, wives, husbands and sisters and friends. As such we most affectionately address you.

Two hundred and twenty-seven years ago the first of our injured race were brought to the shores of America. They came not with glad spirits to select their homes in the New World. They came not with their own consent, to find an unmolested enjoyment of the blessings of this fruitful soil. . . . Neither did they come flying upon the wings of Liberty to a land of freedom. But they came with broken hearts from their beloved native land and were doomed to unrequited toil and deep degradation. Nor did the evil of their bondage end at their emancipation by death. Succeeding generations inherited their chains, and millions have come from eternity into time, and have returned again to the world of spirits, cursed and ruined by American Slavery.

[T]he time has come when you must act for yourselves. It is an old and true saying that, "if hereditary bondsmen would be free, they must themselves strike the blow." You can plead your own cause and do the work of emancipation better than any others. The nations of the Old World are moving in the great cause of universal freedom, and some of them at least will, ere long, do you justice. The combined powers of Europe have placed their broad seal of disapprobation upon the African slave trade. But in the slaveholding parts of the United States the trade is as brisk as ever. They buy and sell you as though you were brute beasts. The North has done much; her opinion of slavery in the abstract is known. But in regard to the South, we adopt the opinion of the *New York Evangelist*—"We have advanced so far, that the cause apparently waits for a more effectual door to be thrown open that has been yet." . . . [G]o to your lordly enslavers and tell them plainly that you are determined to be free. Appeal to their sense of justice and tell them that they have no more right to oppress you than you have to enslave them. Entreat them to remove the grievous burdens which they have imposed upon you, and to remunerate you for your labor. . . . Inform them that all you desire is freedom, and that nothing else will suffice. Do this, and forever after cease to toil for the heartless tyrants, who give you no other reward but stripes and abuse. If they then commence the work of death, they, and not you, will be responsible for the consequences. You had far better all die—die immediately—than live slaves and entail your wretchedness upon your posterity. If you would be free in this generation, here is your only hope. However much you and all of us may desire it, there is not much hope of redemption without the shedding of blood. If you must bleed, let it all come at once—rather die freemen than live to be slaves. It is impossible, like the children of Israel, to make a grand exodus from the land of bondage. The Pharaohs are on both sides of the blood-red waters!

Where is the blood of your fathers? Has it all run out of your veins? Awake, awake; millions of voices are calling you! Your dead fathers speak to you from their graves. Heaven, as with a voice of thunder, call on you to arise from the dust.

Let your motto be Resistance! Resistance! Resistance! No oppressed people have ever secured their liberty without resistance. What kind of resistance you had better make you must decide by the circumstances that surround you, and according to the suggestion of expediency. Brethren, adieu! Trust in the living God. Labor for the peace of the human race, and remember that you are three millions!

◆ EDITORIAL FROM THE FIRST EDITION OF *THE NORTH STAR* (1847)

The first edition of Frederick Douglass's newspaper The North Star *was published on December 3, 1847, in Rochester, New York. Douglass, an escaped slave and leader in the abolitionist movement, dedicated his paper to the cause of blacks in America—as displayed in this, the paper's first editorial.*

To Our Oppressed Countrymen

We solemnly dedicate the *North Star* to your cause, our long oppressed and plundered fellow countrymen. May God bless the offering to your good! It shall fearlessly assert your rights, faithfully proclaim your wrongs, and earnestly demand for you instant and even-handed justice. Giving no quarter to slavery at the South, it will hold no truce with oppressors at the North. While it shall boldly advocate emancipation for our enslaved brethren, it will omit no opportunity to gain for the nominally free, complete enfranchisement. Every effort to injure or degrade you or your cause—originating wheresoever, or with whomsoever—shall find in it a constant, unswerving and inflexible foe.

We shall energetically assail the ramparts of Slavery and Prejudice, be they composed of church or state, and seek the destruction of every refuge of lies, under which tyranny may aim to conceal and protect itself. . . .

While our paper shall be mainly Anti-Slavery, its columns shall be freely opened to the candid and decorous discussions of all measures and topics of a moral and humane character, which may serve to enlighten, improve, and elevate mankind. Temperance, Peace, Capital Punishment, Education,—all subjects claiming the attention of the public mind may be freely and fully discussed here.

While advocating your rights, the *North Star* will strive to throw light on your duties: while it will not fail to make known your virtues, it will not shun to discover your faults. To be faithful to our foes it must be faithful to ourselves, in all things.

Remember that we are one, that our cause is one, and that we must help each other, if we would succeed. We have drunk to the dregs the bitter cup of slavery; we have worn the heavy yoke; we have sighed beneath our bonds, and writhed beneath the bloody lash;—cruel mementoes of our oneness are indelibly marked in our living flesh. We are one with you under the ban of prejudice and proscription—one with you under the slander of inferior—one with you in social and political disfranchisement. What you suffer, we suffer; what you endure, we endure. We are indissolubly united, and must fall or flourish together. . . .

We shall be the advocates of learning, from the very want of it, and shall most readily yield the deference due to men of education among us; but shall always bear in mind to accord most merit to those who have labored hardest, and overcome most, in the praiseworthy pursuit of knowledge, remembering "that the whole need not a physician, but they that are sick," and that "the strong ought to bear the infirmities of the weak."

Brethren, the first number of the paper is before you. It is dedicated to your cause. Through the kindness of our friends in England, we are in possession of an excellent printing press, types, and all other materials necessary for printing a paper. Shall this gift be blest to our good, or shall it result in our injury? It is for you to say. With your aid, cooperation and assistance, our enterprise will be entirely successful. We pledge ourselves that no effort on our part shall be wanting, and that no subscriber shall lose his subscription—*"The North Star* Shall live."

◆ FUGITIVE SLAVE ACT CH. 60, 9 STAT. 462 (1850)

For almost 15 years the provisions of the Missouri Compromise had quieted the debate over the expansion of slavery in the United States. However, following the annexation of Texas in 1845 and the ending of the war with Mexico in 1848, the question of expansion reignited tensions between pro-slavery forces and opponents to the institution.

With Southern members of Congress threatening to withdraw, a compromise was reached in 1850 between advocates of expression and their rivals. The compromise, a package of five statutes, attempted to address the major points of the sectional conflict. One of the provisions of the compromise, which was supported by many Southerners, was a strengthening of the existing federal fugitive slave law. On September 18, 1850, an act amending the 1793 fugitive slave statute was signed

This illustration depicts an escaped slave being returned to his owner in chains (The Library of Congress).

into law. Both the 1850 and the 1793 acts were finally repealed on June 28, 1864.

Section 5. That it shall be the duty of all marshals and deputy marshals to obey and execute all warrants and precepts issued under the provisions of this act, when to them directed; and should any marshal or deputy marshal refuse to receive such warrant, or other process, when tendered, or to use all proper means diligently to execute the same, he shall, on conviction thereof, be fined in the sum of one thousand dollars, to the use of such claimant, . . . and after arrest of such fugitive, by such marshal or his deputy, or whilst at any time in his custody under the provisions of this act, should such fugitive escape, whether with or without the assent of such marshal or his deputy, such marshal shall be liable, on his official bond, to be prosecuted for the benefit of such claimant, for the full value of the service or labor of said fugitive in the State, Territory, or District whence he escaped: and the better to enable the said commissioners, when thus appointed, to execute their duties faithfully and efficiently, in conformity with the requirements of the Constitution of the United States and of this act, they are hereby authorized and empowered, within their counties respectively, to appoint, . . . any one or more suitable persons, from time to time, to execute all such warrants and other processes as may be issued by them in the lawful performance of their respective duties. . . .

Section 6. That when a person held to service or labor in any State or Territory of the United States, has heretofore or shall hereafter escape into another State or Territory of the United States, the person or persons to whom such service or labor may be due,. . . may pursue and reclaim such fugitive person, either by procuring a warrant from some one of the courts, judges, or commissioners aforesaid, of the proper circuit, district, or county, for the apprehension of such fugitive from service or labor, or by seizing and arresting such fugitive, where the same can be done without process, and by taking, or causing such person to be taken, forthwith before such court, judge, or commissioner, whose duty it shall be to hear and determine the case of such claimant in a summary manner; and upon satisfactory proof being made, by deposition of affidavit, in writing, to be taken and certified by such court, judge, or commissioner, or by other satisfactory testimony, duly taken and certified by some court,. . . and with proof, also by affidavit, of the identity of the person whose service or labor is claimed to be due as aforesaid, that the person so arrested does in fact owe service or labor to the person or persons claiming him or her, in the State or Territory from which such fugitive may have escaped as aforesaid, and that said person escaped, to make out and deliver to such claimant, his or her agent or attorney, a certificate setting forth the substantial facts as to the service or labor due from such fugitive to the claimant, and of his or her escape from the State or Territory in which he or she was arrested, with authority to such claimant,. . . to use such reasonable force and restraint as may be necessary, under the circumstances of the case, to take and remove such fugitive person back to the State or Territory whence he or she may have escaped as aforesaid.

Section 7. That any persons who shall knowingly and willingly obstruct, hinder, or prevent such claimant, his agent or attorney, or any person or persons lawfully assisting him, her, or them, from arresting such a fugitive from service or labor, either with or without process as aforesaid, or shall rescue, or attempt to rescue, such fugitive from service or labor, from the custody of such claimant,. . . or other person or persons lawfully assisting as aforesaid, when so arrested,. . . or shall aid, abet, or assist such person so owing service or labor as aforesaid, directly or indirectly, to escape from such claimant,. . . or shall harbor or conceal such fugitive, so as to prevent the discovery and arrest of such person, after notice or knowledge of the fact that such person was a fugitive from service or labor. . . shall, for either of said offenses, be subject to a fine not exceeding one thousand dollars, and imprisonment not exceeding six months. . . ; and shall moreover forfeit and pay, by way of civil damages to the party injured by such illegal conduct, the sum of one thousand dollars, for each fugitive so lost as aforesaid. . . .

Section 9. That, upon affidavit made by the claimant of such fugitive. . . that he has reason to apprehend that such fugitive will be rescued by force from his or their possession before he can be taken beyond the limits of the State in which the arrest is made, it shall be the duty of the officer making the arrest to retain such fugitive in his custody, and to remove him to the State whence he fled, and there to deliver him to said claimant, his agent, or attorney. And to this end, the officer aforesaid is hereby authorized and required to employ so many persons as he may deem necessary to overcome such force, and to retain them in his service so long as circumstances may require.

◆ ACT TO SUPPRESS THE SLAVE TRADE IN THE DISTRICT OF COLUMBIA CH. 63, 9 STAT. 467 (1850)

Although the importation of new slaves from Africa had been outlawed in 1808, the breeding and trading of slaves was still a big business; the Washington, Maryland, and Virginia area served as headquarters to some of the nation's largest traders.

The renewed debate in Congress over the expansion of slavery during the late 1840s led to what has been referred to as the Compromise of 1850—a package of five resolutions, one of which was the 1850 Fugitive Slave Act. Another of the provisions, a concession to the anti-slavery forces, was an act abolishing the slave trade in the District of Columbia.

Be it enacted,. . . That from and after January 1, 1851, it shall not be lawful to bring into the District of Columbia any slave whatsoever, for the purpose of being sold, or for the purpose of being placed in depot, to be subsequently transferred to any other State or place to be sold as merchandise. And if any slave shall be brought into the said District by its owner, or by the authority or consent of its owner, contrary to the provisions of this act, such slave shall thereupon become liberated and free.

◆ NARRATIVE OF SOJOURNER TRUTH, "BOOK OF LIFE" (1851) (EXCERPT)

In 1851 Sojourner Truth initiated a lecturing tour in western New York, accompanied by several distinguished abolitionists. To speak against slavery during this period was both unpopular and unsafe. Abolitionist meetings were frequently disrupted by the pro-slavery forces, and their lives threatened. During such times, Sojourner Truth was known to fearlessly maintain her ground, and by her stately manner and well-timed remarks she would disperse the mob and restore order.

After several months in western New York, she traveled to Akron, Ohio, in order to speak before a less-than-

Sojourner Truth (The Library of Congress)

receptive audience at a woman's rights convention. Fearing negative publicity through an association with Sojourner Truth and the abolitionist movement, the conventioneers pleaded with Frances D. Gage, presiding member of the convention, not to allow Truth to lecture. On the second day, as the conventioneers struggled with the disruptive male clergy of various denominations, Truth slowly rose from her seat and moved towards the podium. Ignoring the requests of her fellow conventioneer, Gage introduced Truth to the audience. A profound hush fell across the audience as Sojourner Truth spoke these words:

Well, children, where there is so much racket there must be something out of kilter. I think that between the Negroes of the South and the women of the North all talking about rights, the white women will be in a fix pretty soon. But what's all this talk about? That man over there says that women need to be helped into carriages and lifted over ditches, and to have the best place everywhere. Nobody ever helps me into carriages, or over mud puddles, or gives me any best place [and raising herself to her full height and her voice to a pitch like rolling thunder, she asked], and ar'n't I a woman? Look at me! Look at my arm! [and she bared her right arm to the shoulder, showing her tremendous muscular power.] I have plowed, and planted, and gathered into barns, and no man could head me—and ar'n't I a woman? I could work as much and eat as much as a man (when I could get it), and bear de lash as well—and ar'n't I a woman? I have borne thirteen children and seen most all sold off into slavery, and when I cried out with a mother's grief, none but Jesus heard—and ar'n't I a woman? [The cheering was long and loud.]

◆ FREDERICK DOUGLASS'S INDEPENDENCE DAY ADDRESS (1852)

In 1852, over three million African Americans were being held as slaves in the United States. Knowing this and understanding the irony implicit in the notion of a holiday commemorating the independence of the United States, Frederick Douglass lost little time in laying bare the contradiction inherent in allowing slavery to exist within a society professedly dedicated to individual freedom.

Fellow Citizens

Pardon me, and allow me to ask, why am I called upon to speak here today? What have I or those I represent to do with your national independence? Are the great principles of political freedom and of natural justice, embodied in that Declaration of Independence, extended to us? And am I, therefore, called upon to bring our humble offering to the national altar, and to confess the benefits, and express devout gratitude for the blessings resulting from your independence to us?

Would to God, both for your sakes and ours, that an affirmative answer could be truthfully returned to these questions. Then would my task be light, and my burden easy and delightful. For who is there so cold that a nation's sympathy could not warm him? Who so obdurate and dead to the claims of gratitude, that would not thankfully acknowledge such priceless benefits? Who so stolid and selfish that would not give his voice to swell the hallelujahs of a nation's jubilee, when the chains of servitude had been torn from his limbs? I am not that man. . .

I am not included within the pale of this glorious anniversary! Your high independence only reveals the immeasurable distance between us. The blessings in which you this day rejoice are not enjoyed in common. The rich inheritance of justice, liberty, prosperity, and independence bequeathed by your fathers is shared by you, not by me. The sunlight that brought life and healing to you has brought stripes and death to me. This Fourth of July is *yours*, not *mine*. You may rejoice, I must mourn. To drag a man in fetters into the grand illuminated temple of liberty, and call upon him to join you in joyous anthems, were inhuman mockery and sacrilegious irony. Do you mean, citizens, to mock me, by asking me to speak today?. . .

Fellow citizens, above your national, tumultuous joy, I hear the mournful wail of millions, whose chains, heavy and grievous yesterday, are today rendered more intolerable by the jubilant shouts that reach them. If I do forget, if I do not remember those bleeding children of sorrow this day, "may my right hand forget her cunning, and may my tongue cleave to the roof of my mouth!" To forget them, to pass lightly over their wrongs, and to chime in with the popular theme, would be treason most scandalous and shocking, and would make me a reproach before God and the world. My subject, then, fellow citizens, is "American Slavery." I shall see this day and its popular characteristics from the slave's point of view. Standing here, identified with the American bondman, making his wrongs mine, I do not hesitate to declare, with all my soul, that the character and conduct of this nation never looked blacker to me than on this Fourth of July. Whether we turn to the declarations of the past, or to the professions of the present, the conduct of the nation seems equally hideous and revolting. America is false to the past, false to the present, and solemnly binds herself to be false to the future. Standing with God and the crushed and bleeding slave on this occasion, I will, in the name of humanity, which is outraged, in the name of Liberty, which is fettered, in the name of the Constitution and the Bible, which are disregarded and trampled upon, dare to call in question and to denounce, with all the emphasis I can command, everything that serves to perpetuate slavery—the great sin and shame of America! "I will not equivocate; I will not excuse"; I will use the severest language I can command, and yet not one word shall escape me that any man, whose judgment is not blinded by prejudice, or who is not at heart a slave-holder, shall not confess to be right and just.

But I fancy I hear some of my audience say it is just in this circumstances that you and your brother Abolitionists fail to make a favorable impression on the public mind. Would you argue more and denounce less, would you persuade more and rebuke less, your cause would be much more likely to succeed. But, I submit, where all is plain there is nothing to be argued. What point in the anti-slavery creed would you have me argue? On what branch of the subject do the people of this country need light? Must I undertake to prove that the slave is a man? That point is conceded already. Nobody doubts it. The slave-holders themselves acknowledge it in the enactment of laws for their government. They acknowledge it when they punish disobedience on the part of the slave. There are seventy-two crimes in the State of Virginia, which, if committed by a black man (no matter how ignorant he be), subject him to the punishment of death,

while only two of these same crimes will subject a white man to like punishment. What is this but the acknowledgment that the slave is a moral, intellectual, and responsible being? The manhood of the slave is conceded. It is admitted in the fact that the Southern statute-books are covered with enactments, forbidding, under severe fines and penalties, the teaching of the slave to read and write. When you can point to any such laws in reference to the beasts of the field, then I may consent to argue the manhood of the slave. When the dogs in your streets, when the fowls of the air, when the cattle on your hills, when the fish of the sea, and the reptiles that crawl, shall be unable to distinguish the slave from a brute, then I will argue with you that the slave is a man!

For the present it is enough to affirm the equal manhood of the Negro race. Is it not astonishing that, while we are plowing, planting, and reaping, using all kinds of mechanical tools, erecting houses, constructing bridges, building ships, working in metals of brass, iron, copper, silver, and gold; that while we are reading, writing, and ciphering, acting as clerks, merchants, and secretaries, having among us lawyers, doctors, ministers, poets, authors, editors, orators, and teachers; that while we are engaged in all the enterprises common to other men—digging gold in California, capturing the whale in the Pacific, feeding sheep and cattle on the hillside, living, moving, acting, thinking, planning, living in families as husbands, wives, and children, and above all, confessing and worshipping the Christian God, and looking hopefully for life and immortality beyond the grave—we are called upon to prove that we are men?

Would you have me argue that man is entitled to liberty? That he is the rightful owner of his own body? You have already declared it. Must I argue the wrongfulness of slavery? Is that a question for republicans? Is it to be settled by the rules of logic and argumentation, as a matter beset with great difficulty, involving a doubtful application of the principle of justice, hard to understand? How should I look today in the presence of Americans, dividing and subdividing a discourse, to show that men have a natural right to freedom, speaking of it relatively and positively, negatively and affirmatively? To do so would be to make myself ridiculous, and to offer an insult to your understanding. There is not a man beneath the canopy of heaven who does not know that slavery is wrong *for him.*

What! Am I to argue that it is wrong to make men brutes, to rob them of their liberty, to work them without wages, to keep them ignorant of their relations to their fellow men, to beat them with sticks, to flay their flesh with the lash, to load their limbs with irons, to hunt them with dogs, to sell them at auction, to sunder their families, to knock out their teeth, to burn their flesh, to starve them into obedience and submission to their masters? Must I argue that a system thus marked with blood and stained with pollution is wrong? No; I will not. I have better employment for my time and strength than such arguments would imply.

What, then, remains to be argued? Is it that slavery is not divine; that God did not establish it; that our doctors of divinity are mistaken? There is blasphemy in the thought. That which is inhuman cannot be divine. Who can reason on such a proposition? They that can, may; I cannot. The time for such argument is past.

At a time like this, scorching irony, not convincing argument, is needed. Oh! had I the ability, and could I reach the nation's ear, I would today pour out a fiery stream of biting ridicule, blasting reproach, withering sarcasm, and stern rebuke. For it is not light that is needed, but fire; it is not the gentle shower, but thunder. We need the storm, the whirlwind, and the earthquake. The feeling of the nation must be quickened; the conscience of the nation must be startled; the hypocrisy of the nation must be exposed; and its crimes against God and man must be denounced.

What to the American slave is your Fourth of July? I answer, a day that reveals to him more than all other days of the year, the gross injustice and cruelty to which he is the constant victim. To him your celebration is a sham; your boasted liberty an unholy license; your national greatness, swelling vanity; your sounds of rejoicing are empty and heartless; your denunciation of tyrants, brass-fronted impudence; your shouts of liberty and equality, hollow mockery; your prayers and hymns, your sermons and thanksgivings, with all your religious parade and solemnity, are to him mere bombast, fraud, deception, impiety, and hypocrisy—a thin veil to cover up crimes which would disgrace a nation of savages. There is not a nation of the earth guilty of practices more shocking and bloody than are the people of these United States at this very hour.

Go where you may, search where you will, roam through all the monarchies and despotisms of the Old World, travel through South America, search out every abuse and when you have found the last, lay your facts by the side of the every-day practices of this nation, and you will say with me that, for revolting barbarity and shameless hypocrisy, America reigns without a rival.

◆ DRED SCOTT V. SANDFORD 19 HOWARD 393 (1857)

In 1835, Dred Scott, born a slave in Virginia, became the property of John Emerson, an Army doctor, in the slave state of Missouri. From there, he was taken into the free state of Illinois and later to the free territory of Minnesota. In 1847, Scott instituted suit in the circuit court of St. Louis County, Missouri, arguing that he should be given his freedom by virtue of his having resided on free soil. After nine years, his case was certified to the U.S. Supreme Court, where five of the nine justices were Southerners.

Under the terms of the Missouri Compromise, Missouri was allowed to join the Union with a slave population of almost 10,000; Maine was admitted as a free state. However, the compromise also prohibited the expansion of slavery into any part of the Louisiana Territory north of Latitude 36 °30'. It was here, into Illinois and the territory of Wisconsin, that Dred Scott's master brought him, and in 1846 Scott sued his master for his freedom.

After numerous delays, trials, and retrials, the case reached the U.S. Supreme Court in 1856. Hearing this case, the Court was not only faced with the question as to whether Scott was a free man, as a result of his sojourn in a free territory, but it also had to consider whether Congress had the authority under the Constitution to outlaw slavery in the territories. Although each of the nine justices delivered a separate opinion, the opinion of Chief Justice Roger Brooke Taney has been generally accepted as the Court's ruling on the matter.

In delivering his opinion, Chief Justice Roger Brooke Taney declared that, by virtue of both the Declaration of Independence and the Constitution, African Americans could not be regarded as citizens of the United States. Moreover, the Court could not deprive slaveholders of their right to take slaves into any part of the Union, North or South. In effect, therefore, the Missouri Compromise, as well as other anti-slavery legislation, was declared to be unconstitutional.

The question is simply this: Can a negro, whose ancestors were imported into this country and sold as slaves, become a member of the political community formed and brought into existence by the constitution of the United States, and as such become entitled to all the rights, and privileges, and immunities, guaranteed by that instrument to the citizen?. . . .

The words "people of the United States" and "citizens" are synonymous terms, and mean the same thing. They both describe the political body who, according to our republican institutions, form the sovereignty, and who hold the power and conduct the government through their representatives. They are what we familiarly call the "sovereign people," and every citizen is one of this people, and a constituent member of this sovereignty. The question before us is, whether the class of persons described in the plea in abatement compose a portion of this people, and are constituent members of this sovereignty? We think they are not, and that they are not included, and were not intended to be included, under the word "citizens" in the constitution, and can therefore claim none of the rights and privileges which that instrument provides for and secures to citizens of the United States. On the contrary, they were at that time considered as a subordinate and inferior class of beings, who had been subjugated by the dominant race, and, whether emancipated or not, yet remained subject to their authority, and had no rights or privileges. . . .

It is not the province of the court to decide upon the justice or injustice, the policy or impolicy, of these laws. The decision of that question belonged to the political or law-making power; to those who formed the sovereignty and framed the constitution. The duty of the court is to interpret the instrument they have framed, with the best lights we can obtain on the subject, and to administer it as we find it, according to its true intent and meaning when it was adopted.

In discussing this question, we must not confound the rights of citizenship which a State may confer within its own limits, and the rights of citizenship as member of the Union. It does not by any means follow, because he has all the rights and privileges of a citizen of a State, that he must be a citizen of the United States. He may have all of the rights and privileges of the citizen of a State, and yet not be entitled to the rights and privileges of a citizen in any other State. For, previous to the adoption of the constitution of the United States, every State had the undoubted right to confer on whomsoever it pleased the character of citizen, and to endow him with all its rights. But this character of course was confined to the boundaries of the State, and gave him no rights or privileges in other States beyond those secured to him by the laws of nations and the comity of States. Nor have the several States surrendered the power of conferring these rights and privileges by adopting the constitution of United States. . . .

It is very clear, therefore, that no State can, by any act or law of its own, passed since the adoption of the constitution, introduce a new member into the political community created by the constitution of the United States. It cannot make him a member of this community by making him a member of its own. And for the same reason it cannot introduce any person, or description of persons, who were not intended to be embraced in this new political family, which the constitution brought into existence, but were intended to be excluded from it.

The question then arises, whether the provisions of the constitution, in relation to the personal rights and privileges to which the citizen of a State should be entitled, embraced the negro African race, at that time in this country, or who might afterwards be imported, who had then or should afterwards be made free in any State;

and to put it in the power of a single State to make him a citizen of the United States, and endue him with the full rights of citizenship in every other State without consent? Does the constitution of the United States act upon him whenever he shall be made free under the laws of a State, and raised there to the rank of a citizen, and immediately clothe him with all the privileges of a citizen in every other State, and in its own courts?

The court thinks the affirmative of these propositions cannot be maintained. And if it cannot, the plaintiff in error could not be a citizen of the State of Missouri, within the meaning of the constitution of the United States, and, consequently, was not entitled to sue in its courts.

It is true, every person, and every class and description of persons, who were at the time of the adoption of the constitution recognized as citizens in the several States, became also citizens of this new political body; but none other; it was formed by them, and for them and their posterity, but for no one else. And the personal rights and privileges guaranteed to citizens of this new sovereignty were intended to embrace those only who were then members of the several State communities, or who should afterwards by birthright or otherwise become members, according to the provisions of the constitution and the principles on which it was founded. . . .

In the opinion of the court, the legislation and histories of the times, and the language used in the declaration of independence, show, that neither the class of persons who had been imported as slaves, nor their descendants, whether they had become free or not, were then acknowledged as a part of the people, nor intended to be included in the general words used in that memorable instrument. . . .

. . . The government of the United States had no right to interfere for any other purpose but that protecting the rights of the owner, leaving it altogether with the several States to deal with this race, whether emancipated or not, as each State may think justice, humanity, and the interests and safety of society, require. . . .

The act of Congress, upon which the plaintiff relies, declares that slavery and involuntary servitude, except as a punishment for crime, shall be forever prohibited in all that part of the territory ceded by France, under the name of Louisiana, which lies north of thirty-six degrees thirty minutes north latitude and not included within the limits of Missouri. And the difficulty which meets us at the threshold of this part of the inquiry is whether Congress was authorized to pass this law under any of the powers granted to it by the Constitution; for, if the authority is not given by that instrument, it is the duty of this Court to declare it void and inoperative and incapable of conferring freedom upon anyone who is held as a slave under the laws of any one of the states. . . .

We do not mean . . . to question the power of Congress in this respect. The power to expand the territory of the United States by the admission of new states is plainly given; and in the construction of this power by all the departments of the government, it has been held to authorize the acquisition of territory, not fit for admission at the time, but to be admitted as soon as its population and situation would entitle it to admission. It is acquired to become a state and not to be held as a colony and governed by Congress with absolute Authority; and, as the propriety of admitting a new state is committed to the sound discretion of Congress, the power to acquire territory for that purpose, to be held by the United States until it is in a suitable condition to become a state upon an equal footing with the other states, must rest upon the same discretion. . . .

But the power of Congress over the person or property of a citizen can never be a mere discretionary power under our Constitution and form of government. The powers of the government and the rights and privileges of the citizen are regulated and plainly defined by the Constitution itself. . . .

These powers, and others, in relation to rights of person, which it is not necessary here to enumerate, are, in express and positive terms, denied to the general government; and the rights of private property have been guarded with equal care. Thus the rights of property are united with the rights of person and placed on the same ground by the Fifth Amendment to the Constitution, which provides that no person shall be deprived of life, liberty, and property without due process of law. And an act of Congress which deprives a citizen of the United States of his liberty of property, without due process of law, merely because he came himself or brought his property into a particular territory of the United States, and who had committed no offense against the law, could hardly be dignified with the name of due process of law. . . .

It seems, however, to be supposed that there is a difference between property in a slave and other property and that different rules may be applied to it in expounding Constitution of the United States. And the laws and usages of nations, and the writings of eminent jurists upon the relation of master and slave and their mutual rights and duties, and the powers which governments may exercise over it, have been dwelt upon in the argument.

But, in considering the question before us, it must be borne in mind that there is no law of nations standing between the people of the United States and their government and interfering with their relation to each other. The powers of the government and the rights of the citizen under it are positive and practical regulations plainly written down. The people of the United States have delegated to it certain enumerated powers and forbidden it to exercise others. It has no power over the person of property of a citizen but what the citizens of the United States have granted. And no laws or usages of other nations, or reasoning of statesmen of jurists upon the relations of master and slave, can enlarge the powers of the government or take from the citizens the rights they have reserved. And if the Constitution recognizes the right of property of the master in a slave, and makes no distinction between that description of property and other property owned by a citizen, no tribunal, acting under the authority of the United States, whether it be legislative, executive, or judicial, has a right to draw such a distinction or deny to it the benefit of the provisions and guaranties which have been provided for the protection of private property against the encroachments of the government.

Now, as we have already said in an earlier part of this opinion, upon a different point, the right of property in a slave is distinctly and expressly affirmed in the Constitution. The right to traffic in it, like an ordinary article of merchandise and property, was guaranteed to the citizens of the United States, in every state that might desire it, for twenty years. And the government in express terms is pledged to protect it in all future time if the slave escapes from his owner. That is done in plain words—too plain to be misunderstood. And no word can be found in the Constitution which gives Congress a greater power over slave property or which entitles property of that kind to less protection than property of any other description. The only power conferred is the power coupled with the duty of guarding and protecting the owner in his rights.

Upon these considerations it is the opinion of the court that the act of Congress which prohibited a citizen from holding and owning property of this kind in the territory of the United States north of the line therein mentioned is not warranted by the Constitution and is therefore void; and that neither Dred Scott himself, nor any of his family, were made free by being carried into this territory; even if they had been carried there by the owner with the intention of becoming a permanent resident. . . .

◆ THE EMANCIPATION PROCLAMATION NO. 17, 12 STAT. 1268 (1863)

In an attempt to bring an end to the Civil War, President Abraham Lincoln, acting on his authority as

President Abraham Lincoln seated with several other men during the first reading of the Emancipation Proclamation (The Library of Congress).

commander-in-chief, on September 22, 1862 issued a warning that slavery would be abolished in any state that continued to rebel. With the war still raging, Lincoln issued the Emancipation Proclamation on January 1, 1863, freeing slaves in those states that had seceded from the Union. The proclamation did not apply, however, to those areas occupied by Union forces—there remained some 800,000 slaves unaffected by the provisions of the document.

By the President of the United States of America: A Proclamation

Whereas on the 22d day of September, A.D. 1862, a proclamation was issued by the President of the United States, containing, among other things, the following, to wit:

"That on the 1st day of January, A.D. 1863, all persons held as slaves within any State or designated part of a State the people whereof shall then be in rebellion against the United States shall be then, henceforward, and forever free; and the executive government of the United States, including the military and naval authority thereof, will recognize and maintain the freedom of such persons and will do no act or acts to repress such

persons, or any of them, in any efforts they may make for their actual freedom."

"That the executive will on the 1st day of January aforesaid, by proclamation, designated the States and parts of States, if any, which the people thereof, respectively, shall then be in rebellion against the United States; and the fact that any State or the people thereof shall on that day be in good faith represented in the Congress of the United States by members chosen thereto at elections wherein a majority of the qualified voters of such States shall have participated shall, in the absence of strong countervailing testimony, be deemed conclusive evidence that such State and the people thereof are not then in rebellion against the United States.":

Now, therefore, I, Abraham Lincoln, President of the United States, by virtue of the power in me vested as Commander-in-Chief of the Army and Navy of the United States in time of actual armed rebellion against the authority and government of the United States, and as a fit and necessary war measure for suppressing said rebellion, do, on this 1st day of January, A.D. 1863, and in accordance with my purpose so to do, publicly proclaimed for the full period of one hundred days from the first day above mentioned, order and designate as the States and parts of States wherein the people thereof, respectively, are this day in rebellion against the United States the following, to wit:

Arkansas, Texas, Louisiana (except the parishes of St. Bernard, Plaquemines, Jefferson, St. John, St. Charles, St. James, Ascension, Assumption, Terrebonne, Lafourche, St. Mary, St. Marti, and Orleans, including the city of New Orleans), Mississippi, Alabama, Florida, Georgia, South Carolina, North Carolina, and Virginia (except the forty-eight counties designated as West Virginia, and also the counties of Berkeley, Accomac, Northampton, Elizabeth City, York, Princess Anne, and Northfolk, including the cities of Norfolk and Portsmouth), and which excepted parts are for the present left precisely as if this proclamation were not issued.

And by virtue of the power and for the purpose aforesaid, I do order and declare that all persons held as slaves within said designated States and parts of States are, and henceforward shall be, free; and that the Executive Government of the United States, including the military and naval authorities thereof, will recognize and maintain the freedom of said persons.

And I hereby enjoin upon the people so declared to be free to abstain from all violence, unless in necessary self-defense; and I recommend to them that, in all cases when allowed, they labor faithfully for reasonable wages.

And I further declare and make known that such persons of suitable condition will be received into the armed service of the United States to garrison forts, positions, stations, and other places, and to man vessels of all sorts in said service.

And upon this act, sincerely believed to be an act of justice, warranted by the Constitution upon military necessity, I invoke the considerate judgment of mankind and the gracious favor of Almighty God.

◆ FREEDMEN'S BUREAU ACT CH. 90, 13 STAT. 507 (1865)

On March 3, 1865, Congress passed legislation designed to provide basic health and educational services to former slaves and to administer abandoned land in the South. Under the act, the Bureau of Refugees, Freedmen and Abandoned Lands, commonly referred to as the Freedmen's Bureau, was created.

An Act to Establish a Bureau for the Relief of Freedmen and Refugees

Be it enacted, That there is hereby established in the War Department, to continue during the present war of rebellion, and for one year thereafter, a bureau of refugees, freedmen, and abandoned lands, to which shall be committed, as hereinafter provided, the supervision and management of all abandoned lands and the control of all subjects relating to refugees and freedmen from rebel states, or from any district of country within the territory embraced in the operations of the army, under such rules and regulations as may be prescribed by the head of the bureau and approved by the President. The said bureau shall be under the management and control of a commissioner to be appointed by the President, by and with the advice and consent of the Senate.

Section 2. That the Secretary of War may direct such issue of provisions, clothing, and fuel, as he may deem needful for the immediate and temporary shelter and supply of destitute and suffering refugees and freedmen and their wives and children, under such rules and regulations as he may direct.

Section 3. That the President may, by and with the advice and consent of the Senate, appoint an assistant commissioner for each of the states declared to be in insurrection, not exceeding ten in number, who shall, under the direction of the commissioner, aid in the execution of the provisions of this act. . . . And any military officer may be detailed and assigned to duty under this act without increase of pay of allowances. . . .

Section 4. That the commissioner, under the direction of the President, shall have authority to set apart, for the use of loyal refugees and freedmen, such tracts of land within the insurrectionary states as shall have been abandoned, or to which the United States shall have acquired title by confiscation or sale, or otherwise, and to every male citizen, whether refugee or freedman, as aforesaid, there shall be assigned not more than forty acres of such land, and the person to whom it was so assigned shall be protected in the use and enjoyment of the land for the term of three years at an annual rent not exceeding six per centum upon the value of such land, as it was appraised by the state authorities in the year eighteen hundred and sixty, for the purpose of taxation, and in case no such appraisal can be found, then the rental shall be based upon the estimated value of the land in said year, to be ascertained in such manner as the commissioner may by regulation prescribe. At the end of said term, or at any time during said term, the occupants of any parcels so assigned may purchase the land and receive such title thereto as the United States can convey, upon paying therefor the value of the land, as ascertained and fixed for the purpose of determining the annual rent aforesaid. . . .

◆ AMENDMENT THIRTEEN TO THE UNITED STATES CONSTITUTION (1865)

Ratified December 18, 1865, the Thirteenth Amendment formally abolishes slavery within the United States.

Section 1. Neither slavery nor involuntary servitude, except as a punishment for crime whereof the party shall have been duly convicted, shall exist within the United States, or any place subject to their jurisdiction.

Section 2. Congress shall have power to enforce this article by appropriate legislation.

◆ BLACK CODES OF MISSISSIPPI (1865)

Following emancipation many states sought to impose restrictions on African Americans to prevent them from enjoying equal social status with whites. These restrictions were designed to not only hold African Americans in a subordinate condition, but to impose restrictions upon them not unlike those which prevailed before the Civil War. Black codes imposed heavy penalties for "vagrancy," "insulting gestures," curfew violations, and "seditious speeches." In November of 1865, Mississippi was the first state to enact such laws.

An Act to Confer Civil Rights on Freedmen, and for other Purposes

Section 1. All freedmen, free negroes and mulattoes may sue and be sued, implead and be impleaded, in all the courts of law and equity of this State, and may acquire personal property, and choses in action, by descent or purchase, and may dispose of the same in the same manner and to the same extent that white persons may: Provided, That the provisions of this section shall not be so construed as to allow any freedman, free negro or mulatto to rent or lease any lands or tenements except in incorporated cities or towns, in which places the corporate authorities shall control the same.

Section 2. All freedmen, free negroes and mulattoes may intermarry with each other, in the same manner and under the same regulations that are provided by law for white persons: Provided, that the clerk of probate shall keep separate records of the same.

Section 3. All freedmen, free negroes or mulattoes who do now and have herebefore lived and cohabited together as husband and wife shall be taken and held in law as legally married, and the issue shall be taken and held as legitimate for all purposes; and it shall not be lawful for any freedman, free negro or mulatto to intermarry with any white person; nor for any person to intermarry with any freedman, free negro or mulatto; and any person who shall so intermarry shall be deemed guilty of felony, and on conviction thereof shall be confined in the State penitentiary for life; and those shall be deemed freedmen, free negroes and mulattoes who are of pure negro blood, and those descended from a negro to the third generation, inclusive, though one ancestor in each generation may have been a white person.

Section 4. In addition to cases in which freedmen, free negroes and mulattoes are now by law competent witnesses, freedmen, free negroes or mulattoes shall be competent in civil cases, when a party or parties to the suit, either plaintiff or plaintiffs, defendant or defendants; also in cases where freedmen, free negroes and mulattoes is or are either plaintiff or plaintiffs, defendant or defendants. They shall also be competent witnesses in all criminal prosecutions where the crime charged is alleged to have been committed by a white person upon or against the person or property of a freedman, free negro or mulatto: Provided, that in all cases said witnesses shall be examined in open court, on the stand; except, however, they may be examined before the grand jury, and shall in all cases be subject to the rules and tests of the common law as to competency and credibility.

Section 5. Every freedman, free negro and mulatto shall, on the second Monday of January, one thousand eight hundred and sixty-six, and annually thereafter, have a lawful home or employment, and shall have written evidence thereof as follows, to wit: if living in any incorporated city, town, or village, a license from the mayor thereof; and if living outside of an incorporated city, town, or village, from the member of the board of police of his beat, authorizing him or her to do irregular and job work; or a written contract, as provided in Section 6 in this act; which license may be revoked for cause at any time by the authority granting the same.

Section 6. All contracts for labor made with freedmen, free negroes and mulattoes for a longer period than one month shall be in writing, and a duplicate, attested and read to said freedman, free negro or mulatto by a beat, city or county officer, or two disinterested white persons of the county in which the labor is to be performed, of which each party shall have one: and said contracts shall be taken and held as entire contracts, and if the laborer shall quit the service of the employer before the expiration of his term of service, without good cause, he shall forfeit his wages for that year up to the time of quitting.

Section 7. Every civil officer shall, and every person may, arrest and carry back to his or her legal employer any freedman, free negro, or mulatto who shall have quit the service of his or her employer before the expiration of his or her term of service without good cause; and said officer and person shall be entitled to receive for arresting and carrying back every deserting employee aforesaid the sum of five dollars, and ten cents per mile from the place of arrest to the place of delivery; and the same shall be paid by the employer, and held as a set off for so much against the wages of said deserting employee: Provided, that said arrested party, after being so returned, may appeal to the justice of the peace or member of the board of police of the county, who, on notice to the alleged employer, shall try summarily whether said appellant is legally employed by the alleged employer, and has good cause to quit said employer. Either party shall have the right of appeal to the county court, pending which the alleged deserter shall be remanded to the alleged employer or otherwise disposed of, as shall be right and just; and the decision of the county court shall be final.

Section 8. Upon affidavit made by the employer of any freedman, free negro or mulatto, or other credible person, before any justice of the peace or member of the board of police, that any freedman, free negro or mulatto legally employed by said employer has illegally deserted said employment, such justice of the peace or member of the board of police issue his warrant or warrants, returnable before himself or other such officer, to any sheriff, constable or special deputy, commanding him to arrest said deserter, and return him or her to said employer, and the like proceedings shall be had as provided in the preceding section; and it shall be lawful for any officer to whom such warrant shall be directed to execute said warrant in any county in this State; and that said warrant may be transmitted without endorsement to any like officer of another county, to be executed and returned as aforesaid; and the said employer shall pay the costs of said warrants and arrest and return, which shall be set off for so much against the wages of said deserter.

Section 9. If any person shall persuade or attempt to persuade, entice, or cause any freedman, free negro or mulatto to desert from the legal employment of any person before the expiration of his or her term of service, or shall knowingly employ any such deserting freedman, free negro or mulatto, or shall knowingly give or sell to any such deserting freedman, free negro or mulatto, any food, raiment, or other thing, he or she shall be guilty of a misdemeanor, and, upon conviction, shall be fined not less than twenty-five dollars and not more than two hundred dollars and costs; and if the said fine and costs shall not be immediately paid, the court shall sentence said convict to not exceeding two months imprisonment in the county jail, and he or she shall

moreover be liable to the party injured in damages: Provided, if any person shall, or shall attempt to, persuade, entice, or cause any freedman, free negro or mulatto to desert from any legal employment of any person, with the view to employ said freedman, free negro or mulatto without the limits of this State, such costs; and if said fine and costs shall not be immediately paid, the court shall sentence said convict to not exceeding six months imprisonment in the county jail.

Section 10. It shall be lawful for any freedman, free negro, or mulatto, to charge any white person, freedman, free negro or mulatto by affidavit, with any criminal offense against his or her person or property, and upon such affidavit the proper process shall be issued and executed as if said affidavit was made by a white person, and it shall be lawful for any freedman, free negro, or mulatto, in any action, suit or controversy pending, or about to be instituted in any court of law equity in this State, to make all needful and lawful affidavits as shall be necessary for the institution, prosecution or defense of such suit or controversy.

Section 11. The penal laws of this state, in all cases not otherwise specially provided for, shall apply and extend to all freedmen, free negroes and mulattoes. . . .

An Act to Regulate the Relation of Master and Apprentice, as Relates to Freedmen, Free Negroes, and Mulattoes

Section 1. It shall be the duty of all sheriffs, justices of the peace, and other civil officers of the several counties in this State, to report to the probate courts of their respective counties semiannually, at the January and July terms of said courts, all freedmen, free negroes, and mulattoes, under the age of eighteen, in their respective counties, beats, or districts, who are orphans, or whose parent or parents have not the means or who refuse to provide for and support said minors; and thereupon it shall be the duty of said probate court to order the clerk of said court to apprentice said minors to some competent and suitable person on such terms as the court may direct, having a particular care to the interest of said minor: Provided, that the former owner of said minors shall have the preference when, in the opinion of the court, he or she shall be a suitable person for that purpose.

Section 2. The said court shall be fully satisfied that the person or persons to whom said minor shall be apprenticed shall be a suitable person to have the charge and care of said minor, and fully to protect the interest of said minor. The said court shall require the said master or mistress to execute bond and security, payable to the State of Mississippi, conditioned that he or she shall furnish said minor with sufficient food and clothing; to treat said minor humanely; furnish medical attention in case of sickness; teach, or cause to be taught, him or her to read and write, if under fifteen years old, and will conform to any law that may be hereafter passed for the regulation of the duties and relation of master and apprentice: Provided, that said apprentice shall be bound by indenture, in case of males, until they are twenty-one years old, and in case of females until they are eighteen years old.

Section 3. In the management and control of said apprentices, said master or mistress shall have the power to inflict such moderate corporeal chastisement as a father or guardian is allowed to infliction on his or her child or ward at common law: Provided, that in no case shall cruel or inhuman punishment be inflicted.

Section 4. If any apprentice shall leave the employment of his or her master or mistress, without his or her consent, said master or mistress may pursue and recapture said apprentice, and bring him or her before any justice of the peace of the county, whose duty it shall be to remand said apprentice to the service of his or her master or mistress; and in the event of a refusal on the part of said apprentice so to return, then said justice shall commit said apprentice to the jail of said county, on failure to give bond, to the next term of the county court; and it shall be the duty of said court at the first term thereafter to investigate said case, and if the court shall be of opinion that said apprentice left the employment of his or her master or mistress without good cause, to order him or her to be punished, as provided for the punishment of hired freedmen, as may be from time to time provided for by law for desertion, until he or she shall agree to return to the service of his or her master or mistress: Provided, that the court may grant continuances as in other cases: And provided further, that if the court shall believe that said apprentice had good cause to quit his said master or mistress, the court shall discharge said apprentice from said indenture, and also enter a judgment against the master or mistress for not more than one hundred dollars, for the use and benefit of said apprentice, to be collected on execution as in other cases.

Section 5. If any person entice away any apprentice from his or her master or mistress, or shall knowingly employ an apprentice, or furnish him or her food or clothing without the written consent of his or her master or mistress, or shall sell or give said apprentice spirits without such consent, said person so offending shall be guilty of a misdemeanor, and shall, upon conviction there of before the county court, be punished as provided for the punishment of persons enticing from their employer hired freedmen, free negroes or mulattoes.

Section 6. It shall be the duty of all civil officers of their respective counties to report any minors within their respective counties to said probate court who are subject to be apprenticed under the provisions of this act, from time to time as the facts may come to their knowledge, and it shall be the duty of said court from time to time as said minors shall be reported to them, or otherwise come to their knowledge, to apprentice said minors as hereinbefore provided.

Section 9. It shall be lawful for any freedman, free negro, or mulatto, having a minor child or children, to apprentice the said minor child or children, as provided for by this act.

Section 10. In all cases where the age of the freedman, free negro, or mulatto cannot be ascertained by record testimony, the judge of the county court shall fix the age. . . .

An Act to Amend the Vagrant Laws of the State

Section 1. All rogues and vagabonds, idle and dissipated persons, beggars, jugglers, or persons practicing unlawful games or plays, runaways, common drunkards, common night-walkers, pilferers, lewd, wanton, or lascivious persons, in speech or behavior, common railers and brawlers, persons who neglect their calling or employment, misspend what they earn, or do not provide for the support of themselves or their families, or dependents, and all other idle and disorderly persons, including all who neglect all lawful business, habitually misspend their time by frequenting houses of ill-fame, gaming-houses, or tippling shops, shall be deemed and considered vagrants, under the provisions of this act, and upon conviction thereof shall be fined not exceeding one hundred dollars, with all accruing costs, and be imprisoned, at the discretion of the court, not exceeding ten days.

Section 2. All freedmen, free negroes and mulattoes in this State, over the age of eighteen years, found on the second Monday in January, 1866, or thereafter, with no lawful employment or business, or found unlawfully assembling themselves together, either in the day or night time, and all white persons assembling themselves with freedmen, free negroes or mulattoes, or usually associating with freedmen, free negroes or mulattoes, on terms of equality, or living in adultery or fornication with a freed woman, freed negro or mulatto, shall be deemed vagrants, and on conviction thereof shall be fined in a sum not exceeding, in the case of a freedman, free negro or mulatto, fifty dollars, and a white man two hundred dollars, and imprisonment at the discretion of the court, the free negro not exceeding ten days, and the white man not exceeding six months.

Section 3. All justices of the peace, mayors, and aldermen of incorporated towns, counties, and cities of the several counties in this State shall have jurisdiction to try all questions of vagrancy in their respective towns, counties, and cities, and it is hereby made their duty, whenever they shall ascertain that any person or persons in their respective towns, and counties and cities are violating any of the provisions of this act, to have said party or parties arrested, and brought before them, and immediately investigate said charge, and, on conviction, punish said party or parties, as provided for herein. And it is hereby made the duty of all sheriffs, constables, town constables, and all such like officers, and city marshals, to report to some officer having jurisdiction all violations of any of the provisions of this act, and in case any officer shall fail or neglect any duty herein it shall be the duty of the county court to fine said officer, upon conviction, not exceeding one hundred dollars, to be paid into the county treasury for county purposes.

Section 4. Keepers of gaming houses, houses of prostitution, prostitutes, public or private, and all persons who derive their chief support in the employments that militate against good morals, or against law, shall be deemed and held to be vagrants.

Section 5. All fines and forfeitures collected by the provisions of this act shall be paid into the county treasury for general county purposes, and in case of any freedman, free negro or mulatto shall fail for five days after the imposition of any or forfeiture upon him or her for violation of any of the provisions of this act to pay the same, that it shall be, and is hereby, made the duty of the sheriff of the proper county to hire out said freedman, free negro or mulatto, to any person who will, for the shortest period of service, pay said fine and forfeiture and all costs: Provided, a preference shall be given to the employer, if there be one, in which case the employer shall be entitled to deduct and retain the amount so paid from the wages of such freedman, free negro or mulatto, then due or to become due; and in case freedman, free negro or mulatto cannot hire out, he or she may be dealt with as a pauper.

Section 6. The same duties and liabilities existing among white persons of this State shall attach to freedmen, free negroes or mulattoes, to support their indigent families and all colored paupers; and that in order to secure a support for such indigent freedmen, free negroes, or mulattoes, it shall be lawful, and is hereby made the duty of the county police of each county in this State, to levy a poll or capitation tax on each and every freedman, free negro, or mulatto, between the ages of eighteen and sixty years, not to exceed the sum of one dollar annually to each person so taxed, which tax, when collected, shall be paid into the county treasurer's hands, and constitute a fund to be called the Freedman's Pauper Fund, which shall be applied by the commissioners of the poor for the maintenance of the poor of the freedmen, free negroes and mulattoes of this State, under such regulations as may be established by the boards of county police in the respective counties of this State.

Section 7. If any freedman, free negro, or mulatto shall fail or refuse to pay any tax levied according to the provisions of the sixth section of this act, it shall be *prima facie* evidence of vagrancy, and it shall be the duty of the sheriff to arrest such freedman, free negro, or mulatto, or such person refusing or neglecting to pay such tax, and proceed at once to hire for the shortest time such delinquent taxpayer to any one who will pay the said tax, with accruing costs, giving preference to the employer, if there be one.

Section 8. Any person feeling himself or herself aggrieved by judgment of any justice of the peace, mayor, or alderman in cases arising under this act, may within five days appeal to the next term of the county court of the proper county, upon giving bond and security in a sum not less than twenty-five dollars nor more than one hundred and fifty dollars, conditioned to appear and prosecute said appeal, and abide by the judgment of the county court; and said appeal shall be tried *de novo* in the county court, and the decision of the said court shall be final. . . .

◆ CIVIL RIGHTS ACT CH. 31, 14 STAT. 27 (1866)

This act, enacted April 9, 1866, was designed to protect recently freed African Americans from black codes and other repressive state and local legislation. It was intended to provide all citizens with basic civil rights including the right to make and enforce contracts, to bring suits in court, to purchase and sell real and personal property, and to enjoy security of person and property.

An Act to protect all Persons in the United States in their Civil Rights, and furnish the Means of their Vindication

Be it enacted. . . That all persons born in the United States and not subject to any foreign power, excluding Indians not taxed, are hereby declared to be citizens of the United States; and such citizens, of every race and color, without regard to any previous condition of slavery or involuntary servitude, except as a punishment for crime whereof the party shall have been duly convicted, shall have the same right in every State and Territory in the United States, to make and enforce contracts, to sue, be parties, and give evidence, to inherit, purchase, lease, sell, hold, and convey real and personal property, and to full and equal benefit of all laws and proceedings for the security of person and property, as is enjoyed by white citizens, and shall be subject to like punishment, pains, and penalties, and to none other, any law, statute, ordinance, regulation, or custom, to the contrary notwithstanding.

Section 2. *And be it further enacted*, That any person who, under color or any law, statute, ordinance, regulation, or custom, shall subject, or cause to be subjected, any inhabitant of any State or Territory to the deprivation of any right secured or protected by this act, or to different punishment, pains, or penalties on account of such person having any time been held in a condition of slavery or involuntary servitude, except as a punishment for crime whereof the party shall have been duly convicted, or by reason of his color or race, than is prescribed for the punishment of white persons, shall be deemed guilty of a misdemeanor, and, on conviction, shall be punished by fine not exceeding one thousand dollars, or imprisonment not exceeding one year, or both, in the discretion of the court. . . .

◆ AMENDMENT FOURTEEN TO THE UNITED STATES CONSTITUTION (1868)

This amendment, ratified July 23, 1868, provided a definition of both national and state citizenship. When the Supreme Court heard the case Dred Scott v. Sandford *in 1857, it ruled that Africans imported into this country as slaves, and their descendants, were not and could never become citizens of the United States. The passage of the Fourteenth Amendment resolved the question of African American citizenship.*

The amendment also reversed what had been the traditional federal-state relationship in the area of citizen's rights. The Fourteenth Amendment provides for the protection of the privileges of national citizenship, and basic civil rights, and guarantees for all citizens equal protection under the law. It also provides the federal government with authority to intervene in cases where state governments have been accused of violating the constitutional rights of individuals.

Section 1. All persons born or naturalized in the United States, and subject to the jurisdiction thereof, are citizens of the United States and of the State wherein they reside. No state shall make or enforce any law which shall abridge the privileges or immunities of citizens of the United States; nor shall any State deprive any person of life, liberty, or property, without due process of law; nor deny to any person within its jurisdiction the equal protection of the laws.

Section 2. Representatives shall be apportioned among the several States according to their respective numbers, counting the whole number of persons in each State, excluding Indians not taxed. But when the right to vote at any election for the choice of electors for President and Vice President of the United States, Representatives in Congress, the Executive and Judicial officers of a State, or the members of the Legislature thereof, is denied to any of the male inhabitants of such State, being twenty-one years of age, and citizens of the United States, or in any way abridged, except for participation in rebellion, or other crime, the basis of representation therein shall be reduced in the proportion which the number of such male citizens shall bear to the whole number of male citizens twenty-one years of age in such State.

Section 3. No person shall be a Senator or Representative in Congress, or elector of President and Vice President, or hold any office, civil or military, under the United States, or under any State, who, having previously taken an oath, as a member of Congress, or as an office of the United States, or as a member of any State legislature, or as an executive or judicial officer of any State, to support the Constitution of the United States, shall have engaged in insurrection or rebellion against the same, or given aid or comfort to the enemies thereof. But Congress may by a vote of two-thirds of each House, remove such disability.

Section 4. The validity of the public debt of the United States, authorized by law, including debts incurred for payment of pensions and bounties for services in suppressing insurrection or rebellion, shall not be questioned. But neither the United States nor any State shall assume or pay any debt or obligation incurred in aid of insurrection or rebellion against the United States, or any claim for the loss or emancipation of any slave; but all such debts, obligations and claims shall be held illegal and void.

Section 5. The Congress shall have power to enforce, by appropriate legislation, the provisions of this article.

◆ AMENDMENT FIFTEEN TO THE UNITED STATES CONSTITUTION (1870)

The Fifteenth Amendment, ratified March 30, 1870, was intended to protect the right of all citizens to vote. However, the amendment was not successful in ending techniques designed to prevent African Americans from voting; many state and local governments continued to employ such tactics as the use of grandfather clauses, literacy tests, "white primaries," and poll taxes as prerequisites to, or deterrents to voting.

Section 1. The right of citizens of the United States to vote shall not be denied or abridged by the United States or by any State on account of race, color, or previous conditions of servitude.

Section 2. The Congress shall have power to enforce this article by appropriate legislation.

◆ KU KLUX KLAN ACT CH. 22, 17 STAT. 13 (1871)

Following the Civil War, white terrorist groups began to spring up throughout the South. These early organizations, consisting mainly of Confederate veterans still obsessed with the goals and aspirations of their Southern heritage, terrorized blacks who sought increased participation in their communities and whites who aided them. Known as the Knights of the White Camelia, the Jayhawkers, or the Ku Klux Klan, by 1871 these groups had become well organized. The Ku Klux Klan Act of 1871 was an attempt by Congress to end intimidation and violence by such organizations. The law, however, failed to exterminate the Klan or to eliminate the continued use of terrorist tactics against blacks and those whites who gave support to black concerns.

Be it enacted. . . that any person who, under color of any law, statute, ordinance, regulation, custom, or usage of any State, shall subject, or cause to be subjected, any person within the jurisdiction of the United States to the deprivation of any rights, privileges, or immunities secured by the Constitution of the United States; shall any such law, statute, ordinance, regulation, custom, or usage of the state to the contrary notwithstanding, be liable to the party injured in any action at law, suit in equity, or other proper proceeding for redress; such proceeding to be prosecuted in the several district or circuit courts of the United States, with and subject to the same rights of appeal, review upon error, and other remedies provided in like cases in such courts, under the provisions of the [Civil Rights Act of April 9, 1866]. . . and the other remedial laws of the United States which are in their nature applicable in such cases.

Section 2. That if two or more persons within any State or Territory of the United States shall conspire together to overthrow, or to put down, or to destroy by force the government of the United States, or to levy war against the United States or to oppose by force the authority of the government of the United States, or by force, intimidation, or threat to prevent. . . any person

from accepting or holding any office or trust or place of confidence under the United States, or from discharging the duties thereof. . . or to injure him in his person or property on account of his lawful discharge of the duties of his office, or to injure his person while engaged in the lawful discharge of the duties of his office, or. . . to deter any party or witness in any court of the United States from attending such court, or from testifying in any matter pending in such court fully, freely, and truthfully, or to injure any party or witness in his person or property on account of his having so attended or testified, or by force, intimidation, or threat to influence the verdict, presentment, or indictment, of any juror or grand juror in any court of the United States, or to injure such juror in his person or property on account of any verdict, presentment, or indictment lawfully assented to by him, or on account of his being or having been such juror, or shall conspire together, or go in disguise upon the public highway or upon the premises of another for the purpose, either directly or indirectly, of depriving any person or any class of persons of the equal protection of the laws, or of equal privileges or immunities under the laws, or for the purpose of preventing or hindering the constituted authorities of any State from giving or securing to all persons within such State the equal protection of the laws, or shall conspire together for the purpose of in any manner impeding, hindering, obstructing, or defeating the due course of justice in any State or Territory, with the intent to deny to any citizen of the United States the due and equal protection of the laws, or to injure any person in his person or in his property for lawfully enforcing the right of any person or class of persons to the equal protection of the laws, or by force, intimidation, or threat to prevent any citizen of the United States lawfully entitled to vote from giving his support or advocacy in a lawful manner. . . or to injure any such citizen in his person or property on account of such support or advocacy, each and every person so offending shall be deemed guilty of a high crime. . . .

Section 3. That in all cases where insurrection, domestic violence, unlawful combinations, or conspiracies in any State shall so obstruct or hinder the execution of the laws thereof, and of the United States, as to deprive any portion or class of the people of such State of any of the rights, privileges, or immunities, or protection, named in the Constitution and secured by this act, and the constituted authorities of such State shall either be unable to protect, or shall from any cause fail in or refuse protection of the people in such rights, such facts will be deemed a denial by such State of the equal protection of the laws to which they are entitled under the Constitution of the United States; and in all such cases, or whenever any such insurrection, violence,

Ku Klux Klan members encircle a burning cross in Edinburg, Mississippi (AP/Wide World Photos, Inc.).

unlawful combination, or conspiracy shall oppose or obstruct the laws of the United States or the due execution thereof, or impede or obstruct the due course of justice under the same, it shall be lawful for the President, and it shall be his duty to take such measures, by the employment of the militia or the land and naval forces of the United States, or either, or by other means, as he may deem necessary for the suppression of such insurrection, domestic violence, or combinations; and any person who shall be arrested under the provisions of this and the preceding section shall be delivered to the marshal of the proper district, to be dealt with according to law.

Section 4. That whenever in any State or part of a State the unlawful combinations named in the preceding section of this act shall be organized and armed, and so numerous and powerful as to be able, by violence, to either overthrow or set at defiance the constituted authorities of such State, and of the United States within such State, or when the constituted authorities are in complicity with, or shall connive at the unlawful purpose of, such powerful and armed combinations; and whenever, by reason of either or all of the causes aforesaid, the conviction of such offender and the preservation of the public safety shall become in such district impracticable, in every such case such combinations shall be deemed a rebellion against the government of the United States, and during the continuation of such rebellion, and within the limits of the district which shall be so under the sway thereof, such limits to be prescribed by proclamation, it shall be lawful for the President of the United States, when in his judgment the public safety shall require it, to suspend the privileges of the writ of habeas corpus, to the end that such rebellion may be overthrown. . . .

Section 6. That any person, or persons, having knowledge that any of the wrongs conspired to be done and mentioned in the second section of this act are about to be committed, and having power to prevent or aid in preventing the same, shall neglect or refuse so to do, and such wrongful act shall be committed, such person or persons shall be liable to the person injured, or his legal representatives, for all damages caused by any such wrongful act which such first-named person or persons by reasonable diligence could have prevented; and such damages may be recovered in an action on the case in the proper circuit court of the United States, and any number of persons guilty of such wrongful neglect or refusal may be joined as defendants in such action. . . .

◆ CIVIL RIGHTS ACT OF 1875 CH. 114, 18 STAT. 335 (1875)

The Civil Rights Act of 1875 concerned itself primarily with the prohibition of racial discrimination in places of public accommodation. Eight years later, however, the U.S. Supreme Court addressed the issue. Ruling in a set of disputes, which came to be known as the Civil Rights Cases, the Court declared the law unconstitutional, stating that Congress did not have the authority to regulate the prevalent social mores of any state.

An Act to Protect All Citizens in Their Civil and Legal Rights.

Whereas it is essential to just governments we recognize the equality of all men before the law, and hold that it is the duty of government in its dealings with the people to mete out equal and exact justice to all, of whatever nativity, race, color, or persuasion, religious or political; and it being the appropriate object of legislation to enact great fundamental principles into law: Therefore, *Be it enacted*, That all persons within the jurisdiction of the United States shall be entitled to the full and equal enjoyment of the accommodations, advantages, facilities, and privileges of inns, public

conveyances on land or water, theaters, and other places of public amusement; subject only to the conditions and limitations established by law, and applicable alike to citizens of every race and color, regardless of any previous condition of servitude.

Section 2. That any person who shall violate the foregoing section by denying to any citizen, except for reasons by law applicable to citizens of every race and color, and regardless of any previous condition of servitude, the full enjoyment of any of the accommodations, advantages, facilities, or privileges in said section enumerated, or by aiding or inciting such denial, shall, for every such offense, forfeit and pay the sum of five hundred dollars to the person aggrieved thereby . . . and shall also, for every such offense, be deemed guilty of a misdemeanor, and upon conviction thereof, shall be fined not less than five hundred nor more than one thousand dollars, or shall be imprisoned not less than thirty days nor more than one year. . . .

Section 4. That no citizen possessing all other qualifications which are or may be prescribed by law shall be disqualified for service as grand or petit juror in any court of the United States, or of any State, on account of race, color, or previous condition of servitude; and any officer or other person charged with any duty in the selection or summoning of jurors who shall exclude or fail to summon any citizen for the cause aforesaid shall, on conviction thereof, be deemed guilty of a misdemeanor, and be fined not more than five thousand dollars.

Section 5. That all cases arising under the provisions of this act . . . shall be renewable by the Supreme Court of the U.S., without regard to the sum in controversy. . . .

◆ FREDERICK DOUGLASS'S SPEECH ON WOMAN SUFFRAGE (1888) (EXCERPT)

In July 1848 Frederick Douglass was one of the few men present at the initial woman's rights convention at Seneca Falls, New York, and it was he who encouraged outspoken feminist Elizabeth Cady Stanton to press for suffrage and who seconded the resolution proposed by Stanton that it was "the duty of the women of this country to secure to themselves their sacred right to the elective franchise." However, in later years, Douglass split ranks with Stanton and Anthony over philosophical differences regarding the Fifteenth Amendment and other matters. Yet, Douglass remained a staunch advocate for the right of women to vote.

In April 1888, Douglass gave a speech before the International Council of Women in Washington, DC. In his message to the conventioneers, Douglass reflected on his role at the Seneca Falls convention and strongly endorsed woman suffrage. Douglass also in-

A portrait of Frederick Douglass taken by early African American photographer James P. Ball (The Library of Congress).

sisted that it is women, not men, who should be the primary spokespersons for the suffrage cause. The text of Douglass's address appeared in the Woman's Journal *on April 14, 1888.*

Mrs. President, Ladies and Gentlemen:—I come to this platform with unusual diffidence. Although I have long been identified with the Woman's Suffrage movement, and have often spoken in its favor, I am somewhat at a loss to know what to say on this really great and uncommon occasion, where so much has been said.

When I look around on this assembly, and see the many able and eloquent women, full of the subject, ready to speak, and who only need the opportunity to impress this audience with their views and thrill them with "thoughts that berate and words that burn," I do not feel like taking up more than a very small space of your time and attention, and shall not. I would not, even now, presume to speak, but for the circumstances of my early connection with the cause, and of having been called upon to do so by one whose voice in this Council we all gladly obey. Men have very little business here as speakers, anyhow; and if they come here at all they should take back benches and wrap themselves in

silence. For this is an International Council, not of men, but of women, and woman should have all the say in it. This is her day in court.

I do not mean to exalt the intellect of woman above man's; but I have heard many men speak on this subject; some of them the most eloquent to be found anywhere in the country; and I believe no man, however gifted with thought and speech, can voice the wrongs and present the demands of women with the skill and effect, with the power and authority of woman herself. The man struck is the man to cry out. Woman knows and feels her wrongs as man cannot know and feel them, and she also knows as well as he can know, what measures are needed to redress them. I grant all the claims at this point. She is her own best representative. We can neither speak for her, nor vote for her, nor act for her, nor be responsible for her; and the thing for men to do in the premises is just to get out of her way and give her the fullest opportunity to exercise all the powers inherent in her individual personality, and allow her to do it as she herself shall elect to exercise them. Her right to be and to do is as full, complete and perfect as the right of any man on earth. I say of her, as I say of the colored people, "Give her fair play, and hands off."

There is to-day, however, a special reason for omitting argument. This is the end of the fourth decade of the woman suffrage movement, a kind of jubilee which naturally turns our minds to the past.

The history of the world has given to us many sublime undertakings, but none more sublime than this. It was a great thing for the friends of peace to organize in opposition to war; it was a great thing for the friends of temperance to organize against intemperance; it was a great thing for humane people to organize in opposition to slavery; but it was a much greater thing, in view of all the circumstances, for woman to organize herself in opposition to her exclusion from participation in government. . . . Men took for granted all that could be said against intemperance, war and slavery. But no such advantage was found in the beginning of the cause of suffrage for women. On the contrary, everything in her condition was supposed to be lovely, just as it should be. She had no rights denied, no wrongs to redress. She herself had no suspicion but that all was going well with her.

There are few facts in my humble history to which I look back with more satisfaction than to the fact, recorded in the history of the woman-suffrage movement, that I was sufficiently enlightened at that early day, and when only a few years from slavery, to support your resolution for woman suffrage. I have done very little in this world in which to glory except this one act—and I certainly glory in that. When I ran away from slavery, it was for myself; when I advocated emancipation, it was for my people, but when I stood up for the rights of woman, self was out of the question, and I found a little nobility in the act.

In estimating the forces with which this suffrage cause has had to contend during these forty years, the fact should be remembered that relations of long standing beget a character in the parties to them in the favor of the continuance.

The relation of man to woman has the advantage of all the ages behind it. Those who oppose a readjustment of this relation tell us that what is always was and always will be, world without end. But we have heard this old argument before, and if we live very long we shall hear it again. When any aged error shall be assailed, and any old abuse is to be removed, we shall meet this same old argument. Man has been so long the king and woman the subject—man has been so long accustomed to command and woman to obey—that both parties to the relation have been hardened into their respective places, and thus has been piled up a mountain of iron against woman's enfranchisement.

The universality of man's rule over woman is another factor in resistance to the woman-suffrage movement. We are pointed to the fact that men have not only always ruled over women, but that they do so rule everywhere, and they easily think that thing that is done everywhere must be right. Though the fallacy of this reasoning is too transparent to need refutation, it still exerts a powerful influence.

All good causes are mutually helpful. The benefits accruing from this movement for the equal rights of woman are not confined or limited to woman only. They will be shared by every effort to promote the progress and welfare of mankind everywhere and in all ages.

◆ IDA B. WELLS-BARNETT'S SPEECH ON THE LYNCH LAW IN ALL ITS PHASES (1893) (EXCERPT)

Ida B. Wells-Barnett began organizing and lecturing in support of an international campaign against lynching after a mob destroyed the offices of her newspaper the Memphis Free Speech *on May 27, 1892. In both her speeches and writings, she used graphic, detailed descriptions of certain lynchings and scrutinized the media accounts through which her audiences were most likely to have heard of them. In her speech in Boston's Tremont Temple on February 13, 1893, Wells-Barnett again speaks out against lynchings and suggests a remedy for ending the heinous practice.*

The race problem or negro question, as it has been called, has been omnipresent and all-pervading since long before the Afro-American was raised from the

Ida B. Wells-Barnett

degradation of the slave to the dignity of the citizen. It has never been settled because the right methods have not been employed in the solution. . . . The operations of law do not dispose of negroes fast enough, and lynching bees have become the favorite pastime of the South. As excuse for the same, a new cry, as false as it is foul, is raised in an effort to blast race character, a cry which has proclaimed to the world that virtue and innocence are violated by Afro-Americans who must be killed like wild beasts to protect womanhood and childhood.

In the past ten years over a thousand colored men, women and children have been butchered, murdered and burnt in all parts of the South. The details of these horrible outrages seldom reach beyond the narrow world where they occur. Those who commit the murders write the reports, and hence these lasting blots upon the honor of a nation cause but a faint ripple on the outside world. They arouse no great indignation and call forth no adequate demand for justice. The victims were black, and the reports are so written as to make it appear that the helpless creatures deserved the fate which overtook them.

Persons unfamiliar with the condition of affairs in the Southern States do not credit the truth when it is told to them. They cannot conceive how such a condition of affairs prevails so near them with steam power, telegraph wires and printing presses in daily and hourly touch with the localities where such disorder reigns.

The right of the Afro-American to vote and hold office remains in the Federal Constitution, but is destroyed in the constitution of the Southern states. Having destroyed the citizenship of the man, they are now trying to destroy the manhood of the citizen. All their laws are shaped to this end;—school laws, railroad car regulations, those governing labor liens on crops,—every device is adopted to make slaves of free men and rob them of their wages. Whenever a malicious law is violated in any of its parts, any farmer, any railroad conductor, or merchant can call together a posse of his neighbors and punish even with death the black man who resists and the legal authorities sanction what is done by failing to prosecute and punish the murders. The Repeal of the Civil Rights Law removed their last barrier and the black man's last bulwark and refuge. The rule of the mob is absolute.

Those who know this recital to be true, say there is nothing they can do—they cannot interfere and vainly hope by further concession to placate the imperious and dominating part of our country in which this lawlessness prevails. Because this country has been almost rent in twain by internal dissension, the other sections seem virtually to have agreed that the best way to heal the breach is to permit the taking away of civil, political, and even human rights, to stand by in silence and utter indifference while the South continues to wreak fiendish vengeance on the irresponsible cause. They pretend to believe that with all the machinery of law and government in its hands; with the jails and penitentiaries and convict farms filled with pretty race criminals; with the well-known fact that no negro has ever been known to escape conviction and punishment for any crime in the South—still there are those who try to justify and condone the lynching of over a thousand black men in less than ten years—an average of one hundred a year. The public sentiment of the country, by its silence in press, pulpit and in public meetings has encouraged this state of affairs, and public sentiment is stronger than law.

Do you ask the remedy? A public sentiment strong against lawlessness must be aroused. Every individual can contribute to this awakening. When a sentiment against lynch law as strong, deep and mighty as that roused against slavery prevails, I have no fear of the result. It should be already established as a fact and not as a theory, that every human being must have a fair trial for his life and liberty, no matter what the charge against him. When a demand goes up from fearless and persistent reformers from press and pulpit, from industrial and moral associations that this shall be so from Maine to Texas and from ocean to ocean, a way will be found to make it so.

◆ BOOKER T. WASHINGTON'S "ATLANTA COMPROMISE" SPEECH (1895)

Booker T. Washington, a major voice in the movement for the advancement of African Americans, was often criticized for encouraging blacks to cultivate peaceful coexistence with whites. Washington advocated the use of technical and industrial self-help programs—even if such programs tended to discount the importance of the cultivation of intellectual and aesthetic values. In an address to the 1895 Atlanta Exposition, Washington outlined his philosophy.

Mr. President and Gentlemen of the Board of Directors and Citizens:

One-third of the population of the South is of the Negro race. No enterprise seeking the material, civil, or moral welfare of this section can disregard this element of our population and reach the highest success. I but convey to you, Mr. President and Directors, the sentiment of the masses of my race when I say that in no way have the value and manhood of the American Negro been more fittingly and generously recognized than by the managers of this magnificent Exposition at every stage of its progress. It is a recognition that will do more to cement the friendship of the two races than any occurrence since the dawn of our freedom.

Not only this, but the opportunity here afforded will awaken among us a new era of industrial progress. Ignorant and inexperienced, it is not strange that in the first years of our new life we began at the top instead of at the bottom; that a seat in Congress or the State Legislature was more sought than real estate or industrial skill; that the political convention or stump speaking had more attractions than starting a dairy farm or truck garden.

A ship lost at sea for many days suddenly sighted a friendly vessel. From the mast of the unfortunate vessel was seen a signal: "Water, water; we die of thirst!" The answer from the friendly vessel at once came back: "Cast down your bucket where you are." A second time the signal, "Water, water; send us water!" ran up from the distressed vessel, and was answered: "Cast down your bucket where you are." And a third and fourth signal for water was answered: "Cast down your bucket where you are." The captain of the distressed vessel, at last heeding the injunction, cast down his bucket, and it came up full of fresh, sparkling water from the mouth of the Amazon River. To those of my race who depend on bettering their condition in a foreign land, or who underestimate the importance of cultivating friendly relations with the Southern white man, who is their next door neighbor, I would say: "Cast down your bucket where you are"—cast it down in making friends in every manly way of the people of all races by whom we are surrounded.

Cast it down in agriculture, mechanics, in commerce, in domestic service, and in the professions. And in this connection it is well to bear in mind that whatever other sins the South may be called to bear, when it comes to business, pure and simple, it is in the South that the Negro is given a man's chance in the commercial world, and in nothing is this Exposition more eloquent than in emphasizing this chance. Our greatest danger is, that in the great leap from slavery to freedom we may overlook the fact that the masses of us are to live by the productions of our hands, and fail to keep in mind that we shall prosper in proportion as we learn to dignify and glorify common labor, and put brains and skill into the common occupations of life; shall prosper in proportion as we learn to draw the line between the superficial and the substantial, the ornamental gewgaws of life and the useful. No race can prosper till it learns that there is as much dignity in tilling a field as in writing a poem. It is at the bottom of life we must begin, and not at the top. Nor should we permit our grievances to overshadow our opportunities.

To those of the white race who look to the incoming of those of foreign birth and strange tongue and habits for the prosperity of the South, were I permitted, I would repeat what I say to my own race, "Cast down your bucket where you are." Cast it down among the 8,000,000 Negroes whose habits you know, whose fidelity and love you have tested in days when to have proved treacherous meant the ruin of your firesides. Cast down your bucket among those people who have, without strikes and labor wars, tilled your fields, cleared your forests, builded your railroads and cities, and brought forth treasures from the bowels of the earth, and helped make possible this magnificent representation of the progress of the South. Casting down your bucket among my people, helping and encouraging them as you are doing on these grounds, and, with education of head, hand and heart, you will find that they will buy your surplus land, make blossom the waste place in your fields, and run your factories. While doing this, you can be sure in the future, as in the past, that you and your families will be surrounded by the most patient, faithful, law-abiding, and unresentful people that the world has seen. As we have proved our loyalty to you in the past, in nursing your children, watching by the sick bed of your mothers and fathers, and often following them with tear-dimmed eyes to their graves, so in the future, in our humble way, we shall stand by you with a devotion that no foreigner can approach, ready to lay down our lives, if need be, in defense of yours, interlacing our industrial, commercial, civil, and religious life with yours in a way that shall make the interests of both races one. In all things that are purely social we can be as separate as the fingers, yet one as the hand in all things essential to mutual progress.

There is no defense or security for any of us except in the highest intelligence and development of all. If anywhere there are efforts tending to curtail the fullest growth of the Negro, let these efforts be turned into stimulating, encouraging, and making him the most useful and intelligent citizen. Effort or means so invested will pay a thousand percent interest. These efforts will be twice blessed—"blessing him that gives and him that takes."

There is no escape through law of man or God from the inevitable:

> The laws of changeless justice bind Oppressor with oppressed; And close as sin and suffering joined We march to fate abreast.

Nearly sixteen millions of hands will aid you in pulling the load upwards, or they will pull against you the load downwards. We shall constitute one-third and more of the ignorance and crime of the South, or one-third its intelligence and progress; we shall contribute one-third to the business and industrial prosperity of the South, or we shall prove a veritable body of death, stagnating, depressing, retarding every effort to advance the body politic.

Gentlemen of the Exposition, as we present to you humble effort at an exhibition of our progress, you must not expect over much. Starting thirty years ago with ownership here and there in a few quilts and pumpkins and chickens (gathered from miscellaneous sources), remember the path that has led from these to the invention and production of agricultural implements, buggies, steam engines, newspapers, books, statuary, carving, paintings, the management of drug stores and banks, has not been trodden without contact with thorns and thistles. While we take pride in what we exhibit as a result of our independent efforts, we do not for a moment forget that our part in this exhibition would fall far short of your expectations but for the constant help that has come to our educational life, not only from the Southern States, but especially from Northern philanthropists, who have made their gifts a constant stream of blessing and encouragement.

The wisest among my race understand that the agitation of questions of social equality is the extremist folly, and that progress in the enjoyment of all the privileges that will come to us must be the result of severe and constant struggle rather than of artificial forcing. No race that has anything to contribute to the markets of the world is long in any degree ostracized. It is important and right that all privileges of the law be ours, but it is vastly more important that we be prepared for the exercise of those privileges. The opportunity to earn a dollar in a factory just now is worth infinitely more than the opportunity to spend a dollar in an opera house.

In conclusion, may I repeat that nothing in thirty years has given us more hope and encouragement, and drawn us so near to you of the white race, as this opportunity offered by the Exposition; and here bending, as it were, over the altar that represents the results of the struggle of your race and mine, both starting practically empty-handed three decades ago, I pledge that, in your effort to work out the great and intricate problem which God has laid at the doors of the South, you shall have at all time the patient, sympathetic help of my race; only let this be constantly in mind that, while from representations in these buildings of the product of field, of forest, of mine, of factory, letters, and art, much good will come, yet far above and beyond material benefits will be that higher good, that let us pray God will come, in a blotting out of sectional differences and racial animosities and suspicions, in a determination to administer absolute justice, in a willing obedience among all classes to the mandates of law. This, coupled with our material prosperity, will bring into our beloved South a new heaven and a new earth.

◆ PLESSY V. FERGUSON 163 US 537 (1896)

On February 23, 1869, the Louisiana state legislature enacted a law prohibiting segregation on public transportation. In 1878, ruling in the case Hall v. DeCuir, *the U.S. Supreme Court declared that state governments could not prohibit segregation on common carriers. Twelve years later, the Court hearing the case* Louisville, New Orleans and Texas Railway v. Mississippi *approved a state statute requiring segregation on intrastate carriers.*

In 1896, the Court once again faced the issue of segregation on public transportation. Homer Adolph Plessy, an African American traveling by train from New Orleans to Covington, Louisiana, was arrested when he refused to ride in the "colored" railway coach; Louisiana state law required that "separate but equal" accommodations be maintained in public facilities for blacks and whites. In its majority opinion, the Court declared that "separate but equal" accommodations constituted a "reasonable" use of state police power and that the Fourteenth Amendment "could not have been intended to abolish distinctions based on color, or to enforce social. . . equality, or a commingling of the two races upon terms unsatisfactory to either."

In effect, the Court's ruling had significantly reduced the authoritativeness of the Fourteenth and Fifteenth Amendments to the Constitution, which were designed to provide African Americans specific rights and protections. The "separate but equal" doctrine paved the way for segregation of African Americans in all walks of life and stood until the Brown v. Board of Education of Topeka *decision of 1954.*

Justice Brown delivered the opinion of the Court.

This case turns upon the constitutionality of an act of the General Assembly of the state of Louisiana, passed in 1890, providing for separate railway carriages for the white and colored races. . . .

The constitutionality of this act is attacked upon the ground that it conflicts both with the Thirteenth Amendment of the Constitution, abolishing slavery, and the Fourteenth Amendment, which prohibits certain restrictive legislation on the part of the states.

1. That it does not conflict with the Thirteenth Amendment, which abolished slavery and involuntary servitude, except as a punishment for crime, is too clear for argument. Slavery implies involuntary servitude—a state of bondage; the ownership of mankind as a chattel, or at least the control of the labor and services of one man for the benefit of another, and absence of a legal right to the disposal of his own person, property, and services. . . .

A statute which implies merely a legal distinction between the white and colored races—a distinction which is founded in the color of the two races, and which must always exist so long as white men are distinguished from the other race by color—has no tendency to destroy the legal equality of the two races, or reestablish a state of involuntary servitude. Indeed, we do not understand that the Thirteenth Amendment is strenuously relied upon by the plaintiff in error in this connection.

2. By the Fourteenth Amendment, all persons born or naturalized in the United States, and subject to the jurisdiction thereof, are made citizens of the United States and of the state wherein they reside; and the states are forbidden from making or enforcing any law which shall abridge the privileges or immunities of citizens of the United States, or shall deprive any person of life, liberty, or property without due process of law, or deny to any person within their jurisdiction the equal protection of the laws. . . .

The object of the amendment was undoubtedly to enforce the absolute equality of the two races before the law, but in the nature of things it could not have been intended to abolish distinctions based upon color, or to enforce social, as distinguished from political, equality, or a commingling of the two races upon terms unsatisfactory to either. Laws permitting, and even requiring, their separation in places where they are liable to be brought into contact do not necessarily imply the inferiority of either race to the other, and have been generally, if not universally, recognized as within the competency of the state legislatures in the exercise of their police power. The most common instance of this is connected with the establishment of separate schools for white and colored children, which has been held to be a valid exercise of the legislative power even by courts of states where the political rights of the colored race have been longest and most earnestly enforced. . . .

So far, then, as a conflict with the Fourteenth Amendment is concerned, the case reduces itself to the question whether the statute of Louisiana is a reasonable regulation, and with respect to this there must necessarily be a large discretion on the part of the legislature. In determining the question of reasonableness it is at liberty to act with reference to the established usages, customs, and traditions of the people, and with a view to the promotion of their comfort, and the preservation of the public peace and good order. Gauged by this standard, we cannot say that a law which authorizes or even requires the separation of the two races in public conveyances is unreasonable or more obnoxious to the Fourteenth Amendment than the acts of Congress requiring separate schools for colored children in the District of Columbia, the constitutionality of which does not seem to have been questioned, or the corresponding acts of state legislatures.

We consider the underlying fallacy of the plaintiff's argument to consist in the assumption that the enforced separation of the two races stamps the colored race with a badge of inferiority. If this be so, it is not by reason of anything found in the act, but solely the colored race chooses to put that construction upon it. The argument necessarily assumes that if, as has been more than once the case, and is not unlikely to be so again, the colored race should become the dominant power in the state legislature, and should enact a law in precisely similar terms, it would thereby relegate the white race to an inferior position. We imagine that the white race, at least, would not acquiesce in this assumption. The argument also assumes that social prejudices may be overcome by legislation and that equal rights cannot be secured to the Negro except by an enforced commingling of the two races. We cannot accept this proposition. If the two races are to meet upon terms of social equality, it must be the result of natural affinities, a mutual appreciation of each other's merits, and a voluntary consent of individuals. . . . Legislation is powerless to eradicate racial instincts or to abolish distinctions based upon physical differences, and the attempt to do so can only result in accentuating the difficulties of the present situation. If the civil and political rights of

both races be equal, one cannot be inferior to the other civilly or politically. If one race be inferior to the other socially, the Constitution of the United States cannot put them upon the same plane.

It is true that the question of the proportion of colored blood necessary to constitute a colored person, as distinguished from a white person, is one upon with there is a difference of opinion in the different states, some holding that any visible admixture of black blood stamps the person as belonging to the colored race. . . others that it depends upon the preponderance of blood. . . and still others that the pre-dominance of white blood must only be in the proportion of three-fourths. . . .But these are questions to be determined under the laws of each state and are not properly put in issue in this case. Under the allegations of his petition it may undoubtedly become a question of importance whether, under the laws of Louisiana, the petitioner belongs to the white or colored race.

The judgment of the court below is therefore, *Affirmed*.

Justice Harlan Dissenting

In respect of civil rights, common to all citizens, the Constitution of the United States does not, I think, permit any public authority to know the race of those entitled to be protected in the enjoyment of such rights. Every true man has pride of race, and under appropriate circumstances with the rights of others, his equals before the law, are not to be affected, it is his privilege to express such pride and to take such action based upon it as to him seems proper. But I deny that any legislative body or judicial tribunal may have regard to the race of citizens when the civil rights of those citizens are involved. Indeed, such legislation, as that here in question, is inconsistent not only with that equality of rights which pertains to citizenship, national and state, but with the personal liberty enjoyed by everyone within the United States.

The Thirteenth Amendment does not permit the withholding or the deprivation of any right necessarily inhering in freedom. It not only struck down the institution of slavery as previously existing in the United States, but it prevents the imposition of any burdens or disabilities that constitute badges of slavery or servitude. It decreed universal civil freedom in this country. This Court has so adjudged. But that amendment having been found inadequate to the protection of the rights of those who had been in slavery, it was followed by the Fourteenth Amendment, which added greatly to the dignity and glory of the American citizenship, and to the security of personal liberty, by declaring that "all persons born or naturalized in the United States, and subject to the jurisdiction thereof, are citizens of the United States and of the state wherein they reside," and that "no state shall make or enforce any law which shall abridge the privileges or immunities of citizens of the United States; nor shall any state deprive any person of life, liberty, or property without due process of law, nor deny to any person within its jurisdiction the equal protection of the laws." These two amendments, if enforced according to their true intent and meaning, will protect all the civil rights that pertains to freedom and citizenship. Finally, and to the end that no citizen should be denied, on account of his race, the privilege of participating in the political control of his country, it was declared by the Fifteenth Amendment that "the right of citizens of the United States to vote shall not be denied or abridged by the United States or by any state on account of race, color, or previous condition of servitude."

These notable additions to the fundamental law were welcomed by the friends of liberty throughout the world. They removed the race line from our governmental systems.

It was said in argument that the statute of Louisiana does not discriminate against either race but prescribes a rule applicable alike to white and colored citizens. But this argument does not meet the difficulty. Everyone knows that the statute in question had its origin in the purpose, not so much to exclude white persons from railroad cars occupied by blacks, as to exclude colored people from coaches occupied by or assigned to white persons. Railroad corporations of Louisiana did not make discrimination among whites in the matter of accommodation for travelers. The thing to accomplish was, under the guise of giving equal accommodation for whites and blacks, to compel the latter to keep to themselves while traveling in railroad passenger coaches. No one would be wanting in candor as to assert the contrary. The fundamental objections, therefore, to the statute is that it interferes with the personal freedom of citizens. If a white man and a black man choose to occupy the same public conveyance on a public highway, it is their right to do so, and no government, proceeding alone on grounds of race, can prevent it without infringing the personal liberty of each.

It is one thing for railroad carriers to furnish, or to be required by law to furnish, equal accommodations for all whom they are under a legal duty to carry. It is quite another thing for government to forbid citizens of the white and black races from traveling in the same public conveyance, and to punish officers of railroad companies for permitting persons of the two races to occupy the same passenger coach. If a state can prescribe, as a rule of civil conduct, that whites and blacks shall not travel as passengers in the same railroad coach, why may it not so regulate the use of the streets of its cities and towns as to compel white citizens to keep on one side of a street and black citizens to keep on the other? Why may it not, upon like grounds, punish whites and blacks who ride together in streetcars or in open vehicles on a public road or street? Why may it not require sheriffs to assign whites to one side of a courtroom and blacks to the other? And why may it not also prohibit the commingling of the two races in the galleries of legislative halls or in public assemblages convened for the consideration of the political questions of the day? Further, if this statute of Louisiana is consistent with the personal liberty of citizens, why may not the state require the separation in railroad coaches of native and naturalized citizens of the United States, or of Protestants and Roman Catholics?

The answer given as the argument to these questions was that regulations of the kind they suggest would be unreasonable and could not, therefore, stand before the law. Is it meant that the determination of questions of legislative power depends upon the inquiry whether the statute whose validity is questioned is, in the judgment of the courts, a reasonable one, taking all the circumstances into consideration? A statute may be unreasonable merely because a sound public forbade its enactment. But I do not understand that the courts have anything to do with the policy or expediency of legislation. The white race deems itself to be the dominant race in this country. And so it is, in prestige, in achievements, in education, in wealth, and in power. So, I doubt not, it will continue to be for all time, if it remains true to its great heritage and holds fast to the principles of constitutional liberty. But in view of the Constitution, in the eye of the law, there is in this country no superior, dominant, ruling class of citizens. There is no caste here. Our Constitution is color-blind and neither knows nor tolerates classes among citizens. In respect of civil rights all citizens are equal before the law. The humblest is the peer of the most powerful. The law regards man as a man and takes no account of his surroundings or of his color when his civil rights, as guaranteed by the supreme law of the land, are involved. It is, therefore, to be regretted that this high tribunal, the final expositor of the fundamental law of the land, has reached the conclusion that it is competent for a state to regulate the enjoyment by citizens of their civil rights solely upon the basis of race. . . .

The sure guarantee of the peace and security of each is the clear, distinct, unconditional recognition by our governments, national and state, of every right that inheres in civil freedom, and of the equality before the law of all citizens of the United States without regard to race. State enactments, regulating the enjoyment of civil rights, upon the basis of race, and cunningly devised legitimate results of the war, under the pretense of recognizing equality of rights, can have no other result than to render permanent peace impossible, and to keep alive a conflict of races, the continuance of which must do harm to all concerned. . . .

The arbitrary separation of citizens, on the basis of race, while they are on a public highway, is a badge of servitude wholly inconsistent with the civil freedom and the equality before the law established by the Constitution. It cannot be justified upon any legal grounds.

If evils will result from the commingling of the two races upon public highways established for the benefit of all, they will be infinitely less than those that will surely come from state legislation regulating the enjoyment of civil rights upon the basis of race. We boast of the freedom enjoyed by our people above all other peoples. But it is difficult to reconcile that boast with a state of the law which, practically, puts the brand of servitude and degradation upon a large class of our fellow-citizens, our equals before the law. The thin disguise of "equal" accommodations for passengers in railroad coaches will not mislead anyone, nor atone for the wrong this day has done. . . .

I am of opinion that the statute of Louisiana is inconsistent with the personal liberty of citizens, white and black, in that state, and hostile to both the spirit and letter of the Constitution of the United States. If laws of like character should be enacted in the several states of the Union, the effect would be in the highest degree mischievous. Slavery, as an institution tolerated by law, would, it is true, have disappeared from our country, but there would remain a power in the states, by sinister legislation, to interfere with the full enjoyment of the blessings of freedom; to regulate civil rights, common to all citizens, upon the basis of race, and to place in a condition of legal inferiority a large body of American citizens, now constituting a part of the political community called the People of the United States, for whom, and by whom through representatives, our government is administered. Such a system is inconsistent with the guarantee given by the Constitution to each state of a republican form of government, and may be stricken down by congressional action, constitutional or laws of any state to the contrary notwithstanding.

For the reasons stated, I am constrained to withhold my assent from the opinion and judgment of the majority. . . .

◆ "LIFT EVERY VOICE AND SING" (1901)

Originally intended for use in a program given by a group of Jacksonville, Florida school children to celebrate Lincoln's birthday, "Lift Every Voice and Sing" has become known as the "black national anthem." The song's words, written by poet and civil rights leader James Weldon Johnson, serve as a tribute to African American heritage. The song's music was composed by Johnson's brother and songwriting partner, J. Rosamond Johnson.

Lift every voice and sing Till earth and heaven ring, Ring with the harmonies of Liberty; Let our rejoicing rise High as the listening skies, Let it resound loud as the rolling sea. Sing a song full of the faith that the dark past has taught us, Sing a song full of the hope that the present has brought us, Facing the rising sun of our new day begun Let us march on till victory is won.

Stony the road we trod, Bitter the chastening rod, Felt in the days when hope unborn had died; Yet with a steady beat, Have not our weary feet Come to the place for which our fathers sighed? We have come over a way that with tears has been watered, We have come, treading our path through the blood of the slaughtered Out from the gloomy past, Till now we stand at last Where the white gleam of our bright star is cast.

God of our weary years, God of our silent tears, Thou who has brought us thus far on the way; Thou who has by Thy might Led us into the light, Keep us forever in the path, we pray. Lest our feet stray from the places, Our God, where We met Thee, Lest, our heart's drunk with the wine of the world, We forget Thee; Shadowed beneath Thy hand, May we forever stand, True to our God, True to our native land.

◆ MARCUS GARVEY'S SPEECH AT LIBERTY HALL, NEW YORK CITY (1922)

Marcus Garvey, black nationalist and founder of the Universal Negro Improvement Association, dedicated his life to uplifting Africans throughout the world. In this 1922 address, Garvey outlined the goals of the Universal Negro Improvement Association.

Over five years ago the Universal Negro Improvement Association placed itself before the world as the movement through which the new and rising Negro would give expression of his feelings. This Association adopts an attitude not of hostility to other races and peoples of the world, but an attitude of self-respect.

. . . Wheresoever human rights are denied to any group, wheresoever justice is denied to any group, there the U.N.I.A. finds a cause. And at this time among all the peoples of the world, the group that suffers most from injustice, the group that is denied most of those rights that belong to all humanity, is the black group. . . even so under the leadership of the U.N.I.A., we are marshalling the 400,000,000 Negroes of the world to fight for the emancipation of the race and of the redemption of the country of our fathers.

We represent a new line of thought among Negroes. Whether you call it advanced thought or reactionary thought, I do not care. If it is reactionary for people to seek independence in government, then we are reactionary. If it is advanced thought for people to seek liberty and freedom, then we represent the advanced school of thought among the Negroes of this country. We of the U.N.I.A. believe that what is good for the other folks is good for us. If government is something that is worth while; if government is something that is appreciable and helpful and protective to others, then we also want to experiment in government. We do not mean a government that will make us citizens without rights or subjects without consideration. We mean a kind of government that will place our race in control, even as other races are in control of their own government.

. . . The U.N.I.A. is not advocating the cause of church building, because we have a sufficiently large number of churches among us to minister to the spiritual needs of the people, and we are not going to compete with those who are engaged in so splendid a work; we are not engaged in building any new social institutions,. . . because there are enough social workers engaged in those praiseworthy efforts. We are not engaged in politics because we have enough local politicians,. . . and the political situation is well taken care of. We are not engaged in domestic politics, in church building or in social uplift work, but we are engaged in nation building.

In advocating the principles of this Association we find we have been very much misunderstood and very much misrepresented by men from within our own race, as well as others from without. Any reform movement that seeks to bring about changes for the benefit of humanity is bound to be misrepresented by those who have always taken it upon themselves to administer to, and lead the unfortunate. . . .

. . . The Universal Negro Improvement Association stands for the Bigger Brotherhood; the Universal Negro Improvement Association stands for human rights, not only for Negroes, but for all races. The Universal Negro Improvement Association believes in the rights of not only the black race, the white race, the yellow race and the brown race. The Universal Negro Improvement Association believes that the white man has as much right to be considered, the yellow man has as much right to be considered, the brown man has as much right to be considered as the black man of Africa. In view of the fact that the black man of Africa has contributed as much to the world as the white man of Europe, and the brown man and yellow man of Asia, we of the Universal Negro Improvement Association demand that the white, yellow and brown races give to the black man his place in the civilization of the world. We ask for nothing more than the rights of 400,000,000 Negroes. We are not

seeking, as I said before, to destroy or disrupt the society or the government of other races, but we are determined that 400,000,000 of us shall unite ourselves to free our motherland from the grasp of the invader. . . .

The Universal Negro Improvement Association is not seeking to build up another government within the bounds or borders of the United States of America. The Universal Negro Improvement Association is not seeking to disrupt any organized system of government, but the Association is determined to bring Negroes together for the building up of a nation of their own. And why? Because we have been forced to it. We have been forced to it throughout the world; not only in America, not only in Europe, not only in the British Empire, but wheresoever the black man happens to find himself, he has been forced to do for himself.

To talk about Government is a little more than some of our people can appreciate. . . .The average man. . . seems to say, "why should there be need for any other government?" We are French, English or American. But we of the U.N.I.A. have studied seriously this question of nationality among Negroes—this American nationality, this British nationality, this French, Italian or Spanish nationality, and have discovered that it counts for nought when that nationality comes in conflict with the racial idealism of the group that rules. When our interests clash with those of the ruling faction, then we find that we have absolutely no rights. In times of peace, when everything is all right, Negroes have a hard time, wherever we go, wheresoever we find ourselves, getting those rights that belong to us in common with others whom we claim as fellow citizens; getting that consideration that should be ours by right of the constitution, by right of the law, but in the time of trouble they make us all partners in the cause, as happened in the last war. . . .

We have saved many nations in this manner, and we have lost our lives doing that before. Hundreds of thousands—nay, millions of black men, lie buried under the ground due to that old-time camouflage of saving the nation. We saved the British Empire; we saved the French Empire; we saved this glorious country more than once; and all that we have received for our sacrifices, all that we have received for what we have done, even in giving up our lives, is just what you are receiving now, just what I am receiving now.

You and I fare no better in America, in the British Empire, or any other part of the white world; we fare no better than any black man wheresoever he shows his head. . . .

The U.N.I.A. is reversing the old-time order of things. We refuse to be followers anymore. We are leading ourselves. That means, if any saving is to be done. . . we are going to seek a method of saving Africa first. Why? And why Africa? Because Africa has become the grand prize of the nations. Africa has become the big game of the nation hunters. Today Africa looms as the greatest commercial, industrial and political prize in the world.

The difference between the Universal Negro Improvement Association and the other movements of this country, and probably the world, is that the Universal Negro Improvement Association seeks independence of government while the other organizations seek to make the Negro a secondary part of existing governments. We differ from the organizations in America because they seek to subordinate the Negro as a secondary consideration in a great civilization, knowing that in America the Negro will never reach his highest ambition, knowing that the Negro in America will never get his constitutional rights. All other organizations which are fostering the improvement of Negroes in the British Empire know that the Negro in the British Empire will never reach the height of his constitutional rights. What do I mean by constitutional rights in America? If the black man is to reach the height of his ambition in this country—if the black man is to get all of his constitutional rights in America—then the black man should have the same chance in the nation as any other man to become president of the nation, or a street cleaner in New York. If the black man in the British Empire is to have all his constitutional rights it means that the Negro in the British Empire should have at least the same right to become premier of Great Britain as he has to become a street cleaner in the city of London. Are they prepared to give us such political equality? You and I can live in the United States of America for 100 more years, and our generations may live for 200 years or for 5000 more years, and so long as there is a black and white population, when the majority is on the side of the white race, you and I will never get political justice or get political equality in this country. Then why should a black man with rising ambition, after preparing himself in every possible way to give expression to that highest ambition, allow himself to be kept down by racial prejudice within a country? If I am as educated as the next man, if I am as prepared as the next man, if I have passed through the best schools and colleges and universities as the other fellow, why should I not have a fair chance to compete with the other fellow for the biggest position in the nation?. . .

We are not preaching a propaganda of hate against anybody. We love the white man; we love all humanity. . . ..The white man is as necessary to the existence of the Negro as the Negro is necessary to his existence. There is a common relationship that we cannot escape. Africa has certain things that Europe wants, and Europe has certain things that Africa wants. . . it is impossible

for us to escape it. Africa has oil, diamonds, copper, gold and rubber and all the minerals that Europe wants, and there must be some kind of relationship between Africa and Europe for a fair exchange, so we cannot afford to hate anybody.

The question often asked is what does it require to redeem a race and free a country? If it takes man power, if it takes scientific intelligence, if it takes education of any kind, or if it takes blood, then the 400,000,000 Negroes of the world have it.

It took the combined power of the Allies to put down the mad determination of the Kaiser to impose German will upon humanity. Among those who suppressed his mad ambition were two million Negroes who have not yet forgotten how to drive men across the firing line. . . when so many white men refused to answer to the call and dodged behind all kinds of excuses, 400,000 black men were ready without a question. It was because we were told it was a war of democracy; it was a war for the liberation of the weaker peoples of the world. We heard the cry of Woodrow Wilson, not because we liked him so, but because the things he said were of such a nature that they appealed to us as men. Wheresoever the cause of humanity stands in need of assistance, there you will find the Negro ever ready to serve.

He has done it from the time of Christ up to now. When the whole world turned its back upon the Christ, the man who was said to be the Son of God, when the world cried out "Crucify Him," when the world spurned Him and spat upon Him, it was a black man, Simon, the Cyrenian, who took up the cross. Why? Because the cause of humanity appealed to him. When the black man saw the suffering Jew, struggling under the heavy cross, he was willing to go to His assistance, and he bore that cross up to the heights of Calvary. In the spirit of Simon, the Cyrenian, 1900 years ago, we answered the call of Woodrow Wilson, the call to a larger humanity, and it was for that we willingly rushed into the war. . . .

We shall march out, yes, as black American citizens, as black British subjects, as black French citizens, as black Italians or as black Spaniards, but we shall march out with a greater loyalty, the loyalty of race. We shall march out in answer to the cry of our fathers, who cry out to us for the redemption of our own country, our motherland, Africa.

We shall march out, not forgetting the blessings of America. We shall march out, not forgetting the blessings of civilization. We shall march out with a history of peace before and behind us, and surety that history shall be our breast-plate, for how can a man fight better than knowing that the cause for which he fights is righteous?. . . Glorious shall be the battle when the time comes to fight for our people and our race.

We should say to the millions who are in Africa to hold the fort, for we are coming 400,000,000 strong.

◆ EXECUTIVE ORDER NO. 8802, 3 C.F.R., 1938–1943 COMP. P. 957 (1941)

Issued by President Franklin D. Roosevelt on June 25, 1941, Executive Order 8802 was intended to eliminate discriminatory practices in the defense industry during World War II (1941–1945).

Whereas it is the policy of the United States to encourage full participation in the national defense program by all citizens of the United States, regardless of race, creed, color, or national origin, in the firm belief that the democratic way of life within the Nation can be defended successfully only with the help and support of all groups within its borders; and

Whereas there is evidence that available and needed workers have been barred from employment in industries engaged in defense production solely because of considerations of race, creed, color, or national origin, to the detriment of workers' morale and of national unity:

Now, Therefore, by virtue of the authority vested in me by the Constitution and the statues, and as a prerequisite to the successful conduct of our national defense production effort, I do hereby reaffirm the policy of the United States that there shall be no discrimination in the employment of workers in defense industries or Government because of race, creed, color, or national origin, and I do hereby declare that it is the duty of employers and of labor organizations, in furtherance of said policy and of this order, to provide for the full and equitable participation of all workers in defense industries, without discrimination because of race, creed, color, or national origin;

And it is hereby ordered as follows:

1. All departments and agencies of the Government of the United States concerned with vocational and training programs for defense production shall take special measures appropriate to assure that such programs are administered without discrimination because of race, creed, color, or national origin;

2. All contracting agencies of the Government of the United States shall include in all defense contracts hereafter negotiated by them a provision obligating the contractor not to discriminate against any worker because of race, creed, color, or national origin;

3. There is established in the Office of Production Management a Committee on Fair Employment Practice, which shall consist of a chairman and four other members to be appointed by the President. The Chair-

man and members of the Committee shall serve as such without compensation but shall be entitled to actual and necessary transportation, subsistence and other expenses incidental to performance of their duties. The Committee shall receive and investigate complaints of discrimination in violation of the provisions of this order and shall take appropriate steps to redress grievances which it finds to be valid. The Committee shall also recommend to the several departments and agencies of the Government of the United States and to the President all measures which may be deemed by it necessary or proper to effectuate the provisions of this order.

◆ EXECUTIVE ORDER NO. 9981, 3 C.F.R. 1943–1948 COMP. P. 720 (1948)

Signed by President Harry S. Truman on July 26, 1948, Executive Order 9981 ended segregation in the Armed Forces of the United States.

Whereas it is essential that there be maintained in the armed services of the United States the highest standards of democracy, with equality of treatment and opportunity for all those who serve in our country's defense:

Now, therefore, by virtue of the authority vested in me as President of the United States, by the Constitution and the statutes of the United States, and as Commander-in-Chief of the armed services, it is hereby ordered as follows:

1. It is hereby declared to be the policy of the President that there shall be equality of treatment and opportunity for all persons in the armed services without regard to race, color, religion or national origin. This policy shall be put into effect as rapidly as possible, having due regard to the time required to effectuate any necessary changes without impairing efficiency or morals.

2. There shall be created in the National Military Establishment an advisory committee to be known as the President's Committee on Equality of Treatment and Opportunity in the Armed Services, which shall be composed of seven members to be designated by the President.

3. The Committee is authorized on behalf of the President to examine into the rules, procedures and practices of the armed services in order to determine in what respect such rules, procedure and practices may be altered or improved with a view to carrying out the policy of this order. The Committee shall confer and advise with the Secretary of the Army, the Secretary of the Air Force, and shall make such recommendations to the President and to said Secretaries as in the judgment of the Committee will effectuate lthe policy hereof.

4. All executive departments and agencies of the Federal Government are authorized and directed to cooperate with the Committee in its work, and to furnish the Committee such information or the services of such persons as the Committee may require in the performance of its duties.

5. When requested by the Committee to do so, persons in the armed services or in any of the executive departments and agencies of the Federal Government shall testify before the Committee and shall make available for the use of the Committee such documents and other information as the Committee may require.

6. The Committee shall continue to exist until such time as the President shall terminate its existence by Executive order.

◆ BROWN V. BOARD OF EDUCATION OF TOPEKA 347 U.S. 483 (1954)

Beginning in the late 1930s, the U.S. Supreme Court began to review numerous cases dealing with segregation in public education; by the 1950s it had become evident that segregated educational facilities were not equal.

In 1938, ruling in the case Missouri ex rel. Gaines v. Canada, *the Court ruled that states were required to provide equal educational facilities for African Americans within its boundaries. (The state of Missouri at that time had maintained a practice of providing funds for African Americans to attend graduate and professional schools outside of the state, rather than provide facilities itself.) Taking an even greater step, in 1950 the Court in* Sweatt v. Painter *ruled that a separate law school for African Americans provided by the state of Texas violated the equal protection clause of the Fourteenth Amendment.*

In 1952, five different cases, all dealing with segregation in public schools but with different facts and from different places, reached the U.S. Supreme Court. Four of the cases, Brown v. Board of Education of Topeka *(out of Kansas),* Briggs v. Elliott *(out of South Carolina),* Davis v. Prince Edward County School Board *(out of Virginia), and* Gebhart v. Belton *(out of Delaware) were considered together; the fifth case* Bolling v. Sharpe *coming out of the District of Columbia, was considered separately (since the district is not a state).*

After hearing initial arguments, the Court found itself unable to reach an agreement. In 1953, the Court heard reargument. Thurgood Marshall, legal counsel for the National Association for the Advancement of Colored People Legal Defense and Education Fund, presented arguments on behalf of the African American students. On May 17, 1954, the Court unanimous-

Prior to the *Brown v. Board of Education, Topeka* decision, African American children were often subjected to inferior educational facilities (The Library of Congress).

ly ruled that segregation in all public education deprived minority children of equal protection under the Fourteenth Amendment. (In the Bolling *case, the Court determined that segregation violated provisions of the Fifth Amendment, since the Fourteenth Amendment is expressly directed to the states.)*

Chief Justice Warren delivered the opinion of the Court.

These cases come to us from the States of Kansas, South Carolina, Virginia and Delaware. They are premised on different facts and different local conditions, but a common legal question justifies their consideration together in this consolidated opinion.

In each of these cases, minors of the Negro race, through their legal representatives, seek the aid of the courts in obtaining admission to the public schools of their community on a nonsegregated basis. In each instance, they had been denied admission to schools attended by white children under laws requiring or permitting segregation according to race. This segregation was alleged to deprive the plaintiffs of the equal protection of the laws under the Fourteenth Amendment. In each of the cases other than the Delaware case, a three-judge federal district court denied relief to the plaintiffs on the so-called "separate but equal" doctrine announced by this Court in this Court in *Plessy v. Ferguson....* Under that doctrine, equality of treatment is accorded when the races are provided substantially equal facilities, even though these facilities be separate. In the Delaware case, the Supreme Court of Delaware adhered to that doctrine, but ordered that the plaintiffs be admitted to the white schools because of their superiority to the Negro schools.

The plaintiffs contend that segregated public schools are not "equal" and cannot be made "equal," and that hence they are deprived of the equal protection of the laws. Because of the obvious importance of the question presented, the Court took jurisdiction. Argument was heard in the 1952 Term, and reargument was heard this Term on certain questions propounded by the Court.

Reargument was largely devoted to the circumstances surrounding the adoption of the Fourteenth Amendment in 1868. It covered exhaustively consideration of the Amendment in Congress, ratification by the states, then existing practices in racial segregation, and the views of proponents and opponents of the Amendment. This discussion and our own investigation convince us that, although these sources cast some light, it is not enough to resolve the problem with which we are faced. At best, they are inconclusive. The most avid proponents of the post-War Amendments undoubtedly intended them to remove all legal distinctive among "all persons born or naturalized in the United States." Their opponents, just as certainly, were antagonistic to both the letter and the spirit of the Amendments and wished them to have the most limited effect. What others in Congress and the state legislatures had in mind cannot be determined with any degree of certainty.

An additional reason for the inconclusive nature of the Amendment's history, with respect to segregated schools, is the status of public education at that time. In the South, the movement toward free common schools, supported by general taxation, had not yet taken hold. Education of white children was largely in the hands of private groups. Education of Negroes was almost non-existent, and practically all of the race were illiterate. In fact, any education of Negroes was forbidden by law in some states. Today, in contrast, many Negroes have achieved outstanding success in the arts and sciences as well as in the business and professional world. It is true that public school education at the time of the Amendment had advanced further in the North, but the effect of the Amendment on Northern States was generally ignored by the congressional debates. Even in the North, the conditions of public education did not approximate those existing today. The curriculum was usually rudimentary; ungraded schools were common in rural areas; the school term was but three months a year in many states; and compulsory school attendance was virtually unknown. As a consequence, it is not surprising that there should be so little in the history of the Fourteenth Amendment relating to its intended effect on public education.

In the first cases in this Court construing the Fourteenth Amendment, decided shortly after its adoption, the Court interpreted it as proscribing all state imposed discriminations against the Negro race. The doctrine of "separate but equal" did not make its appearance in this Court until 1896 in the case of *Plessy v. Ferguson...* involving not education but transportation. American courts have since labored with the doctrine for over half a century. In this Court, there have been six cases involving the "separate but equal" doctrine in the field of public education. In *Cumming v. County Board of Education...* and *Gong Lum v. Rice...* the validity of the doctrine itself was not challenged. In more recent cases, all on the graduate school level, inequality was found in that specific benefits enjoyed by white students were denied to Negro students of the same educational qualifications. In none of these cases [*Missouri ex rel. Gaines v. Canada, Sipuel v. University of Oklahoma, Sweatt v. Painter,* and *McLaurin v. Oklahoma State Regents*] was it necessary to reexamine the doctrine to grant relief to the Negro plaintiff. And in *Sweatt v. Painter...* the Court expressly reserved decision on the question whether *Plessy v. Ferguson* should be held inapplicable to public education.

In the instant cases, that question is directly presented. Here, unlike *Sweatt v. Painter,* there are findings below that the Negro and white schools involved have been equalized, or are being equalized, with respect to buildings, curricula, qualifications and salaries of teacher, and other "tangible" factors. Our decision, therefore, cannot turn on merely a comparison of these tangible factors in the Negro and white schools involved in each of the cases. We must look instead to the effect of segregation itself on public education.

In approaching this problem, we cannot turn the clock back to 1868 when the Amendment was adopted, or even to 1896 when *Plessy v. Ferguson* was written. We must consider public education in the light of its full development and its present place in American life throughout the Nation. Only in this way can it be determined if segregation in public schools deprives these plaintiffs of the equal protection of the laws.

Today, education is perhaps the most important function of state and local governments. Compulsory school attendance laws and the great expenditures for education both demonstrate our recognition of the importance of education to our democratic society. It is required in the performance of our most basic public responsibilities, even service in the armed forces. It is the very foundation of good citizenship. Today it is a principal instrument in awakening the child to cultural values, in preparing him for later professional training, and in helping him to adjust normally to his environment. In these days, it is doubtful that any child may reasonably be expected to succeed in life if he is denied the opportunity of an education. Such an opportunity, where the state has undertaken to provide it, is a right which must be made available to all on equal terms.

We come then to the question presented: Does segregation of children in public schools solely on the basis of race, even though the physical facilities and other "tangible" factors may be equal, deprive the children of the minority group of equal educational opportunities? We believe that it does.

In *Sweatt v. Painter* in finding that a segregated law school for Negroes could not provide them equal educational opportunities, this Court relied in large part on "those qualities which are incapable of objective measurement but which make for greatness in the law school." In *McLaurin v. Oklahoma State Regents* . . . the Court, in requiring that a Negro admitted to a white graduate school be treated like all other students, again resorted to intangible considerations: ". . . his ability to study, to engage in discussions and exchange views with other students, and, in general, to learn his profession." Such considerations apply with added force to children in grade and high schools. To separate them from others of similar age and qualifications solely because of their race generates a feeling of inferiority as to their status in the community that may affect their hearts and minds in a way unlikely ever to be undone. The effect of this separation on their educational opportunities was well stated by a finding in the Kansas case by a court which nevertheless felt compelled to rule against the Negro plaintiffs:

> "Segregation of white and colored children in public school has a detrimental effect upon the colored children. The impact is greater when it has the sanction of the law; for the policy of separating the races is usually interpreted as denoting the inferiority of the negro group. A sense of inferiority affects the motivation of a child to learn. Segregation with the sanction of law, therefore, has a tendency to [retard] the educational and mental development of Negro children and to deprive them of some of the benefits they would receive in racial[ly] integrated school systems."

Whatever may have been the extent of psychological knowledge at the time of *Plessy v. Ferguson*, this finding is amply supported by modern authority. Any language in *Plessy v. Ferguson* contrary to this finding is rejected.

We conclude that in the field of public education the doctrine of "separate but equal" has no place. Separate educational facilities are inherently unequal. Therefore, we hold that the plaintiffs and others similarly situated for whom the actions have brought are, by reason of the segregation complained of, deprived of the equal protection of the laws guaranteed by the Fourteenth Amendment. This disposition makes unnecessary any discussion whether such segregation also violates the Due Process Clause of the Fourteenth Amendment.

Because these are class actions, because of the wide applicability of this decision, and because of the great variety of local conditions, the formulation of decrees in these presents problems of considerable complexity. On reargument, the consideration of appropriate relief was necessarily subordinated to the primary question— the constitutionality of segregation in public education. We have now announced that such segregation is a denial of the equal protection of the laws. In order that we may have the full assistance of the parties in formulating decrees, the cases will be restored to the docket, and the parties are requested to present further argument on Questions 4 and 5 previously propounded by the Court for the reargument this Term. The Attorney General of the United States is again invited to participate. The Attorneys General of the states requiring or permitting segregation in public education will also be permitted to appear as amici curiae upon request to do so by September 15, 1954, and submission of briefs by October 1, 1954.

It is so ordered.

◆ *THE SOULS OF BLACK FOLKS: ESSAYS AND SKETCHES* BY W.E.B. DU BOIS (1955) (EXCERPT)

Many scholars believe that among prominent civil rights leader W.E.B. Du Bois' greatest achievements, his writings truly stand out. Throughout his lifetime, he penned many books and essays expressing his beliefs about racial assimilation, cooperation, and the use of education to end prejudice. Among these notable writings is The Souls of Black Folk, *an extremely popular analysis of the problem of race as it relates to African Americans throughout society.*

After the Egyptian and Indian, the Greek and Roman, the Teuton and Mongolian, the Negro is sort of seventh son, born with a veil, and gifted with second-sight in this American world,—a world which yields him no true self-consciousness, but only lets him see himself through the revelation of the other world. It is a peculiar sensation, this double-consciousness, this sense of always looking at one's self through the eyes of others, of measuring one's soul by the tape of a world that looks on in amused contempt and pity. One ever feels his twoness,—an American, a Negro; two souls, two thoughts, two unreconciled strivings; two warring ideals in one dark body, whose dogged strength alone keeps it from being torn asunder.

The history of the American Negro is the history of this strife,—this longing to attain self-conscious manhood, to merge his double self into a better and truer self. In this merging he wishes neither of the older selves to be lost. He would not Africanize America, for America has too much to teach the world and Africa. He would not bleach his Negro soul in a flood of white Americanism, for he knows that Negro blood has a message for the world. He simply wishes to make it possible for a man to be both a Negro and an American, without being cursed and spit upon by his fellows, without having the doors of Opportunity closed roughly in his face.

◆ MARY MCLEOD BETHUNE'S LAST WILL AND TESTAMENT (1955) (EXCERPT)

Prior to her death on May 18, 1955, educator and Bethune-Cookman College founder Mary McLeod Bethune composed her "Last Will and Testament," which was published posthumously in Ebony *magazine. Although a tireless fighter for equality and educational opportunities for African Americans, she continuously eschewed rhetorical militancy in favor of a doctrine of universal love, as demonstrated by the following text.*

Sometimes as I sit communing in my study I feel that death is not far off. I am aware that it will overtake me before the greatest of my dreams—full equality for the Negro in our time is realized. . . . The knowledge that my work has been helpful to many fills me with joy and great satisfaction.

Sometimes I ask myself if I have any other legacy to leave. Truly, my worldly possessions are few. . . . Perhaps in them there is something of value. So, as my life draws to a close, I will pass them on to Negroes everywhere in the hope that an old woman's philosophy may give them inspiration. Here, then, is my legacy.

I leave you love. Love builds. It is positive and helpful.

I leave you great hope. The Negro's growth will be great in the years to come.

I leave you the challenge of developing confidence in one another. As long as Negroes are hemmed into racial blocs by prejudice and pressure, it will be necessary for them to band together for economic betterment.

I leave you a thirst for education. Knowledge is the prime need of the hour.

I leave you a respect for the uses of power. We live in a world which respects power above all things. Power, intelligently directed, can lead to more freedom.

I leave you faith. Faith is the first factor in a life devoted to service. Without faith, nothing is possible. With it, nothing is impossible. Faith in God is the greatest power, but great, too, is faith in oneself.

I leave you racial dignity. I want Negroes to maintain their human dignity at all costs. We, as Negroes, must recognize that we are the custodians as well as the heirs of a great civilization.

I leave you a desire to live harmoniously with your fellow men. The problem of color is world-wide. It is found in Africa and Asia, Europe, and South America. I appeal to American Negroes—North, South, East and West—to recognize their common problems and unite to solve them.

I leave you finally a responsibility to our young people. The world around us really belongs to youth, for youth will take over its future management.

If I have a legacy to leave my people, it is my philosophy of living and serving. As I face tomorrow, I am content, for I think I have spent my life well. I pray now that my philosophy may be helpful to those who share my vision of a world of Peace, Progress, Brotherhood and Love.

◆ CIVIL RIGHTS ACT OF 1957, PUB.L. NO. 85–315, 71 Stat. 634 (1957)

This act, signed by President Eisenhower on September 9, 1957, was the first piece of comprehensive legislation in the area of civil rights since the Civil Rights Act of 1875, which the Supreme Court in 1883 declared unconstitutional. The new act provided for the creation of a Commission on Civil Rights, extended the jurisdiction of the federal district courts to include civil action arising out of the act, and empowered the U.S. Attorney General to take action in cases where rights secured by the act were believed to have been violated.

An Act to provide means of further securing and protecting the civil rights of persons within the jurisdiction of the United States.

Part I—Establishment of the Commission on Civil Rights

Sec. 101. (a) There is created in the executive branch of the Government a Commission on Civil Rights (hereinafter called the "Commission").

(b) The Commission shall be composed of six members who shall be appointed by the President by and with the advice and consent of the Senate. Not more than three of the members shall at any one time be of the same political party.

(c) The President shall designate one of the members of the Commission as Chairman and one as Vice Chairman. The Vice Chairman shall act as Chairman in the absence or disability of the Chairman, or in the event of a vacancy in that office.

(d) Any vacancy in the Commission shall not affect its powers and shall be filled in the same manner, and subject to the same limitation with respect to party affiliations as the original appointment was made. . . .

Part IV—To Provide Means of Further Securing and Protecting the Right to Vote

Sec. 131. Section 2004 of the Revised Statutes (42 U.S.C. 1971), is amended as follows:

. . . No person, whether acting under cover of law or otherwise, shall intimidate, threaten, coerce, or attempt to intimidate, or coerce any other person for the purpose of interfering with the right of such other person to vote as he may choose, or of causing such other person to vote, for, or to vote as he may choose, or of causing such other person to vote for, or not to vote for, any candidate for the office of President, Vice President, presidential elector, Member of the Senate, or Member of the House of Representatives, Delegates or Commissioners from the Territories or possessions, at any general, special, or primary election held solely or in part for the purpose of selecting or electing any such candidate.

. . . Whenever any person has engaged or there are reasonable grounds to believe that any person is about to engage in any act or practice which would deprive any right or privilege secured by subsection (a) or (b), the Attorney General may institute for the United States, or in the name of the United States, a civil action or other proper proceeding for preventive relief, including an application for a permanent or temporary injunction, restraining order, or other order. In any proceeding hereunder the United States shall be liable for costs the same as a private person. . . .

◆ EXECUTIVE ORDER NO. 10730, 3 C.F.R. 1954–1958 COMP. P. 388 (1957)

In September of 1957, Arkansas Governor Orval Faubus mobilized the Arkansas National Guard in an effort to prevent African American students from entering Little Rock's Central High School. As a result, on September 24, President Dwight D. Eisenhower issued an executive order authorizing the use of the National Guard and the Air National Guard of the United States to assist in desegregation in Little Rock.

Whereas on September 23, 1957, I issued Proclamation No. 3204 reading in part as follows:

Whereas certain persons in the State of Arkansas, individually and in unlawful assemblages, combinations, and conspiracies, have wilfully obstructed the enforcement of orders of the United States District Court for the Eastern District of Arkansas with respect to matters relating to enrollment and attendance at public schools, particularly at Central High School, located in Little Rock School District, Little Rock, Arkansas; and

Whereas such wilful obstruction of justice hinders the execution of the laws of that State and of the United States, and makes it impracticable to enforce such laws by the ordinary course of judicial proceedings; and

Whereas such obstruction of justice constitutes a denial of the equal protection of the laws secured by the Constitution of the United States and impedes the course of justice under those laws;

Now, therefore, I, Dwight D. Eisenhower, President of the United States, under and by virtue of the authority vested in me by the Constitution and Statutes of the United States, including Chapter 15 of Title 10 of the United States Code, particularly sections 332, 333 and 334 thereof, do command all persons engaged in such obstruction of justice to cease and desist therefrom, and to disperse forthwith, and

Whereas the command contained in that Proclamation has not been obeyed and wilful obstruction of enforcement of said court orders still exists and threatens to continue:

Now, therefore, by virtue of the authority vested in me by the Constitution and Statutes of the United States, including Chapter 15 of Title 10, particularly sections 332, 333 and 334 thereof, and section 301 of Title 3 of the United States Code, it is hereby ordered as follows:

Section 1. I hereby authorize and direct the Secretary of Defense to order into the active military service of the United States as he may deem appropriate to carry out the purposes of this Order, any or all of the units of the National Guard of the United States and of the Air National Guard of the United States within the State of Arkansas to serve in the active military service of the United States for an indefinite period and until relieved by appropriate orders.

Section 2. The Secretary of Defense is authorized and directed to take all appropriate steps to enforce any orders of the United States District Court for the Eastern District of Arkansas for the removal of obstruction of justice in the State of Arkansas with respect to matters relating to enrollment and attendance at public schools in the Little Rock School District, Little Rock, Arkansas. In carrying out the provisions of this section, the Secretary of Defense is authorized to use the units, and members thereof, ordered into the active military service of the United States pursuant to Section 1 of this Order.

Section 3. In furtherance of the enforcement of the aforementioned orders of the United States District Court for the Eastern District of Arkansas, the Secretary of Defense is authorized to use such of the armed forces of the United States as he may deem necessary.

Federal troops escorting African American students to class at Little Rock's Central High School (AP/Wide World Photos, Inc.).

Section 4. The Secretary of Defense is authorized to delegate to the Secretary of the Army or the Secretary of the Air Force, or both, any of the authority conferred upon him by this Order.

◆ CIVIL RIGHTS ACT OF 1960, PUB.L. NO. 86–449, 74 Stat. 86 (1960)

This act, signed by President Eisenhower on May 6, 1960, further defined civil rights violations and outlined penalties connected with such violations. It guaranteed the provision of criminal penalties in the event a suspect crosses state lines to avoid legal process for the actual or attempted bombing or burning of any vehicle or building, and provided penalties for persons who obstructed or interfered with any order of a federal court.

An Act to enforce constitutional rights, and for other purposes.

Title II

Sec. 201. Chapter 49 of title 18, United States Code, is amended by adding at the end thereof a new section as follows:

Section 1074. Flight to avoid prosecution for damaging or destroying any building or other real or personal property.

. . . Whoever moves or travels in interstate or foreign commerce with intent either (1) to avoid prosecution, or custody, or confinement after conviction, under the laws of the place from which he flees, for willfully attempting to or damaging or destroying by fire or explosive any building, structure, facility, vehicle, dwelling house, synagogue, church, religious center or educational institution, public or private, or (2) to avoid giving testimony in any criminal proceeding relating to any such offense shall be fined not more than $5,000 or imprisoned not more than five years, or both.

. . . Violations of this section may be prosecuted in the Federal judicial district in which the original crime was alleged to have been committed or in which the person was held in custody or confinement. . . .

Sec. 203. Chapter 39 of title 18 of the United States Code is amended by adding at the end thereof the following new section:

Section 837. Explosives; illegal use or possession; and, threats or false information concerning attempts to damage or destroy real or personal property by fire or explosives.

. . . Whoever transports or aids and abets another in transporting in interstate or foreign commerce any explosive, with the knowledge or intent that it will be used to damage or destroy any building or other real or personal property for the purpose of interfering with its use for educational, religious, charitable, residential, business, or civic objectives or of intimidating any person pursuing such objectives, shall be subject to imprisonment for not more than one year, or a fine of not more than $1,000 or both; and if personal injury results shall be subject to imprisonment for not more than ten years or a fine of not more than $10,000, or both; and if death results shall be subject to imprisonment for any term of years or for life, but the court may impose the death penalty if the jury so recommends.

. . . The possession of an explosive in such a manner as to evince an intent to use, or the use of, such explosive, to damage or destroy any building or other real or personal property used for educational, religious, charitable, residential, business, or civic objectives or to intimidate any person pursuing such objectives, creates rebuttable presumptions that the explosive was transported in interstate or foreign commerce or caused to be transported in interstate or foreign commerce by the person so possessing or using it, or by a person aiding or abetting the person so possessing or using it: Provided, however, that no person may be convicted under this section unless there is evidence independent of the presumptions that this section has been violated.

. . . Whoever, through the use of the mail, telephone, telegraph, or other instrument of commerce, willfully imparts or conveys, or causes to be imparted or conveyed, any threat, or false information knowing the same to be false, concerning an attempt or alleged attempt being made, or to be made, to damage or destroy any building or other real or personal property for the purpose of interfering with its use for educational, religious, charitable, residential, business, or civic objectives, or of intimidating any person pursuing such objectives, shall be subject to imprisonment for not more than one year or a fine of not more than $1,000, or both.

◆ EXECUTIVE ORDER NO. 11053, 3 C.F.R. 1959–1963 COMP P.645 (1962)

On September 30, 1962, riots erupted on the campus of the University of Mississippi when Governor Ross Barnett attempted to block the court-ordered admission of African American student James H. Meredith.

President John F. Kennedy quickly responded by authorizing the use of federal troops to restore order.

Whereas on September 30, 1962, I issued Proclamation No. 3497 reading in part as follows:

Whereas the Governor of the State of Mississippi and certain law enforcement officers and other officials of that State, and other persons, individually and in unlawful opposing and obstructing the enforcement of orders entered by the United States District Court for the Southern District of Mississippi and the United States Court of Appeals for the Fifth Circuit; and

Whereas such unlawful assemblies, combinations, and conspiracies oppose and obstruct the execution of the laws of the United States, impede the course of justice under those laws and make it impracticable to enforce those laws in the State of Mississippi by the ordinary course of judicial proceedings; and

Whereas I have expressly called the attention of the Governor of Mississippi to the perilous situation that exists and to his duties in the premises, and have requested but have not received from him adequate assurances that the orders of the courts of the United States will be obeyed and that law and order will be maintained:

Now, therefore, I, John F. Kennedy, President of the United States, under and by virtue of the authority vested in me by the Constitution and laws of the United States, including Chapter 15 of Title 10 of the United States Code, particularly sections 332, 333 and 334 thereof, do command all persons engaged in such obstructions of justice to cease and desist therefrom to disperse and retire peaceably forth-with; and

Whereas the commands contained in that proclamation have not been obeyed and obstruction of enforcement of those court orders still exists and threatens to continue:

Now, therefore, by virtue of the authority vested in me by the Constitution and laws of the United States, including Chapter 15 of Title 10, particularly Sections 332, 333 and 334 thereof, and Section 301 of Title 3 of the United States Code, it is hereby ordered as follows:

Section 1. The Secretary of Defense is authorized and directed to take all appropriate steps to enforce all orders of the United States District Court for the Southern District of Mississippi and the United States Court of Appeals for the Fifth Circuit and to remove all obstructions of justice in the State of Mississippi.

Section 2. In furtherance of the enforcement of the aforementioned orders of the United States District Court for the Southern District of Mississippi and the United States Court of Appeals for the Fifth Circuit, the Secretary of Defense is authorized to use such of the armed forces of the United States as he may deem necessary.

Section 3. I hereby authorize the Secretary of Defense to call into the active military service of the United States, as he may deem appropriate to carry out the purposes of this order, any or all of the units of the Army National Guard and of the Air National Guard of the State of Mississippi to serve in the active military service of the United States for an indefinite period and until relieved by appropriate orders. In carrying out the provisions of Section 1, the Secretary of Defense is authorized to use the units, and members thereof, ordered into the active military service of the United States pursuant to this section.

Section 4. The Secretary of Defense is authorized to delegate to the Secretary of the Army or the Secretary of the Air Force, or both, any of the authority conferred upon him by this order.

◆ THE BIRMINGHAM MANIFESTO (1963)

In 1963, a series of events in Birmingham, Alabama made known the plight of African Americans to the nation at large. African American citizens were arrested en masse during peaceful demonstrations—demonstrations which were crushed by police dogs and firehoses. The Manifesto, dated April 3, 1963, embodied the hope of the African American community in Birmingham that law, order, and peace would somehow prevail.

The patience of an oppressed people cannot endure forever. The Negro citizens of Birmingham for the last several years have hoped in vain for some evidence. . . [of the]. . . resolution of our just grievances.

Birmingham is part of the United States and we are bona fide citizens. Yet the history of Birmingham reveals that very little of the democratic process touches the life of the Negro in Birmingham. We have been segregated racially, exploited economically, and dominated politically. Under the leadership of the Alabama Christian Movement for Human Rights, we sought relief by petition for the repeal of city ordinances requiring segregation and the institution of a merit hiring policy in city employment. We were rebuffed. We then turned to the system of the courts. We weathered set-back after set-back, with all of its costliness, finally winning the terminal, bus, parks and airport cases. The bus decision has been implemented begrudging and the parks decision prompted the closing of all municipally-owned recreational facilities with the exception of the zoo and Legion Field. . . .

We have always been a peaceful people, bearing our oppression with superhuman effort. Yet we have been the victims of repeated violence, not only that inflicted by the hoodlum element but also that inflicted by the blatant misuse of police power. . . . For years, while our homes and churches were being bombed, we heard nothing but the rantings and ravings of racist city officials.

The Negro protest for equality and justice has been a voice crying in the wilderness. Most of Birmingham has remained silent, probably out of fear. In the meanwhile, our city has acquired the dubious reputation of being the worst big city in race relations in the United States. Last fall, for a flickering moment, it appeared that sincere community leaders from religion, business and industry discerned the inevitable confrontation in race relations approaching. Their concern for the city's image and commonwealth of all its citizens did not run deep enough. Solemn promises were made, pending a postponement of direct action, that we would be joined in a suit seeking the relief of segregation ordinances. Some merchants agreed to desegregate their restrooms as a good faith start, some actually complying, only to retreat shortly thereafter. We hold in our hands now, broken faith and broken promises. We believe in the American Dream of democracy, in the Jeffersonian doctrine that "all men are created equal and are endowed by their Creator with certain inalienable rights, among these being life, liberty and the pursuit of happiness."

Twice since September we have deferred our direct action thrust in order that a change in city government would not be made in the hysteria of a community crisis. We act today in full concert with our Hebraic-Christian traditions, the law of morality and the Constitution of our nation. The absence of justice and progress in Birmingham demands that we make a moral witness to give our community a chance to survive. We demonstrate our faith that we believe that the beloved community can come to Birmingham. We appeal to the citizenry of Birmingham, Negro and white, to join us in this witness for decency, morality, self-respect and human dignity. Your individual and corporate support can hasten the day of "liberty and justice for all." This is Birmingham's moment of truth in which every citizen can play his part in her larger destiny. . . .

◆ MARTIN LUTHER KING'S SPEECH AT THE LINCOLN MEMORIAL, WASHINGTON, DC (1963)

On August 28, 1963, some 250,000 people gathered at the Lincoln Memorial in Washington, DC, in order to raise the nation's consciousness and to demonstrate on behalf of the civil legislation being debated in Congress. It was during this demonstration that Dr. Martin Luther King, Jr. gave the "I Have a Dream" speech.

I am happy to join with you today in what will go down in history as the greatest demonstration for freedom in the history of our nation.

Five score years ago, a great American, in whose symbolic shadow we stand today, signed the Emancipation Proclamation. This momentous decree came as a great beacon of light of hope to millions of Negro slaves who had been seared in the flames of withering injustice. It came as a joyous daybreak to end the long night of their captivity.

But one hundred years later, the Negro is still not free. One hundred years later, the life of the Negro is still sadly crippled by the manacles of segregation and the chains of discrimination. One hundred years later, the Negro lives on a lonely island of poverty in the midst of a vast ocean of material prosperity. One hundred years later, the Negro is still languished in the corners of American society and finds himself an exile in his own land. So we have come here today to dramatize a shameful condition.

In a sense we have come to our nation's capitol to cash a check. When the architects of our republic wrote the magnificent words of the Constitution and the Declaration of Independence, they were signing a promissory note to which every American was to fall heir. This note was a promise that all men, yes black men as well as white men, would be guaranteed the unalienable rights of life, liberty, and the pursuit of happiness. It is obvious today that America has defaulted on this promissory note insofar as her citizens of color are concerned. Instead of honoring this sacred obligation, America has given the Negro people a bad check: a check which has come back marked "insufficient funds." But we refuse to believe that the bank of justice is bankrupt. We refuse to believe that there are insufficient funds in the great vaults of opportunity of this nation. So we have come to cash this check—a check that will give us upon demand the riches of freedom and the security of justice.

We have also come to this hallowed spot to remind America of the fierce urgency of now. This is not the time to engage in the luxury of cooling off or to take the tranquilizing drug of gradualism. Now is the time to make real the promises of democracy. Now is the time to rise from the dark and desolate valley of segregation to the sunlit path of racial justice. Now is the time to lift our nation from the quicksands of racial injustice to the solid rock of brotherhood. Now is the time to make justice a reality for all of God's children.

It would be fatal for the nation to overlook the urgency of the moment and to underestimate the determination of the Negro. This sweltering summer of the Negro's legitimate discontent will not pass until there is an invigorating autumn of freedom and equality. Nine-teen hundred and sixty-three is not an end, but a beginning. Those who hope that the Negro needed to blow off steam, and will now be content will have a rude awakening if the Nation returns to business as usual. There will neither be rest nor tranquility in America until the Negro is granted his citizenship rights. The whirlwinds of revolt will continue to shake the foundations of our Nation until the bright day of justice emerges.

But there is something that I must say to my people who stand on the warm threshold which leads into the palace of justice. In the process of gaining our rightful place we must not be guilty of wrongful deeds. Let us not seek to satisfy our thirst for freedom by drinking from the cup of bitterness and hatred.

We must forever conduct our struggle on the high plane of dignity and discipline. We must not allow our creative protest to degenerate into physical violence. Again and again we must rise to the majestic heights of meeting physical force with soul force. The marvelous new militancy which has engulfed the Negro community must not lead us to a distrust of all white people, for many of our white brothers, as evidenced by their presence here today, have come to realize that their destiny is tied up with our destiny and their freedom is inextricably bound to our freedom. We cannot walk alone.

And as we walk, we must make the pledge that we shall always march ahead. We cannot turn back. There are those who are asking the devotees of civil rights, "when will you be satisfied?" We can never be satisfied as long as the Negro is the victim of the unspeakable horrors of police brutality. We can never be satisfied as long as our bodies, heavy with the fatigue of travel, cannot gain lodging in the motels of the highways and the hotels of the cities. We cannot be satisfied as long as the Negro's basic mobility is from a smaller ghetto to a larger one. We can never be satisfied as long as our children are stripped of their self-hood and robbed of their dignity by signs reading "For Whites Only." We can never be satisfied as long as a Negro in Mississippi cannot vote and a Negro in New York believes he has nothing for which to vote. No. No, we are not satisfied, and we will not be satisfied until justice rolls down like waters, and righteousness like a mighty stream.

I am not unmindful that some of you have come here out of great trials and tribulations. Some of you have come fresh from narrow jail cells. Some of you have come from areas where your quest for freedom left you battered by the storms of persecution and staggered by the winds of police brutality. You have been the victims of creative suffering. Continue to work with the faith that unearned suffering is redemptive.

Go back to Mississippi, go back to Alabama, go back to South Carolina, go back to Georgia, go back to Louisiana, go back to the slums and ghettos of our northern cities, knowing that somehow this situation can and will be changed. Let us not wallow in the valley of despair.

I say to you today, my friends, that in spite of the difficulties and frustrations of the moment, I still have a dream. It is a dream deeply rooted in the American dream. I have a dream that one day this nation will rise up and live out the true meaning of its creed: "We hold these truths to be self-evident—that all men are created equal."

I have a dream that one day on the red hills of Georgia the sons of former slaves and the sons of former slaveowners will be able to sit down together at the table of brotherhood. I have a dream that one day even the state of Mississippi, a desert state sweltering with the heat of injustice and oppression, will be transformed into an oasis of freedom and justice.

I have a dream that my four little children will one day live in a nation where they will not be judged by the color of their skin but by the content of their character.

I have a dream today.

I have a dream that one day the state of Alabama, whose governor's lips are presently dripping with the words of interposition and nullification, will be transformed into a situation where little black boys and black girls will be able to join hands with little white boys and white girls and walk together as sisters and brothers.

I have a dream today.

I have a dream that one day every valley shall be exalted, every hill and mountain shall be made low, the rough places will be made plain, and the crooked places will be made straight, and the glory of the Lord shall be revealed, and all flesh shall see it together.

This is our hope. This is the faith with which I return to the South. With this faith we will be able to transform the jangling discords of our nation into a beautiful symphony of brotherhood. With this faith we will be able to work together, to pray together, to struggle together, to go to jail together, to stand up for freedom together, knowing that we will be free one day.

This will be the day when all of God's children will be able to sing the new meaning "My country 'tis of thee, sweet land of liberty, of thee I sing. Land where my fathers died, land of the pilgrim's pride, from every mountainside, let freedom ring."

And if America is to be a great nation this must become true. So let freedom ring from the prodigious hilltops of New Hampshire! Let freedom ring from the mighty mountains of New York! Let freedom ring from the heightening Alleghenies of Pennsylvania!

Let freedom ring from the snowcapped Rockies of Colorado!

Let freedom ring from the curvaceous peaks of California!

But not only that; let freedom ring from Stone Mountain of Georgia!

Let freedom ring from Lookout Mountain of Tennessee.

Let freedom ring from every hill and mole hill of Mississippi. From every mountainside, let freedom ring.

When we let freedom ring, when we let it ring from every village and every hamlet, from every state and every city, we will be able to speed up that day when all God's children—black men and white men, Jews and Gentiles, Protestants and Catholics—will be able to join hands and sing in the words of that old Negro spiritual, Free at last! Free at last! Thank God almighty, we are free at last!

◆ AMENDMENT TWENTY-FOUR TO THE UNITED STATES CONSTITUTION (1964)

By 1964, when the Twenty-Fourth Amendment was ratified, most states had already discontinued the use of the poll tax, which had proved to be one of the most effective means of keeping African Americans from the polls—only the states of Alabama, Arkansas, Mississippi, Texas, and Virginia still implemented such a tax. The amendment, proposed in 1962, banned the use of poll taxes as a prerequisite to participating in federal elections; ruling in the case Harper v. Virginia Board of Elections, *the U.S. Supreme Court banned the use of poll taxes in state elections.*

Section 1. The right of citizens of the United States to vote in any primary or other election for President or Vice President, for electors for President or Vice President, or for Senator or Representative in Congress, shall not be denied or abridged by the United States or any State by reason of failure to pay any poll tax or other tax.

Section 2. The congress shall have power to enforce this article by appropriate legislation.

◆ CIVIL RIGHTS ACT OF 1964, PUB. L. NO. 88–352, 78 STAT. 241 (1964)

This civil rights act was signed by President Lyndon B. Johnson on July 2, 1964, although it had been initiated by President John F. Kennedy in June of 1963. More comprehensive than previous acts, the 1964 act contained 11 titles covering the areas of voting rights, access to public facilities, federal aid to schools engaged in the process of desegregation, discrimination in federally funded programs, and discrimination in employment. The act also strengthened earlier voter registration protection; made racial discrimination in restaurants, hotels, and motels illegal; provided for equal access to public parks, pools, and other facilities; outlined unlawful employment practice; and mandated the creation of a federal Equal Employment Opportunity Commission.

An Act to enforce the constitutional right to vote, to confer jurisdiction upon the district courts of the United States to provide injunctive relief against discrimination in public accommodations, to authorize the Attorney General to institute suits to protect constitutional rights in public facilities and public education, to extend the Commission on Civil Rights, to prevent discrimination in federally assisted programs, to establish a Commission on Equal Employment Opportunity, and for other purposes.

Title I—Voting Rights

Sec. 101. Section 2004 of the Revised Statutes (42 U.S.C. 1971). . . is further amended as follows:. . . .

. . . "No Person acting under color of law shall—"

"(A) In determining whether any individual is qualified under State law or laws to vote in any Federal election, apply any standard, practice, or procedure different from the standards, practices, or procedures applied under such law or laws to other individuals within the same county, parish, or similar political subdivision who have been found by State officials to be qualified to vote;"

"(B) deny the right of any individual to vote in any Federal election because of an error or omission on any record or paper relating to any application, registration, or other act requisite to voting, if such error or omission is not material in determining whether such individual is qualified under State law to vote in such election; or"

"(C) employ any literacy test as a qualification for voting in any Federal election unless (I) such test is administered to each individual and is conducted wholly in writing, and (II) a certified copy of the test and of the answers given by the individual is furnished to him within twenty-five days of the submission of his request made within the period of time during which records and papers are required to be retained and preserved pursuant to title III of the Civil Rights Act of 1960 (42 U.S.C. 1974–74e; 74 Stat. 88). . . ."

Sec. 201. (a) All persons shall be entitled to the full and equal enjoyment of the goods, services, facilities, privileges, advantages, and accommodations of any place of public accommodation, as defined in this section, without discrimination or segregation on the ground of race, color, religion, or national origin.

(b) Each of the following establishments which serves the public is a place of public accommodation within the meaning of this title if its operations affect commerce, or if discrimination or segregation by it is supported by State action:

(1) any inn, hotel, motel, or other establishment which provides lodging to transient guests, other than an establishment located within a building which contains not more than five rooms for rent or hire and which is actually occupied by the proprietor of such establishment as his residence;

(2) any restaurant, cafeteria, lunchroom, lunch counter, soda fountain, or other facility principally engaged in selling food for consumption on the premises, including, but not limited to, any such facility located on the premises of any retail establishment; or any gasoline station;

(3) any motion picture house, theater, concert hall, sports arena, stadium or other place of exhibition or entertainment; and

(4) any establishment (A)(I) which is physically located within the premises of any establishment otherwise covered by this subsection, or (II) within the premises of which is physically located any such covered establishment, and (B) which holds itself out as serving patrons of such covered establishment. . . .

(e) The provisions of this title shall not apply to a private club or other establishment not in fact open to the public, except to the extent that the facilities of such establishment are made available to the customers or patrons of an establishment within the scope of subsection (b).

Sec. 206. (a) Whenever the Attorney General has reasonable cause to believe that any person or group of persons is engaged in a pattern or practice of resistance to the full enjoyment of any of the rights secured by this title, and that the pattern or practice is of such a nature and is intended to deny the full exercise of the rights herein described, the Attorney General may bring a civil action in the appropriate district court of the United States. . . .

Title IV—Desegregation of Public Education

Sec. 407. (a) Whenever the Attorney General receives a complaint in writing—

(1) signed by a parent or group of parents to the effect that his or their minor children, as members of a class of persons similarly situated, are being deprived by a school board of the equal protection of the laws, or

(2) signed by an individual, or his parent, to the effect that he has been denied admission to or not permitted to continue in attendance at a public college by reason of race, color, religion, or national origin and the Attorney General believes the complaint is meritorious and certifies that the signer or signers of such complaint are unable, in his judgment, to initiate and maintain appropriate legal proceedings for relief and that the institution of an action will materially further the orderly achievement of desegregation in public education, the Attorney General is authorized, after giving notice of such complaint to the appropriate school board or college authority and after certifying that he is satisfied that such board or authority has had a reasonable time to adjust the conditions alleged in such complaint, to institute for or in the name of the United States a civil action in any appropriate district court of the United States against such parties and for such relief as may be appropriate. . . .

Title VI—Nondiscrimination In Federally-Assisted Programs

Sec. 601. No person in the United States shall, on the ground of race, color, or national origin, be excluded from participation in, be denied the benefits of, or be subjected to discrimination under any program or activity receiving Federal financial assistance. . . .

Title VII—Equal Employment Opportunity

Sec. 703. (a) It shall be an unlawful employment practice for an employer—

(1) to fail or refuse to hire or to discharge any individual, or otherwise to discriminate against any individual with respect to his compensation, terms, conditions, or privileges of employment, because of such individual's race, color, religion, sex, or national origin; or

(2) to limit, segregate, or classify his employees in any way which would deprive or tend to deprive any individual of employment opportunities or otherwise adversely affect his status as an employee, because of such individual's race, color, religion, sex, or national origin.

(b) It shall be an unlawful employment practice for an employment agency to fail or refuse to refer for employment, or otherwise to discriminate against, any individual because of his race, color, religion, sex, or national origin, or to classify or refer for employment any individual on the basis of his race, color, religion, sex, or national origin.

(c) It shall be an unlawful employment practice for a labor organization—

(1) to exclude or to expel from its membership, or otherwise to discriminate against, any individual because of his race, color, religion, sex, or national origin;

(2) to limit, segregate, or classify its membership, or to classify or fail or refuse to refer for employment any individual, in any way which would deprive or tend to deprive any individual of employment opportunities, or would limit such employment opportunities or otherwise adversely affect his status as an employee or as an applicant for employment, because of such individual's race, color, religion, sex, or national origin; or

(3) to cause or attempt to cause an employer to discriminate against an individual in violation of this section.

(d) It shall be an unlawful employment practice for any employer, labor organization, or joint labor-management committee controlling apprenticeship or other training or retraining, including on-the-job training programs to discriminate against any individual because of his race, color, religion, sex, or national origin in admission to, or employment in, any program established to provide apprenticeship or other training.

(e) Notwithstanding any other provision of this title, (1) it shall not be an unlawful employment practice for an employer to hire and employ employees, for an employment agency to classify, or refer for employment any individual, for a labor organization to classify its membership or to classify or refer for employment any individual, or for an employer, labor organization, or joint labor-management committee controlling apprenticeship or other training or retraining programs to admit or employ any individual in any such program, on the basis of his religion, sex, or national origin in those certain instances where religion, sex, or national origin is a bona fide occupational qualification reasonably necessary to the normal operation of that particular business or enterprise. . . .

Sec. 705. (1) There is hereby created a Commission to be known as the Equal Employment Opportunity Commission, which shall be composed of five members, not more than three of whom shall be members of the same political party, who shall be appointed by the President by and with the advice and consent of the Senate. . . .

◆ EXECUTIVE ORDER NO. 11246, 3 C.F.R., 1964–1965 COMP. P.339–348 (1965)

On September 24, 1965, President Lyndon B. Johnson issued the following executive order, prohibiting discrimination in government employment and government contracting.

Under and by virtue of the authority vested in me as President of the United States by the Constitution and statutes of the United States, it is ordered as follows:

Part I—Nondiscrimination in Government Employment

Section 101. It is the policy of the Government of the United States to provide equal opportunity in Federal employment for all qualified persons, to prohibit discrimination in employment because of race, creed, color, or national origin, and to promote the full realization of equal employment opportunity through a positive, continuing program in each executive department and agency. The policy of equal opportunity applies to every aspect of Federal employment policy and practice.

Section 102. The head of each executive department and agency shall establish and maintain a positive program of equal employment opportunity for all civilian employees and applicants for employment within his jurisdiction in accordance with the policy set forth in Section 101.

Section 103. The Civil Service Commission shall supervise and provide leadership and guidance in the conduct of equal employment opportunity programs for the civilian employees of and applications for employment within the executive departments and agencies and shall review agency program accomplishments periodically. In order to facilitate the achievement of a model program for equal employment opportunity in the Federal service, the Commission may consult from time to time with such individuals, groups, or organizations as may be of assistance in improving the Federal program and realizing the objectives of this part.

Section 104. The Civil Service Commission shall provide for the prompt, fair, and impartial consideration of all complaints of discrimination in Federal employment on the basis of race, creed, color, or national origin. Procedures for the consideration complaints shall include at least one impartial review within the executive department or agency and shall provide for appeal to the Civil Service Commission.

Section 105. The Civil Service Commission shall issue such regulations, orders, and instructions as it deems necessary and appropriate to carry out its responsibilities under this Part, and the head of each executive department and agency shall comply with the regulations, orders, and instructions issued by the Commission under this Part.

Part II—Nondiscrimination In Employment By Government Contractors And Subcontractors

Section 201. The Secretary of Labor shall be responsible for the administration of Parts II and III of this Order and shall adopt such rules and regulations and issue such orders as he deems necessary and appropriate to achieve the purposes thereof.

Section 202. Except in contracts exempted in accordance with Section 204 of this Order, all Government contracting agencies shall include in every Government contract hereafter entered into the following provisions:

"(1) The contractor will not discriminate against any employee or applicant for employment because of race, creed, color, or national origin. The contractor will take affirmative action to ensure that applicants are employed, and that employees are treated during employment, without regard to their race, creed, color, or national origin. Such action shall include, but not be limited to the following: employment, upgrading, demotion, or transfer; recruitment or recruitment advertising; layoff or termination; rates of pay or other forms of compensation; and selection for training, including apprenticeship. The contractor agrees to post in conspicuous places, available to employees and applicants for employment, notices to be provided by the contracting officer setting forth the provisions of this nondiscrimination clause."

"(2) The contractor will, in all solicitations or advertisements for employees placed by or on behalf of the contractor, state that all qualified applicants will receive consideration for employment without regard to race, creed, color, or national origin. . . ."

Part III—Nondiscrimination Provisions In Federally Assisted Construction Contracts

Section 301. Each executive department and agency which administers a program involving Federal financial assistance shall require as a condition for approval of any grant, contract, loan, insurance, or guarantee thereunder, which may involve a construction contract, that the applicant for Federal assistance undertake and agree to incorporate, or cause to be incorporated, into all construction contracts paid for in whole or in part with funds obtained from the Federal Government or borrowed on the credit of the Federal Government pursuant to such grant, contract, loan, insurance, or guarantee, or undertaken pursuant to any Federal program involving such grant, contract, loan, insurance, or guarantee, the provisions prescribed for Government contracts by Section 202 of this Order or such modification thereof, preserving in substance the contractor's obligations thereunder, as may be approved by the Secretary of Labor, together with such additional provisions as the Secretary deems appropriate to establish and protect the interest of the United States in the enforcement of those obligations. . . .

◆ VOTING RIGHTS ACT OF 1965 PUB.L. NO. 89–110, 79 STAT. 437 (1965)

Signed by President Lyndon B. Johnson on August 6, 1965, the Voting Rights Act was an outgrowth of the protest demonstrations organized by African Americans to draw attention to discriminatory voter-registration practices in several Southern states. The 1965 law abolished literacy, knowledge, and character tests as qualifications for voting; empowered federal registrars to register potential voters in any county where, in the judgments of the Attorney General of the United States, registrars were indeed necessary to enforce the Fifteenth Amendment; and gave the Attorney General of the United States the right to take whatever legal action be deemed necessary to eliminate any equivalent of the poll tax.

Although the single aim of the Voting Rights Act of 1965 was African American enfranchisement in the South, obstacles to registration and voting faced by all minorities were affected. Its potential as a tool for Hispanic Americans, however, was not fully realized for nearly a decade.

An Act to enforce the Fifteenth Amendment to the Constitution of the United States, and for other purposes.

Section 2. No voting qualification or prerequisite to voting, or standard, practice, or procedure shall be imposed or applied by any State or political subdivision to deny or abridge the right of any citizen of the United States to vote on account of race or color.

Section 4. (a) To assure that the right of citizens of the United States to vote is not denied or abridged on account of race or color, no citizen shall be denied the right to vote in any Federal, State, or local election because of his failure to comply with any test or device in any State with respect to which the determinations have been made under subsection (b) or in any political subdivision with respect to which such determinations have been made as a separate unit, unless the United States District Court for the District of Columbia in an action for a declaratory judgment brought by such State or subdivision against the United States has determined that no such test or device has been used during the five years preceding the filing of the action for the purpose or with the effect of denying or abridging the right to vote on account of race or color: *Provided,* That no such declaratory judgment shall issue with respect to any plaintiff for a period of five years after the entry of a final judgment of any court of the United States, other than the denial of a declaratory judgment under this section, whether entered prior to or after the enactment of this Act, determining that denials or abridgments of the right to vote on account of race or color through the use of such tests or devices have occurred anywhere in the territory of such plaintiff. . . .

(d) For purposes of this section no State or political subdivision shall be determined to have engaged in the use of tests or devices for the purpose or with the effect of denying or abridging the right to vote on account of race or color if (1) incidents of such use have been few in number and have been promptly and effectively corrected by State or local action, (2) the continuing effect of such incidents has been eliminated, and (3) there is no reasonable probability of their recurrence in the future. . . .

Section 10. (a) The Congress finds that the requirement of the payment of a poll tax as a precondition to voting (I) precludes persons of limited means from voting or imposes unreasonable financial hardship upon such persons as a precondition to their exercise of the franchise, (II) does not bear a reasonable relationship to any legitimate State interest in the conduct of elections, and (III) in some areas has the purpose or effect of denying persons the right to vote because of race or color. Upon the basis of these findings, Congress declares that the constitutional right of citizens to vote is denied or abridged in some areas by the requirement of the payment of a poll tax as a precondition to voting. . . .

Section 11. (a) No person acting under color of law shall fail or refuse to permit any person to vote who is entitled to vote under any provision of this Act or is otherwise qualified to vote, or willfully fail or refuse to tabulate, count, and report such person's vote.

(b) No person, whether acting under color of law or otherwise, shall intimidate, threaten, or coerce, or attempt to intimidate, threaten or coerce any person for voting or attempting to vote, or intimidate, threaten, or coerce, or attempt to intimidate, threaten, or coerce any person for urging or aiding any person to vote or attempt to vote, or intimidate, threaten, or coerce any person for exercising any powers or duties under section 3 (a), 6, 8, 9, 10, or 12 (e). . . .

Section 14. (1) The terms "vote" or "voting" shall include all action necessary to make a vote effective in any primary, special, or general election, including, but not limited to, registration, listing pursuant to this Act, or other action required by law prerequisite to voting, casting a ballot, and having such ballot counted properly and included in the appropriate totals of votes cast with respect to candidates for public or party office and propositions for which votes are received in an election. . . .

Sec. 17. Nothing in this Act shall be construed to deny, impair, or otherwise adversely affect the right to vote of any person registered to vote under the law of any state or political subdivision. . . .

◆ THE BLACK PANTHER MANIFESTO (1966)

The Black Panther Party relied on a strict and uncompromising regimen to mold its members into a unified and cohesive revolutionary force. Similar to the Nation of Islam, the party denounced all intoxicants, drugs, and artificial stimulants "while doing party work." The intellectual fare of every party member was the ten-point program, which every member was obliged to know, understand, and even to commit to memory.

1. We want FREEDOM. We want power to determine the destiny of our Black Community.

We believe that black people will not be free until we are able to determine our destiny.

2. We want full employment for our people.

We believe that the federal government is responsible and obligated to give every man employment or a guaranteed income. We believe that if the white American businessman will not give full employment, then the means of production should be taken from the businessmen and placed in the community so that the people of the community can organize and employ all of its people and give a high standard of living.

3. We want an end to the robbery by the CAPITALIST of our Black Community.

We believe that this racist government has robbed us and now we are demanding the overdue debt of forty acres and two mules. Forty acres and two mules was promised 100 years ago as restitution for slave labor and mass murder of black people. We will accept the payment in currency which will be distributed to our many communities. The Germans are now aiding the Jews in Israel for the genocide of the Jewish people. The Germans murdered six million Jews. The American racist has taken part in the slaughter of over fifty million black people, therefore, we feel that this is a modest demand that we make.

4. We want decent housing, fit for shelter of human beings.

We believe that if the white landlords will not give decent housing to our black community, then the housing and the land should be made into cooperatives so that our community, with government aid, can build and make decent housing for its people.

5. We want education for our people that exposes the true nature of this decadent American society. We want education that teaches us our true history and our role in the present-day society.

We believe in an educational system that will give to our people a knowledge of self. If a man does not have knowledge of himself and his position in society and the world, then he has little chance to relate to anything else.

6. We want all black men to be exempt from military service.

We believe that Black people should not be forced to fight in the military service to defend a racist government that does not protect us. We will not fight and kill other people of color in the world who, like black people, are being victimized by the white racist government of America. We will protect ourselves from the force and violence of the racist police and the racist military, by whatever means necessary.

7. We want an immediate end to POLICE BRUTALITY and MURDER of black people.

We believe we can end police brutality in our black community by organizing black self-defense groups that are dedicated to defending our black community from racist police oppression and brutality. The Second Amendment to the Constitution of the United States gives a right to bear arms. We therefore believe that all black people should arm themselves for self-defense.

8. We want freedom for all black men held in federal, state, county and city prisons and jails.

We believe that all black people should be released from the many jails and prisons because they have not received a fair and impartial trial.

Black Panthers demonstrating outside a Manhattan, New York courthouse during the murder trial of the "Harlem Six" (The New York Amsterdam News).

9. We want all black people when brought to trial to be tried in court by a jury of their peer group or people from their black communities, as defined by the constitution of the United States.

We believe that the courts should follow the United States Constitution so that black people will receive fair trials. The 14th Amendment of the U.S. Constitution gives a man a right to be tried by his peer group. A peer is a person from a similar economic, social, religious, geographical, environmental, historical and racial background. To do this the court will be forced to select a jury from the black community from which the black defendant came. We have been, and are being tried by all-white juries that have no understanding of the "average reasoning man" of the black community.

10. We want land, bread, housing, education, clothing, justice and peace. And as our major political objective, a United Nations-supervised plebiscite to be held

throughout the black colony in which only black colonial subjects will be allowed to participate, for the purpose of determining the will of black people as to their national destiny.

When, in the course of human events, it becomes necessary for one people to dissolve the political bands which have connected them with another, and to assume, among the powers of the earth, the separate and equal station to which the laws of nature and nature's God entitle them, a decent respect to the opinions of mankind requires that they should declare the causes which impel them to the separation.

We hold these truths to be self-evident, that all men are created equal; that they are endowed by their Creator with certain inalienable rights; that among these are life, liberty, and the pursuit of happiness.

That, to secure these rights, governments are instituted among them, deriving their just powers from the consent of the governed; that, whenever any form of government becomes destructive of these ends, it is the right of the people to alter or to abolish it, and to institute a new government, laying its foundation on such principles, and organizing its powers in such form, as to them shall seem most likely to effect their safety and happiness.

Prudence, indeed, will dictate that governments long established should not be changed for light and transient causes; and, accordingly, all experience hath shown, that mankind are more disposed to suffer, while evils are sufferable, than to right themselves by abolishing the forms to which they are accustomed. But, when a long train of abuses and usurpations, pursuing invariably the same object, evinces a design to reduce them under absolute despotism, it is their right, it is their duty, to throw off such government, and to provide new guards for their future security.

◆ CIVIL RIGHTS ACT OF 1968 PUB.L. NO. 90–284, TITLES VIII & IX, 82 STAT. 284 (1968)

Title VIII of Public Law 90–284, the Civil Rights Act of 1968, is better known as the Fair Housing Act. It was signed by President Lyndon B. Johnson on April 11, 1968, and created a national housing policy. The act made discrimination in the sale or rental or financing of housing illegal, and empowered the U.S. Attorney General to take action in such cases.

Title VIII—Fair Housing

Sec. 801. It is the policy of the United States to provide, within constitutional limitations, for fair housing throughout the United States.

Section 804. As made applicable by section 803 and except as exempted by sections 803(b) and 807, it shall be unlawful—

(a) to refuse to sell or rent after the making of a bona fide offer, or to refuse to negotiate for the sale or rental of, or otherwise make unavailable or deny, a dwelling to any person because of race, color, religion, or national origin.

(b) to discriminate against any person in the terms, conditions, or privileges of sale or rental of a dwelling, or in the provision of services or facilities in connection there-with, because of race, color, religion, or national origin.

(c) to make, print, or publish or cause to be made, printed, or published any notice, statement, or advertisement, with respect to the sale or rental of a dwelling that indicates any preference, limitation, or discrimination based on race, color, religion, or national origin, or an intention to make any such preference, limitation, or discrimination.

(d) to represent to any person because of race, color, religion, or national origin that any dwelling is not available for inspection, sale, or rental when such dwelling is in fact so available.

(e) for profit, to induce or attempt to induce any person to sell or rent any dwelling by representations regarding the entry or prospective entry into the neighborhood of a person or persons of a particular race, color, religion, or national origin.

Sec. 805. After December 31, 1968, it shall be unlawful for any bank, building and loan association, insurance company or other corporation, association, firm or enterprise whose business consists in whole or in part in the making of commercial real estate loans, to deny a loan or other financial assistance to a person applying therefor for the purpose of purchasing, constructing, improving, repairing, or maintaining a dwelling, or to discriminate against him in the fixing of the amount, interest rate, duration, or other terms or conditions of such loan or other financial assistance, because of the race, color, religion, or national origin of such person or of any person associated with him in connection with such loan or other financial assistance or the purposes of such loan or other financial assistance, or of the present or prospective owners, leases, tenants, or occupants of the dwelling or dwellings in relation to which such loan or other financial assistance is to be made or given. . . .

Title IX—Prevention of Intimidation in Fair Housing Cases

Section 901. Whoever, whether or not acting under color of law, by force or threat of force willfully injures, intimidates or interferes with, or attempts to injure, intimidate or interfere with—

(a) any person because of his race, color, religion or national origin and because he is or has been selling, purchasing, renting, financing, occupying, or contracting or negotiating for the sale, purchase, rental, financing or occupation of any dwelling, or applying for or participating in any service, organization, or facility relating to the business of selling or renting dwellings; or

(b) any person because he is or has been, or in order to intimidate such person or any other person or any class of persons from—

(1) participating, without discrimination on account of race, color, religion or national origin, in any of the activities, services, organizations or facilities described in subsection 901(a). . . .

◆ BARBARA JORDAN'S SPEECH ON PRESIDENTIAL IMPEACHMENT PROCEEDINGS (1974) (EXCERPT)

On July 25, 1974, Congresswoman Barbara Jordan appeared on television to offer her position on the impeachment of the President of the United States, Richard Nixon. Solemn, exhausted, she hunched over four annotated amended pages of her personal notes, as well as four pages of historical impeachment criteria set against the president's conduct. Her black-rimmed glasses reflected the glare of the lighting in the room as she examined her notes. At that moment, she improvised her speech while looking into the television cameras.

"We the people"—it is a very eloquent beginning. But when the Constitution of the United States was completed on the seventeenth of September in 1787, I was not included in that "We the people." I felt for many years that somehow George Washington and Alexander Hamilton just left me out by mistake. But through the process of amendment, interpretation, and court decision, I have finally been included in "We the people."

It is wrong, I suggest, it is a misreading of the Constitution for any member here to assert that for a member to vote for an Article of Impeachment means that the member must be convinced that the President should be removed from office. The Constitution doesn't say that. The powers relating to impeachment are an essential check in the hands of this body, the legislature, against and upon the encroachment of the Executive. In establishing the division between the two branches of the legislature, the House and the Senate, assigning to one the right to accuse and the other the right to judge, the

framers of this Constitution were very astute. They did not make the accusers and the judges the same persons.

We know the nature of impeachment. We have been talking about it for a while now. "It is chiefly designed for the President and his high ministers" to somehow be called into account. It is designed to "bridle" the Executive if he engages in excesses. It is designed as a method of national "inquest into the conduct of public men. . . ." The nature of impeachment is a narrowly channeled exception to the separation of powers maxim; the Federal Convention of 1787 said that. It limited impeachment to "high crimes and misdemeanors" and discounted and opposed the term "maladministration."

The drawing of political lines goes to the motivation behind impeachment; but impeachment must proceed within the confines of the constitutional term "high crimes and misdemeanors."

What the President did know on the twenty-third of June was the prior activities of E. Howard Hunt, which included his participation in the break-in of Daniel Ellsberg's psychiatrist, which included Howard Hunt's participation in the Dita Beard ITT affair, which included Howard Hunt's fabrication of cables, designed to discredit the Kennedy administration.

We have heard time and time again that the evidence reflects payment to the defendants of money. The President has knowledge that these funds were being paid and that these were funds collected for the 1972 presidential campaign.

Beginning shortly after the Watergate break-in and continuing to the present time, the President has engaged in a series of public statements and actions designed to thwart the lawful investigation by government prosecutors. Moreover, the President has made public announcements and assertions bearing on the Watergate case which the evidence will show he knows to be false. . . .

James Madison said, again at the Constitutional Convention: "A president is impeachable if he attempts to subvert the Constitution."

The Constitution charges that President with the task of taking care that the laws be faithfully executed, and yet the President has counseled his aides to commit perjury, willfully disregarded the secrecy of grand jury proceedings, concealed surreptitious entry, attempted to compromise a federal judge while publicly displaying his cooperation with the processes of criminal justice. . . .

If the impeachment provision in the Constitution of the United States will not reach the offenses charged here, then perhaps that eighteenth-century Constitution should be abandoned to a twentieth-century paper shredder. Has the President committed offenses and planned and directed and acquiesced in a course of conduct which the Constitution will not tolerate? That is the question. We know that. We know the question. We should now forthwith proceed to answer the question. It is reason and not passion which must guide our deliberations, guide our debate, and guide our decision.

◆ PRESIDENT GEORGE BUSH'S MESSAGE TO THE SENATE RETURNING WITHOUT APPROVAL THE CIVIL RIGHTS ACT OF 1990 26 WEEKLY COMP. PRES.DOC. 1632–34 (OCT. 22, 1990)

In June of 1989, the U.S. Supreme Court delivered opinions in several cases dealing with seniority systems and racial discrimination in employment. Ruling in the cases Lorance v. ATT Technologies Inc., Martin v. Wilks, Patterson v. McLean Credit Union, *and* Wards Cove Packing Co. v. Antonio, *the Court appeared to reverse earlier civil rights rulings. Civil rights organizations were quick to protest the rulings; opponents of the ruling, including the NAACP Legal Defense and Educational Fund, the Leadership Conference on Civil Rights, the American Civil Liberties Union, and the National Organization of Women, argued that the Court had undermined the protection granted by federal civil rights and equal employment legislation.*

On October 16 and 17, 1990, both houses of Congress approved a bill designed to reverse the Court's ruling. On October 22, President Bush vetoed the bill, claiming that the bill's provisions would encourage employers to establish hiring quotas.

To the Senate of the United States.

I am today returning without my approval [Separate Bill] 2104, the "Civil Rights Act of 1990." I deeply regret having to take this action with respect to a bill bearing such a title, especially since it contains certain provisions that I strongly endorse.

Discrimination, whether on the basis of race, national origin, sex, religion, or disability, is worse than wrong. It is a fundamental evil that tears at the fabric of our society, and one that all Americans should and must oppose. That requires rigorous enforcement of existing antidiscrimination laws. . . .

. . . Despite the use of the term "civil rights" in the title of S. 2104, the bill actually employs a maze of highly legalistic language to introduce the destructive force of quotas into our Nation's employment system. Primarily through provisions governing cases in which employment practices are alleged to have unintentionally caused the disproportionate exclusion of members of certain groups, S. 2104 creates powerful incentives for employers to adopt hiring and promotion quotas. These incentives are created by the bill's new and very technical rules of litigation, which will make it difficult for employers to defend legitimate employment practices. In many cases, a defense against unfounded allegations will be impossible. Among other problems, the plaintiff often need not even show that any of the employer's practices caused a significant statistical disparity. In other cases, the employer's defense is confined to an unduly narrow definition of "business necessity" that is significantly more restrictive than that established by the Supreme Court in *Griggs v. Duke Power Co.* and in two decades of subsequent decisions. Thus, unable to defend legitimate practices in court, employers will be driven to adopt quotas in order to avoid liability.

Proponents of S. 2104 assert that it is needed to overturn the Supreme Court's *Wards Cove Packing Co. v. Antonio* decision and restore the law that had existed since the Griggs case in 1971. S. 2104, however, does not in fact codify Griggs or the Court's subsequent decisions prior to Ward Cove. Instead, S. 2104 engages in a sweeping rewrite of two decades of Supreme Court jurisprudence, using language that appears in no decision of the Court and that is contrary to principles acknowledged even by the Justice Stevens' dissent in Wards Cove: "The opinion in Griggs made it clear that a neutral practice that operates to exclude minorities is nevertheless lawful if it serves a valid business purpose."

I am aware of the dispute among lawyers about the proper interpretation of certain critical language used in this portion of S. 2104. The very fact of this dispute suggests that the bill is not codifying the law developed by the Supreme Court in Griggs and subsequent cases. This debate, moreover, is a sure sign that S. 2104 will lead to years—perhaps decades—of uncertainty and expensive litigation. It is neither fair nor sensible to give the employers of our country a difficult choice between using quotas and seeking a clarification of the law through costly and very risky litigation.

D. 3205 contains several other unacceptable provisions as well. One section unfairly closes the courts, in many instances, to individuals victimized by agreements, to which they were not a party, involving the use of quotas. Another section radically alters the remedial provisions in Title VII of the Civil Rights Act of 1964, replacing measures designed to foster conciliation and settlement with a new scheme modeled on a tort system widely acknowledged to be in a state of crisis. The bill also contains a number of provisions that will create unnecessary and inappropriate incentives for litigation. These include unfair retroactivity rules; attorneys fee provisions that will discourage settlements; unreasonable new statutes of limitation; and a "rule of construction" that will make it extremely difficult to know how courts can be expected to apply the law. In order to assist the Congress regarding legislation in this area, I enclose herewith a memorandum from the Attorney General explaining in detail the defects that make S. 2104 unacceptable.

Our goal and our promise has been equal opportunity and equal protection under the law. That is a bedrock principle from which we cannot retreat. The temptation to support a bill—any bill—simply because its title includes the words "civil rights" is very strong. This impulse is not entirely bad. Presumptions have too often run the other way, and our Nation's history on racial questions cautions against complacency. But when our efforts, however well intentioned, result in quotas, equal opportunity is not advanced but thwarted. The very commitment to justice and equality that is offered as the reason why this bill should be signed requires me to veto it. . . .

George Bush

The White House,

October 22, 1990

◆ CIVIL RIGHTS ACT OF 1991 PUB.L. NO. 102–166, 105 STAT 1071 (1991)

After vetoing Congress' 1990 civil rights legislation, the Bush administration joined both houses of Congress in working on alternative bills. Following months of negotiation, the Senate passed Senate Bill 1745 on October 30; the House passed the bill on November 7. On November 21, President George Bush signed the Civil Rights Act of 1991.

This act is designed to provide additional remedies to deter harassment and intentional discrimination in the workplace, to provide guidelines for the adjudication of cases arising under Title VII . . . and to expand the scope of civil rights legislation weakened by Supreme Court decisions, particularly the Court's ruling in *Wards Cove Packing Co. v. Antonio*, 490 US 642 (1989).

Sec. 2. Findings

The Congress finds that—

(1) additional remedies under Federal law are needed to deter unlawful harassment and intentional discrimination in the workplace;

(2) the decision of the Supreme Court in *Wards Cove Packing Co. v. Antonio*, 490 U.S. 642 (1989) has weakened the scope and effectiveness of Federal civil rights protections; and

(3) legislation is necessary to provide additional protections against unlawful discrimination in employment.

Sec. 3. Purposes.

The purposes of this Act are—

(1) to provide appropriate remedies for intentional discrimination and unlawful harassment in the workplace;

(2) to codify the concepts of "business necessity" and "job related" enunciated by the Supreme Court in *Griggs v. Duke Power Co.*, 401 U.S. 424 (1971), and in the other Supreme Court decisions prior to *Wards Cove Packing Co. v. Antonio*, 490 U.S. 642 (1989);

(3) to confirm statutory authority and provide statutory guidelines for the adjudication of disparate impact suits under title VII of the Civil Rights Act of 1964 (42 U.S.C. 2000e et seq.); and

(4) to respond to recent decisions of the Supreme Court by expanding the scope of relevant civil rights statutes in order to provide adequate protection to victims of discrimination.

Title I—Federal Civil Rights Remedies

Sec. 105. Burden of Proof in Disparate Impact Cases.

(a) Section 703 of the Civil Rights Act of 1964 (42 U.S.C. 2000e–2) is amended by adding at the end the following new subsection:

. . . An unlawful employment practice based on disparate impact is established under this title only if—

. . . A complaining party demonstrates that a respondent used a particular employment practice that causes a disparate impact on the basis of race, color, religion, sex, or national origin and the respondent fails to demonstrate that the challenged practice is job related for the position in question and consistent with business necessity. . . .

. . . With respect to demonstrating that a particular employment practice causes a disparate impact as described in subparagraph

(A)(I), the complaining party shall demonstrate that each particular challenged employment practice causes a disparate impact, except that if the complaining party can demonstrate to the court that the elements of a respondent's decisionmaking process are not capable of separation for analysis, the decisionmaking process may be analyzed as one employment practice.

. . . If the respondent demonstrates that a specific employment practice does not cause the disparate impact, the respondent shall not be required to demonstrate that such practice is required by business necessity. . . .

Sec. 106. Prohibition Against Discriminatory Use of Test Scores.

Section 703 of the Civil Rights Act of 1964 (42 U.S.C. 2000e–2) (as amended by section 105) is further amended by adding at the end of the following new subsection:

. . . It shall be an unlawful employment practice for a respondent, in connection with the selection or referral of applicants or candidates for employment or promotion, to adjust the scores of, use different cutoff scores for, or otherwise alter the results of, employment related tests on the basis of race, color, religion, sex, or national origin. . . .

Title II—Glass Ceiling

Sec. 202 Findings and Purpose.

(a) Findings—Congress finds that—

(1) despite a dramatically growing presence in the workplace, women and minorities remain underrepresented in management and decision-making positions in business;

(2) artificial barriers exist to the advancement of women and minorities in the workplace;

(3) United States corporations are increasingly relying on women and minorities to meet employment requirements and are increasingly aware of the advantages derived from a diverse work force;

(4) the "Glass Ceiling Initiative" undertaken by the Department of Labor, including the release of the report entitled "Report on the Glass Ceiling Initiative," has been instrumental in raising public awareness of—

(A) the underrepresentation of women and minorities at the management and decision-making levels in the United States work force;

(B) the underrepresentation of women and minorities in line functions in the United States work force;

(C) the lack of access for qualified women and minorities to credential-building developmental opportunities; and

(D) the desirability of eliminating artificial barriers to the advancement of women and minorities to such levels;

(f) the establishment of a commission to examine issues raised by the Glass Ceiling Initiative would help—

(A) focus greater attention on the importance of eliminating artificial barriers to the advancement of women and minorities to management and decision-making positions in business; and

(B) promote work force diversity. . . .

◆ THE MILLION MAN MARCH/DAY OF ABSENCE MISSION STATEMENT (1995) (EXCERPT BY DR. MAULANA KARENGA)

I. Introduction

The Black men and women, the organizations and persons, participating in this historic Million Man March and Day of Absence held in Washington, DC, on October 16, 1995, on the eve of the 21st century, and supported by parallel activities in cities and towns throughout the country: *conscious* of the critical juncture of history in which we live and the challenges it poses for us; *concerned* about increasing racism and the continuing commitment to white supremacy in this country; deteriorating social conditions, degradation of the environment and the impact of these on our community, the larger society and the world; *committed* to the ongoing struggle for a free and empowered community, a just society and a better world; *recognizing* that the country and government have made a dangerous and regressive turn to the right and are producing policies with negative impact on people of color, the poor and the vulnerable; *realizing* that every man and woman and our community have both the right and responsibility to resist evil and contribute meaningfully to the creation of a just and good society; *reaffirming* the best values of our social justice tradition which require respect for the dignity and rights of the human person, economic justice, meaningful political participation, shared power, cultural integrity, mutual respect for all peoples, and uncompromising resistance to social forces and structures which deny or limit these; *declare* our commitment to assume a new and expanded responsibility in the struggle to build and sustain a free and empowered community, a just society and a better world. We are aware that we make this commitment in an era in which this is needed as never before and in which we cannot morally choose otherwise.

In doing this, we self-consciously emphasize the priority need of Black men to stand up and assume this new and expanded responsibility without denying or minimizing the equal rights, role and responsibility of Black women in the life and struggle of our people.

Our priority call to Black men to stand up and assume this new and expanded sense of responsibility is based on the realization that the strength and resourcefulness of the family and the liberation of the people require it;

that some of the most acute problems facing the Black community within are those posed by Black males who have not stood up; that the caring and responsible father in the home; the responsible and future-focused male youth; security in and of the community; the quality of male/female relations, and the family's capacity to avoid poverty and push the lives of its members forward all depend on Black men's standing up;

that in the context of a real and principled brotherhood, those of us who have stood up, must challenge others to stand also; and that unless and until Black men stand up, Black men and women cannot stand together and accomplish the awesome tasks before us.

II. The Historical Significance of the Project

This Million Man March, forming a joint project with its companion activity, The Day of Absence, speaks to who we are, where we stand and what we are compelled to do in this hour of meeting and posing challenges. Its significance lies in the fact that:

1. It is a timely and necessary state of challenge both to ourselves and the country in a time of increasing racism, attacks on hard won gains, and continually deteriorating conditions for the poor and vulnerable and thus an urgent time for transformative and progressive leadership;

2. It is a declaration of the resolve of Black men, in particular and the Black community in general, to mobilize and struggle to maintain hard won gains, resist evil and wrong wherever we find it and to continue to push our lives and history forward;

3. It is a reaffirmation of our self-understanding as a people that we are our own liberators, that no matter how numerous or sincere our allies are, the greatest burdens to be borne and the most severe sacrifices to be made for liberation are essentially our own;

4. It is an effective way to refocus and expand discussion on critical issues confronting our people, this country and the world and put forth our positions on them;

5. It is both an example and encouragement of operational unity; unity in diversity, unity without uniformity, and unity on principle and in practice for the greater good;

6. It is a galvanizing and mobilizing process to raise consciousness, cultivate commitment and lay the groundwork for increased positive social, political and economic activity;

7. And finally, it is a necessary continuation of our ancient and living moral tradition of speaking truth to power and seeking power for the vulnerable, justice for the injured, right for the wronged and liberation for the oppressed. . . .

VII. Continuing Practice and Projects

38. The Million Man March and Day of Absence can only have lasting value if we continue to work and struggle beyond this day. Thus, our challenge is to take the spirit of this day, the process of mobilization and the possibilities of organization and turn them into ongoing structures and practices directed toward our liberation and flourishing as a people.

39. Central to sustaining and institutionalizing this process is:

a. the follow-up development of an expanded Black political agenda and the holding of a Black Political Convention to forge this agenda for progressive political change;

b. a massive and ongoing voter registration of Black people as independents; using our vote to insist and insure that candidates address the Black agenda; and creating and sustaining a progressive independent political movement;

c. the building and strengthening of Black united fronts and collective leadership structures like the National African American Leadership Summit to practice and benefit from operational unity in our addressing local, national and international issues;

d. the establishment of a Black Economic Development Fund to enhance economic development, cultivate economic discipline and cooperative practices and achieve economic self-determination;

e. the reaffirmation and strengthening of family through quality male/female relations based on principles of equality, complementarity, mutual respect and shared responsibility in love, life and struggle; and through loving and responsible parenthood that insists on discipline and achievement, provides spiritual, moral and cultural grounding and through expanding rites of passage programs, mentorships and increasing adoptions;

f. the ongoing struggle for reparations in the fullest sense, that is to say: public admission, apology and recognition of the Holocaust of African Enslavement and appropriate compensation by the government; and support for the Conyers Reparations Bill on the Holocaust;

g. the continuing struggle against police abuse, government suppression, violations of civil and human rights and the industrialization of prisons; and in support of the freedom of all political prisoners, prisoners' rights and their efforts to transform themselves into worthy members of the community;

h. the critical task of organizing the community as a solid wall in the struggle against drugs, crime and violence in the community which we see as interrelated and which must be joined with the struggle to reduce and end poverty, increase employment, strengthen fatherhood, motherhood and family, support parents, provide education and prevention programs, and expose and reject those who deal in death for the community.

None of this denies external sources of drugs nor stops us from demanding uniform sentencing and penalties for those involved in the drug trade on the local, national and international level, but it compels us to stand up and take responsibility for the life we must live in spite of external impositions;

i. continuing and expanding our support for African-centered independent schools through joining their boards, enrolling our children, being concerned and active parents, donating time, services and monies to them and working in various other ways to insure that they provide the highest level of culturally-rooted education; and intensifying and broadening the struggle for quality public education through heightened parental concern and involvement and social activism which insist on a responsible administration, professional and committed teachers, continuing faculty and staff development; safe pleasant, encouraging and fully-equipped campuses and an inclusive and culture-respecting curriculum which stresses mastery of knowledge as well as critical thinking, academic excellence, social responsibility and an expanded sense of human possibility;

j. continuing and reinforced efforts to reduce and eliminate negative media approaches to and portrayals of Black life and culture; to organize a sustained and effective support for positive models, messages and works; to achieve adequate and dignified representation of Blacks in various media and in various positions in these media; to expand support for and development of independent Black media; and to challenge successful and notable African Americans in various media to support all these efforts;

k. strengthening and supporting organizations and institutions of the Black community concerned with the uplifting and liberation of our people by joining as families and persons, volunteering service, giving donations and providing and insisting on the best leadership possible;

l. building appropriate alliances with other peoples of color, supporting their liberation struggles and just demands and engaging in mutually supportive and mutually beneficial activities to create and sustain a just and good society;

m. standing in solidarity with other African peoples and other Third World peoples in their struggles to free themselves, harness their human and material resources and live full and meaningful lives;

n. reaffirming in the most positive ways the value and indispensability of the spiritual and ethical grounding of our people in accomplishing the historical tasks confronting us by freeing and renewing our minds and

reaffirming our commitment to the good, the proper and the beneficial, by joining as families and persons the faith communities of our choice, supporting them, living the best of our traditions ourselves and challenging other members and the leadership to do likewise and constantly insisting that our faith communities give the best of what we have to offer to build the moral community and just society we struggle for as a people;

o. and finally, embracing and practicing a common set of principles that reaffirm and strengthen family, community and culture, The Nguzo Saba (The Seven Principles): Umoja (Unity); Kujichagulia (Self-Determination); Ujima (Collective Work and Responsibility); Ujamaa (Cooperative Economics); Nia (Purpose); Kuumba (Creativity); and Imani (Faith).

For full text of the Mission Statement, contact University of Sankore Press, 2560 W. 54th St., Los Angeles, CA 9004; phone (800) 997–2656; fax (213) 299–0261.

◆ THE PRESIDENT'S INITIATIVE ON RACE—THE ADVISORY BOARD'S REPORT TO THE PRESIDENT (1998) (EXCERPT)

On June 13, 1997, President Clinton established the seven-member President's Advisory Board to the President's Initiative on Race. Headed by historian John Hope Franklin, the advisory board was given the responsibilities of promoting national dialogue on race issues, increasing the nation's understanding of the history and future of race relations, identifying and creating plans to calm racial tension and promote increased opportunity for all Americans, and addressing crime and the administration of justice.

On September 18, 1998, the advisory board concluded its work and presented its recommendations to President Clinton. Its report One America in the 21st Century: Forging a New Future *recommended that the President institute a standing advisory board to build upon its foundation and for a public education program to underscore the "common values" of a diverse multiracial nation.*

Introduction

America's greatest promise in the 21st century lies in our ability to harness the strength of racial diversity. Our greatest challenge is to work as one community to define ourselves with pride as a multi-racial democracy. At the end of the 20th century, America has emerged as the worldwide symbol of opportunity and freedom through leadership that constantly strives to give meaning to the fundamental principles of our Constitution. Those principals of justice, opportunity, equality, and

John Hope Franklin served as head of the President's Initiative on Race (Fisk University Library).

inclusion must continue to guide the planning for our future.

The Advisory Board and Its Mandate

Members of the Advisory Board to the President's Initiative on Race have spent the past 15 months engaged in a process designed to examine race relations in America. Through study, dialogue, and action we have begun to engage the American people in a focused examination of how racial differences have affected our society and how to meet the racial challenges that face us. Our task was to take this necessary first step in the President's effort to articulate and realize a vision of a more just society.

In June 1997, through Executive Order No. 13050, President Clinton appointed Dr. John Hope Franklin (chairman), Linda Chavez-Thompson, Reverend Dr. Suzan D. Johnson Cook, Thomas H. Kean, Angela E. Oh, Bob Thomas, and William F. Winter to serve as members of the Advisory Board.

. . . [T]he Board forged ahead to meet the objectives set out by the President through his Executive Order. Those objectives included the following:

Promote a constructive national dialogue to confront and work through the challenging issues that surround race.

Increase the Nation's understanding of our recent history of race relations and the course our Nation is charting on issues of race relations and racial diversity.

Bridge racial divides by encouraging community leaders to develop and implement innovative approaches to calming racial tensions.

Identify, develop, and implement solutions to problems in areas in which race has a substantial impact, such as education, economic opportunity, housing, health care, and the administration of justice.

In addition, the Advisory Board examined issues related to race and immigration, the impact of the media on racial stereotyping, and enforcement of civil rights laws.

We wish to make it clear that this Report is not a definitive analysis of the state of race relations in America today. . . . Rather, we were engaged in the task of assisting with the initial stages of this new America's journey toward building a more just society in the 21st century.

Accomplishments, Challenges, and Opportunities

. . . Many challenges lie ahead. As America's racial diversity grows, the complexity of giving meaning to the promise of America grows as well. It is these challenges that signal where opportunities may exist. This report attempts to frame the challenges, identify the opportunities, and recommended action. It provides an overview of information gathered from communities across the Nation, including diverse points of view about racial differences and controversial issues that are currently being debated and ideas for how strong leadership can continue to move our Nation closer to its highest aspirations.

Report Overview

. . . Although this Report concludes our year-long exploration of race and racism, our work is only the foundation for building one America. The work that lies ahead cannot be accomplished by a single group. Our experience has provided the Nation with the chance to identify leaders in many parts of this country, working in numerous fields, who will promote a vision of a unified, strong, and just society. The Race Initiative affirmed the efforts of Americans who have been, are, and will continue to give meaning to the words "justice," "equality," "dignity," "respect," and "inclusion." We urge bold and decisive action to further the movement toward "redeeming the promise of America."

4

African American Landmarks

As far back as the establishment of first permanent European settlement in America, African Americans have made significant contributions to the social, economic, scientific, and cultural development of this country. The American landscape is covered with sites commemorating this African American experience. From the war for independence, through the conflicts fought on the western frontier, and on to more recent battles, sites have been established to commemorate African American participation in the defense of this nation. The African American quest for knowledge has been embodied at the first institutions organized to educate them in this country. The trail from slavery to freedom can be retraced by way of the many markers noting stations along the Underground Railroad. Other sites commemorate the achievements of African Americans in the arts and sciences or in pursuit of equal rights. Landmarks, unlike most textual documents, stand through time as public testaments to the strength and courage of African Americans.

◆ ALABAMA

Birmingham

Sixteenth Street Baptist Church
1530 Sixth Ave. at Sixteenth St., N.

Wallace A. Rayfield, a local African American architect, designed the present sanctuary, and in 1911 Windham Brothers Construction Company, a local African American contractor, constructed the building. The church has continued to serve as a center for activities in the community. The church received national attention during the middle of the racial unrest of the 1960s, when four African American children—Addie Mae Collins, Denise McNair, Cynthia Wesley, and Carol Robertson—were killed in a bomb explosion near the

sanctuary on September 15, 1963. The tragedy spurred Birmingham to address its racial problems and led to greater racial unity nationwide. The building was declared a national historic landmark on September 17, 1980.

Florence

William Christopher Handy Birthplace
620 W. College St.

W. C. Handy, composer of "St. Louis Blues," was born in 1873. The cabin in which he was born was moved from its original site to its current location in Florence, Alabama. The restored cabin, constructed circa 1845, contains his piano, trumpet, and other mementos.

Montgomery

Civil Rights Memorial
400 Washington Ave., corner of Hull St.

This black granite monument is presented as a wall with water cascading over the words of Martin Luther King, Jr., "Until justice rolls down like waters and righteousness like a mighty steam." The names of forty civil rights martyrs are inscribed on a circular stone that is also presented. The memorial, commissioned by the Southern Poverty Law Center, was designed by architect Maya Lin and dedicated in 1989.

Dexter Avenue King Memorial Baptist Church and Pastorium
Church, 454 Dexter Ave.; pastorium, 309 S. Jackson St.

The Dexter Avenue King Memorial Baptist Church, erected in 1878, was the church where Martin Luther King, Jr. organized the 1955 boycott of Montgomery's segregated bus system. Although the pastorium was damaged by a bomb on January 31, 1956, the boycott continued and spurred the 1956 Supreme Court ruling that bus segregation was illegal. It was this boycott that brought King into national prominence as a civil rights leader.

King pastored at the church from 1954 to 1959. The church houses a mural depicting scenes of the Civil Rights movement, as well as a library that includes personal mementoes of King and his family. The church was declared a national historic landmark on July 1, 1974. Restoration of the pastorium, erected circa 1912, was in progress in 1990. The King family furnishings are to be returned to the pastorium when the cottage is open to the public.

Selma

Brown Chapel African Methodist Episcopal Church and King Monument
410 Martin Luther King, Jr., St.

The church is housed in an imposing red brick structure with twin towers. It was organized in 1866 and moved to its present site in 1908. Brown Chapel was closely allied with the Civil Rights movement of the 1960s; in 1965 it became the center for the Southern Christian Leadership Conference's (SCLC) voting rights campaign. Early in 1965 the church served as headquarters for the SCLC, housed rallies for Martin Luther King, Jr. and other SCLC leaders, and was the site for planning demonstrations including the ill-fated demonstration on March 7 known as "Bloody Sunday." The voting campaign spurred the passage of the Voting Rights Act of 1965. Brown Chapel was declared a national historic landmark on February 4, 1982.

Edmund Pettis Bridge
Broad St., U.S. 80

On Sunday, March 7, 1965, three hundred civil rights demonstrators started out from Selma, Alabama, on what was to be a 55-mile march to Montgomery, Alabama, protesting the denial of voting rights to African Americans who had attempted to register in Selma. Reaching the Edmund Pettis Bridge, the marchers were met by state troopers—the orders to deploy the troopers had been issued by Governor George Wallace to enforce his executive order forbidding such demonstrations. The unarmed marchers were turned back by tear gas and night sticks resulting in numerous injuries.

On March 21, a second march started out, organized by the Rev. Martin Luther King, Jr.; this march concluded five days later on the steps of the state capitol building in Montgomery. The two demonstrations aroused national concern and hastened Congress to pass a new voting rights bill.

Built in 1940, the Pettis Bridge marks the site of an important era in African American history. A marker depicting the struggle at the bridge is located near Broad Street.

Talladega

Talladega College and Swayne Hall
627 W. Battle St.

The first college for African Americans in Alabama, Talladega College was founded by the American Missionary Association in 1867 as a primary school. The school pursued a liberal arts program at a time when vocational education dominated African American institutions. Its Savery Library houses three fresco panels known as the celebrated *Amistad Murals* by Hale Woodruff, who studied in France under the renowned Henry Ossawa Tanner.

Swayne Hall, built in 1857, is the oldest building on the campus of Talladega College. The building was constructed by slave labor before the school was established and transferred to the college in 1867. It was declared a national historic landmark on December 2, 1974.

Tuskegee

Tuskegee University

Tuskegee Institute (now Tuskegee University), a world-renowned center for agricultural research and extension work, first opened on July 4, 1881, with a $2,000 appropriation from the Alabama state legislature. It consisted of a single shanty, a student body of thirty, and one teacher—Booker T. Washington. Tuskegee functioned originally as a normal school for the training of African American teachers, the first of its kind established in the United States. Eventually, it specialized in agricultural and manual training, areas which were to make both the school and Booker T. Washington famous.

In 1882, Washington moved the school to a one hundred-acre plantation and began a self-help program that enabled students to finance their education. Most of the early buildings were built with the aid of student labor.

Next to Washington, the most notable person to be associated with the institute was George Washington Carver, who became its director of agricultural research in 1896. Carver persuaded many Southern farmers to cultivate peanuts, sweet potatoes, and other crops instead of cotton, which was rapidly depleting the soil. Ultimately, Carver's research programs helped develop 300 derivative products from peanuts and 118 from

Chapel at Tuskegee Institute in Tuskegee, Alabama (AP/Wide World Photos, Inc.).

sweet potatoes. At one point, he even succeeded in making synthetic marble from wood pulp.

Today, Tuskegee covers nearly five thousand acres and has more than 150 buildings. There are more than 27 landmarks associated with Washington and Carver. Places to visit include the Founder's Marker (i.e., the site of Washington's original shanty), the Oaks (i.e., Washington's home), the Booker T. Washington Monument, gravesites for Washington (and two of his wives) and Carver, and the George Washington Carver Museum, which houses the scientist's plant, mineral, and bird collections and exhibits of various products that he developed. Tuskegee is also home to the George Washington Carver Foundation, a research center founded by Carver in 1940. Tuskegee was declared a national historic landmark on June 23, 1965.

◆ ALASKA

Fairbanks

Mattie Crosby's Home

One of the few African American pioneers of Alaska, Mattie Crosby first came to the territory in 1900 with a Maine family that adopted her. During this period, some African Americans came into the territory during the era of the Gold Rush, while others were occasionally seen on board ships that brought in supplies. However, for nearly 17 years, Mattie Crosby lived in Fairbanks, Alaska, without meeting another African American.

◆ ARIZONA

Tombstone

John Swain Grave Site
Boot Hill Cemetery

Born a slave in 1845, John Swain went to Tombstone, Arizona, in 1879 as a cowhand in the employ of John Slaughter. Swain was an expert rider and one of several African Americans to work for Slaughter.

In 1884, Swain is said to have fought and lost a one-round boxing match with John L. Sullivan, then heavyweight champion of the world. He died just three months short of his one hundredth birthday and was buried with honors by the citizens of Tombstone. A special tablet stands on the grave site, commemorating the close ties between Swain and Slaughter.

◆ ARKANSAS

Little Rock

Central High School
1500 Park St., corner of Fourteenth and Park Sts.

In the fall of 1957, the first major confrontation over implementation of the Supreme Court's 1954 ruling in outlawing racial segregation in public schools took place at Central High School in Little Rock, Arkansas. The school was built in 1927.

Upon their arrival for classes on September 23, 1957, African American students were turned away by the Arkansas National Guard on the order of Arkansas Governor Orval Faubus. President Dwight D. Eisenhower responded to the crisis by issuing an executive order on September 24, which called for the use of federal troops to enforce the court's order to desegregate public schools.

Ish House
1600 Scott St.

The home of Jefferson Ish was constructed in 1880. Jefferson Ish worked to ensure high quality education for African Americans in the area. After his death, the Ish School was established in the city to honor him. One of his sons, G. W. Ish, became an innovative physician and provided health care for local residents, as well as students at Philander Smith College. G.W. Ish also introduced isoniazid and streptomycin to treat pulmonary tuberculosis. The Ish home was designated a national historic landmark on January 3, 1978.

Philander-Smith College
812 W. 13th St.

In 1877 this institution was opened under the sponsorship of the African Methodist Episcopal Church as Walder College in Little Rock, Arkansas. After receiving a large donation that enabled the school to construct a permanent brick edifice, the college was renamed.

◆ CALIFORNIA

Allensworth

Allensworth Colony

Established as an all-African American community, the town of Allensworth was founded by Allen Allensworth in 1910. Now a state park, this landmark serves as a memorial to its founder.

Allen Allensworth, as a slave just prior to the Civil War, was a well-known racing jockey in Louisville, Kentucky. With the beginning of the Civil War, Allensworth was allowed to enter the Navy, where he advanced to the rank of chief petty officer. Following the war, Allensworth studied for the ministry and returned to the military service as chaplain of the famed 24th U.S. Infantry. Around 1900 he migrated to California, where he dedicated himself to improving the status of African Americans.

Arcadia

Santa Anita Race Track

Santa Anita Race Track is located on the former site of the E. J. "Lucky" Baldwin Ranch, at which John Fisher, a former slave, was a prominent breeder and trainer. Fisher, a native of St. Louis, was at first reluctant to follow Baldwin to California out of fear of Native Americans, but was eventually persuaded to join him. He later became a foreman on the ranch.

Beckwourth

Beckwourth Pass

Beckwourth Pass, which runs through the Sierra Nevada Mountains in Beckwourth, California, was discovered by Jim Beckwourth, one of a number of African American traders and trappers dubbed "mountain men" by chroniclers of American history. The log cabin that he built as his home in 1852 still stands near the Plumas County hamlet named for him.

Hornitos

Gold Mining Camp

This was the home of Moses Rodgers, a successful and affluent African American mine owner who was one of the finest engineers and metallurgists in the state. Rodgers was one of several African American miners who struck it rich in gold and quartz.

Red Bluff

Oak Hill Cemetery

This is the burial place of Aaron Coffey, the only black member of the Society of California Pioneers. Coffey, the descendant of an officer who fought under Jackson at New Orleans, came to California as a slave in 1849. By day, he worked for his master; by night, as a cobbler, he accumulated money toward his $1,000 emancipation fee. Betrayed by his owner, he was forced to return to Missouri, where he was again sold. Coffey pleaded with his new master to allow him to return to California and earn the necessary money to free himself and his family, which he had left behind as collateral. Upon accomplishing that mission, Coffey returned to Red Bluff, took up farming, and settled down to a contented family life.

Sacramento

St. Andrew's African Methodist Episcopal Church
2131 Eighth St.

St. Andrew's was the first African Methodist Episcopal congregation in California. Organized in a private residence in 1850, within four years the congregation had founded a school for African, Asian, and Native American children in the church's basement.

San Francisco

Leidesdorff St.

This street in San Francisco, California, is named for William Alexander Leidesdorff, a wealthy and influential California pioneer of African and Danish ancestry and a native of the Danish West Indies. A merchant, Leidesdorff operated the first steamer to pass through the Golden Gate Strait. Leidesdorff was later appointed U.S. vice-consul and ultimately became a civic and educational leader in San Francisco.

◆ COLORADO

Central City

"Aunt Clara" Brown's Chair
Central City Opera House Eureka St.

"Aunt Clara" Brown, believed to have been the first African American resident of the Colorado Territory, was born a slave in Virginia. Brown moved to Missouri, where her husband and children were sold before she gained freedom through her master's last will and testament. From Missouri, she headed for Kansas and then for the gold fields of Colorado, where she opened the territory's first laundry. She soon began putting aside money from her earnings towards the purchase of her family's freedom.

Even when the Emancipation Proclamation set her immediate family free, she nonetheless returned to Missouri and brought a group of 38 relatives back to Central City. She remained in the mining community for the rest of her life, nursing the sick and performing other charitable works.

Brown died in 1877 and was buried with honors by the Colorado Pioneers Association, of which she was a member. The Central City Opera House Association dedicated a chair to her in 1932.

Inter-Ocean Hotel in Denver, Colorado.

Denver

Inter-Ocean Hotel
16th and Market Sts.

Built by Barney Ford, the Inter-Ocean Hotel in Denver, Colorado, was once a showplace for millionaires and presidents. Ford, an African American entrepreneur active during the Gold Rush days, joined the fight over the organization of the Colorado Territory and the question of statehood. Originally allowed to vote, Ford saw this privilege abrogated by the territorial constitution and, as a result, sought to delay statehood for the territory until African American voting rights were reinstated. Enlisting the aid of the famed Massachusetts abolitionist Senator Charles Sumner, Ford urged President Andrew Johnson to veto the bill for statehood.

After Ford retired, he spent the remainder of his life in Denver, where he died in 1902. He is buried alongside his wife, Julia, in Denver's Riverside Cemetery.

Justina Ford House/Black American West Museum
3091 California St.

Justina Ford was the first African American doctor in Denver. Upon her arrival in 1902 until 1952, she remained the city's only African American woman doctor. Unable to practice in the local hospital at first, her home, built in 1890, became her office as well. Ford, a family doctor and general practitioner, attracted patients from various races. During her career of over fifty years, she delivered more than seven thousand babies and became known as "the baby doctor." The Black American West Museum purchased the Ford home in 1986 to house the museum and to preserve the memory of Ford and her work. The museum includes photographs, memorabilia, and other documents on African American cowboys. The museum also shows how African Americans helped settle the West.

Pueblo

El Pueblo Museum
905 S. Prairie Ave.

The El Pueblo museum houses a replica of the Gantt-Blackwell Fort, which Jim Beckwourth, African American explorer, scout, and trader, claimed to have founded in 1842. The validity of the claim has not been established, as Beckworth had something of a reputation as a teller of tall tales.

◆ CONNECTICUT

Canterbury

Prince Goodin Homestead

This parcel of land in Canterbury was once the home of Prince Goodin, a free African American who fought with the British against the French in the French and Indian War. Goodin enlisted in 1757, after hearing a fiery speech by Canterbury's Rev. James Cogswell that stressed the danger of encroachment against "properties, liberties, religion, and our lives." While serving at Fort William Henry, he was captured during a French attack upon the fort and taken to Montreal, where he was sold into slavery. After three years of captivity, Goodin was freed when the British took the city in 1760.

Prudence Crandall House
Junction of Connecticut Rtes. 14 and 169

The Crandall House, built in 1805, became a school for Canterbury residents in 1831. The admittance of Sarah Harris, a black woman, caused local resentment. Subsequently, Prudence Crandall dismissed her white students and converted the school into a training facility for prospective black teachers. Twenty such students were in residence in 1833. Still in protest, local shopkeepers refused to sell goods to Crandall. The Connecticut General Assembly passed a black law in May 1833 restricting African Americans from outside instruction in private schools without town approval. Crandall ignored the law and, though jailed, her conviction was set aside due to technical errors. She closed the school in September 1834. The Crandall House was designated a national historic landmark on July 17, 1991.

Enfield

Paul Robeson Residence
1221 Enfield St.

Purchased by Paul Robeson and his wife in 1940, this residence served as their home until 1953. Robeson, a singer, actor, and civil rights activist, is best known for his roles in the film *The Emperor Jones* and the musical and film version of *Show Boat*.

Farmington

First Church of Christ
75 Main St.

When in 1839 the mutinied Cuban slave ship *Amistad* landed off the coast of Connecticut, abolitionists in the area demanded protection for the Africans. The First Church of Christ in Farmington, Connecticut, served as the center of community life for the *Amistad* insurrectionists while they awaited trial. The church was designated a national historic landmark on December 8, 1976.

Washington

Jeff Liberty Grave Site
Judea Cemetery

Here lies the grave of Jeff Liberty, an African American soldier who served in the Continental Army during the American Revolution. His grave marker, erected by the Sons of the American Revolution, states simply "in remembrance of Jeff Liberty and his colored patriots." Liberty, a slave at the time of the rebellion, asked his owner to be allowed to serve in the struggle for independence. His request granted, he fought throughout the revolution with an all-black regiment and was granted freedman status at the end of the war.

◆ DELAWARE

Wilmington

Asbury Methodist Episcopal Church
Third and Walnut Sts.

The Asbury Methodist Episcopal Church was dedicated in 1789 by the distinguished orator Bishop Francis Asbury. Tradition has it that on one occasion a number of the town's leading citizens, many of whom were eager to hear Asbury preach, but considered Methodism socially beneath them, stayed outside within hearing distance of the sermon, refusing to enter the church. The listeners were impressed by the eloquence of the man they heard—but, as it turned out, the voice they heard was not that of the bishop, but of his African American servant Harry Hosier (also known as "Black Harry") whose compelling testimony reached heir ears and

Jeff Liberty's grave marker in Washington, Connecticut.

The unveiling of the Mary McLeod Bethune Memorial statue in 1974 (AP/Wide World Photos, Inc.).

inspired their admiration. In its early years, the church welcomed African American members. However, by 1805 African Americans had left this church, driven out by the decision of white worshippers to confine African American members to the gallery.

◆ DISTRICT OF COLUMBIA

Mary McLeod Bethune Memorial
Lincoln Park

The Mary McLeod Bethune Memorial, unveiled in 1974, is the first monument to an African American or a woman to be erected on public land in the nation's capital. Bethune, an educator, was concerned about the children of the laborers working on the Florida East Coast Railroad. Thus, in 1904, she established the Daytona Normal and Industrial Institute for African American girls. In 1926, she merged the institute with the Cookman Institute of Jacksonville to form the Bethune-Cookman College.

The monument, located in Lincoln Park, DC, is inscribed with the following words:

I leave you love, I leave you hope. I leave you the challenge of developing confidence in one another. I leave you a thirst for education. I leave you respect for the use of power. I leave you faith. I leave you racial dignity.

Bethune Museum and Archives
1318 Vermont Ave., NW

Named for Mary McLeod Bethune, the Bethune Museum and Archives, located in the Bethune Council House, was opened in November 1979 and was granted national historic site status in April 1982. The Bethune Museum and Archives is a fully independent nonprofit organization that works to document the contributions made by African American women to society and to enrich the lives of America's children through educational material programs and other services. The Council House was built circa 1885.

Blanche K. Bruce House
909 M St., NW

Blanche K. Bruce, from Mississippi, was the first African American to serve a full term in the U.S. Senate.

Born in Farmville, Virginia, Bruce learned the printer's trade in Missouri. In 1861, prior to the Civil War, he escaped to Hannibal, Missouri, and set up a school for African Americans. He studied at Oberlin College in Ohio and, after moving to Mississippi, became a wealthy planter. A Republican, Bruce was elected by the Mississippi state legislature to the U.S. Senate in 1874. The Blanche K. Bruce House was designated a national historic landmark on May 15, 1975.

Ralph Bunche House
1510 Jackson St., NE

Ralph Bunche had a long association with Howard University, where he served on the faculty and organized the political science department. While living in the District of Columbia, he commissioned local African American architect Holyard Robinson to design his residence. Later, Bunche was appointed undersecretary general of the United Nations. He won the Nobel Peace Prize in 1950. The house was designated a national historic landmark on September 30, 1993.

Mary Ann Shadd Cary House
1421 W St., NW

Between 1881 and 1886, this three-story brick house, located in Washington, DC, served as the residence of Mary Ann Shadd Cary, the first African American woman to co-edit a newspaper *The Provincial Freeman*. In 1883, she became one of the first African American women to earn a law degree. Cary, a lecturer, writer, educator, lawyer, and abolitionist, appeared before audiences throughout the country, usually speaking on the topics of slavery and women's suffrage. The house was designated a national historic landmark on December 8, 1976.

Frederick Douglass House
1411 W St., SE

Cedar Hill, the twenty-room colonial mansion in which Frederick Douglass lived for the last 13 years of his life, has been preserved as a monument to the great nineteenth-century abolitionist. In 1964, it was declared a national historic landmark. Credit for the restoration and preservation of the home belongs largely to the National Association of Colored Women's Clubs, which worked hand-in-hand with the Douglass Association. The Caring Institute, an organization that honors caring people, now occupies the site.

Edward Kennedy "Duke" Ellington Birthplace
1212 T St., NW

Born April 29, 1899, Duke Ellington was one of the world's great jazz composers, pianists, and bandleaders.

It has been said of him that "the man is the music, the music is the man."

Emancipation Statue
Lincoln Park
E. Capitol St.

Former slaves were responsible for financing and erecting the oldest memorial to Abraham Lincoln in the Washington, DC area. Following Lincoln's assassination in 1865, the first five dollars for the statue were donated by a Mrs. Charlotte Scott of Marietta, Ohio. Contributions were soon pouring in, whereupon Congress finally set aside grounds for Thomas Bell's statue depicting Lincoln breaking slavery's chains. The memorial was dedicated on April 14, 1876—the eleventh anniversary of Lincoln's assassination.

Charlotte Forten Grimké House
1608 R St., NW

Charlotte Forten Grimké, born of wealthy free African American parents in Philadelphia, was among the first wave of Northerners engaged in educating African Americans in the occupied Union territories of the South. Her activities as an activist, writer, poet, and educator forged a path for other African American women. The house, built circa 1880, was designated a national historic landmark on May 11, 1976.

General Oliver Otis Howard House
604 Howard Pl., Howard University

Howard University is named in honor of Union General Oliver Otis Howard, once head of the Freedmen's Bureau, and his residence is one of four original university buildings still standing at this institution. The recently restored house—a brick residence with a mansard roof, dormer windows, and three and one-half-story tower—was privately built for General Howard between 1867 and 1869. It was declared a national historic landmark on February 12, 1974.

Howard University
2400 Sixth St., NW

Howard University, founded in 1867, is the largest institution of higher learning established for African Americans immediately following the Civil War.

Covering more than fifty acres, the campus is situated on one of the highest elevations in the District of

Frederick Douglass's house in Washington, DC (National Park Service).

Columbia. Among the historic buildings are Andrew Rankin Memorial Chapel (1895), Freedmen's Hospital (1909), and the Founders Library. Founders Library contains more than 300,000 volumes and includes the Moorland-Spingarn Collection, one of the finest collections on African American life and history in the United States.

LeDroit Park Historic District
Boundary approximates Florida and Rhode Island Aves., 2nd and Elm Sts., and Howard University.

A subdivision created in 1873, the land was part of that purchased as a site for Howard University and the excess was then sold to Amzi L. Barber, the school's acting president and son-in-law of real estate brokers LeDroit Langdon, and Andrew Langdon. Approximately sixty-five houses had been built in the park by 1887 and included various styles from Italianate villas to Gothic cottages. Originally an exclusive white community, in 1893 the area became racially integrated. Afterwards, many whites moved out, and it was almost totally occupied by African Americans. Among the African American residents were Judge Robert H. Terrell and

his wife, Mary Church Terrell, Paul Laurence Dunbar, and much later Mayor Walter Washington. The park was declared a national historic landmark district on February 25, 1974.

Lincoln Memorial
Foot of Twenty-third St. NW, in W. Potomac Park on the Mall

The Lincoln Memorial, dedicated in 1922, has been the site of several important events underscoring African Americans' quest for dignity and struggle for equal opportunity. In 1939, when singer Marian Anderson was refused permission to appear at Constitution Hall by the Daughters of the American Revolution, she performed an Easter Sunday concert on the steps of the Lincoln Memorial before a crowd of 75,000. Her rendition of "Nobody Knows the Trouble I've Seen" prompted NAACP Executive Secretary Walter White to foresee the advent of "a new affirmation of democracy." Another such pivotal event involved the 1963 March on Washington, which was climaxed by the Rev. Martin Luther King, Jr.'s "I Have A Dream" speech. The memorial was

Emancipation Statue in Washington, DC.

designated a national historic landmark on October 15, 1966.

Metropolitan African Methodist Episcopal Church
1518 M St., NW

Completed in 1886, this Victorian, Gothic-style church was designed by architect George Dearing. The church had two forerunners: Israel Bethel A.M.E. (1821) and Union Bethel A.M.E. (1938). On July 6, 1838, Union Bethel was officially sanctioned by the Baltimore Conference, marking the founding of the Metropolitan AME Church. In 1872 the name was officially changed to Metropolitan African Methodist Episcopal Church. The new church building, which, according to the conference, had to be built "in close proximity" to the Capitol, was dedicated on May 30, 1886. Present at the ceremony were Bishop Daniel Payne, Frederick Douglass, and Francis Cardozo. The building has been the site of funeral services for many prominent African Americans, as well as the place for church service during the inauguration of President Bill Clinton. These services

were an official part of the inaugural events, the first to be held at an African American church. It was declared a national historic landmark on July 26, 1973.

Miner Normal School
2565 Georgia Ave., NW

Myrtilla Miner's School for Colored Girls was established in 1851 as a model teaching facility for young African American women. It was the district's only school dedicated solely to teacher training. Although the Miner School, as it was known, operated for a time in different locations, in 1875 it was temporarily affiliated with Howard University's Normal Department. The District of Columbia built a new Miner School—a semipublic school—in 1877 and ten years later it was incorporated into the local public school system. Congress expanded the school into a four-year degree-granting institution in 1929, known as Miner Teachers College. In 1955, the school merged with the local white teacher's college to become the District of Columbia Teachers College. This operation ceased in 1977, when the college merged with two other institutions to become the University of the District of Columbia. The school was designated a national historic landmark on October 11, 1991.

M Street High School
128 M St., NW

The Fifteenth Street Presbyterian Church was the birthplace of M Street High School in 1870. The school was originally known as the Preparatory High School for Colored Youth. It moved to several locations until Congress saw a need for an elite school for its African American population and appropriated money to construct a facility for this purpose. The building was completed in 1891 and was one of the first high schools in the nation built with public funds to serve African Americans. The faculty was well educated and the school offered business and college preparatory classes that were superior to lower level programs in many U.S. colleges and universities. Graduates who became distinguished leaders included Carter G. Woodson and Rayford Logan. Among the early principals were Robert Terrell, Anna Julia Cooper, and Mary Church Terrell. The new Dunbar High School, built in 1916, became the new high school for African Americans, while M Street took junior high school status. School integration in 1954 eliminated the need for a separate facility for African Americans. The school was designated a national historic landmark on October 23, 1986.

National Museum of African Art
950 Independence Ave., SW

A part of the Smithsonian Institution, the National Museum of African Art maintains exhibitions, research components, and public programs on the art and culture of sub-Saharan Africa. The museum was established in 1964 and incorporated as a bureau of the Smithsonian in 1979.

African American Civil War Memorial
Vermont Ave. and U St., NW

The "Spirit of Freedom" statue was unveiled on July 18, 1998, in the Shaw neighborhood of Northwest Washington, DC. It is the centerpiece of the African American Civil War Memorial. Designed by sculptor Ed Hamilton of Louisville, Kentucky, who won a nationwide competition to do the work, the monument is the first to honor and salute African American soldiers and their white officers who fought and died in the Civil War. The memorial, designed by Paul S. Devrouax and landscape architect Edward D. Dunson, is located in a pie-shaped site nearly one block long. The "Spirit of Freedom" is a nine-foot-high 3,000 pound bronze sculpture in a semi-circular arc and high relief. The exterior consists of three infantrymen and a sailor working together to fight for family and freedom. The "Spirit of Freedom," depicted as a woman with eyes closed and hands crossed over her chest, is positioned above the men to guide and protect them. In addition to the statue, the granite walls of the memorial are inscribed with nearly 209,000 names of the Civil War veterans.

Mary Church Terrell House
326 T St., NW

Built in 1907, this house served as the residence of Mary Church Terrell, who achieved national prominence as an early educator, the first president of the National Association of Colored Women, and a civil rights and women's rights activist. She spoke at the 60th anniversary of the First Women's Rights Convention in Seneca Falls, New York. Her lecture in German delivered in 1903 at the International Congress of Women led her to the nationwide lecture circuit. The Terrell House was designated a national historic landmark on May 15, 1975.

St. Luke's Episcopal Church
15th and Church Sts., NW

From 1879 until 1934, the pulpit of St. Luke's Episcopal Church was filled by Alexander Crummell, an African American scholar who became a leading spokesman for African and African American liberation. He was the founder of the American Negro Academy, established with the intention of forming a cadre of African American intellectuals and scholars. The church, located in Washington, DC, was designated a national historic landmark on May 11, 1976.

Tidal Basin Bridge

Designed and constructed by African American engineer Archie Alphonso Alexander, the Tidal Basin Bridge is one of Washington's major tourist attractions. Alexander, born in Ottumwa, Iowa, in 1888, later became the first Republican governor of the U.S. Virgin Islands in 1954.

Carter G. Woodson House and the Association for the Study of Negro Life and History
1538 Ninth St., NW

Founded in 1915, the Association for the Study of Negro Life and History was formed to study and preserve the historical record of African American culture. The pioneer behind the association was Carter G. Woodson, who operated the organization out of his home until his death in 1950.

A scholar and lecturer, Woodson began publication of the *Journal of Negro History* in 1916. Ten years later, Woodson initiated the observance of "Negro History Week," to be celebrated in February as close as possible to the birthdays of both Frederick Douglass and Abraham Lincoln, during which African American leaders would be appropriately honored. Negro History Week has grown into what is now Black History Month.

The Woodson house, built circa 1890, was designated a national historic landmark on May 11, 1976. Today, the organization is headquartered at 1401 14th Street, NW and is known as the Association for the Study of Afro-American Life and History.

◆ FLORIDA

Daytona Beach

Bethune-Cookman College
640 Second Ave.

One of the leading institutions in the South for the training of African American teachers, Bethune-Cookman College was founded in 1904 by Mary McLeod Bethune on "faith and a dollar-and-a-half." The school was first known as Daytona Normal and Industrial Institute for Negro Girls.

Bethune served as advisor to Presidents Franklin D. Roosevelt and Harry S. Truman and directed the Division of Negro Affairs in Roosevelt's National Youth Administration. She was one of the most influential women in the United States between the two world wars.

Mary McLeod Bethune House
Bethune-Cookman College

The two-story frame house belonging to the African American activist and educator Mary McLeod Bethune was built in 1920 on the campus of the school that she established in 1904. The house was proclaimed a national historic landmark on December 2, 1974.

Eatonville

Eatonville, Zora Neale Hurston Memorial Park and Marker
11 People St.

Incorporated in 1887, Eatonville claims to be one of the oldest all-African American community in America. The fourth mayor of the town, John Hurston, a former slave, was the father of the town's most celebrated resident, Zora Neale Hurston. She is highly recognized today as a folklorist, anthropologist, and noted writer of the Harlem Renaissance. Still virtually all-African American, Eatonville is the site of the Zora Neale Hurston festivals held each January to celebrate Hurston's life and work. In addition, a marker has been placed in the Zora Neale Hurston Memorial Park.

Fort Pierce

Zora Neale Hurston House
1734 School Court St.

Zora Neale Hurston lived and worked in this one-story concrete house in Fort Pierce. Her gravesite in a segregated cemetery in Fort Pierce was unmarked until August 1973, when writer Alice Walker placed a stone at the approximate site of her burial. The home in which she lived from 1957, when she worked as reporter and journalist for a local African American weekly newspaper and continued to write until she died in 1960, was designated a national historic landmark on December 4, 1991.

Key West

Dry Tortugas

African American artisans and laborers worked in the construction of Dry Tortugas, a fort in Key West, Florida, which helped control the Florida straits. The largest all-masonry fortification in the western world, it served as a prison until 1873. Among the prisoners was Samuel A. Mudd, a physician who had set John Wilkes Boothe's broken leg after the assassination of Abraham Lincoln.

Fort George Island

Kingsley Plantation

Zephaniah Kingsley traded extensively in slaves, and the headquarters for his operation was on this plantation on Fort George Island. The oldest known plantation in Florida, the Kingsley Plantation was established in 1763. The plantation, which has been restored as a museum, displays exhibits and furnishings that depict the plantation and island life during the period from 1763 to 1783. The site was added to the national park system on February 16, 1988, a part of the Timucuan Ecological and Historic Preserve. On September 29, 1970, it was designated a national historic landmark.

Franklin County

Fort Gadsen

In 1814, the British built the fort as a base for recruiting Seminole Indians and runaway slaves during the War of 1812. The British abandoned it to their allies in 1815, along with its artillery and military supplies. It became known as the Negro Fort and British Fort and served as a beacon for rebellious slaves and a threat to supply vessels on the river. On May 15, 1975, the British fort was named a national historic landmark.

Olustee

Olustee Battlefield Historic Memorial

This site commemorates the largest Civil War battle in Florida's history. Also known as the Battle of Ocean Pond (1864), many African American troops fought bravely for the Union cause. The site was acquired by the state of Florida in 1909. The monument was built in 1912 and dedicated in 1913, just 49 years after the battle.

◆ GEORGIA

Andersonville

Andersonville Prison

Andersonville, the infamous Confederate prison in Andersonville, Georgia where thousands of Union soldiers perished as a result of the brutal manner in which they were confined, is now a national monument. Corporal Henry Gooding of the black 54th Massachusetts regiment was imprisoned here, where he died on July 19, 1864. It was Corporal Gooding who had started a protest regarding the pay of African American soldiers, going over the heads of military brass to write President Lincoln. At that time the pay of African American was a flat $7 per month. For whites, it ranged from $9 to $30. Encouraged by Colonel Robert Shaw, the African American soldiers of the 54th refused to accept any remuneration unless it were equal to that of white comrades. This financial inequity was subsequently rectified, but Cor-

Ebenezer Baptist Church in Atlanta, Georgia (AP/Wide World Photos, Inc.).

Martin Luther King, Jr. memorial in Atlanta, Georgia (Michael Ochs Archives).

poral Gooding died at Andersonville without ever having drawn a day's pay.

Atlanta

Clark Atlanta University Center District

Atlanta University was founded in 1865, holding its first classes for freed slaves in abandoned railway cars. Clark College was founded four years later. The two schools were incorporated in 1988. The Clark Atlanta University System includes the other traditionally African American colleges located in the immediate vicinity: Morris Brown (1881), Morehouse (1867), and Spelman (1881), and the Interdenominational Theological Seminary (1946).

Fountain Hall (formerly Stone Hall), built in 1882 and located on the Morris Brown campus, is the oldest building in the complex. It was named a national historic landmark on December 2, 1974.

Ebenezer Baptist Church
407 Auburn Ave.

A Gothic-revival building constructed in 1922, Ebenezer Baptist Church had as its associate pastor the

Rev. Martin Luther King, Jr. It was from this church that King's movement radiated outward to the rest of the South, organizing chapters of the Southern Christian Leadership Conference (SCLC), the civil rights coalition of which he served as president.

When King was assassinated on April 4, 1968, funeral services were held in this church. As millions watched on television, mourners lined up for miles behind the mule drawn wagon that carried King from Ebenezer to Morehouse College, his alma mater. There, the eulogies were delivered, and more than 150,000 mourners paid their last respects.

Martin Luther King Jr. National Historic District
Auburn Ave.

The district, which consists of several blocks of Atlanta's Auburn Avenue and Boulevard, includes Martin Luther King, Jr.'s birthplace—a two-story Queen Anne style house built in 1895—and grave site, and the church where King served as assistant pastor. The environs of his childhood are largely intact. Private efforts to create a living monument to King and his beliefs have been carried on primarily through the Martin Luther King, Jr. Center for Non-Violent Social Change, Inc. The Martin Luther King Historic District was designated a national historic landmark on May 5, 1977. In 1980 the district became a unit of the national park system.

South View Cemetery

Martin Luther King, Jr., was laid to rest in South View Cemetery, where a marble crypt was inscribed with the words he used to conclude his famous speech delivered on the occasion of the 1963 March on Washington— "Free at last, free at last, thank God Almighty I'm free at last."

South View cemetery was founded in 1886 by African Americans who balked at a prevailing policy requiring that they be buried in the rear of the municipal cemetery.

Sweet Auburn Historic District
Auburn Ave.

Although only a remnant of its original one-mile expanse has survived, the Sweet Auburn district typified the rapid growth of African American enterprise in the post-Civil War period. Forced to adjust to segregated residential and commercial patterns, wealthy African Americans settled in the area once known as Wheat Street and the "richest Negro street in the world." The district survives as a center of African American business and social activity. The district was designated a national historic landmark district on December 8, 1976.

Augusta

Laney-Walker North Historic District
Bounded by D'Antignac; Seventh, Twiggs, Phillips, and Harrison Sts., Walton Way, and Laney-Walker Blvd.

Developed during the nineteenth century as a self-sufficient, working-class community, the Laney-Walker district includes good examples of such houses as the plantation plain, shotgun, double pen, Victorian cottage, and an indigenous Augusta house. Prominent African American residents of the area were novelist Frank Yerby, educator and Haines Normal and Industrial Institute-founder Lucy C. Laney, minister and church-founder Charles T. Walker, and numerous physicians, merchants, builders, and business people. Businesses in the district are important landmarks in Augusta's African American community. Examples are the Pilgrim Health and Life Insurance Company (1898) and the Penny Savings Bank (1910). The area was designated a national historic landmark district on September 5, 1985.

Columbus

"Blind Tom" Marker
U.S. Rte. 27A

This marks the grave site of the famous African American pianist "Blind Tom" Bethune. Born Thomas Green Bethune, son of a slave, he was a prodigy whose astonishing talent brought him into the salons of Europe, where royalty marveled at his virtuoso performances.

Gertrude Pridgett "Ma" Rainey House
805 5th Ave.

The Rainey House was the retirement residence of Ma Rainey, who was recognized as "Mother of the Blues." She made her singing debut at age 14. In 1904, she married William "Pa" Rainey of the Rabbit Foot Minstrels and became known as "Ma." The team performed with various minstrels until they separated.

Ma Rainey worked out of Chicago during the 1920s and early 1930s and continued to tour the South. She had already won a national following as gospel and blues performer long before she made her first recording in 1924. Rainey retired in 1934. She returned to Columbus in 1935 and lived in the house that she had earlier purchased for her mother. She died in 1939 and was buried in the local Potterdale Cemetery. The Rainey House was declared a national historic landmark on November 18, 1992.

Bragg Smith Grave Site and Memorial
Columbus Colored Cemetery
Fourth St. and Seventh Ave.

This memorial, located in the Columbus Colored Cemetery, was built in memory of Bragg Smith, who was killed while attempting to rescue a city engineer trapped in a caved-in structure. The marble memorial is believed to have been the first civic memorial in the country dedicated to an African American.

Savannah

First Bryan Baptist Church
559 W. Bryan St.

The land on which Bryant Church was build is considered the oldest real estate in the country continuously owned by African Americans. Deeds for the land are dated September 4, 1793. Andrew Bryan formed the First African Baptist Church in Savannah on January 20, 1788, and pastored the congregation that became First Bryan Baptist Church in 1799. He remained there until his death in 1812.

Inside the First Bryan Baptist Church is a memorial dedicated to the Rev. George Liele, a former slave and the first African American Baptist missionary. His work took him up and down the Savannah River, from Augusta to Savannah, several times a year, where he preached to slaves. One of the slaves that he converted and baptized was Andrew Bryan, for whom the church was named.

Woodbury

Red Oak Creek Covered Bridge
North of Woodbury on Huel Brown Rd.

This 1840 structure is 412 feet long and was built by African American bridge builder Horace King, a former slave. King continued to work for his white master, John Goodwin, a contractor, after he was freed in 1848. One of the few extant in the state, the bridge is believed to be the oldest structure of its type in Georgia and the longest covered bridge span in the state. King built other bridges in west Georgia as well as the bridge across the Chattahoochee River in Columbus. The Red Oak Covered Bridge was designated a national historic landmark on May 7, 1973.

◆ ILLINOIS

Chicago

Robert S. Abbott House
4742 Martin Luther King Dr.

This house was occupied by Robert Stengstacke Abbott from 1926 until his death in 1940. Under Abbott, the *Chicago Defender*, a newspaper targeted to African American readers, encouraged African Americans in the South to migrate northward, particularly to Chicago. Probably more than any other publication, the *Defender* was responsible for the large northward migration of African Americans during the first half of the twentieth century. The house was named a national historic landmark on December 8, 1976.

***Chicago Bee* Building**
3647–3655 S. State St.

The *Chicago Bee* Building was the last major structure built in Chicago's Black Metropolis, near State and 35th streets on the Near South Side. African American entrepreneur Anthony Overton had the structure built to house his newspaper, the *Chicago Bee*. Opened in 1931, the building also housed his Overton Hygenic Manufacturing Company. It was the first building designed in the late 1920s Art Deco style and was one of the most picturesque structures in the metropolis. The building was designated a national historic landmark on April 30, 1986.

Oscar Stanton DePriest House
4536–4538 S. Dr. Martin Luther King Jr. Dr.

This house served as the residence of the first African American elected to the House of Representatives from a northern state. Oscar DePriest was born in Florence, Alabama, but moved with his family to Kansas and later to Chicago. While in Chicago, he worked as a real estate broker and, in 1928, he was elected to the U.S. House of Representatives, where he served three terms. Following his tenure, he returned to the real estate business, but remained politically active in Chicago—including serving as vice-chairman of the Cook County Republican Committee. The DePriest house was designated a national historic landmark on May 15, 1975.

Milton L. Olive Park
Lake Shore Dr.

Milton L. Olive Park was dedicated by Chicago Mayor Richard Daley in honor of the first African American soldier to be awarded a Congressional Medal of Honor during the Vietnam War. Olive died in action after exhibiting extraordinary heroism, having saved the lives of several other soldiers exposed to a live grenade.

Jean Baptiste Point Du Sable Homesite
401 N. Michigan Ave.

Jean Baptiste Point Du Sable, born in Haiti to a French mariner father and a black mother, immigrated to French Louisiana and became a fur trapper. He established trading posts on the sites of the present cities of Michigan City, Indiana; Peoria, Illinois; and Port Huron, Michigan—but the most important post was on the site of Chicago, Illinois. This site, where he constructed a log home for his wife and family, is recognized as the first settlement in the Chicago area. In 1796, Du Sable sold his Chicago home and went to live with his son in St. Charles, where he died in 1814.

The homesite was designated a national historic landmark on May 11, 1976. The site of Du Sable's home is marked by a plaque on the northeast approach to the Michigan Avenue Bridge. Two other plaques recognizing Du Sable exist—one in the Chicago Historical Society, the other in the lobby of Du Sable High School, at 49th and State Streets.

Provident Hospital and Training School
500 E. 51st St. and Vincennes Ave.

The original Provident Hospital and Training School was established as the first training school for African American nurses in the United States. It was founded by Daniel Hale Williams, the renowned surgeon who performed one of the first successful operations on the human heart in 1893. The current hospital was opened in 1933.

Quinn Chapel of the AME Church
2401 S. Wabash Ave.

Quinn Chapel is the oldest African American congregation in Chicago. Its history dates to 1844, when several local African Americans organized a weekly, nonsectarian prayer group that met in a member's home. The group was organized in 1847 as a congregation of the AME Church and was named for William Paul Quinn, bishop, circuit rider, and key figure in the western advance of the church. The church would serve as a focal point for the social and humanitarian life of Chicago's elite African Americans. Erected in 1892, the church structure was declared a national historic landmark on September 4, 1979.

Underground Railroad Marker
9955 S. Beverly Ave.

This marks one of many transit points used by slaves escaping from the South to Canada.

Victory Monument
35th St. and S. Parkway

Sculpted by Leonard Crunelle, Victory Monument honors the African American soldiers of Illinois who served in World War I. The monument and tomb of Stephen A. Douglas, once the owner of much of the land in the area, is also located near 35th Street.

Ida B. Wells-Barnett House
3624 S. Dr. Martin Luther King Jr. Dr.

This house was the home of the 1890s fiery journalist, civil rights advocate, and crusader for African American women, Ida Wells-Barnett. Wells-Barnett was exiled from the South, after writing scathing articles about lynchings and race relations in Memphis, Tennessee, where her career in journalism began. She organized women's clubs in New England and Chicago and the Alpha Suffrage Club in Chicago. Wells-Barnett was a founder of the National Association for the Advancement of Colored People (NAACP). The Wells-Barnett House was designated a national historic landmark on May 30, 1974.

Daniel Hale Williams House
445 E. 42nd St.

This house was the home of one of America's first African American surgeons, whose accomplishments include performing one of the first successful heart operations in 1893 and establishing quality medical facilities for African Americans. Daniel Hale Williams was born in Hollidaysburg, Pennsylvania. He had managed a barber shop prior to apprenticing under Henry Palmer, who was surgeon-general of Wisconsin. Williams received his medical degree from Chicago Medical College in 1883 and later opened an office in Chicago; he was the first African American to win a fellowship from the American College of Surgeons. The Williams house was designated a national historic landmark on May 15, 1975.

Quincy

Father Augustine Tolton Grave Site
St. Peter's Cemetery
Broadway and 32nd St.

The Father Augustine Tolton grave site marks the resting place of the first African American to be ordained as a Roman Catholic priest. Ordained in 1886, Father Tolton opened a school for African American children, was pastor at St. Joseph's Church in Quincy, and later served as pastor at St. Monica's Church in Chicago. He died in 1897.

◆ INDIANA

Bloomingdale

Underground Railroad Marker
U.S. Rte. 41

This marks one of several points once used to assist fugitive slaves seeking freedom and safety into Canada. One such slave, William Trail, liked Indiana so much he decided to stay and go into farming. His efforts were successful, and he became one of many prosperous farmers active in Union County, Indiana.

Fountain City

Levi Coffin House
113 U.S. 27, N.

Born in North Carolina in 1798, Levi Coffin, a Quaker abolitionist who was also known as "The President of the Underground Railroad," used his own home in Fountain City as a way station for runaway slaves. Between 1827 and 1847, Coffin hid more than three hundred slaves heading for Illinois, Michigan, or Canada. The home was built in 1839, altered in 1910, then restored to its former design.

Coffin left Fountain City for Ohio, where he continued his activities, eventually helping over 3,000 slaves escape from the South—he was still engaged in the resettlement of former slaves long after the Civil War had ended. Coffin died in Avondale, Ohio, in 1877.

Indianapolis

Madame C. J. Walker Building
617 Indiana Ave.

The Walker Building was constructed in 1927, the headquarters for the prosperous firm of Madame C. J. Walker (1867–1919). The Art Deco structure was architecturally significant and incorporated African, Egyptian, and Moorish motifs in its design. It housed a number of businesses, including a theater, pharmacy, ballroom, and the Walker Beauty College, where thousands of Walker's successful beauty agents were trained.

Walker's firm manufactured 75 beauty products, as well as training programs, beauty schools, and shops nationwide. Her hair care business catapulted her into fame and wealth, and many called her the nation's first African American woman millionaire. She also gave generously to various charities. The Walker Building was designated a national historic landmark on July 17, 1991.

◆ IOWA

Clinton

Underground Railroad Marker
Sixth and S. Second Sts.

Before the Lafayette Hotel was built, the small house that once stood at this location had been a point of shelter and sustenance for fugitive slaves escaping from Missouri (Iowa was a free territory by virtue of both the Northwest Ordinance of 1787 and the Missouri Compromise of 1820). Many Quakers, who had come to the state before the Civil War, took great pains to maintain an efficient and effective Underground Railroad network.

Des Moines

Fort Des Moines Provisional Army Officer Training School
Southwest Ninth St.

Fort Des Moines Provisional Army Officer Camp was opened on June 15, 1917, for the purpose of training talented African American soldiers for officer's rank. On October 14, 1917, 639 African American soldiers were commissioned as second lieutenants and assigned to the American Expeditionary Forces being sent to France to fight in World War I. African American units, led by men trained at the school, were assembled in France as the 92nd Division. The camp was abandoned at the end of the war, and the site was designated a national historic landmark on May 30, 1974.

Sioux City

Pearl Street

Sioux City was a refuge for many slaves escaping from Missouri. Pearl Street, once the city's main thoroughfare, was named for an African American who had arrived in the town by boat more than a century earlier and achieved widespread popularity as a cook.

◆ KANSAS

Beeler

George Washington Carver Homestead

Along Route K–96 in Ness County lies the plot of land once homesteaded by George Washington Carver, the famed African American agricultural scientist. He spent two years here before attending college in Iowa. The homestead was designated a national historic landmark on November 23, 1977.

Nicodemus

Nicodemus Historic District
U.S. 24 (Site approximates North St., E. Bend Rd., South St., and Seventh St.)

Located two miles west of the Rooks-Graham county line, the Nicodemus Historic District is the last of three now virtually deserted colonies that were founded by the Exodusters—a group of African American homesteaders that migrated from the South to Kansas during the 1870s. A principal leader of the mass migration was Tennessee's former slave Benjamin "Pap" Singleton, who established 11 colonies in Kansas between 1873 and 1880. The name "Nicodemus" was derived from a slave who, according to legend, foretold the coming of the Civil War.

Arriving in 1877, the first settlers lived in dugouts and burrows during the cold weather. From the outset, they were plagued by crop failures. Although never more than five hundred in number, they managed nonetheless to establish a community with teachers, ministers, and

Early migrants to the Nicodemus, Kansas settlement.

civil servants. The state of Kansas has commemorated this site with a historical marker located in a roadside park in Nicodemus. The district was designated a national historic landmark on January 7, 1976.

Osawatomie

John Brown Memorial State Park
Tenth and Main Sts.

This state park, named in honor of insurrectionist John Brown, contains the cabin in which he lived and engaged in abolitionist activities during his brief sojourn in Kansas. The cabin, built in 1854 on a site about one mile west of town, was dismantled, moved, and reconstructed in the park in 1912. In1928 it was covered with a stone pergola. The park was designated a national historic landmark on March 24, 1971.

Topeka

Brown v. Board of Education National Historic Landmark
330 Western Ave.

The historic area includes Sumner and Monroe elementary schools, both associated with the landmark Supreme Court case. In 1951, Linda Brown, who at first traveled a considerable distance to study at the all-African American Monroe Elementary School, was refused enrollment in Sumner Elementary School be-

cause she was African American. What followed was the landmark case *Brown v. Board of Education of Topeka*. Upon hearing the case, the U.S. Supreme Court concluded that "separate education facilities are inherently unequal," striking down the 1896 *Plessy v. Ferguson* decision and giving the legal basis for desegregation in public schools. Sumner was designated a national historic landmark on May 4, 1987, and Monroe was included in 1991. The combined designation became a part of the national park system in 1993.

◆ KENTUCKY

Berea

Lincoln Hall
Berea College

Opened in 1855, Berea College was the first college established in the United States for the specific purpose of educating blacks and whites together. The school's Lincoln Hall, built in 1887, was designated as a national historic landmark on December 2, 1974.

Louisville

Kentucky Derby Museum
Churchill Downs, 704 Central Ave.

Materials relating to early African American jockeys, who played an important part in racing history, are in the museum. Isaac Murphy, the first jockey to ride three Kentucky Derby horses to victory, is among those represented.

Louisville Free Public Library, Western Colored Branch
604 S. 10th St.

The library, established in 1905, was the first public library in the nation built exclusively for African Americans. It was financed by Andrew Carnegie and played an important role in advancing African American culture in Louisville. Thomas F. Blue, the first librarian, opened a library education program at the facility in 1908 to prepare African Americans for positions in the library. The building was declared a national historic landmark on December 6, 1975.

Simpsonville

Lincoln Institute Complex
Off U.S. Rte. 60

Lincoln Institute was Kentucky's leading center for the education of African American students in secondary school between 1908 and 1938. Whitney M. Young, Sr. directed the school. When a state law in 1904 ordered Berea College to close its doors to biracial education, the college founded the Lincoln Institute. Kentucky's schools were integrated in the 1950s and the institute became obsolete. It closed on 1965. On December 12, 1988, the complex was designated a national historic landmark.

Whitney M. Young, Jr. Birthplace
Off U.S. Rte. 60

Whitney M. Young, Jr. was born in a simple, two-story frame building near Simpsonville. He grew up on the campus of the Lincoln Institute. Later, Young worked with the Urban League in Minnesota and Omaha, then became dean of social work at Atlanta University (now Clark Atlanta). In 1961, Young was appointed executive director of the National Urban League, a position he held until 1971, when he died in Lagos, Nigeria. On April 27, 1984, the house in which he was born and lived was declared a national historic landmark.

◆ LOUISIANA

Alexandria

Arna Wendell Bontemps House
1327 3rd St.

Arna Wendell Bontemps was born in this modest Queen Anne Revival style cottage in 1906 and remained there until his family relocated to California. Bontemps relocated to New York City in 1923 and became active as a Harlem Renaissance writer. Later he taught in Huntsville, Alabama, and in Chicago. He moved to Nashville, Tennessee in 1943, to become head librarian at Fisk University and remained there until he retired in 1965. He was then professor at the University of Illinois, Chicago Circle, as it was known then, and curator of the James Weldon Johnson Collection at Yale University. He returned to Fisk as writer-in-residence, the position that he held when he died on June 4, 1973. In his lifetime he wrote numerous books, poems, and articles. His birthplace, now a museum, was designated a national historic landmark on September 13, 1993.

Melrose

Melrose Plantation
Rte. 119

The Yucca Plantation, known after 1875 as Melrose Plantation, was established in 1794 by Marie Therese Coincoin, a former slave and wealthy businesswoman. The African House located on the plantation, a unique structure with an umbrella-like roof, is believed to be of direct African derivation. Melrose is also associated with Clementine Hunter, one of its African American workers, whose paintings of the plantation and its activities made her a famous folk painter. The site and its various buildings were declared a national historic landmark on April 16, 1984.

New Orleans

James H. Dillard House
571 Audubon St.

This house served as the home of James Dillard from 1894 to 1913. Dillard played an important role in African American education in the nineteenth century, strengthening vocational and teacher training programs. Dillard's home was designated a national historic landmark on December 2, 1975. Dillard University, founded in 1869, was named for this educator.

Flint-Goodrich Hospital of Dillard University
Intersection of Louisiana Ave. and LaSalle St.

The hospital was founded in 1911 and became the medical unit of Dillard University. In the 1930s the hospital was the only institution in the state that offered internships to African American students preparing to become doctors. Flint-Goodrich was also the city's sole health care facility that admitted African Americans. It was significant for its contributions to tuberculosis testing and treatment, infant and maternal care, and syphilis treatment. The hospital was designated a national historic landmark on January 13, 1989.

Louisiana State Museum

The Louisiana State Museum contains a tablet inscribed in the memory of Norbert Rillieux, inventor of the sugar evaporating pan that revolutionized the sugar refining industry.

Port Hudson

Port Hudson Siege Marker

Located near the Mississippi River some 25 miles north of Baton Rouge, Port Hudson was the scene of many heroic acts by African American soldiers during the Civil War including Louisiana's celebrated regiment of African Americans, the Native Guards.

◆ MAINE

Portland

John B. Russwurm House
238 Ocean Ave.

Russwurm, the second African American to receive a college degree, graduated from Bowdoin College in 1826. He co-edited the nation's first African American newspaper *Freedom's Journal*, then emigrated to Liberia. The historic house where he lived from 1812 to 1827, the only surviving structure closely tied to Russwurm, was designated a national historic landmark on July 21, 1983.

◆ MARYLAND

Annapolis

Banneker-Douglass Museum
84 Franklin St.

This museum, located in the city's historic district, is dedicated to the African American surveyor and inventor Benjamin Banneker and the abolitionist Frederick Douglass, both born in Maryland.

Matthew Henson Plaque
Maryland State House

The Matthew Henson Plaque honors the memory of the only man to accompany Admiral Robert E. Peary on all of his polar expeditions. On April 6, 1909, Henson became the first man actually to reach the North Pole. Peary himself, barely able to walk, arrived after Henson had taken a reading of his position and proudly planted the U.S. flag.

Thurgood Marshall Statue

A seven-foot bronze statue of Supreme Court Justice Thurgood Marshall was unveiled in Annapolis in November 1996. It is the state's first memorial dedicated to an African American.

Baltimore

Benjamin Banneker Marker
Westchester Ave. at Westchester School

This marker in Baltimore, Maryland, is a tribute to Benjamin Banneker, the black mathematician, astronomer, and inventor who, in 1792, produced an almanac regarded as among the most reliable. His scientific knowledge led to his assignment as a member of the surveying and planning team that helped lay out the nation's capital.

Beulah M. Davis Collection
Soper Library
Morgan State University

Morgan State University houses an interesting collection of artifacts on Benjamin Banneker, noted astronomer, compiler of almanacs, and—together with Pierre-Charles L'Enfant—surveyor of the District of Columbia. It also houses a number of artifacts on Frederick Douglass and Matthew Henson.

Frederick Douglass Monument
Morgan State University

On the campus of Morgan State University is the Frederick Douglass memorial statue created by the noted African American sculptor James Lewis. The work, completed in 1956, stands 12 feet tall with pedestal. Its simple inscription reads "Frederick Douglass 1817–1895 Humanitarian, Statesman."

Rockville

Uncle Tom's Cabin

This is the site of the log cabin believed to have been the birthplace of Josiah Henson, the escaped slave immortalized as Uncle Tom in Harriet Beecher Stowe's famous abolitionist study.

Born in 1789, Henson was sold at auction at an early age and transferred among many masters until he managed to escape in 1830. After setting up a community for fugitive slaves in Dawn, Canada, Henson frequently returned to the South to liberate others. Meeting with Stowe, Henson outlined his slave experiences, which later formed the bases for her celebrated story—in the introduction to Henson's autobiography, published some years later, she acknowledged his story as the source of her own tale.

◆ MASSACHUSETTS

Boston

Abiel Smith School and Museum of Afro-American History
46 Joy St.

Now housing the Museum of Afro-American History, this building, built in 1834, was the site of the city's first school for African American children.

African American National Historic Site
Museum of Afro American History, Dudley Station, Box 5

This site includes the Black Heritage Trail and contains the largest concentration of pre-Civil War African American history sites anywhere in the United States. Among them are the African Meeting House (the oldest extant African American church building in New England), the Smith Court residences (typical of African American families and built between 1799 and 1853), the Abiel Smith School (built in 1834), and the home of Lewis Hayden (the most documented of Boston's Underground Railroad stations). Hayden was an escaped slave from Kentucky who helped recruit the all-black 54th Massachusetts Regiment. Congress authorized the African American National Historic Site on October 10,

1980. The National Park Services coordinates it components; the site is federally-owned.

African Meeting House
8 Smiths Court

This is the site of the first black church in Boston and oldest surviving black church building in the United States. It was designated a national historic site on May 30, 1974, and is a part of the Boston African American National Historic Site.

Bunker Hill Monument

Standing in the Charlestown district of Boston, Massachusetts, the Bunker Hill Monument commemorates the famous Revolutionary War battle which—contrary to popular belief—was actually fought on Breed's Hill on June 17, 1775. A number of African Americans fought alongside the colonists during the battle including Peter Salem, Salem Poor, Titus Coburn, Cato Howe, Alexander Ames, Seymour Burr, Pomp Fiske, and Prince Hall, founder of the Negro Masonic order.

Crispus Attucks Monument

The Crispus Attucks Monument, located in the Boston Common, was dedicated in 1888 to the five victims of the Boston Massacre—Crispus Attucks, Samuel Maverick, James Caldwell, Samuel Gray, and Patrick Carr. The site of the Massacre is marked by a plaque on State Street, near the Old State House.

Attucks is believed by many historians to have been the same man who, in 1750, was advertised as a runaway black slave from Framingham, Massachusetts. Although a stranger to Boston, he led a group that converged on a British garrison, which was quartered in King Street to help enforce the Townshend Acts. One of the soldiers of the garrison panicked and fired, and Attucks was the first to fall. Gray and Caldwell were also killed on the same spot; Maverick and Carr died later of wounds sustained during the clash. The British soldiers were later tried for murder but acquitted. The five men are buried a few blocks away in Granary Burying Ground, together with such famous Revolutionary figures as John Adams and John Hancock, as well as Governor William Bradford of Plymouth Colony.

William C. Nell House
3 Smith Court

From the 1830s to the end of the Civil War, William C. Nell was one of the leading African American abolitionists. Born in Boston, he studied law in the office of William I. Bowditch. Nell refused to take an oath to be admitted to the bar because he did not want to support the Constitution of the United States, which compro-

Crispus Attucks Monument in Boston, Massachusetts (AP/Wide World Photos, Inc.).

mised on the issue of slavery. He then began organizing meetings and lecturing in support of the anti-slavery movement. The Nell house was designated a national historic landmark on May 11, 1976.

Colonel Robert Gould Shaw Monument
Beacon and Park Sts.

Executed by the famed sculptor Augustus Saint-Gaudens, the Shaw monument depicts Colonel Robert

Monument honoring Union Colonel Robert Gould Shaw and the famed 54th Massachusetts Volunteers.

Gould Shaw and the 54th Massachusetts Volunteers, an African American regiment that served in the Union Army during the Civil War. The regiment particularly distinguished itself in the battle for Fort Wagner, during which Colonel Shaw was killed. Sergeant William H. Carney's valiant exploits during this battle later earned him the Medal of Honor.

Cambridge

Maria Baldwin House
196 Prospect and H Sts.

This house was the permanent address of Maria Baldwin from 1892 until her death in 1922. Baldwin served as principal and later as "master" of the Agassiz School in Cambridge, as a leader in such organizations as the League for Community Service, as a gifted and popular speaker on the lecture circuit, and as a sponsor of charitable activities such as establishing the first kindergarten in Atlanta, Georgia. Baldwin exemplified the achievements that were attainable by an African American in a predominantly white society. The house was designated as a national historic landmark on May 11, 1976.

Phillis Wheatley Folio
Harvard University

During her celebrated trip to England in 1773, Phillis Wheatley was presented with a folio edition of John Milton's *Paradise Lost*, which now is housed in the library of Harvard University in Cambridge, Massachusetts.

Wheatley, who came to America in 1761 as a child aged seven or eight, made rapid strides in mastering the English language and, by the time she was 14, had already completed her first poem. Always in delicate health, she died in Boston on December 5, 1784.

Central Village

Paul Cuffe Memorial

Paul Cuffe, son of a freedman, was born in 1759 and became a prosperous merchant seaman. Cuffe resolved to use his wealth and position to campaign for the extension of civil rights to African Americans. On one occasion, he refused to pay his personal property tax on the grounds that he was being denied full citizenship rights. A court of law eventually upheld his action, whereupon he was granted the same privileges and immunities enjoyed by white citizens of the state. In 1815, Cuffe transported 38 African Americans to Sierra Leone in what was intended to launch a systematic attempt to repatriate the African American inhabitants of the United States. However, with the growth of abolitionist sentiment, the repatriation movement lost favor.

Dorchester

William Monroe Trotter House
97 Sawyer Ave.

Built in the late 1880s or 1890s, this balloon-frame rectangular-plan house was the primary home of William Monroe Trotter, journalist, civil rights activist, insurance agent, and mortgage broker. He was a bitter opponent of Booker T. Washington and had a confrontation with Washington in Boston on July 3, 1903, that came to be known as the "Boston riot." Trotter formed the Boston Suffrage League and, in 1901, cofounded and became editor and publisher of the crusading newspaper *The Guardian.* His home was designated a national historic landmark on May 11, 1976.

Great Barrington

W. E. B. Du Bois Homesite
Rte. 23

This location served as the boyhood home of William Edward Burghardt Du Bois from 1868 to 1873. Du Bois, the prominent African American sociologist and writer, was a major figure in the Civil Rights movement during the first half of the twentieth century. Du Bois fought discrimination against African Americans through his writing, as a college professor, and as a lecturer. The Du Bois homesite was designated on May 11, 1976 as a national historic landmark.

Lynn

Jan Ernst Matzeliger Statue

The Matzeliger Statue is one of the few extant memorials to this African American inventor, whose shoe-lace machine revolutionized the industry and made mass-produced shoes a reality in the United States. A native of Dutch Guiana, Matzeliger came to the United States in 1876, learned the cobbler's trade, and set out to design a machine that would simplify shoe manufacturing. Always sickly, he died at an early age, unable to capitalize on his successful patent, which was purchased by the United Shoe Machinery Company of Boston. After his death, Matzeliger was awarded a gold medal at the 1901 Pan-American Exposition.

New Bedford

New Bedford Whaling Museum

The museum maintains a treasury of whaling artifacts and information including the names and histories of African Americans who participated in the whaling industry. The museum also houses versions of the toggle harpoon—invented by Lewis Temple, an African American metalsmith—which revolutionized the whaling industry.

Suffolk County

Paul Cuffe Farm and Memorial
1504 Drift Rd.

Paul Cuffe was a self-educated African American who became a prosperous merchant. He was a pioneer in the struggle for minority rights in the eighteenth and early nineteenth centuries and was active in the movement for black resettlement in Africa. The Paul Cuffe Farm was designated a national historic landmark on May 30, 1974.

◆ MICHIGAN

Battle Creek

Sojourner Truth Grave Site
Oakhill Cemetery

This site in the Oak Hill Cemetery marks the resting place of one of the most powerful abolitionist and lecturers of the nineteenth century, Sojourner Truth. Sojourner settled in Battle Creek after the Civil War, but continued to travel on lecture tours until a few years before her death on November 26, 1883.

Cassopolis

Underground Railroad Marker
Rte. M–60

This marks one of many as rest places used by slaves escaping from the South to Canada. The marker is located approximately two miles east of Cassopolis.

Detroit

Douglass-Brown Marker
William Webb House
E. Congress St.

The Douglass-Brown Marker indicates the site of the William Webb House, where fellow abolitionists Frederick Douglass and John Brown met in March of 1859 to

Sojourner Truth's gravesite in Battle Creek, Michigan.

The Motown Museum in Detroit, Michigan (Corbis Corporation [Bellevue]).

map out the strategy for the raid on the federal armory at Harpers Ferry, West Virginia. Douglass was strongly opposed to this course of action. Nevertheless, on October 16, 1959, Brown's forces seized the fort, only to be overtaken by federal troops two days later.

Ralph Bunche Birthplace
5685 W. Fort St.

A plaque marks the site of the birthplace of the undersecretary general of the United Nations and Nobel

Peace Prize winner, Ralph Bunche, who was born in 1927. Bunche, the first African American to receive this honor, was awarded the prize in 1950 for his work as a United Nations mediator following the Arab-Israeli war of 1948.

Dunbar Hospital
580 Frederick Ave.

The hospital is a landmark in the East Ferry Historic District. In 1918, the townhouse structure became the city's first nonprofit hospital for African Americans, who had inadequate access to mainstream hospitals in Detroit. African American physicians established the Allied Medical Society (later known as the Detroit Medical Society) and raised funds to establish a medical facility, Dunbar Hospital. In 1928, the hospital moved to Brush and Illinois streets and operated as Parkside Hospital until it was lost to urban renewal in 1960. Built in 1892 as a private residence, in 1928 the old Dunbar building served as the home of Charles C. Diggs, Sr. and housed his undertaking business. Later his son, Charles, Jr., made the home his residence. The building was designated a national historic landmark on June 19, 1979.

Elmwood Cemetery
1200 Elmwood

Elmwood Cemetery contains the grave sites of 14 members of the 102nd U.S. Colored Regiment.

Elijah McCoy Home Site
5730 Lincoln

A plaque marks the site of one of Elijah McCoy's residences. McCoy, born in Ontario, Canada, settled in the Detroit area, opening a manufacturing company in 1870. McCoy is best known for his self lubricating device for locomotives and engines.

Second Baptist Church in Detroit, Michigan (Burton Historical Collection).

Motown Museum
2648 W. Grand Blvd.

This location served as the early headquarters of Motown Records, founded in 1958 by songwriter and independent record producer Berry Gordy, Jr. Performers including the Four Tops, Marvin Gaye, the Jackson Five, Martha and the Vandellas, Smokey Robinson, the Supremes, the Temptations, Mary Wells, and Stevie Wonder all played an important part in the early success of Motown. In 1972, the company moved its headquarters from Detroit to Los Angeles, California, but a museum containing restored sound studios and mementos is maintained at this site.

National Museum of the Tuskegee Airmen
Historic Fort Wayne

The museum houses memorabilia of the Tuskegee Airmen, an all-African American unit of fighter pilots active during World War II. The airmen, who were trained at Alabama's Tuskegee Institute (as it was known then), played an important role in the fight against racial discrimination in the armed forces.

Underground Railroad Marker
Second Baptist Church
441 Monroe

One of many stops along the Underground Railroad, the basement of the Second Baptist Church was used to hide runaway slaves. The church, founded in 1836, is one of the oldest African American congregations in the Midwest.

Marshall

Crosswhite Boulder
Michigan Ave. and Mansion St.

The Crosswhite Boulder in Marshall, Michigan marks the site of two confrontations that occurred in 1846 in defense of Adam Crosswhite, a fugitive slave who had fled from Kentucky. The Crosswhite case is said to have been instrumental in the enactment of the Fugitive Slave Law of 1850.

◆ MINNESOTA

Minneapolis-St. Paul

Fort Snelling State Park

Fort Snelling was the outpost in the Wisconsin Territory to which the slave later to become known as Dred Scott was transported from Illinois in 1836. Scott met and married his wife Harriet at the fort and saw his first child born there. Later taken to Missouri by his master, he filed suit for his freedom and became a national figure as his case was tried from 1847 to 1857 before numerous tribunals en route to the U.S. Supreme Court. Scott argued that he should be considered free by virtue of his having previously resided in Illinois and at Fort Snelling.

◆ MISSISSIPPI

Jackson

Farish Street Neighborhood Historic District
Approximate boundary Amite, Mill, Fortification, and
    Lamar Sts.

The district, comprising 695 buildings on 125 acres in downtown Jackson, is the state's largest African American community. A segregated area for African American residents in the 1890s, it soon became known for professionals of local or national prominence. The district gives excellent examples of the vernacular buildings of the period 1860 through the 1940s, although most of the buildings were erected between 1890 and 1930. The

Houston Hall, Lincoln University in Jefferson City, Missouri (AP/Wide World Photos, Inc.).

district was designated a national historic landmark site on March 13, 1980. After that, the boundary increased to include Amite, Lamar, Mill, and Fortification streets and embraced structures built by local African American contractors. The expanded site was designated a national historic landmark on September 18, 1980.

Lorman

Alcorn State University Historic District
Alcorn State University campus

Alcorn State University, founded in 1871, is the oldest African American land grant college in the United States. Land grant status was designated in 1878, and the legislature changed the college's name to Alcorn Agricultural and Mechanical College. The state selected for its first president Hiram R. Revels, a distinguished leader during Reconstruction and the first African American to serve in the U. S. Congress. Buildings in the historic district include Lanier Hall, the Administration Building, and Harmon Hall. The Alcorn district was designated a national historic landmark site on May 20, 1983.

Oakland Chapel on the Alcorn University campus was built in 1838 as one of the first buildings of Oakland College, a white institution. In 1871 the state purchased

the school to educate African Americans. The chapel was designated a national historic landmark on May 11, 1976.

Mound Bayou

Isiah Thornton Montgomery House
W. Main St.

This location served as the home of Isiah Thornton Montgomery, who in 1887 founded Mound Bayou—a place where African Americans could obtain social, political, and economic rights in a white supremacist South. The house, a two-story red brick structure built in 1910, was declared a national historic landmark on May 11, 1976.

Natchez

Natchez National Cemetery

This cemetery, established in 1840, is the final resting place of many African American war dead including landsman Wilson Brown, a Medal of Honor recipient during the Civil War. Brown and seaman John Lawson received their medals for courage in action while serving aboard the U.S.S. *Hartford* in the Mobile Bay engagement of August 5, 1864.

Piney Woods

Piney Woods Country Life School
5096 MS49, 20 miles south of Jackson

Lawrence Clifton Jones established the school in 1909 to provide education for African Americans in Mississippi's back woods. The curriculum combined industrial education and academics. In early 1920s the junior college program prepared future teachers. Jones gained nationwide attention in the 1950s as "The Little Professor of Piney Woods," when he was featured on the television program *This Is Your Life*. Today, enrolled students originate from both Mississippi and distant states as well.

◆ MISSOURI

Diamond

George Washington Carver Birthplace and National Monument
U.S. Rte. 71

Located in a park in Diamond, Missouri, Carver National Monument commemorates the place where the great African American scientist George Washington Carver was born and spent his early childhood. The cabin of his birth no longer exists.

Kidnapped when he was just six weeks old, Carver was eventually ransomed for a horse valued at $300. Raised in Missouri by the family of Moses Carver, his owner, he made his way through Minnesota, Kansas, and Iowa before being "discovered" by Booker T. Washington in 1896. That same year, Carver joined the faculty of Tuskegee Institute, where he conducted most of the research for which he is now famous.

The monument, one of the first created in honor of an African American, consists of a statue of Carver as a boy and encloses several trails leading to places of which he was particularly fond. The park also houses a visitors' center and a museum displaying many of his discoveries and personal belongings. The monument was added to the national park system on October 15, 1966.

Kansas City

Kansas City Jazz Museum

The museum opened in September 1998 as a monument to the music of the city that flourished between the 1920s and 1940s, as well as to spur redevelopment of the abandoned neighborhood where it is located.

Mutual Musicians Association Building
1823 Highland Ave.

This building served as the home of the American Federation of Musicians Local 627 from the 1920s to the 1940s. Its members created the Kansas City style of jazz and included such greats as Count Basie, Hershel Evens, Lester Young, and Charlie Parker.

Jefferson City

Lincoln University

The more than $6,000 raised by the 62nd and 65th U.S. Colored infantries constituted the initial endowment for a 22-square-foot room in which classes were held in 1866 at what is now Lincoln University. Known then as the Lincoln Institute, the school began receiving state aid to expand its teacher training program in 1870. It became a state institution nine years later, and instituted college-level courses in 1887. It has been known as Lincoln University since 1921 and has offered graduate programs since 1940.

St. Louis

Scott Joplin House
2685 Delmar Blvd.; office, 2754 Bacon St.

A composer known as "king of ragtime," Scott Joplin was born in Texarkana, Texas, but he left home to earn a living when he was 14 years of age. In his music he combined Midwestern folk and African American traditions within Western and European forms and provided an important foundation for modern American music. Joplin played piano in the St. Louis and Sedalia, Missouri area, and this house built in the 1890s is the last surviving residence of Joplin. The house, a two-story row house separated into flats, was declared a national historic landmark on December 8, 1976.

Old Courthouse
Broadway and Market Sts.

It was in the Old Courthouse in 1847 that Dred Scott first filed suit to gain his freedom; for the next ten years, the Dred Scott case was a burning political and social issue throughout America. In 1857, the case reached the Supreme Court, where Chief Justice Roger Taney handed down the decision that slaves could not become free by escaping or by being taken into free territory nor could they be considered American citizens. Ironically, a few weeks after the decision was rendered, Scott was set free by his new owner. He died a year later. The site

The Old Courthouse in St. Louis, Missouri (Corbis Corporation [Bellevue]).

was designated a national historic landmark on May 27, 1987.

Homer G. Phillips Hospital
26101 Whittier St.

Built between 1932 and 1936, the hospital provided for the health care of local African Americans. It was also one of the few well-equipped facilities for African Americans from across the country where medical technicians, doctors and nurses could be trained. The hospital was named for the attorney who was successful in the fight to establish the facility. Inadequate municipal support resulting in budgetary problems forced the hospital to close as an acute care facility on August 17, 1979. The building was designated a national historic landmark on September 23, 1982.

◆ MONTANA

Big Horn Station

Fort Manuel Marker

Captain William Clark and his party, which included a slave named York, camped at this site on July 26, 1806, a year before Manuel Lisa established Montana's first trading post. This site also was chosen by Major Andrew Henry as the Rocky Mountain Fur Company's first trading post; the leader of that expedition was Edward Rose, another of the famed African American mountain men and explorers active in the territory.

◆ NEVADA

Reno

Beckwourth Trail

In the early days of pioneer settlement, the barren stretch of trail between Reno and the California line was the last obstacle before passing through to the West Coast. The original trail was laid out by an African American explorer, Jim Beckwourth, one of the legendary mountain men.

◆ NEW HAMPSHIRE

Jaffrey

Amos Fortune Grave Site

This grave site marks the resting place of the eighteenth-century African slave Amos Fortune, who purchased his freedom in 1770 at the age of sixty and went on to become one of the leading citizens of Jaffrey, his adopted hometown. Nine years after purchasing his freedom, Fortune was able to buy freedom for his wife, Violet Baldwin, and his adopted daughter, Celyndia. In 1781, he moved to Jaffrey and worked as a tanner, employing both black and white apprentices. In 1795, six years before his death, Fortune founded the Jaffrey Social Library and, in his will, directed that money be left to the church and to the local school district. (The school fund begun by Fortune is still in existence.)

The Fortune house and barn still stand intact, and both Fortune and his wife lie in the meeting house burial ground. Fortune's freedom papers and several receipt slips for the sale of his leather are on file at the Jaffrey Public Library.

◆ NEW JERSEY

Lawnside

Site of Free Haven

Located just east of the city of Camden, New Jersey, is the town of Lawnside, originally known as Free Haven. The town served as a major stop on the Underground Railroad, and following the Civil War attracted a large population of freed slaves from the South.

Red Bank

T. Thomas Fortune House
94 W. Bergen Pl.

From 1901 to 1915, this location was the home of African American journalist T. Thomas Fortune. Born a slave in Marianna, Florida, Fortune was freed by the Emancipation Proclamation in 1863. He received training as a printer and founded the *New York Age* newspaper. The Fortune House, built between 1860 and 1885, was designated a national historic landmark on December 8, 1976.

◆ NEW MEXICO

Lincoln

Old Court House

During the Lincoln County Cattle War of 1877–1878, Billy the Kid, the notorious outlaw, was held in custody at the Old Court House in Lincoln, New Mexico, now a frontier museum. African American cowhands were involved on both sides of this struggle and, on one occasion, a group of African American cavalry men is said to have surrounded Billy the Kid during a particularly bloody battle.

Zuni

Zuni Pueblo

Zuni Pueblo was discovered in 1539 by Estevanico, a Moorish slave, who was one of the original party of Spanish explorers to land in Tampa Bay in 1528.

Having heard of the legend of the Seven Cities of Gold, reputed to be located in the Southwest, Estevanico signed on as an advance scout for an expedition led by a Father Marco. Often traveling ahead of the main party, Estevanico sent most of his messages back via friendly Indians. His last message—a giant cross emblematic of a major discovery—led the expedition to the Zuni Pueblo, which Estevanico apparently thought formed part of the legendary Seven Cities. By the time the expedition arrived, however, the suspicious Zuni had already put Estevanico to death. Today, Estevanico is credited with the European discovery of the territory comprising the states of Arizona and New Mexico.

◆ NEW YORK

Albany

Emancipation Proclamation
New York State Library

The New York State Library houses President Abraham Lincoln's original draft of the Emancipation Proclamation, which was issued in September 1862. The draft

was purchased by Gerritt Smith, a wealthy abolitionist and patron of the famed revolutionary John Brown. The January 1, 1863, version of the proclamation resides in the National Archives of Washington, DC.

Auburn

Harriet Tubman House
180–182 South St.

Born a slave in Maryland, Harriet Tubman escaped from slavery at the age of 25, only to return to the South at least 19 times to lead others to freedom. Rewards of up to $40,000 were offered for her capture, but she was never arrested nor did she ever lose one of her "passengers" in transit.

During the Civil War, she served as a spy for Union forces. At the close of the war, Tubman settled in this house in Red Bank, New Jersey, years after it had outlived its original function as a major way station on the northbound freedom route of fugitive slaves. In 1953, the house was restored at a cost of $21,000. The house now stands as a monument to the woman believed to have led some three hundred slaves to freedom via the Underground Railroad. The house was designated a national historic landmark on May 30, 1974.

Brooklyn

Ronald McNair Monument
Ronald McNair Park

A nine-foot granite monument of Ronald McNair, African American astronaut who lost his life in the Space Shuttle Challenger accident in 1986, was unveiled in a dedication ceremony in McNair Park in 1994. Created by Brooklyn artist Ogundipe Fayomi, the monument consists of three bronze plaques showing images from his life and achievements. McNair's quote is engraved on one side: "My wish is that we would allow this planet to be the beautiful oasis that she is, and allow ourselves to live more in the peace she generates."

Greater New York City

Abyssinian Baptist Church
132 W. 138th St.

The Abyssinian Baptist Church is one of the oldest and largest African American Baptist congregations in the United States. The church building was completed in 1923, under the leadership of the Rev. Adam Clayton Powell, Sr. In 1937, Powell retired and was succeeded

Abyssinian Baptist Church in New York City (AP/Wide World Photos, Inc.).

by his son Adam Clayton Powell, Jr., who was elected to the U.S. Congress in 1960.

Amsterdam News Founding Place
2293 Seventh Ave.

The *Amsterdam News* was founded on December 4, 1909, in the home of James H. Anderson on 132 West 65th Street in New York City. At that time one of only fifty African American "news sheets" in the country, the *Amsterdam News* had a staff of ten, consisted of six

printed pages, and sold for two cents a copy. Since then, the paper has been printed at several Harlem addresses. This building was designated a national historic landmark on May 11, 1976.

Apollo Theater
253 W. 125th St.

The Apollo Theater in Harlem, once an entertainment mecca for all races, is one of the last great vaudeville houses in the United States. Erected in 1914, the building was designated a national historic landmark on November 17, 1983.

Louis Armstrong House
3456 107th St., Corona, Queens

For years this was the home of Louis Armstrong, the famous jazz musician whose talents entertained millions throughout the world. Whenever Armstrong was at his Corona home in Queens, New York, on a break from his concert dates, he was a favorite with neighborhood youngsters, often entertaining them in his home and on the street. The house was designated a national historic landmark on May 11, 1976.

Ralph Bunche House
115–125 Grosvenor Rd., Kew Gardens, Queens

The house served as the home of Ralph Bunche, the distinguished African American diplomat and undersecretary general to the United Nations. In 1950, Bunche was awarded the Nobel Peace Prize for his contribution to peace in the Middle East. The house was designated a national historic landmark on May 11, 1976.

Will Marion Cook Residence
221 W. 138th St.

This residence in New York City served as the home of the early twentieth century African American composer Will Marion Cook, whom Duke Ellington called "the master of all masters of our people." Cook was born in Washington, DC. He began studying violin at 13 years of age and, at 15, won a scholarship to study with Joseph Joachim at the Berlin Conservatory. Syncopated ragtime music was introduced to theatergoers in New York City for the first time with Cook's operetta *Clorinda*. The residence was designated a national historic landmark on May 11, 1976.

Duke Ellington Statue
Fifth Ave. and 110th St.

A twenty-five foot high cast bronze monument featuring an eight foot high statue of Duke Ellington was unveiled on July 1, 1997, on the northeast corner of Central Park. Designed by sculptor Robert Graham, it is the first public monument in the country honoring the jazz legend and composer. Bobby Short, cabaret performer who led the drive to erect the memorial, said that the location is "a bridge between Duke Ellington's two worlds: The sophisticated world of the Upper East Side and the street world of Harlem."

Edward Kennedy "Duke" Ellington Residence
935 St. Nicholas Ave., Apt. 4A

When Duke Ellington recorded "Take the A Train" to Harlem, he meant just that, because the A train express stops on St. Nicholas Avenue and was the quickest and fastest way for Ellington to get home. This St. Nicholas Avenue address was the long-term residence of Ellington, who has been regarded by critics as the most creative African American composer of the twentieth century. The residence was designated a national historic landmark on May 11, 1976.

Fraunces Tavern
Broad and Pearl Sts.

One of the most famous landmarks in New York City, Fraunces Tavern was bought in 1762 from a wealthy Huguenot by Samuel Fraunces, a West Indian of black and French extraction. Known as the Queen's Head Tavern, it served as a meeting place for numerous patriots.

On April 24, 1774, the Sons of Liberty and the Vigilance Committee met at the tavern to map out much of the strategy later used during the war. George Washington himself was a frequenter of the tavern, as were many of his senior officers. Washington's association with Fraunces continued for a number of years, with Fraunces eventually coming to be known as Washington's "Steward of the Household" in New York City. It was at Fraunces Tavern, in fact, that Washington took leave of his trusted officers in 1783 before retiring to Mount Vernon.

Much of the tavern's original furnishings and decor are still intact. The third floor, now a museum, contains several Revolutionary War artifacts, while the fourth floor holds a historical library featuring paintings by John Ward Dunsmore. A restaurant is maintained on the ground floor.

Freedom National Bank
275 W. 125th St.

Freedom National Bank, Harlem's first African American-chartered and -run commercial bank, was founded in 1965.

Harlem Historic District
Approximating the northern tip of Manhattan

Once the political and cultural hub of black America in the twentieth century, Harlem is primarily known as the major site of the literary and artistic "renaissance" of the 1920s and 1930s. Following the migration of blacks from the South and Caribbean to Harlem in the initial decade of the twentieth century, the city became a nurturing ground for pioneering black intellectual (i.e, literature, art, and black nationalism) and popular (i.e, dance and jazz) movements, as well as a vibrant nightlife centered around such nightclubs as the Cotton Club, Smalls Paradise, and the Savoy Ballroom.

Matthew Henson Residence
Dunbar Apartments, 246 W. 150th St.

This residence served as the home of Matthew Henson, the African American explorer who was an assistant to Robert E. Peary. Henson's best known achievement came in 1909, when he became the first man to reach the North Pole. The residence was designated a national historic landmark on May 15, 1975.

Hotel Theresa
2090 Seventh Ave. at 125th St.

Built in 1913, the Hotel Theresa was once a luxury hotel serving white clientele from lower Manhattan and accommodating "white only" dinner patrons in its luxurious Skyline Room. In 1936, a corporation headed by Love B. Woods tried to take over the hotel and transform it into an African American business establishment. This move failed when Seidenberg Estates, the realtor, set a price beyond the reach of the group. Woods, however, was eventually able to purchase the hotel, which now serves as an office building.

James Weldon Johnson Residence
187 W. 135th St.

From 1925 to 1938, this was the New York City residence of James Weldon Johnson, the versatile African American composer of popular songs as well as poet, writer, general secretary of the NAACP, and civil rights activist. Johnson is best known for composing the song "Lift Every Voice and Sing," which has been called the Negro National Anthem. Johnson was born in Jacksonville, Florida, and studied at Columbia University. The residence was named a national historic landmark on May 11, 1976.

Maiden Lane—The First Slave Revolt in New York

In 1712, on Maiden Lane and William Street, the first organized slave revolt in New York City occurred. Approximately thirty slaves joined and attempted to fight their way to freedom. Many people were injured in the melee that ensued as the slaves escaped to the woods with the militia close behind. Surrounded in the woods, several slaves committed suicide. The rest were captured and subsequently executed.

Malcolm X Residence
23–11 97th St., East Elmhurst, Queens

African American Muslim leader Malcolm X resided at this location with his family from 1954 until his death in 1965. The house, which was owned by the Nation of Islam while he and his family lived there, was the scene of a fire bombing on February 13, 1965. Malcolm X and his family escaped without injury.

Claude McKay Residence
180 W. 135th St.

From 1941 to 1946, this residence in New York City was the home of the African American poet and writer Claude McKay, who has often been called the father of the Harlem Renaissance. McKay was born in Jamaica, British West Indies, and was in Kingston's constabulary prior to coming to the United States. His residence was named a national historic landmark on December 8, 1976.

Florence Mills Residence
220 W. 135th St.

This residence was the home of the popular African American singer who in the 1920s achieved stardom both on Broadway and in Europe. The Florence Mills' residence was designated a national historic landmark on December 8, 1976.

Paul Robeson Residence
555 Edgecomb Ave.

This residence in New York City was the home of the famous African American actor and singer Paul Robeson. In the 1940s and the 1950s, Robeson suffered public condemnation for his socialist political sympathies, even while he was widely acclaimed for his artistic talents. The residence was named a national historic landmark on December 8, 1976.

John Roosevelt "Jackie" Robinson House
5224 Tilden St., Brooklyn

This house served as the home of Jackie Robinson, the baseball player who in 1947 became the first African American to play in the major leagues in the twentieth century. His baseball contract broke down the color barrier to African American participation in professional sports. While a Brooklyn Dodger, Robinson lived for many years in the same borough of New York City where he played baseball. The residence was designated a national historic landmark on May 11, 1976.

St. George's Episcopal Church
Third Ave. and First St.

Located in New York City, this was the church home of Harry Thacker Burleigh, the African American composer, arranger, and singer who helped establish the black spiritual as an integral part of American culture. The church was designated a national historical landmark on December 8, 1976.

Schomburg Center for Research in Black Culture
515 Malcolm X Blvd.

Part of the New York Public Library System, the Schomburg Center for Research in Black Culture is devoted to documenting the black experience around the world. The collection is built around the private library of Arthur A. Schomburg, a Puerto Rican of African descent. It contains books, pamphlets, manuscripts, photographs, art objects, and recordings that cover virtually every aspect of black life—from ancient Africa to present-day United States. The building was designated a national historic landmark on September 21, 1978.

Sugar Hill, Harlem

Sugar Hill is a handsome residential section in uptown Harlem, New York. It is bordered on the west by Amsterdam Avenue, on the north by 160th Street, on the east by Colonial Park, and on the south by 145th Street. An area of tall apartment buildings and private homes, it is peopled largely by middle-class African Americans, sometimes referred to as the "black bourgeoisie." Its only counterparts in the area of central Harlem are Riverton and Lenox Terrace.

Booker T. Washington Plaque
New York University

Booker T. Washington, educator and founder of Tuskegee Institute, is the only African American honored by a plaque in the Hall of Fame at New York University.

Roy Wilkins House
147–15 Village Rd., Jamaica, Queens

This location served as the home of civil rights leader and former NAACP executive secretary Roy Wilkins from 1952 until his death in 1981. Wilkins had served as executive secretary of the NAACP for 22 years before retiring in 1977.

Greenburgh

Villa Lewaro

Designed by the noted African American architect Vertner Woodson Tandy for Madame C. J. Walker, the successful cosmetics manufacturer, Villa Lewaro illustrates the achievements of African Americans in both

Madame C.J. Walker's house in Greenburgh, New York (The Library of Congress).

architecture and business. The Villa Lewaro, built in 1918, was declared a national historic landmark on May 11, 1976. The Building was sold in 1998 and will be used as a tourist attraction.

Lake Placid

John Brown House and Grave Site

Just six miles south of Lake Placid on Route 86A is the farm Brown purchased after he had left Ohio, now the location of his grave. The farm was part of 100,000 acres set aside for both freedmen and slaves by Gerritt Smith, a wealthy abolitionist. Smith hoped to build an independent community peopled by former slaves who had learned farming and other trades. Brown joined Smith in the venture, but the idea failed to take hold and was eventually abandoned. Brown lived there until he joined the free-soil fight in Kansas.

Rochester

Frederick Douglass Monument
Central Ave. and Paul St.

New York Governor Theodore Roosevelt dedicated the Frederick Douglass Monument in 1899, four years after Douglass' death. In Rochester, Douglass edited his newspaper *The North Star*. Douglass was buried in Mount Hope Cemetery, not far from the memorial.

Frederick Douglass Museum and Cultural Center Foundation
300 Main St.

Opened to the general public in April 1999, this museum pays tribute to one of Rochester's most esteemed citizens of the eighteenth century. Among the artifacts contained in the museum are pews from the church that Douglass was memorialized following his death in 1895.

Frederick Douglass statue in Rochester, New York (Schomburg Center for Research in Black Culture).

South Granville

Lemuel Haynes House
Parker Hill Rd., off Rte. 149

This house, located in South Granville, Washington County, New York, was built in 1793. It served as the home of Lemuel Haynes from 1822 to 1833, the first African American ordained minister in the United States. Haynes was also the first African American to minister to a white congregation. The South Granville home site was declared a national historic landmark on May 15, 1975.

◆ NORTH CAROLINA

Durham

North Carolina Mutual Life Insurance Company
114–116 W. Parish St.

This Parish Street address is the home office of North Carolina Mutual Life Insurance Company, an African American-managed enterprise that was founded in 1898 and achieved financial success in an age of Jim Crow.

The business was first located in the Mechanics and Farmers Bank, a six-story structure that symbolized the city's affluent African Americans. Among the outstanding leaders associated with the firm were John Merrick, Charles Clinton Spaulding, and Asa T. Spaulding. The site was declared a national historic landmark on May 15, 1975.

Milton

The Yellow Tavern
Main St., between Lee St. and Farmer's Alley

For more than thirty years, the Yellow Tavern (also known as Union Tavern and the Thomas Day House) was the workshop of Tom Day, one of the great African American artisans and furniture makers of the Deep South prior to the Civil War. Day began making hand-wrought mahogany furniture in 1818 and, within five years, accumulated enough money to convert the old Yellow Tavern into a miniature factory. Both white apprentices and black slaves were taught this skilled trade under his tutelage. Day's artistry was so revered by the citizens of Milton that they went to great pains to secure a special dispensation from a North Carolina law that made it illegal for any free black or mulatto to migrate into the state. The Yellow Tavern, built circa 1910, was declared a national historic landmark by the Department of the Interior on May 15, 1975. Examples of Day's furniture can be seen in the North Carolina State Museum and at North Carolina Agricultural and Technical University in Greensboro.

Raleigh

John Chavis Memorial Park
E. Lenoir and Worth Sts.

This park is named after John Chavis, an African American educator and preacher who founded an interracial school in Raleigh, which later numbered among its graduates several important public figures including senators, congressmen, and governors. As a result of the abortive Nat Turner slave rebellion in 1831, however, African Americans were barred from preaching in North Carolina, obliging Chavis to retire from the pulpit. He died in 1838.

Sedalia

Palmer Memorial Institute Historic District
6135 Burlington Rd., near Rock Creek Dairy Rd.

Charlotte Hawkins Brown, a North Carolina native, founded a school at this site on October 10, 1902, and named it for her friend and benefactor, Alice Freeman

Harriet Beecher Stowe's home in Cincinnati, Ohio (AP/Wide World Photos, Inc.).

Palmer Institute. The school stressed academics, industrial, and vocational education. The school was incorporated on November 23, 1907. By 1916 the school had four buildings and had begun to make its presence felt nationwide. By 1922 it was one of the nation's leading preparatory schools for African American students. The school changed its focus in the 1930s, after the public school system for African Americans improved, and Palmer closed its elementary department and functioned largely as a finishing and college preparatory school. The school closed in 1971. In 1987 the state purchased the site to develop it as a commemorative for African American education. Canary College, the former residence of the school's founder, is the focal point of the site. The site was declared a national historic landmark on October 24, 1988.

◆ OHIO

Akron

John Brown Monument

The John Brown Monument was built in honor of the abolitionist whose ill-fated Harpers Ferry revolt led to his conviction for treason and execution by hanging in 1859.

Cincinnati

Harriet Beecher Stowe House
2950 Gilbert Ave.

The Harriet Beecher Stowe House has been preserved as a memorial to the internationally known author of *Uncle Tom's Cabin*. The house served as the Beecher family residence from 1832 to 1836.

Dayton

Paul Laurence Dunbar House
219 N. Dunbar St.

Paul Laurence Dunbar, the first African American poet after Phillis Wheatley to gain anything approaching a national reputation in the United States, was also the first to concentrate on dialect poetry and exclusively African American themes. His first collection of poetry *Oak and Ivy* was published before he was 20 years old. By 1896, his book *Majors and Minors* had won critical favor in a *Harper's Weekly* review. The Dunbar House was built circa 1890, but Dunbar bought it for his mother in 1903 and lived in it with her until only three years before his death. Dunbar contracted tuberculosis in 1899, and his health continued to fail until his death on February 9, 1906. The house was designated a national historic landmark on June 30, 1980.

Oberlin

John Mercer Langston House
207 E. College St.

Elected township clerk in 1855, John Mercer Langston is believed to have been the first African American to be elected to public office. Langston later served for the Freedman's Bureau, became the first dean of the Howard University Law School, and served as a U.S. Minister Resident to Haiti. The Langston House, which served as Langston's home from 1856 to 1867, was designated a national historic landmark on May 15, 1975.

Oberlin College

Before the Civil War, Oberlin was one of the centers of underground abolitionist planning. The college was one of the first institutions to graduate African Americans and women; three of John Brown's raiding party at Harpers Ferry were identified as African Americans from Oberlin.

After the war, Oberlin was able to devote more time to its stated mission: providing quality education to all regardless of race. Among the distinguished alumni of Oberlin was Blanche K. Bruce, who served a full term in the U.S. Senate (1875–1881).

Ripley

John Rankin House and Museum
Off U.S. 62, west of Ripley

An Underground Railroad station prior to the Civil War, the John Rankin House in Ripley, Ohio, is believed to have been the haven of the fugitive slave on whose story the novelist Harriet Beecher Stowe based the flight incident in *Uncle Tom's Cabin*. The house was built in 1828.

Wilberforce

Colonel Charles Young House
Rte. 42 between Clifton and Stevenson Rds.

This address was the residence of the highest ranking African American officer in World War I and the first African American military attache. Colonel Charles Young was the son of former slaves and was born in Mays Lick,

Kentucky. The Army had declared Young unfit physically because of high blood pressure; to prove that he was physically fit, he rode horseback five hundred miles from Wilberforce to Washington, DC, in 16 days. The Army, however, still stuck by its ruling. The house was declared a national historic landmark on May 30, 1974.

Wilberforce University

Established by the Methodist Church in 1856, Wilberforce University is named for William Wilberforce, an English abolitionist. In 1863, the school was purchased by the African Methodist Episcopal Church; in 1981, the institution was sold to the state of Ohio. Wilberforce is the site of the National Afro-American Museum.

◆ OKLAHOMA

Boley

Boley Historic District
Approximating Seward Avenue, Walnut and Cedar streets, and the southern city limits

This is the largest of the all-African American towns established in Oklahoma to provide African Americans with the opportunity for self-government in an era of white supremacy and segregation. The town was established in 1903 and named for a white official of the Fort Smith and Western Railway, who encouraged a development for the African American railway workers. Residents migrated from Georgia, Texas, Louisiana, Mississippi, Alabama, and Florida. The Boley Historic District was designated a national historic landmark on May 15, 1975.

Ponca City

101 Ranch

During the latter part of the nineteenth century, the 101 Ranch was one of the largest and most famous in the West. The ranch was established in 1879 and, in its prime, it employed several African American cowhands, the most celebrated of whom was Bill Pickett.

The originator of the art of bulldogging or steer wrestling, Pickett also perfected a unique style unlike any used by contemporary rodeo participants. In March 1932, though then in his seventies, Pickett was still active—the last of the original 101 hands. He died on April 21, 1932, after being kicked by a horse, and was buried on a knoll near the White Eagle Monument. The ranch was declared a national historic landmark on May 15, 1975.

Wilberforce University in Wilberforce, Ohio (The Library of Congress).

◆ PENNSYLVANIA

Erie

Harry T. Burleigh Birthplace

A friend of famed Czech composer Antonin Dvorak and a composer/arranger in his own right, Harry T. Burleigh was born in 1866 in Erie, Pennsylvania. Burleigh set to music many of the stirring poems of Walt Whitman and arranged such unforgettable spirituals as *Deep River*. He died in 1949.

Lancaster

Thaddeus Stevens Grave Site
Schreiner's Cemetery
Chestnut and Mulberry Sts.

Senator Thaddeus Stevens of Pennsylvania, a white abolitionist and civil rights activist, was one of the chief architects of the Fourteenth Amendment to the Constitution. Upon his death in 1868, five black and three white pallbearers escorted the body to Washington, DC. Stevens' body lay in state on the same catafalque that had borne the body of Lincoln and was guarded by African American soldiers of the 54th Massachusetts Regiment. Two days later the body was returned to Lancaster, where over 10,000 African Americans attended the funeral. Stevens was buried in Schreiner's Cemetery, a cemetery for African Americans—in his will, he had rejected burial in a white cemetery because of segregationist policy.

Montgomery County

James A. Bland Grave Site
Merion Cemetery

In the Merion Cemetery in Montgomery County, Pennsylvania lies the grave of African American composer James A. Bland, who wrote "Carry Me Back to Old Virginny," now the state song of Virginia. Bland was one of the most popular African American minstrels of the nineteenth century.

Philadelphia

Frances Ellen Watkins Harper House
1006 Bainbridge St.

This was the home of the African American writer and social activist Frances Ellen Watkins Harper, who participated in the nineteenth-century abolition, woman's suffrage, and temperance movements. Harper occupied the residence from 1870 to 1911. The house was named a national historic landmark on December 8, 1976.

Mother Bethel African Methodist Episcopal Church
419 Sixth St.

The current building was erected in 1859; it is the fourth church to be erected on the site where Richard Allen and Absalom Jones founded the Free African Society in 1787. This organization later grew into the African Methodist Episcopal Church, one of the largest African American religious denominations in the United States.

Allen, the first African American bishop, was born a slave and became a minister and circuit rider after winning his freedom. In 1814, he and James Forten organized a force of 2,500 free African Americans to defend Philadelphia against the British. Sixteen years later, Allen organized the first African American convention in Philadelphia and was instrumental in getting the group to adopt a strong platform denouncing slavery and encouraging abolitionist activities. Allen died in 1831 and was buried in the church crypt.

As for Forten, he had been born free in 1766 and, despite his youth, served aboard a Philadelphia privateer during the Revolutionary War. In 1800, he was one of the signers of a petition requesting Congress to alter the Fugitive Slave Act of 1793. Opposed to the idea of resettling slaves in Africa, Forten chaired an 1817 meeting held at Bethel to protest existing colonization schemes. In 1833, he put up the funds that William Lloyd Garrison needed to found *The Liberator*. After his death, Forten's work was continued by his successors, who remained active in the abolitionist cause throughout the Civil War and fought for African American rights during Reconstruction. The Forten home served as a meeting place for many of the leading figures in the movement. The church was named a national historic landmark on May 30, 1974.

Negro Soldiers Monument
West Fairmount Park
Lansdowne Dr.

The Negro Soldiers Monument was erected by the state of Pennsylvania in 1934 to pay tribute to its fallen African American soldiers.

Henry O. Tanner House
2903 W. Diamond St.

Born in Pittsburgh in 1859, Henry Ossawa Tanner was the first African American to be elected to the

National Academy of Design. He became an internationally recognized painter of the nineteenth Century. The Diamond Street residence was the artist's boyhood home. The site is important also to commemorate the work of Tanner's father, Benjamin Tucker Tanner, bishop in the African Methodist Episcopal Church and editor of the *A.M.E. Church Review*. The homesite, a three-story structure, became Tanner's residence about 1872. The house was designated a historical landmark on May 11, 1976.

Bessie Smith Residence
7003 S. Twelfth St.

This location served as home to blues singer Bessie Smith from about 1926 until her death in 1937.

◆ RHODE ISLAND

Portsmouth

Portsmouth served as the site of the only American Revolutionary battle in which an all-African American unit, the First Rhode Island Regiment, participated in 1778.

◆ SOUTH CAROLINA

Beaufort

Robert Smalls House
511 Prince St.

Robert Smalls, a former slave, served in both the state legislature and the U.S. Congress. While in office, Smalls was an advocate for the rights of African Americans. He had lived in Beaufort, South Carolina, both as a slave and as a free man. The Smalls house, a large frame two-story structure built in 1843, was designated a national historic landmark on May 30, 1973.

Charleston

Avery Normal Institute
125 Bull St.

Founded by the American Missionary Association in 1865, the institute moved to Bull Street and provided college preparatory education and teacher training for Charleston's African American community. Francis Cardozo developed it into a prestigious private school.

The school closed in 1954, due to financial difficulties. Today the historic building houses the Avery Research Center for African American History, founded in 1985.

Dubose Hayward House
76 Church St.

Dubose Hayward, the author of *Porgy*, the book upon which George Gershwin's opera *Porgy and Bess* was based, lived here from 1919 to 1924. It was designated a national historic landmark on November 11, 1971.

Old Slave Mart
6 Chalmers St.

The mart was built in 1853 to be used for the auction of slaves and other goods. Originally the mart included two additional lots and three buildings. The buildings were holding points for slaves who were to be sold. The structure that remains is the only known extant facility used as a slave auction gallery in the state. It now houses an African American museum and a gift shop. The building was designated a national historic landmark on May 2, 1975.

Denmark Vesey House
56 Bull St.

This was the residence of Denmark Vesey, a free black Charleston carpenter whose hard work earned him substantial wealth and respect among Charleston's African American community. He planned a slave insurrection, carefully selecting leaders and participants who were believed to be his supporters. His plot for July 14, 1822, was uncovered and Vesey was sentenced to death twelve days before the scheduled coup. The Denmark Vesey House was declared a national historic landmark on May 11, 1976.

Columbia

Chapelle Administration Building, Allen University
1530 Harden St.

The Chapelle Administration Building is located at Allen University, a school founded in 1881. Named for Bishop Richard Allen, the school was established primarily to educate clergy for the African Methodist Episcopal church. The Chapelle building is one of the finest works of John Anderson Lankford, a pioneer African American architect who helped gain recognition for African American architects among the architectural

community. The building was named a national historic landmark on December 8, 1976.

Frogmore

Penn Center Historic District
Rte. 37

Penn School was founded in 1862 and supported by northern missionaries and abolitionists. Ellen Murray of the Pennsylvania Freemen's Relief Association and her friend, Laura Towne, opened the school in Murray's house. As enrollment expanded, the school relocated to Brick Church, then to a site adjacent to the church. The new school was named Penn School. The school provided exceptional education to local African American residents who were denied admission to the white schools. The school also addressed health, agricultural, and financial needs of the African American residents of St. Helena. It collected and preserved the artifacts, musical recordings, oral history, and heritage of the residents. The school closed in 1948, but its buildings still serve the community. The traditions of the facilities are carried on by Penn Community Services, Inc. On December 2, 1974, the area was designated a national historic landmark district.

Georgetown

Joseph H. Rainey House
909 Prince St.

Joseph Hayne Rainey (1832–1887), a former slave, was the first African American to serve in the U.S. House of Representatives. His election, along with the election of Hiram R. Revels, the first African American citizen to be elected to the U.S. Senate in 1870, marked the beginning of African American participation in the federal legislative process. The house, built circa 1760, was designated a national historic landmark on April 20, 1984. Rainey lived in the facility from 1832 to 1887.

Rantowles

Stono River Slave Rebellion Historic Site

This was the site of a 1739 slave insurrection, during which some one hundred slaves escaped. The site, located in Rantowles, South Carolina, was named a national historic landmark on July 4, 1974.

◆ SOUTH DAKOTA

Deadwood

Adams Memorial Museum

Only one of the legendary claimants to the title of "Deadwood Dick" is African American, but he can back his assertion with a colorful autobiography that takes the reader through his childhood in slavery, his early bronco-busting efforts, and his fabled life as a range rider and fighter in the old West. Nat Love claimed he won the title during a public competition held in Deadwood on July 4, 1876. The presence of other African American cowboys, gambling house operators, and escort soldiers in the area during these years, as well as the convincing style of Love's narrative, lend a high degree of credibility to his adventurous tales—although, like Jim Beckwourth, he may have been given to moments of wanton exaggeration.

◆ TENNESSEE

Henning

Alex Haley House
Haley Ave. at S. Church St.

Best known for the television adaptation of his Pulitzer Prize-winning book *Roots*, author Alex Haley has awakened both black and white Americans to the richness of African and African American history and culture. The house, built in 1918 by Haley's grandfather, served as his home from 1921 to 1929 and was where he heard many of the stories that inspired him to write *Roots*. Today the house serves as a museum.

Jackson

Casey Jones Railroad Museum

On Chester Street in Jackson, Tennessee, is found the Casey Jones Railroad Museum, which is filled with memorabilia of a bygone era. Jones was immortalized through the song about Casey Jones' legendary train ride. The song, which became popularized in vaudeville and music halls, was written by Wallace Saunders, an African American fireman aboard Jones' locomotive. The Railroad Museum serves to remind us of the enormous unsung contributions of African Americans to the railroad industry in the United States.

Memphis

Beale Street Historic District
Beale St. from Second to Fourth Sts.

The "blues," a unique black contribution to American music, was born on a Beale Street lined with saloons, gambling halls, and theaters. The street was immortalized by William Christopher Handy, who composed "Beale Street Blues." Beale Street, located in Memphis, Tennessee, was designated a national historic landmark on October 15, 1966.

Nat Love

William Christopher Handy Park

The city of Memphis, Tennessee, pays tribute to famed blues composer William Christopher Handy in the form of a park and a heroic bronze statue overlooking the very same Beale Street that he immortalized in the tune "Beale Street Blues." The statue, showing Handy standing with horn poised, was executed by Leone Tomassi of Italy and was dedicated in 1960, at the close of a memorial campaign instituted by the city shortly after Handy's death in 1958.

Tom Lee Memorial
Beale St.

The thirty-foot high Tom Lee granite memorial was erected in 1954 to honor an African American who, on May 8, 1925, saved the lives of 32 passengers aboard the *M. E. Norman*, an excursion boat that had capsized some twenty miles below Memphis near Cow Island. Alerted to the disaster, Lee pulled 32 people from the water onto his skiff. He was honored for his feat by the Memphis Engineers Club, which provided him with money for the duration of his life. A fund was also raised to purchase him a home. After his death in 1952,

Beale Street in Memphis, Tennessee (AP/Wide World Photos, Inc.).

a committee raised the money needed to erect the memorial.

Lorraine Hotel
406 Mulberry St.

It was on the balcony of the Lorraine Hotel that Martin Luther King, Jr. was assassinated, while emerging from a second-floor room in the presence of a pair of his trusted advisers, Ralph Abernathy and Jesse Jackson. King died in the emergency room of St. Joseph's Hospital on April 4, 1968. The Lorraine closed for business in 1988. It is now operated as the National Civil Rights Museum.

Nashville

Fisk University Historic District

Opened on January 9, 1866, and incorporated on August 22, 1867, Fisk University was founded in Nashville, Tennessee, following the Civil War by the American Missionary Association to provide a liberal arts education for children of former slaves. Fisk School, as it was known then, began operation in former Union army barracks. In 1873, the campus was moved to a new

site, the old Fort Gillem. In 1978, the forty-acre campus was designated a national historic landmark district. Among the historic buildings on campus are the residences once occupied by Arna Bontemps, Elmer S. Imes, Robert Hayden, and John W. Work. Several are Victorian design.

A bronze statue of illustrious Fisk graduate W. E. B. Du Bois, standing with book in hand, is located on the campus.

Jubilee Hall, a Victorian Gothic structure, is the South's first permanent structure built to educate African American students. The Fisk Jubilee Singers set out from Nashville in 1871 to raise money for their school, and in their concerts they introduced the Negro spiritual to the world. The singers raised enough money to save the school and to erect Jubilee Hall, which was dedicated on January 1, 1876. The hall was named a national historic landmark on December 9, 1971.

James Weldon Johnson House
911 18th Ave.

Writer and civil rights leader James Weldon Johnson resided at this location from about 1930 until his death in 1938, teaching literature and writing at Fisk University. Johnson was born in 1871 in Jacksonville, Florida. Johnson, in collaboration with his brother J. Rosamond Johnson, was responsible for creating the song "Lift Every Voice and Sing." Johnson's death mask is in the Fisk University Library, Special Collection.

◆ TEXAS

Amarillo

First Black School

Matthew Bones Hooks was born in central Texas in 1867. The story goes that he rode wild horses at the age of eight, had his first paid job as a cowhand at the age of ten, and later herded cattle for Colonel Charles Goodnight, moving them from Texas to Dodge City, Kansas. Hooks homesteaded in New Mexico, rode broncos in Romfa, Texas, in 1910, and then moved to Amarillo, Texas, where he established the first school for African Americans in that city. The school was in the North Heights section, an all-African American community. He also founded the Dogie Club, an organization for underprivileged boys, in cooperation with the Boy Scouts. He was the only African American member of the old Settlers Association of Amarillo and the first African American of Amarillo to serve on a grand jury.

Houston

Freedmen's Town Historic District
Approximating Genessee St., W. Dallas Ave., Arthur St., and W. Gray St.

The district, also known as the Fourth Ward, includes narrow street and one and two-story frame buildings representing Houston's African American community just after slavery. When Houston's population nearly doubled between 1910 and 1930, the district was the economic center for the African American community. While nearly forty percent of the structures were demolished by the early 1990s, many of these were deteriorating or at risk due to encroachment by city developers.

◆ VIRGINIA

Alexandria

Franklin and Armfield Office
1315 Duke St.

From 1828 to 1836, the office of the Franklin and Armfield slave trading company in Alexandria, Virginia, was the South's largest slave-trading firm. (During the company's operation, Alexandria was part of the District of Columbia.) The building was designated a national historic landmark on June 2, 1978.

Colonial National Historic Park

Jamestown Island, located in Colonial National Historic Park, is where the first African American slaves arrived in the American colonies in 1619. In addition, the park served as the site of the Battle of Yorktown in 1781, a struggle in which three African Americans held combat positions in patriot militia units and worked for the Hessian forces as musicians and servants.

Arlington

Benjamin Banneker Boundary Stone
18th and Van Buren Sts.

The boundary stone in Arlington, Virginia, commemorates the accomplishments of Benjamin Banneker, who helped survey the city of Washington, DC, and who was perhaps the most well-known African American in colonial America. Banneker, a mathematician and scientist, was born in Ellicott Mills, Maryland, and received his early schooling with the aid of a Quaker family. Banneker was a national hero for African Americans, and many schools have been named after him. The boundary stone was declared a national historic landmark on May 11, 1976.

Charles Richard Drew House
2505 First St., S.

Located in Arlington, Virginia, this house served as the home of Charles Richard Drew from 1920 to 1939. Drew, a noted African American physician and teacher, is best remembered for his pioneer work in discovering means to preserve blood plasma. The house was named a national historic landmark on May 11, 1976.

Chatham

Pittsylvania County Courthouse
U.S. Business Rte. 29

The Pittsylvania County Courthouse in Chatham, Virginia, was closely associated with the 1878 case *Ex parte Virginia*. This case, held upon the issue of African American participation on juries, stemmed from a clear attempt by a state official to deny citizens the equal protection of law guaranteed by the Fourteenth Amendment to the Constitution. The courthouse was designated a national historic landmark on May 4, 1987.

Capahosic

Holley Knoll House

From 1935 to 1959, this house served as the retirement home of Robert R. Moton. Moton, who succeeded

Hampton University in Hampton, Virginia.

Booker T. Washington as head of Tuskegee Institute in 1915, guided the school's growth until 1930. He was an influential educator and active in many African American causes.

Glen Allen

Virginia Randolph Cottage
2200 Mountain Rd.

As the first supervisor of the Jeanes Fund, set up by a wealthy Philadelphia Quaker to aid African American education, Virginia Randolph worked to upgrade African American vocational training. The cottage in Glen Allen, Virginia, was named a national historic landmark on December 2, 1974.

Hampton

Hampton University

Founded in 1868 as Hampton Normal and Industrial Institute, this was one of the earliest institutions of higher learning for African Americans in the United

Booker T. Washington's boyhood home in Rocky Mount, Virginia (Corbis Corporation [Bellevue]).

States. Samuel Chapman Armstrong, an agent of the Freedmen's Bureau, persuaded the American Missionary Association to purchase land for the school. Booker T. Washington was one of its graduates who later founded Tuskegee Institute in Alabama, modeling it after the Hampton tradition. Washington also taught for a time at Hampton. The Hampton area and several of its buildings were designated a national historic landmark district on May 30, 1974.

Lynchburg

Anne Spencer House
1313 Pierce St.

Anne Spencer, poet and librarian, was friend and confidante of many Harlem Renaissance luminaries. Her poetry was published largely in the 1920s, when the Harlem Renaissance was in full blossom. She maintained her relationship with the African American cultural leaders of Harlem, and they visited her in the garden that she provided for them. The Spencer home was designated a national historic landmark on December 6, 1976.

Norfolk

Black Civil War Veterans' Memorial
Elmwood Cemetery
Princess Anne Rd.

In a section of Norfolk's Elmwood Cemetery marked by a granite monument lie the grave sites of several African American soldiers who served during the Civil War.

Richmond

Arthur Ashe Statue
Monument Ave.

A 12-foot bronze statue of tennis legend Arthur Ashe was unveiled in his hometown in July 1996. The statue depicts Ashe in a warm-up suit holding books over his head in one hand and a tennis racket in the other. The inscription, taken from a Bible verse, is the opening passage of his autobiography *Days of Grace*: "Since we are surrounded by so great a cloud of witnesses, let us lay aside every weight, and the sin which so easily ensnares us, and let us run with endurance the race that is set before us."

Jackson Ward Historic District

Bounded by Fourth, Marshall, and Smith Streets and the Richmond-Petersburg Turnpike, this was the foremost African American community of the nineteenth and early twentieth centuries and an early center for ethnic social organizations and protective banking institutions. The district was named a national historic landmark on June 2, 1978.

Maggie Lena Walker National Historic Site
110–A E. Leigh St.

In 1903, Maggie Lena Walker, an African American woman, founded the successful Saint Luke Penny Savings Bank and became the first woman to establish and head a bank. In addition to being the first woman president of a bank, she was editor of a newspaper considered to be one of the best journals of its class in America. The house is located in the Jackson Ward Historic District of Richmond; it was declared a national historic landmark May 12, 1975, and it became a part of the national park system on November 10, 1978.

St. Luke Building
900 St. James St.

The Edwardian building, completed in 1903, is national headquarters for the Independent Order of St. Luke, an African American benevolent society founded in Baltimore by Mary Prout, a former slave. The organization helped to ease the transition from slavery to freedom, providing financial aid and guidance to newly freed slaves. The oldest African American-affiliated office building in the city, it houses the Maggie Lena Walker office now preserved as a memorial. The structure was remodeled and enlarged between 1915 and 1920. It was designated a national historic landmark on September 16, 1982.

Fort at Harpers Ferry National Historic Park in West Virginia (AP/Wide World Photos, Inc.).

Rocky Mount

Booker T. Washington National Monument

The Burroughs plantation, on which educator and scholar Booker T. Washington was born, can be found in a two hundred-acre park located 22 miles southeast of Roanoke, Virginia. Born a slave, Washington lived here until the end of the Civil War, when he and his mother moved to Malden, West Virginia.

◆ WASHINGTON

Centralia

George Washington Park

This park is named after a liberated slave who escaped from slavery in Virginia when he was adopted by a white couple and taken to Missouri. He then left Missouri with a wagon train heading for the Pacific Northwest, settling on a homestead along the Chehalis River. Once the location was reached by the Northern Pacific Railroad, Washington laid out a town, setting aside acreage for parks, a cemetery, and churches. Soon over 2,000 lots were in the hands of a thriving population that formed the nucleus of Centerville.

◆ WEST VIRGINIA

Harpers Ferry

Harpers Ferry National Historic Park

Harpers Ferry derives its historical fame from the much publicized anti-slavery raid conducted by John Brown and a party of eighteen men, including five African Americans, from October 16th to 18th, 1859. Brown hoped to set up a fortress and refuge for slaves that he could transform into an important way station for black fugitives en route to Pennsylvania.

Brown lost two of his sons in the battle and was himself seriously wounded. Later tried and convicted of treason, he was hanged at Charles Town on December 2, 1859.

Malden

Booker T. Washington Monument
U.S. Rte. 60

This monument, erected in 1963, marks the site where Booker T. Washington labored for several years in the salt works. At the time, Washington credited his employer, Mrs. Violla Ruffner, with having encouraged him to pursue a higher education at Hampton Institute.

◆ WISCONSIN

Milton

Milton House and Museum
18 S. Jamesville St.

The Milton House, the first structure made of poured concrete in the United States, was once used as a hideaway for fugitive slaves escaping by means of the Underground Railroad.

Portage

Ansel Clark Grave Site
Silver Lake Cemetery

Ansel Clark, "born a slave, died a respected citizen," settled in Wisconsin after the Civil War, in which he served as an impressed laborer in the Confederate cause before escaping. Brought to Portage by a man to whom he had tended in a Union hospital, Clark served as town constable and deputy sheriff. For thirty years he worked in law enforcement, standing up to the town's rough characters and keeping them in line with his "firmness and dignity."

Appendix

◆African American Recipients of Selected Awards
◆African American Federal Judges
◆African American Olympic Medalists

◆ AFRICAN AMERICAN RECIPIENTS OF SELECTED AWARDS

ACADEMY AWARD OF MERIT (OSCAR)— ACADEMY OF MOTION PICTURE ARTS AND SCIENCES

Best Performance by an Actor in a Leading Role

1963 Sidney Poitier, in *Lilies of the Field*

Best Performance by an Actor in a Supporting Role

1982 Louis Gossett, Jr., in *An Officer and a Gentleman*

1989 Denzel Washington, in *Glory*

1996 Cuba Gooding, Jr., in *Jerry Maquire*

Best Performance by an Actress in a Supporting Role

1939 Hattie McDaniel, in *Gone with the Wind*

1990 Whoopi Goldberg, in *Ghost*

Best Original Score

1984 Prince, for *Purple Rain*

1986 Herbie Hancock, for *'Round Midnight*

AMERICAN ACADEMY AND INSTITUTE OF ARTS AND LETTERS AWARD

Art

1946 Richmond Barthé

1966 Romare Bearden

1971 Norman Lewis

Literature

1946 Gwendolyn Brooks; Langston Hughes

1956 James Baldwin

1961 John A. Williams

1970 James A. McPherson

1971 Charles Gordone

1972 Michael S. Harper

1974 Henry Van Dyke

1978 Lerone Bennett, Jr.; Toni Morrison

1985 John Williams

1987 Ernest J. Gaines

1992 August Wilson

Music

1974 Olly Wilson

1981 George Walker

1988 Hale Smith

1991 Tania J. Leon

AUSTRALIAN OPEN

Men's Singles

1970 Arthur Ashe

Men's Doubles

1977 Arthur Ashe

Women's Doubles

1957 Althea Gibson, with Darlene Hard

CONGRESSIONAL GOLD MEDAL

1978 Marian Anderson

1990 Jesse Owens

1994 Colin L. Powell, Jr.

1998 Little Rock Nine: Jean Brown Trickey, Carlotta Walls LaNier, Melba Patillo Beals, Terrence Roberts, Gloria Ray Karlmark, Thelma Mothershed Wair, Ernest Green, Elizabeth Eckford, and Jefferson Thomas

1999 Rosa Louise McCauley Parks

EMMY AWARD—ACADEMY OF TELEVISION ARTS AND SCIENCES

Primetime Awards

Outstanding Lead Actor in a Drama Series

1966 Bill Cosby, in "I Spy" (NBC)

1967 Bill Cosby, in "I Spy" (NBC)

1968 Bill Cosby, in "I Spy" (NBC)

1991 James Earl Jones, in "Gabriel's Fire" (ABC)

1998 Andre Braugher, in "Homicide: Life on the Street" (NBC)

Outstanding Lead Actor in a Comedy, Variety, or Music Series

1959 Harry Belafonte, in "Tonight with Belafonte"

1985 Robert Guillaume, in "Benson" (ABC)

Outstanding Lead Actress in a Comedy, Variety, or Music Series

1981 Isabel Sanford, in "The Jeffersons" (CBS)

Outstanding Lead Actress in a Comedy or Drama Special

1974 Cicely Tyson, in "The Autobiography of Miss Jane Pittman" (CBS)

Outstanding Lead Actress in a Miniseries or Special

1991 Lynn Whitfield, in "The Josephine Baker Story" (HBO)

1997 Alfre Woodard, in "Miss Evers' Boys" (HBO)

Outstanding Supporting Actor in a Comedy, Variety, or Music Series

1979 Robert Guillaume, in "Soap" (ABC)

Outstanding Supporting Actor in a Miniseries or Special

1991 James Earl Jones, in "Heatwave" (TNT)

Outstanding Supporting Actress in a Drama Series

1984 Alfre Woodard, in "Doris in Wonderland" episode of "Hill Street Blues" (NBC)

1991 Madge Sinclair, in "Gabriel's Fire" (ABC)

1992 Mary Alice, in "I'll Fly Away" (NBC)

Outstanding Supporting Actress in a Comedy, Variety, or Music Series

1987 Jackee Harry, in "227"

Outstanding Supporting Actress in a Miniseries or Special

1991 Ruby Dee, in "Decoration Day," *Hallmark Hall of Fame* (NBC)

Outstanding Directing in a Drama Series

1986 Georg Stanford Brown, in "Parting Shots" episode of "Cagney & Lacey" (ABC)

1990 Thomas Carter, in "Promises to Keep" episode of "Equal Justice" (ABC)

1991 Thomas Carter, in "In Confidence" episode of "Equal Justice" (ABC)

1992 Eric Laneuville, in "All God's Children" episode of "I'll Fly Away" (NBC)

Outstanding Producing in a Miniseries or Special

1989 Suzanne de Passe, in "Lonesome Dove"

Outstanding Producing in a Variety, Music, or Comedy Special

1984 Suzanne de Passe, in "Motown 25: Yesterday, Today and Forever"

1985 Suzanne de Passe, in "Motown at the Apollo"

Outstanding Variety, Music, or Comedy Special

1997 "Chris Rock: Bring on the Pain" (HBO)

Outstanding Achievement in Music Composition

1971 Ray Charles, in "The First Nine Months Are the Hardest" (NBC)

1972 Ray Charles, in "The Funny Side of Marriage" (NBC)

Outstanding Achievement in Music Composition for a Series

1977 Quincy Jones and Gerald Fried, in "Roots" (ABC)

Outstanding Choreography

1981 Debbie Allen, for "Come One, Come All" episode of "Fame"

1982 Debbie Allen, for "Class Act" episode of "Fame"

1989 Debbie Allen, for "Motown 30: What's Goin' On!"

Daytime Awards

Outstanding Talk Show

1987 "The Oprah Winfrey Show"

1988 "The Oprah Winfrey Show"

1989 "The Oprah Winfrey Show"

1991 "The Oprah Winfrey Show"

1992 "The Oprah Winfrey Show"

1994 "The Oprah Winfrey Show"

1995 "The Oprah Winfrey Show"

1996 "The Oprah Winfrey Show"

1997 "The Oprah Winfrey Show"

Outstanding Talk Show Host

1987 Oprah Winfrey, "The Oprah Winfrey Show"

1991 Oprah Winfrey, "The Oprah Winfrey Show"

1992 Oprah Winfrey, "The Oprah Winfrey Show"

1993 Oprah Winfrey, "The Oprah Winfrey Show"

1994 Oprah Winfrey, "The Oprah Winfrey Show"

1995 Oprah Winfrey, "The Oprah Winfrey Show"

1996 Montel Williams, "The Montel Williams Show"

Sports Awards

Outstanding Sports Personality/Studio Host

1998 James Brown (Fox Sports Network)

Outstanding Sports Event Analyst

1997 Joe Morgan (ESPN/NBC)

Outstanding Sports Journalism

1995 "Broken Promises" and "Pros and Cons" episodes of "Real Sports with Bryant Gumbel"

1998 "Diamond Buck$" and "Winning at All Costs" episodes of "Real Sports with Bryant Gumbel"

Hall of Fame Award

1992 Bill Cosby

1994 Oprah Winfrey

FRENCH OPEN

Men's Doubles

1971 Arthur Ashe

Women's Singles

1956 Althea Gibson

Women's Doubles

1956 Althea Gibson

1999 Venus and Serena Williams

GRAMMY AWARDS—NATIONAL ACADEMY OF RECORDING ARTS AND SCIENCES

Record of the Year

1963 *I Can't Stop Loving You,* by Count Basie

1967 *Up, Up and Away,* by 5th Dimension

1969 *Aquarius/Let the Sun Shine In*, by 5th Dimension

1972 *The First Time Ever I Saw Your Face*, by Roberta Flack

1973 *Killing Me Softly with His Song*, by Roberta Flack

1976 *This Masquerade*, by George Benson

1983 *Beat It*, by Michael Jackson

1984 *What's Love Got To Do with It?*, by Tina Turner

1985 *We Are the World*, by USA For Africa; produced by Quincy Jones

1988 *Don't Worry, Be Happy*, by Bobby McFerrin

1991 *Unforgettable*, by Natalie Cole with Nat "King" Cole

1993 *I Will Always Love You*, by Whitney Houston

1995 *Kiss From a Rose* by Seal

Album of the Year

1973 *Innervisions*, by Stevie Wonder; produced by Stevie Wonder

1974 *Fulfillingness' First Finale*, by Stevie Wonder; produced by Stevie Wonder

1976 *Songs in the Key of Life*, by Stevie Wonder; produced by Stevie Wonder

1983 *Thriller*, by Michael Jackson; produced by Quincy Jones

1984 *Can't Slow Down*, by Lionel Richie; produced by Lionel Richie and James Anthony Carmichael

1990 *Back on the Block*, by Quincy Jones; produced by Quincy Jones

1991 *Unforgettable*, by Natalie Cole

1999 *The Miseducation of Lauryn Hill*, by Lauryn Hill; produced by Lauryn Hill

HEISMAN MEMORIAL TROPHY—DOWNTOWN ATHLETIC CLUB OF NEW YORK CITY, INC.

1961 Ernie Davis, Syracuse University, TB

1965 Michael Garrett, University of Southern California, TB

1968 O. J. Simpson, University of Southern California, TB

1972 Johnny Rodgers, University of Nebraska, FL

1974 Archie Griffin, University of Ohio State, HB

1975 Archie Griffin, University of Ohio State, HB

1976 Anthony (Tony) Dorsett, University of Pittsburgh, HB

1977 Earl Campbell, University of Texas, FB

1978 Billy Sims, University of Oklahoma, HB

1979 Charles White, University of Southern California, TB

1980 George Rogers, University of South Carolina, HB

1981 Marcus Allen, University of Southern California, TB

1982 Herschel Walker, University of Georgia, HB

1983 Mike Rozier, University of Nebraska, TB

1985 Bo Jackson, Auburn University, TB

1987 Tim Brown, University of Notre Dame, FL

1988 Barry Sanders, Oklahoma State University, HB

1989 Andre Ware, University of Houston, QB

1991 Desmond Howard, University of Michigan, WR

1993 Charlie Ward, Florida State University, QB

1994 Rashaan Salaam, Colorado, RB

1995 Eddie George, Ohio State, RB

1997 Charles Woodson, University of Michigan, DB/R

1998 Ricky Williams, University of Texas at Austin, TB

CLARENCE L. HOLTE LITERARY PRIZE (BIANNUAL)—CO-SPONSORED BY THE PHELPS-STOKES FUND AND THE SCHOMBURG CENTER FOR RESEARCH IN BLACK CULTURE OF THE NEW YORK PUBLIC LIBRARY

1979 Chancellor Williams, for *The Destruction of Black Civilization: Great Issues of a Race from 4500 B.C. to 2000 A.D.*

1981 Ivan Van Sertima, for *They Came Before Columbus*

1983 Vincent Harding, for *There Is a River: The Black Struggle for Freedom in America*

1985 No award

1986 John Hope Franklin, for *George Washington Williams: A Biography*

1988 Arnold Rampersad, for *The Life of Langston Hughes, Volume 1 (1902-1941): I, Too, Sing America*

KENNEDY CENTER HONORS—JOHN F. KENNEDY CENTER FOR THE PERFORMING ARTS

1978 Marian Anderson

1979 Ella Fitzgerald

1980 Leontyne Price

1981 William "Count" Basie

1983 Katherine Dunham

1984 Lena Horne

1986 Ray Charles

1987 Sammy Davis, Jr.

1988 Alvin Ailey

1989 Harry Belafonte

1990 Dizzy Gillespie

1991 Fayard and Harold Nicholas

1992 Lionel Hampton

1993 Arthur Mitchell; Marion Williams

1994 Aretha Franklin

1995 B. B. King; Sidney Poitier

1996 Benny Carter

1997 Jessye Norman

1998 Bill Cosby

MARTIN LUTHER KING, JR. NONVIOLENT PEACE PRIZE—MARTIN LUTHER KING, JR. CENTER FOR NONVIOLENT SOCIAL CHANGE, INC.

1973 Andrew Young

1974 Cesar Chavez

1975 John Lewis

1976 Randolph Blackwell

1977 Benjamin E. Mays

1978 Kenneth D. Kaunda; Stanley Levison

1979 Jimmy Carter

1980 Rosa Parks

1981 Ivan Allen, Jr.

1982 Harry Belafonte

1983 Sir Richard Attenborough; Martin Luther King, Sr.

1984 No award

1985 No award

1986 Bishop Desmond Tutu

1987 Corazon Aquino

1988 No award

1989 No award

1990 Mikhail Gorbachev

1991 No award

1992 No award

1993 Jesse Jackson

MISS AMERICA—MISS AMERICA ORGANIZATION

1984 Vanessa Williams (New York); Suzette Charles (New Jersey)

1990 Debbye Turner (Missouri)

MISS BLACK AMERICA—J. MORRIS ANDERSON PRODUCTION COMPANY

1968 Sandy Willliams (Pennsylvania)

1969 G. O. Smith (New York)

1970 Stephanie Clark (District of Columbia)

1971 Joyce Warner (Florida)

1972 Linda Barney (New Jersey)

1973 Arnice Russell (New York)

1974 Von Gretchen Sheppard (California)

1975 Helen Ford (Mississippi)

1976 Twanna Kilgore (District of Columbia)

1977 Claire Ford (Tennessee)

1978 Lydia Jackson (New Jersey)

1979 Veretta Shankle (Mississippi)

1980 Sharon Wright (Illinois)

1981 Pamela Jenks (Massachusetts)

1982 Phyllis Tucker (Florida)

1983 Sonia Robinson (Wisconsin)

1984 Lydia Garrett (South Carolina)

1985 Amina Fakir (Michigan)

1986 Rachel Oliver (Massachusetts)

1987 Leila McBride (Colorado)

1989 Paula Swynn (District of Columbia)

1990 Rosie Jones (Connecticut)

1991 Sharmelle Sullivan (Indiana)

1992 Marilyn DeShields

1993 Pilar Ginger Fort

1994 Karen Wallace

1995 Asheera Ahmad

MISS USA—MADISON SQUARE GARDEN TELEVISION PRODUCTIONS

1990 Carole Gist (Michigan)

1992 Shannon Marketic

1993 Kenya Moore (Michigan)

1994 Frances Louise "Lu" Parker

1995 Chelsi Smith (Texas)

1996 Ali Landry

MS. OLYMPIA WINNERS— INTERNATIONAL FEDERATION OF BODYBUILDERS, WOMEN'S BODYBUILDING CHAMPIONS

1983 Carla Dunlap

1990 Lenda Murray

1991 Lenda Murray

1992 Lenda Murray

1993 Lenda Murray

1994 Lenda Murray

1995 Lenda Murray

MR. OLYMPIA WINNERS— INTERNATIONAL FEDERATION OF BODYBUILDERS, MEN'S BODYBUILDING CHAMPIONS

1967 Sergio Oliva

1968 Sergio Oliva

1982 Chris Dickerson

1984 Lee Haney

1985 Lee Haney

1986 Lee Haney

1987 Lee Haney

1988 Lee Haney

1989 Lee Haney

1990 Lee Haney

1991 Lee Haney

1998 Ronnie Coleman

NATIONAL BASEBALL HALL OF FAME

1962 Jackie Robinson

1969 Roy Campanella

1971 Leroy R. "Satchel" Paige

1972 Josh Gibson; Walter "Buck" Leonard

1973 Roberto W. Clemente; Monte Irvin

1974 James T. "Cool Papa" Bell

1975 William "Judy" Johnson

1976 Oscar M. Charleston

1977 Ernest Banks; Martin Dihigo; John H. Lloyd

1979 Willie Mays

1981 Andrew "Rube" Foster; Robert T. Gibson

1982 Hank Aaron; Frank Robinson

1983 Juan A. Marichal

1985 Lou Brock

1986 Willie L. "Stretch" McCovey

1987 Ray Dandridge; Billy Williams

1988 Willie Stargell

1990 Joe Morgan

1991 Rod Carew; Ferguson Jenkins

1993 Reggie Jackson

1995 Leon Day

1996 Bill Foster

1997 Willie Wells

1998 Larry Doby

1999 Orlando Cepeda; Joe Williams

NATIONAL BASKETBALL HALL OF FAME

1972 Robert Douglass

1974 Bill Russell

1976 Elgin "The Big E" Baylor; Charles Cooper

1978 Wilt Chamberlain

1979 Oscar Robertson

1981 Clarence Gaines; Willis Reed

1983 Sam Jones

1984 Nate Thurmond

1986 Walt "Clyde" Frazier

1987 Wes Unseld

1988 William "Pop" Gates; K.C. Jones; Lenny Wilkins (player)

1989 Dave Bing; Elvin Hayes; Earl "The Pearl" Monroe

1990 Nate "Tiny" Archibald

1991 Lusia Harris-Stewart; Connie Hawkins; Bob Lanier

1992 Walt Bellamy; Julius "Dr. J" Erving; Calvin Murphy

1994 Kareem Abdul-Jabbar; Cheryl Miller

1995 George Gervin; David Thompson

1996 Alex English

1998 Marques Haynes, Lenny Wilkins (coach)

1999 Wayne Embry, John Thompson

NATIONAL BOOK AWARD—NATIONAL BOOK FOUNDATION

1953 Ralph Ellison, for *Invisible Man*, Fiction

1969 Winthrop D. Jordan, for *White over Black: American Attitudes toward the Negro, 1550-1812*, History and Biography

1983 Gloria Naylor, for *The Women of Brewster Place*, First Novel; Joyce Carol Thomas, for *Marked By Fire*, Children's Literature; Alice Walker, for *The Color Purple*, Fiction

1990 Charles Johnson, for *Middle Passage*, Fiction

1991 Melissa Fay Green, for *Praying for Sheetrock*, Nonfiction

1992 Edward P. Jones, for *Lost in the City*, Fiction

NATIONAL MEDAL OF ARTS—NATIONAL ENDOWMENT FOR THE ARTS

1985 Ralph Ellison (writer); Leontyne Price (singer)

1986 Marian Anderson (singer)

1987 Romare Bearden (artist); Ella Fitzgerald (singer)

1988 Gordon Parks (photographer and film director)

1989 Katherine Dunham (choreographer); Dizzy Gillespie (musician)

1990 Riley "B. B." King (musician)

1991 James Earl Jones (actor); Billy Taylor (musician)

1994 Harry Belafonte (singer)

1995 Gwendolyn Brooks (poet); Ossie Davis (actor); Ruby Dee (actress)

1996 The Harlem Boys Choir (chorale); Lionel Hampton (musician)

1997 Betty Carter (singer)

1998 Fats Domino (singer)

NATIONAL SOCIETY OF ARTS AND LETTERS GOLD MEDAL OF MERIT AWARD

1982 Andre Watts (music)

NATIONAL TRACK AND FIELD HALL OF FAME—THE ATHLETICS CONGRESS OF THE USA

1974 Ralph Boston; Lee Calhoun; Harrison Dillard; Rafer Johnson; Jesse Owens; Wilma Rudolph; Malvin Whitfield

1975 Ralph Metcalfe

1976 Robert Hayes; Hayes Jones

1977 Robert Beamon; Andrew W. Stanfield

1978 Tommie Smith; John Woodruff

1979 Jim Hines; William DeHart Hubbard

1980 Wyomia Tyus

1981 Willye White

1982 Willie Davenport; Eddie Tolan

1983 Lee Evans

1984 Madeline Manning Mims

1986 Henry Barney Ewell

1988 Gregory Bell

1989 Milt Campbell; Edward Temple

1990 Charles Dumas

1994 Cornelius Johnson; Edwin Moses

1995 Valerie Brisco; Florence Griffith Joyner

1997 Evelyn Ashford; Henry Carr; Renaldo Nehemiah

NEW YORK DRAMA CRITICS' CIRCLE AWARD

Best American Play

1959 *A Raisin in the Sun*, by Lorraine Hansberry

1975 *The Taking of Miss Janie*, by Ed Bullins

1982 *A Soldier's Play*, by Charles Fuller

1996 *Seven Guitars*, by August Wilson

Best New Play

1985 *Ma Rainey's Black Bottom*, by August Wilson

1987 *Fences*, by August Wilson

1988 *Joe Turner's Come and Gone*, by August Wilson

1990 *The Piano Lesson*, by August Wilson

NOBEL PEACE PRIZE—NOBEL FOUNDATION

1950 Ralph J. Bunche

1964 Martin Luther King, Jr.

NOBEL PRIZE IN LITERATURE—NOBEL FOUNDATION

1993 Toni Morrison

PRESIDENTIAL MEDAL OF FREEDOM—UNITED STATES EXECUTIVE OFFICE OF THE PRESIDENT

1963 Marian Anderson; Ralph J. Bunche

1964 John L. Lewis; Leontyne Price; A. Philip Randolph

1969 Edward Kennedy "Duke" Ellington; Ralph Ellison; Roy Wilkins; Whitney M. Young, Jr.

1976 Jesse Owens

1977 Martin Luther King, Jr. (posthumously)

1980 Clarence Mitchell

1981 James H. "Eubie" Blake; Andrew Young

1983 James Cheek; Mabel Mercer

1984 Jack Roosevelt "Jackie" Robinson (posthumously)

1985 William "Count" Basie (posthumously); Jerome "Brud" Holland (posthumously)

1987 Frederick Douglass Patterson

1988 Pearl Bailey

1991 Colin L. Powell

1992 Ella Fitzgerald

1993 Arthur Ashe, Jr. (posthumously); Thurgood Marshall (posthumously); Colin L. Powell

1994 Dorothy Height; Barbara Jordan

1995 William Thaddeus Coleman, Jr.; John Hope Franklin; A. Leon Higginbotham, Jr.

1996 John H. Johnson; Rosa Parks

1998 James Farmer

PROFESSIONAL FOOTBALL HALL OF FAME

1967 Emlen Tunnell

1968 Marion Motley

1969 Fletcher "Joe" Perry

1971 Jim Brown

1972 Ollie Matson

1973 Jim Parker

1974 Richard "Night Train" Lane

1975 Roosevelt Brown; Leonard "Lenny" Moore

1976 Leonard "Len" Ford

1977 Gale Sayers; Bill Willis

1980 Herb Adderley; David "Deacon" Jones

1981 Willie Davis

1983 Bobby Bell; Bobby Mitchell; Paul Warfield

1984 Willie Brown; Charley Taylor

1985 O. J. Simpson

1986 Ken Houston; Willie Lanier

1987 Joe Greene; John Henry Johnson; Gene Upshaw

1988 Alan Page

1989 Mel Blount; Art Shell; Willie Wood

1990 Junious "Buck" Buchanan; Franco Harris

1991 Earl Campbell

1992 Lem Barney; John Mackey

1993 Larry Little; Walter Payton

1994 Tony Dorsett; Leroy Kelly

1995 Lee Roy Selmon

1996 Charlie Joiner; Mel Renfro

1997 Mike Haynes

1998 Mike Singletary; Dwight Stephenson

1999 Eric Dickerson; Lawrence Taylor

PULITZER PRIZE—COLUMBIA UNIVERSITY GRADUATE SCHOOL OF JOURNALISM

Biography or Autobiography

1994 *W. E. B. Du Bois: Biography of a Race, 1968–1919*, by David Levering Lewis

Journalism: Commentary

1996 E. R. Shipp

Journalism: Feature Writing

1999 Angelo B. Henderson

Letters: Drama

1970 *No Place To Be Somebody*, by Charles Gordone

1982 *A Soldier's Play*, by Charles Fuller

1987 *Fences*, by August Wilson

1990 *The Piano Lesson*, by August Wilson

Letters: Fiction

1978 *Elbow Room*, by James Alan McPherson

1983 *The Color Purple*, by Alice Walker

1988 *Beloved*, by Toni Morrison

Letters: Poetry

1950 *Annie Allen*, by Gwendolyn Brooks

1987 *Thomas and Beulah*, by Rita Dove

Letters: Special Awards and Citations

1977 Alexander Palmer Haley, for *Roots*

Music: Special Awards and Citations

1976 Scott Joplin

1996 George Walker

1997 Wynton Marsalis

1999 Edward Kennedy "Duke" Ellington (posthmously)

ROCK AND ROLL HALL OF FAME

1986 Chuck Berry; James Brown; Ray Charles; Sam Cooks; Fats Domino; Little Richard; Robert Johnson; Jimmy Yancey

1987 The Coasters; Bo Diddley; Aretha Franklin; Marvin Gaye; Louis Jordan; B.B. King; Clyde McPhalter; Smokey Robinson; Big Joe Turner; T-Bone Walker; Muddy Waters; Jackie Wilson

1988 The Drifters; Barry Gordy, Jr.; The Supremes

1989 The Ink Spots; Otis Redding; Bessie Smith; The Soul Stirrers; The Temptations; Stevie Wonder

1990 Louis Armstrong; Hank Ballard; Charlie Christian; The Four Tops; Holland, Dozier, and Holland; The Platters; Ma Rainey

1991 La Vern Baker; John Lee Hooker; Howlin' Wolf; The Impressions; Wilson Pickett; Jimmy Reed; Ike and Tina Turner

1992 Blue Brand, Booker T. and the M.G.'s; Jimi Hendrix; Isley Brothers; Elmore James; Doc Pomus; Professor Longhair; Sam and Dave

1993 Ruth Brown; Etta James; Frankie Lymon and the Teenagers; Sly and the Family Stone; Dinah Washington

1994 Willie Dixon; Bob Marley; Johnny Otis

1995 Al Green; Martha and the Vandellas; The Orioles

1996 Little Willie John; Gladys Knight and the Pips; The Shirelles

1997 Mahalia Jackson; The Jackson Five; Parliament

1998 Jelly Roll Morton; Lloyd Price

1999 Charles Brown; Curtis Mayfield; The Staple Singers

SPRINGARN MEDAL—NATIONAL ASSOCIATION FOR THE ADVANCEMENT OF COLORED PEOPLE

1915 Ernest E. Just—head of the department of physiology at Howard University Medical School.

1916 Charles Young—major in the United States Army.

1917 Harry T. Burleigh—composer, pianist, singer.

1918 William Stanley Braithwaite—poet, literary critic, editor.

1919 Archibald H. Grimké—former U.S. Consul in Santo Domingo, president of the American Negro Academy, author, president of the District of Columbia branch of the NAACP.

1920 William Edward Burghardt DuBois—author, editor, organizer of the first Pan-African Congress.

1921 Charles S. Gilpin—actor.

1922 Mary B. Talbert—former president of the National Association of Colored Women.

1923 George Washington Carver—head of research and director of the experiment station at Tuskegee Institute.

1924 Roland Hayes—singer.

1925 James Weldon Johnson—former United States Consul in Venezuela and Nicaragua, author, editor, poet; secretary of the NAACP.

1926 Carter G. Woodson—editor, historian; founder of the Association for the Study of Negro Life and History.

1927 Anthony Overton—businessman; president of the Victory Life Insurance Company (the first African American organization permitted to do business under the rigid requirements of the State of New York).

1928 Charles W. Chesnutt—author.

1929 Mordecai Wyatt Johnson—the first African American president of Howard University.

1930 Henry A. Hunt—principal of Fort Valley High and Industrial School, Fort Valley, Georgia.

1931 Richard Berry Harrison—actor.

1932 Robert Russa Moton—principal of Tuskegee Institute.

1933 Max Yergan—secretary of the YMCA in South Africa.

1934 William Taylor Burwell Williams—dean of Tuskegee Institute.

1935 Mary McLeod Bethune—founder and president of Bethune Cookman College.

1936 John Hope—president of Atlanta University.

1937 Walter White—executive secretary of the NAACP.

1939 Marian Anderson—singer.

1940 Louis T. Wright—surgeon.

1941 Richard Wright—author.

1942 A. Philip Randolph—labor leader, international president of the Brotherhood of Sleeping Car Porters.

1943 William H. Hastie—jurist, educator.

1944 Charles Drew—scientist.

1945 Paul Robeson—singer, actor.

1946 Thurgood Marshall—special counsel of the NAACP

1947 Percy Julian—research chemist.

1948 Channing H. Tobias—minister, educator.

1949 Ralph J. Bunche—international civil servant, acting United Nations mediator in Palestine.

1950 Charles Hamilton Houston—chairman of the NAACP Legal Committee.

1951 Mabel Keaton Staupers—leader of the National Association of Colored Graduate Nurses.

1952 Harry T. Moore—state leader of the Florida NAACP.

1953 Paul R. Williams—architect.

1954 Theodore K. Lawless—physician, educator, philanthropist.

1955 Carl Murphy—editor, publisher, civic leader.

1956 Jack Roosevelt Robinson—athlete.

1957 Martin Luther King, Jr.—minister, civil rights leader.

1958 Daisy Bates and the Little Rock Nine—for their pioneer role in upholding the basic ideals of American democracy in the face of continuing harassment and constant threats of bodily injury.

1959 Edward Kennedy "Duke" Ellington—composer, musician, orchestra leader.

1960 Langston Hughes—poet, author, playwright.

1961 Kenneth B. Clark—professor of psychology at the City College of the City University of New York, founder and director of the Northside Center for Child Development, prime mobilizer of the resources of modern psychology in the attack upon racial segregation.

1962 Robert C. Weaver—administrator of the Housing and Home Finance Agency.

1963 Medgar Wiley Evers—NAACP field secretary for Mississippi, World War II veteran.

1964 Roy Wilkins—executive director of the NAACP.

1965 Leontyne Price—singer.

1966 John H. Johnson—founder and president of the Johnson Publishing Company.

1967 Edward W. Brooke III—the first African American to win popular election to the United States Senate.

1968 Sammy Davis, Jr.—performer, civil rights activist.

1969 Clarence M. Mitchell, Jr.—director of the Washington Bureau of the NAACP, civil rights activist.

1970 Jacob Lawrence—artist, teacher, humanitarian.

1971 Leon H. Sullivan—minister.

1972 Gordon Alexander Buchanan Parks—writer, photographer, filmmaker.

1973 Wilson C. Riles—educator.

1974 Damon Keith—jurist.

1975 Hank Aaron—athlete.

1976 Alvin Ailey—dancer, choreographer, artistic director.

1977 Alexander Palmer Haley—author, biographer, lecturer.

1978 Andrew Young—United States Ambassador to the United Nations, diplomat, cabinet member, civil rights activist, minister.

1979 Rosa Parks—community activist.

1980 Rayford W. Logan—educator, historian, author.

1981 Coleman A. Young—mayor of the City of Detroit, public servant, labor leader, civil rights activist.

1982 Benjamin E. Mays—educator, theologian, humanitarian).

1983 Lena Horne—performer, humanitarian.

1984 Tom Bradley—government executive, public servant, humanitarian.

1985 William H. "Bill" Cosby—comedian, actor, educator, humanitarian.

1986 Benjamin Lawson Hooks—executive director of the NAACP.

1987 Percy Ellis Sutton—public servant, businessman, community leader.

1988 Frederick Douglass Patterson—doctor of veterinary medicine, educator, humanitarian, founder of the United Negro College Fund.

1989 Jesse Jackson—minister, political leader, civil rights activist.

1990 L. Douglas Wilder—governor of Virginia.

1991 Colin L. Powell—general in the United States Army, chairman of the Joint Chiefs of Staff.

1992 Barbara C. Jordan—educator, former congresswoman.

1993 Dorothy L. Height—president of the National Council of Negro Women.

1994 Maya Angelou—poet, author, performing artist.

1995 John Hope Franklin—historian.

1996 A. Leon Higginbotham, Jr.—jurist, judge

1997 Carl T. Rowan—journalist.

1998 Myrlie Evers-Williams—former chair, board of directors, NAACP

1999 Earl G. Graves, publisher and media executive

SULLIVAN AWARD—AMATEUR ATHLETIC UNION

1961 Wilma Rudolph

1981 Carl Lewis

1983 Edwin Moses

1986 Jackie Joyner-Kersee

1988 Florence Griffith-Joyner

1991 Mike Powell

1993 Charlie Ward

1996 Michael Johnson

1998 Chamique Holdsclaw

TONY (ANTOINETTE PERRY) AWARD— LEAGUE OF AMERICAN THEATERS AND PRODUCERS

Actor (Dramatic)

1969 James Earl Jones, for *The Great White Hope*

1975 John Kani, for *Sizwe Banzi*; Winston Ntshona, for *The Island*

1987 James Earl Jones, for *Fences*

Supporting or Featured Actor (Dramatic)

1982 Zakes Mokae, for *Master Harold. . . and the Boys*

1992 Larry Fishburne, for *Two Trains Running*

1994 Jeffrey Wright, for *Angels in America*

1996 Ruben Santiago-Hudson, for *Seven Guitars*

Actor (Musical)

1970 Cleavon Little, for *Purlie*

1973 Ben Vereen, for *Pippin*

1982 Ben Harvey, for *Dreamgirls*

1992 Gregory Hines, for *Jelly's Last Jam*

Supporting or Featured Actor (Musical)

1954 Harry Belafonte, for *John Murray Anderson's Almanac*

1975 Ted Rose, for *The Wiz*

1981 Hinton Battle, for *Sophisticated Ladies*

1982 Cleavant Derricks, for *Dreamgirls*

1983 Charles "Honi" Coles, for *My One and Only*

1984 Hinton Battle, for *The Tap Dance Kid*

1991 Hinton Battle, for *Miss Saigon*

1997 Chuck Cooper, for *The Life*

Supporting or Featured Actress (Dramatic)

1977 Trazana Beverley, for *For Colored Girls Who Have Considered Suicide/When the Rainbow Is Enuf*

1987 Mary Alice, for *Fences*

1988 L. Scott Caldwell, for *Joe Turner's Come and Gone*

1997 Lynne Thigpen, for *An American Daughter*

Actress (Musical)

1962 Diahann Carroll, for *No Strings*

1968 Leslie Uggams, for *Hallelujah, Baby*

1974 Virginia Capers, for *Raisin*

1982 Jennifer Holliday, for *Dreamgirls*

1989 Ruth Brown, for *Black and Blue*

1996 Audra McDonald, for *Master Class*

Supporting or Featured Actress (Musical)

1950 Juanita Hall, for *South Pacific*

1968 Lillian Hayman, for *Halleluja, Baby*

1970 Melba Moore, for *Purlie*

1975 Dee Dee Bridgewater, for *The Wiz*

1977 Delores Hall, for *Your Arms's Too Short To Box with God*

1978 Nell Carter, for *Ain't Misbehavin*

1992 Tonya Pinkins, for *Jelly's Last Jam*

1994 Audra McDonald, for *Carousel*

1996 Ann Duquesnay, for *Bring in 'Da Noise, Bring in 'Da Funk*

1997 Lillias White, for *The Life*

Play

1974 *The River Niger*, by Joseph A. Walker

1987 *Fences*, by August Wilson

UNITED STATES MEDAL OF HONOR

Civil War

Army

William H. Barnes, Private, Company C, 38th United States Colored Troops.

Powhatan Beaty, First Sergeant, Company G, 5th United States Colored Troops.

James H. Bronson, First Sergeant, Company D, 5th United States Colored Troops.

William H. Carney, Sergeant, Company C, 54th Massachusetts Infantry, United States Colored Troops.

Decatur Dorsey, Sergeant, Company B, 39th United States Colored Troops.

Christian A. Fleetwood, Sergeant Major, 4th United States Colored Troops.

James Gardiner, Private, Company 1, 36th United States Colored Troops.

James H. Harris, Sergeant, Company B, 38th United States Colored Troops.

Thomas R. Hawkins, Sergeant Major, 6th United States Colored Troops.

Alfred B. Hilton, Sergeant, Company H, 4th United States Colored Troops.

Milton M. Holland, Sergeant, 5th United States Colored Troops.

Alexander Kelly, First Sergeant, Company F, 6th United States Colored Troops.

Robert Pinn, First Sergeant, Company I, 5th United States Colored Troops.

Edward Radcliff, First Sergeant, Company C, 38th United States Colored Troops.

Charles Veal, Private, Company D, 4th United States Colored Troops.

Navy

Aaron Anderson, Landsman, *USS Wyandank*.

Robert Blake, Powder Boy, *USS Marblehead*.

William H. Brown, Landsman, *USS Brooklyn*.

Wilson Brown, *USS Hartford*.

John Lawson, Landsman, *USS Hartford*.

James Mifflin, Engineer's Cook, *USS Brooklyn*.

Joachim Pease, Seaman, *USS Kearsarge*.

Interim Period

Navy

Daniel Atkins, Ship's Cook, First Class, *USS Cushing*.

John Davis, Seaman, *USS Trenton*.

Alphonse Girandy, Seaman, *USS Tetrel*.

John Johnson, Seaman, *USS Kansas*.

William Johnson, Cooper, *USS Adams*.

Joseph B. Noil, Seaman, *USS Powhatan*.

John Smith, Seaman, *USS Shenandoah*.

Robert Sweeney, Seaman, *USS Kearsage, USS Jamestown*.

Western Campaigns

Army

Thomas Boyne, Sergeant, Troop C, 9th United States Cavalry.

Benjamin Brown, Sergeant, Company C, 24th United States Infantry.

John Denny, Sergeant, Troop C, 9th United States Cavalry.

Pompey Factor, Seminole Negro Indian Scouts.

Clinton Greaves, Corporal, Troop C, 9th United States Cavalry.

Henry Johnson, Sergeant, Troop D, 9th United States Cavalry.

George Jordan, Sergeant, Troop K, 9th United States Cavalry.

William McBreyar, Sergeant, Troop K, 10th United States Cavalry.

Isaiah Mays, Corporal, Company B, 24th United States Infantry.

Issac Payne, Private (Trumpeteer) Seminole Negro Indian Scouts.

Thomas Shaw, Sergeant, Troop K, 9th United States Cavalry.

Emanuel Stance, Sergeant, Troop F, 9th United States Cavalry.

Augustus Walley, Private, Troop 1, 9th United States Cavalry.

John Ward, Sergeant, Seminole Negro Indian Scouts.

Moses Williams, First Sergeant, Troop 1, 9th United States Cavalry.

William O. Wilson, Corporal, Troop 1, 9th United States Cavalry.

Brent Woods, Sergeant, Troop B, 9th United States Cavalry.

Spanish-American War

Army

Edward L. Baker, Jr., Sergeant Major, 10th United States Cavalry.

Dennis Bell, Private, Troop H, 10th United States Cavalry.

Fitz Lee, Private, Troop M, 10th United States Cavalry.

William H. Thompkins, Private, Troop G, 10th United States Cavalry.

George H. Wanton, Sergeant, Troop M, 10th United States Cavalry.

Navy

Joseph B. Noil, Non-combatant Service, *USS Powhatan.*

Robert Penn, Fireman, First Class, *USS Iowa.*

World War I

Army

Freddie Stowers, Corporal, Company C, 371st Infantry Regiment, 93rd Infantry Division.

World War II

Army

Vernon Baker, First Lieutenant.

Edward A. Carter, Jr., Staff Sergeant.

John R. Fox, First Lieutenant.

Willy F. James, Jr., Private First Class.

Ruben Rivers, Staff Sergeant.

Charles L. Thomas, First Lieutenant.

George Watson, Private.

Korean War

Army

Cornelius H. Charlton, Sergeant, 24th Infantry Regiment, 25th Division.

William Thompson, Private, 24th Infantry Regiment, 25th Division.

Vietnam War

Army

Webster Anderson, Sergeant, Battery A, 2nd Battalion, 320th Artillery, 101st Airborne Division.

Eugene Ashley, Jr., Sergeant, Company C, 5th Special Forces Group (Airborne), 1st Special Forces.

William M. Bryant, Sergeant First Class, Company A, 5th Special Forces Group, 1st Special Forces.

Lawrence Joel, Specialist Sixth Class, Headquarters and Headquarters Company, 1st Battalion, 173d Airborne Brigade.

Dwight H. Johnson, Specialist Fifth Class, Company B, 1st Battalion, 69th Armor, 4th Infantry Division.

Garfield M. Langhorn, Private First Class, Troop C, 7th Squadron, 17th Cavalry, 1st Aviation Brigade.

Matthew Leonard, Platoon Sergeant, Company B, 1st Battalion, 16th Infantry, 1st Infantry Division.

Donald R. Long, Sergeant, Troop C, 1st Squadron, 4th Cavalry, 1st Infantry Division.

Milton L. Olive III, Private First Class, Company B, 2nd Battalion 503d Infantry, 173d Airborne Brigade.

Riley L. Pitts, Captain, Company C, 2nd Battalion, 27th Infantry, 25th Infantry Division.

Charles C. Rogers, Lieutenant Colonel, 1st Battalion, 5th Infantry, 1st Infantry Division.

Rupert L. Sargent, First Lieutenant, Company B, 4th Battalion, 9th Infantry, 25th Infantry Division.

Clarence E. Sasser, Specialist 5th Class, Headquarters Company, 3rd Battalion, 60th Infantry, 90th Infantry Division.

Clifford C. Sims, Staff Sergeant, Company D, 2nd Battalion, 501st Infantry, 101st Airborne Division.

John E. Warren, Jr., First Lieutenant, Company C, 2nd Battalion, 22d Infantry, 25th Infantry Division.

Marines

James A. Anderson, Jr. Private First Class, 2nd Platoon, Company F, 2nd Battalion, 3rd Marine Division.

Oscar P. Austin, Private First Class, Company E, 7th Marines, 1st Marine Division.

Rodney M. Davis, Company B, First Battalion, 5th Marines, 1st Marine Division.

Robert H. Jenkins, Jr., Private First Class, 3rd Reconnaissance Battalion, 3rd Marine Division.

Ralph H. Johnson, Private First Class, Company A, 1st Reconnaissance Battalion, 1st Marine Division.

UNITED STATES OPEN

Men's Singles

1968 Arthur Ashe

Women's Singles

1957 Althea Gibson
1958 Althea Gibson

Mixed Doubles

1957 Althea Gibson

UNITED STATES POET LAUREATE

1993 Rita Dove (served until 1995)

UNITED STATES POSTAL SERVICE STAMPS ON AFRICAN AMERICAN HISTORY

Louis Armstrong

Benjamin Banneker

William "Count" Basie

James Pierson Beckwourth

Mary McLeod Bethune

James Hubert "Eubie" Blake

Ralph Johnson Bunche

George Washington Carver

Nat "King" Cole

Bessie Coleman

John Coltrane

Allison Davis

Benjamin O. Davis, Sr.

Frederick Douglass

Charles Richard Drew

(W)illiam (E)dward (B)urghardt Du Bois

Jean Baptiste Pointe Du Sable

Paul Laurence Dunbar

Edward Kennedy "Duke" Ellington

Erroll Garner

(W)illiam (C)hristopher Handy

Coleman Hawkins

Matthew Alexander Henson

Billie Holiday

Mahalia Jackson

James Price Johnson

James Weldon Johnson

Robert Johnson

Scott Joplin

Percy Lavon Julian

Ernest Everett Just

Martin Luther King, Jr.

Joe Louis

Hudson William Ledbetter, "Leadbelly"

Roberta Martin

Jan E. Matzeliger

Clyde McPhatter

Charles Mingus

Thelonious Sphere Monk

Ferdinand "Jelly Roll" Morton

James Cleveland "Jesse" Owens

Charlie "Bird" Parker

Bill Pickett

Salem Poor

Gertrude "Ma" Rainey

(A)sa Philip Randolph

Otis Redding

John Roosevelt "Jackie" Robinson

James Andrew "Jimmy" Rushing

Bessie Smith

Henry Ossawa Tanner

Sonny Terry
Sister Rosetta Tharpe
Sojourner Truth
Harriet Tubman
Madame C. J. Walker
Clara Ward
Booker Taliaferro Washington
Dinah Washington
Ethel Waters
Muddy Waters
Ida Bell Wells-Barnett
Josh White
Howlin' Wolf
Carter Godwin Woodson
Whitney Moore Young

WIMBLEDON—ALL ENGLAND LAWN TENNIS AND CROQUET CLUB

Men's Singles

1975   Arthur Ashe

Ladies' Singles

1957   Althea Gibson

1958   Althea Gibson

Ladies' Doubles

1957   Althea Gibson, with Darlene Hard

1958   Althea Gibson, with Maria Bueno

◆ AFRICAN AMERICAN FEDERAL JUDGES

PRESIDENT FRANKLIN D. ROOSEVELT

| 1937 | William H. Hastie* | District Court, Virgin Islands |
| 1939 | Harnian E. Moore* | District Court, Virgin Islands |

PRESIDENT HARRY S TRUMAN

1945	Irvin C. Mollison*	United States Customs Court
1949	William H. Hastie*	Court of Appeals, Third Circuit
1949	Harnian E. Moore (a)*	District Court, Virgin Islands

PRESIDENT DWIGHT D. EISENHOWER

| 1957 | Scovel Richardson* | United States Customs Court |
| 1958 | Walter Gordon* | District Court, Virgin Islands |

PRESIDENT JOHN F. KENNEDY

1961	James B. Parsons**	Senior Judge, District Court, Illinois
1961	Wade M. McCree**	District Court, Michigan
1961	Thurgood Marshall**	Court of Appeals, Second Circuit

PRESIDENT LYNDON B. JOHNSON

1964	Spottswood Robinson**	District Court, District of Columbia
1964	A. Leon Higginbotham**	District Court, Pennsylvania
1965	William B. Bryant	Senior Judge, District Court, District of Columbia
1966	Wade H. McCree*	Court of Appeals, Sixth Court
1966	James L. Watson	United States Customs Court
1966	Constance B. Motley	Senior Judge, District Court, New York
1966	Spottswood Robinson	Senior Judge, Court of Appeals for the Federal Circuit
1966	Aubrey E. Robinson	Chief Judge, District Court, District of Columbia
1967	Damon Keith**	District Court, Michigan
1967	Thurgood Marshall*	Associate Justice, Supreme Court
1967	Joseph C. Waddy**	District Court, District of Columbia

PRESIDENT RICHARD M. NIXON

1969	Almeric Christian**	District Court, Virgin Islands
1969	David W. Williams	Senior Judge, District Court, California
1969	Barrington D. Parker	Senior Judge, District Court, District of Columbia
1971	Lawrence W. Pierce**	District Court, New York
1971	Clifford Scott Green	District Court, Pennsylvania
1972	Robert L. Carter	Senior Judge, District Court, New York
1972	Robert M. Duncan**	Military Court of Appeals
1974	Robert M. Duncan**	District Court, Ohio

PRESIDENT GERALD R. FORD

1974	Henry Bramwell**	Senior Judge, District Court, New York
1976	George N. Leighton**	Senior Judge, District Court, Illinois
1976	Matthew Perry**	Military Court of Appeals
1976	Cecil F. Poole**	District Court, California

PRESIDENT JIMMY CARTER

1978	Almeric Christian (a)**	Chief Judge, District Court, Virgin Islands
1978	U.W. Clemon	District Court, Alabama
1978	Robert F. Collins**	District Court, Louisiana

1978	Julian A. Cook, Jr.	District Court, Michigan
1978	Damon J. Keith	Court of Appeals, Sixth Circuit
1978	A. Leon Higginbotham*	Court of Appeals, Third Circuit
1978	Mary Johnson Lowe	District Court, New York
1978	Theodore McMillian	Court of Appeals, Eighth Circuit
1978	David S. Nelson	District Court, Massachusetts
1978	Paul A. Simmons**	District Court, Pennsylvania
1978	Jack E. Tanner	District Court, Washington
1979	Harry T. Edwards	Court of Appeals for the Federal Circuit
1979	J. Jerome Farris	Court of Appeals, Ninth Circuit
1979	Joseph W. Hatchett	Court of Appeals, Eleventh Circuit
1979	Terry J. Hatter	District Court, California
1979	Joseph C. Howard	District Court, Maryland
1979	Benjamin T. Gibson	District Court, Michigan
1979	James T. Giles	District Court, Pennsylvania
1979	Nathaniel R. Jones	Court of Appeals, Sixth Circuit
1979	Amalya L. Kearse	Court of Appeals, Second Circuit
1979	Gabrielle Kirk McDonald**	District Court, Texas
1979	John Garrett Penn**	District Court, District of Columbia
1979	Cecil F. Poole	Court of Appeals, Ninth Circuit
1979	Matthew J. Perry	District Court, South Carolina
1979	Myron H. Thompson	District Court, Alabama
1979	Anne E. Thompson	District Court, New Jersey
1979	Odell Horton	District Court, Tennessee
1979	Anna Diggs Taylor	District Court, Michigan
1979	Horace T. Ward	District Court, Georgia
1979	Alcee L. Hastings***	District Court, Florida
1980	Clyde S. Cahill, Jr.**	District Court, Missouri
1980	Richard C. Erwin	District Court, North Carolina
1980	Thelton E. Henderson	District Court, California
1980	George Howard, Jr.	District Court, Arkansas
1980	Earl B. Gilliam	District Court, California
1980	Norma Holloway Johnson	District Court, District of Columbia
1980	Consuela B. Marshall	District Court, California
1980	George White	District Court, Ohio

PRESIDENT RONALD REAGAN

1981	Lawrence W. Pierce	Court of Appeals, Second Circuit
1982	Reginald Gibson	United States Court of Claims
1984	John R. Hargrove	District Court, Maryland
1984	Henry Wingate	District Court, Mississippi
1985	Ann Williams	District Court, Illinois
1986	James Spencer	District Court, Virginia
1987	Kenneth Hoyt	District Court, Texas
1988	Herbert Hutton	District Court, Pennsylvania

PRESIDENT GEORGE BUSH

1990	Clarence Thomas**	Court of Appeals for the Federal Circuit
1990	James Ware	District Court, California
1991	Saundra Brown Armstrong	District Court, California
1991	Fernando J. Giatan	District Court, Missouri
1991	Donald L. Graham	District Court, Florida
1991	Sterling Johnson	District Court, New York
1991	J. Curtis Joyner	District Court, Pennsylvania
1991	Timothy K. Lewis	District Court, Pennsylvania

1991	Joe B. McDade	District Court, Illinois
1991	Clarence Thomas	Associate Justice, Supreme Court
1992	Garland E. Burrell, Jr.	District Court, California
1992	Carol Jackson	District Court, Missouri
1992	Timothy K. Lewis	Court of Appeals, Third Circuit

PRESIDENT BILL CLINTON

1993	Henry Lee Adams	District Court, Florida
1993	Wilkie Ferguson	District Court, Florida
1993	Raymond Jackson	District Court, Virginia
1993	Gary Lancaster	District Court, Pennsylvania
1993	Reginald Lindsay	District Court, Massachusetts
1993	Charles Shaw	District Court, Missouri
1994	Deborah Batts	District Court, New York
1994	Franklin Burgess	District Court, Washington
1994	James Beaty, Jr.	District Court, North Carolina
1994	David Coar	District Court, Illinois
1994	Audrey Collins	District Court, California
1994	Clarence Cooper	District Court, Georgia
1994	Michael Davis	District Court, Minnesota
1994	Raymond Finch	District Court, Virgin Islands
1994	Vanessa Gilmore	District Court, Texas
1994	A. Haggerty	District Court, Oregon
1994	Denise Page Hood	District Court, Michigan
1994	Napoleon Jones	District Court, California
1994	Blance Manning	District Court, Illinois
1994	Theodore McKee	Circuit Court, Third Circuit
1994	Vicki Miles‐LaGrange	District Court, Oklahoma
1994	Solomon Oliver, Jr.	District Court, Ohio
1994	Barrington Parker, Jr.	District Court, New York
1994	Judith Rogers	Circuit Court, District of Columbia
1994	W. Louis Sands	District Court, Georgia
1994	Carl Stewart	Circuit Court, Fifth Circuit
1994	Emmet Sullivan	Circuit Court, District of Columbia
1994	William Walls	District Court, New Jersey
1994	Alexander Williams	District Court, Maryland
1995	R. Guy Cole	Circuit Court, Sixth Circuit
1995	Curtis Collier	District Court, Tennessee
1995	Wiley Daniel	District Court, Colorado
1995	Andre Davis	District Court, Maryland
1995	Bernice B. Donald	District Court, Tennessee
1996	Charles N. Clevert, Jr.	District Court, Wisconsin
1996	Joseph A. Greenaway, Jr.	District Court, New Jersey
1997	Eric L. Clay	Circuit Court, Sixth Circuit
1997	Algenon L. Marbley	District Court, Ohio
1997	Martin J. Jenkins	District Court, California
1997	Henry H. Kennedy, Jr.	District Court, District of Columbia
1998	Gregory Sleet	District Court, Delaware
1998	Ivan L.R. Lemelle	District Court, Louisiana
1998	Sam A. Lindsay	District Court, Texas
1998	Johnnie B. Rawlinson	District Court, Nevada
1998	Margaret Seymour	District Court, South Carolina
1998	Richard Roberts	District Court, District of Columbia
1998	Gerald Bruce Lee	District Court, Virginia
1998	Lynn Bush	Court of Federal Claims

1998	Stephan P. Mickle	District Court, Florida
1998	Victoria Roberts	District Court, Michigan
1998	Raner Collins	District Court, Arizona
1998	Ralph Tyson	District Court, Louisiana
1999	William Hibbler	District Court, Illinois

(a) Reappointment

*   Deceased

**   No longer serving

***   Impeached and removed from the court

◆ AFRICAN AMERICAN OLYMPIC MEDALISTS

Place/Year	Athlete	Event	Place	Time/Distance
St. Louis, 1904	George C. Poag	200 M Hurdles	3rd	
	George C. Poag	400 M Hurdles	3rd	
London, 1908	J.B. Taylor	1600 M Relay	1st	3:29.4
Paris, 1924	Dehart Hubbard	Long Jump	1st	24' 5.125"
	Edward Gourdin	Long Jump	2nd	23' 10"
Los Angeles, 1932	Eddie Tolan	100 M Dash	1st	10.3
	Ralph Metcalfe	100 M Dash	2nd	10.3
	Eddie Tolan	200 M Dash	1st	21.2
	Ralph Metcalfe	200 M Dash	3rd	21.5
	Edward Gordon	Long Jump	1st	25' .75"
Berlin, 1936	Jesse Owens	100 M Dash	1st	10.3
	Ralph Metcalfe	100 M Dash	2nd	10.4
	Jesse Owens	200 M Dash	1st	20.7
	Matthew Robinson	200 M Dash	2nd	21.1
	Archie Williams	400 M Run	1st	46.5
	James DuValle	400 M Run	2nd	46.8
	John Woodruff	800 M Run	1st	1:52.9
	Fritz Pollard, Jr.	110 M Hurdles	3rd	14.4
	Cornelius Johnson	High Jump	1st	6'8"
	Jesse Owens	Long Jump	1st	26' 5.75"
	Jesse Owens	400 M Relay	1st	39.8
	Ralph Metcalfe	400 M Relay	1st	39.8
London, 1948	Harrison Dillard	100 M Dash	1st	10.3
	Norwood Ewell	100 M Dash	2nd	10.4
	Norwood Ewell	200 M Dash	1st	21.1
	Mal Whitfield	400 M Run	3rd	46.9
	Willie Steele	Long Jump	1st	25' 8"
	Herbert Douglass	Long Jump	3rd	25' 3"
	Lorenzo Wright	400 M Relay	1st	40.6
	Harrison Dillard	1600 M Relay	1st	3:10.4
	Norwood Ewell	1600 M Relay	1st	3:10.4
	Mal Whitfield	1600 M Relay	1st	3:10.4
	Audrey Patterson	200 M Dash	3rd	25.2
	Alice Coachman	High Jump	1st	5' 6.125"
Helsinki, 1952	Andrew Stanfield	200 M Dash	1st	20.7
	Ollie Matson	400 M Run	3rd	46.8
	Mal Whitfield	800 M Run	1st	1:49.2
	Harrison Dillard	110 M Hurdles	1st	13.7
	Jerome Biffle	Long Jump	1st	24' 10"
	Meredith Gourdine	Long Jump	2nd	24' 8.125"
	Harrison Dillard	400 M Relay	1st	40.1
	Andrew Stanfield	400 M Relay	1st	40.1
	Ollie Matson	400 M Relay	1st	40.1
	Bill Miller	Javelin	2nd	237
	Milton Campbell	Decathlon	2nd	6,975 pts.
	Floyd Patterson	Boxing: Middleweight	1st	
	Norvel Lee	Boxing: Light Heavyweight	1st	
	Nathan Brooks	Boxing: Flyweight	1st	
	Charles Adkins	Boxing: Light Welterweight	1st	
	Barbara Jones	400 M Relay	1st	45.9
Melbourne, 1956	Andrew Stanfield	200 M Dash	2nd	20.7
	Charles Jenkins	400 M Run	1st	46.7
	Lee Calhoun	110 M Hurdles	1st	13.5
	Charles Dumas	High Jump	1st	6' 11.25"
	Gregory Bell	Long Jump	1st	25' 8.25"
	Willye White	Long Jump	2nd	19' 11.75"
	Ira Murchison	400 M Relay	1st	39.5
	Leamon King	400 M Relay	1st	39.5
	Charles Jenkins	400 M Relay	1st	39.5
	Lou Jones	1600 M Relay	1st	3:04.8

Place/Year	Athlete	Event	Place	Time/Distance
	Milton Campbell	Decathlon	1st	7,937 pts.
	Rafer Johnson	Decathlon	2nd	7,587 pts.
	K.C. Jones	Men's Basketball	1st	
	Bill Russell	Men's Basketball	1st	
	James Boyd	Boxing: Light Heavyweight	1st	
	Mildred McDaniel	High Jump	1st	5' 9.25"
	Margaret Matthews	400 M Relay	3rd	44.9
	Isabelle Daniels	400 M Relay	3rd	44.9
	Mae Faggs	400 M Relay	3rd	44.9
	Wilma Rudolph	400 M Relay	3rd	44.9
Rome, 1960	Les Carney	200 M Dash	2nd	20.6
	Lee Calhoun	110 M Hurdles	1st	13.8
	Willie May	110 M Hurdles	2nd	13.8
	Hayes Jones	110 M Hurdles	3rd	14
	Otis Davis	400 M Run	1st	44.9
	John Thomas	High Jump	3rd	7' .25"
	Ralph Boston	Long Jump	1st	26' 7.75"
	Irvin Robertson	Long Jump	2nd	26' 7.25"
	Otis Davis	1600 M Relay	1st	3:02.2
	Rafer Johnson	Decathlon	1st	8,392 pts.
	Oscar Robertson	Men's Basketball	1st	
	Walt Bellamy	Men's Basketball	1st	
	Bob Boozer	Men's Basketball	1st	
	Wilbert McClure	Boxing: Light Middleweight	1st	
	Cassius Clay	Boxing: Light Heavyweight	1st	
	Edward Crook	Boxing: Middleweight	1st	
	Quincelon Daniels	Boxing: Light Welterweight	3rd	
	Earlene Brown	Shot Put	3rd	53' 10.25"
	Wilma Rudolph	100 M Dash	1st	11
	Wilma Rudolph	200 M Dash	1st	24
	Martha Judson	400 M Relay	3rd	44.5
	Lucinda Williams	400 M Relay	3rd	44.5
	Barbara Jones	400 M Relay	3rd	44.5
	Wilma Rudolph	400 M Relay	3rd	44.5
Tokyo, 1964	Robert Hayes	100 M Dash	1st	9.9
	Henry Carr	200 M Dash	1st	20.3
	Paul Drayton	200 M Dash	2nd	20.5
	Hayes Jones	110 M Hurdles	1st	13.6
	Robert Hayes	400 M Relay	1st	39
	Paul Drayton	400 M Relay	1st	39
	Richard Stebbins	400 M Relay	1st	39
	John Thomas	High Jump	2nd	7' 1.75"
	John Rambo	High Jump	3rd	7' 1"
	Ralph Boston	Long Jump	2nd	26' 4"
	Walt Hazzard	Men's Basketball	1st	
	Lucius Jackson	Men's Basketball	1st	
	Charles Brown	Boxing: Featherweight	3rd	
	Ronald Harris	Boxing: Lightweight	3rd	
	Joe Frazier	Boxing: Heavyweight	1st	
	Robert Carmody	Boxing: Flyweight	3rd	
	Wyomia Tyus	100 M Dash	1st	11.4
	Edith McGuire	100 M Dash	2nd	11.6
	Edith McGuire	200 M Dash	1st	23
	Wyomia Tyus	400 M Relay	2nd	43.9
	Edith McGuire	400 M Relay	2nd	43.9
	Willye White	400 M Relay	2nd	43.9
	Marilyn White	400 M Relay	2nd	43.9
Mexico City, 1968	Jim Hines	100 M Dash	1st	9.9
	Charles Greene	100 M Dash	3rd	10
	Tommie Smith	200 M Dash	1st	19.8
	John Carlos	200 M Dash	3rd	20
	Lee Evans	400 M Run	1st	43.8

Place/Year	Athlete	Event	Place	Time/Distance
	Larry James	400 M Run	2nd	43.9
	Ron Freeman	400 M Run	3rd	44.4
	Willie Davenport	110 M Hurdles	1st	13.3
	Ervin Hall	110 M Hurdles	2nd	13.4
	Jim Hines	400 M Relay	1st	38.2
	Charles Greene	400 M Relay	1st	38.2
	Mel Pender	400 M Relay	1st	38.2
	Ronnie Ray Smith	400 M Relay	1st	38.2
	Wyomia Tyus	400 M Relay	1st	42.8
	Barbara Ferrell	400 M Relay	1st	42.8
	Margaret Bailes	400 M Relay	1st	42.8
	Mildrette Netter	400 M Relay	1st	42.8
	Lee Evans	1600 M Relay	1st	2:56.1
	Vince Matthews	1600 M Relay	1st	2:56.1
	Ron Freeman	1600 M Relay	1st	2:56.1
	Larry James	1600 M Relay	1st	2:56.1
	Edward Caruthers	High Jump	2nd	7' 3.5"
	Bob Beamon	Long Jump	1st	29' 2.5"
	Ralph Boston	Long Jump	3rd	26' 9.25"
	Spencer Haywood	Men's Basketball	1st	
	Charlie Scott	Men's Basketball	1st	
	Michael Barrett	Men's Basketball	1st	
	James King	Men's Basketball	1st	
	Calvin Fowler	Men's Basketball	1st	
	John Baldwin	Boxing: Light Middleweight	3rd	
	Alfred Jones	Boxing: Middleweight	3rd	
	Albert Robinson	Boxing: Featherweight	2nd	
	Ronald Harris	Boxing: Lightweight	1st	
	James Wallington	Boxing: Light Welterweight	3rd	
	George Foreman	Boxing: Heavyweight	1st	
	Wyomia Tyus	100 M Dash	1st	11
	Barbara Ferrell	100 M Dash	2nd	11.1
	Madeline Manning	800 M Run	1st	2:00.9
Munich, 1972	Robert Taylor	100 M Dash	2nd	10.24
	Larry Black	200 M Dash	2nd	20.19
	Vince Matthews	400 M Run	1st	44.66
	Wayne Collett	400 M Run	2nd	44.80
	Rod Milburn	110 M Hurdles	1st	13.24
	Eddie Hart	400 M Relay	1st	38.19
	Robert Taylor	400 M Relay	1st	38.19
	Larry Black	400 M Relay	1st	38.19
	Gerald Tinker	400 M Relay	1st	38.19
	Randy Williams	Long Jump	1st	27' .25"
	Arnie Robinson	Long Jump	3rd	26' 4"
	Jeff Bennet	Decathlon	3rd	7,974 pts.
	Wayne Collett	400 M Dash	2nd	44.80
	Marvin Johnson	Boxing: Middleweight	3rd	
	Ray Seales	Boxing: Light Welterweight	1st	
	Cheryl Toussain	1600 M Relay	2nd	3:25.2
	Mable Fergerson	1600 M Relay	2nd	3:25.2
	Madeline Manning	1600 M Relay	2nd	3:25.2
Montreal, 1976	Millard Hampton	200 M Dash	2nd	20.29
	Dwayne Evans	200 M Dash	3rd	20.43
	Fred Newhouse	400 M Run	2nd	44.40
	Herman Frazier	400 M Run	3rd	44.95
	Willie Davenport	110 M Hurdles	3rd	13.38
	Edwin Moses	400 M Hurdles	1st	47.64
	Millard Hampton	400 M Relay	1st	38.83
	Steve Riddick	400 M Relay	1st	38.83
	Harvey Glance	400 M Relay	1st	38.83
	John Jones	400 M Relay	1st	38.83
	Herman Frazier	1600 M Relay	1st	2:58.7

Place/Year	Athlete	Event	Place	Time/Distance
	Benny Brown	1600 M Relay	1st	2:58.7
	Maxie Parks	1600 M Relay	1st	2:58.7
	Fred Newhouse	1600 M Relay	1st	2:58.7
	Arnie Robinson	Long Jump	1st	27′ 4.75″
	Randy Williams	Long Jump	2nd	26′ 7.25″
	James Butts	Triple Jump	2nd	56 8.5″
	Phil Ford	Men's Basketball	1st	
	Adrian Dantley	Men's Basketball	1st	
	Walter Davis	Men's Basketball	1st	
	Quinn Buckner	Men's Basketball	1st	
	Kenneth Carr	Men's Basketball	1st	
	Scott May	Men's Basketball	1st	
	Philip Hubbard	Men's Basketball	1st	
	Johnny Tate	Boxing: Heavyweight	3rd	
	Leo Randolph	Boxing: Flyweight	1st	
	Howard David	Boxing: Lightweight	1st	
	Sugar Ray Leonard	Boxing: Light Welterweight	1st	
	Michael Spinks	Boxing: Middleweight	1st	
	Leon Spinks	Boxing: Light Heavyweight	1st	
	Rosalyn Bryant	1600 M Relay	2nd	3:22.8
	Shelia Ingram	1600 M Relay	2nd	3:22.8
	Pamela Jiles	1600 M Relay	2nd	3:22.8
	Debra Sapenter	1600 M Relay	2nd	3:22.8
	Lusia Harris	Women's Basketball	2nd	
	Charlotte Lewis	Women's Basketball	2nd	
Los Angeles, 1984	Carl Lewis	100 M Dash	1st	9.9
	Sam Graddy	100 M Dash	2nd	10.19
	Carl Lewis	200 M Dash	1st	19.80
	Kirk Baptiste	200 M Dash	2nd	19.96
	Alonzo Babers	400 M Run	1st	44.27
	Antonio McKay	400 M Run	3rd	44.71
	Earl Jones	800 M Run	3rd	1:43.83
	Roger Kingdom	110 M Hurdles	1st	13.20
	Greg Foster	110 M Hurdles	2nd	13.23
	Edwin Moses	400 M Hurdles	1st	47.75
	Danny Harris	400 M Hurdles	2nd	48.13
	Sam Graddy	400 M Relay	1st	37.83
	Ron Brown	400 M Relay	1st	37.83
	Calvin Smith	400 M Relay	1st	37.83
	Carl Lewis	400 M Relay	1st	37.83
	Sunder Nix	1600 M Relay	1st	2:57.91
	Roy Armstead	1600 M Relay	1st	2:57.91
	Alonzo Babers	1600 M Relay	1st	2:57.91
	Antonio McKay	1600 M Relay	1st	2:57.91
	Michael Carter	Shot Put	1st	21.09 m
	Carl Lewis	Long Jump	1st	8.54 m
	Al Joyner	Triple Jump	1st	17.26 m
	Mike Conley	Triple Jump	2nd	17.18 m
	Evelyn Ashford	100 M Dash	1st	10.97
	Alice Brown	100 M Dash	2nd	11.13
	Valerie Brisco-Hooks	200 M Dash	1st	21.81
	Florence Griffith	200 M Dash	2nd	22.04
	Valerie Brisco-Hooks	400 M Run	1st	48.83
	Chandra Cheeseborough	400 M Run	2nd	49.05
	Kim Gallagher	800 M Run	2nd	1:58.63
	Benita Fitzgerald-Brown	100 M Hurdles	1st	12.84
	Kim Turner	100 M Hurdles	2nd	12.88
	Judi Brown	400 M Hurdles	2nd	55.20
	Valerie Brisco-Hooks	1600 M Relay	1st	3:18.29
	Chandra Cheeseborough	1600 M Relay	1st	3:18.29
	Lillie Leatherwood	1600 M Relay	1st	3:18.29
	Sherri Howard	1600 M Relay	1st	3:18.29

Place/Year	Athlete	Event	Place	Time/Distance
	Jackie Joyner	Heptathlon	2nd	6,386 pts.
	Tyrell Biggs	Boxing: Super Heavyweight	1st	
	Henry Tillman	Boxing: Heavyweight	1st	
	Frank Tate	Boxing: Light Middleweight	1st	
	Virgil Hill	Boxing: Middleweight	2nd	
	Evander Holyfield	Boxing: Light Heavyweight	3rd	
	Steven McCrory	Boxing: Flyweight	1st	
	Meldrick Taylor	Boxing: Featherweight	1st	
	Pernell Whitaker	Boxing: Lightweight	1st	
	Jerry Page	Boxing: Light Welterweight	1st	
	Mark Breland	Boxing: Welterweight	1st	
	Patrick Ewing	Men's Basketball	1st	
	Vern Fleming	Men's Basketball	1st	
	Michael Jordan	Men's Basketball	1st	
	Sam Perkins	Men's Basketball	1st	
	Alvin Robertson	Men's Basketball	1st	
	Wayman Tisdale	Men's Basketball	1st	
	Leon Wood	Men's Basketball	1st	
	Cathy Boswell	Women's Basketball	1st	
	Teresa Edwards	Women's Basketball	1st	
	Janice Lawrence	Women's Basketball	1st	
	Pamela McGee	Women's Basketball	1st	
	Cheryl Miller	Women's Basketball	1st	
	Lynette Woodard	Women's Basketball	1st	
Seoul, 1988	Carl Lewis	100 M Dash	1st	9.92
	Calvin Smith	100 M Dash	2nd	9.99
	Joe DeLoach	200 M Dash	1st	19.75
	Carl Lewis	200 M Dash	2nd	19.79
	Steve Lewis	400 M Run	1st	43.87
	Butch Reynolds	400 M Run	2nd	43.93
	Danny Everett	400 M Run	3rd	44.09
	Roger Kingdom	110 M Hurdles	1st	12.98
	Tonie Campbell	110 M Hurdles	3rd	13.38
	Andre Phillips	400 M Hurdles	1st	47.19
	Edwin Moses	400 M Hurdles	3rd	47.56
	Butch Reynolds	1600 M Relay	1st	2:56.16
	Steve Lewis	1600 M Relay	1st	2:56.16
	Antonio McKay	1600 M Relay	1st	2:56.16
	Danny Everett	1600 M Relay	1st	2:56.16
	Carl Lewis	Long Jump	1st	8.72 m
	Mike Powell	Long Jump	2nd	8.49 m
	Larry Myricks	Long Jump	3rd	8.27 m
	Florence Griffith-Joyner	100 M Dash	1st	10.54
	Evelyn Ashford	100 M Dash	2nd	10.83
	Florence Griffith-Joyner	200 M Dash	1st	21.34
	Shelia Echols	400 M Relay	1st	41.98
	Florence Griffith-Joyner	400 M Relay	1st	41.98
	Evelyn Ashford	400 M Relay	1st	41.98
	Alice Brown	400 M Relay	1st	41.98
	Jackie Joyner-Kersee	Long Jump	1st	24' 3.5"
	Jackie Joyner-Kersee	Heptathlon	1st	7,291 pts.
	Denean Howard-Hill	1600 M Relay	2nd	3:15.51
	Valerie Brisco	1600 M Relay	2nd	3:15.51
	Diane Dixon	1600 M Relay	2nd	3:15.51
	Florence Griffith-Joyner	1600 M Relay	2nd	3:15.51
	Kim Gallagher	800 M Run	3rd	1:56.91
	Andrew Maynard	Boxing: Light Heavyweight	1st	
	Ray Mercer	Boxing: Heavyweight	1st	
	Kennedy McKinney	Boxing: Bantamweight	1st	
	Riddick Bowe	Boxing: Super Heavyweight	2nd	
	Roy Jones	Boxing: Middleweight	2nd	
	Kenny Monday	Wrestling: Freestyle	1st	

Place/Year	Athlete	Event	Place	Time/Distance
	Nate Carr	Wrestling: Freestyle	3rd	
	Zina Garrison	Tennis: Doubles	1st	
	Zina Garrison	Tennis: Singles	3rd	
	Tom Goodwin	Baseball	1st	
	Ty Griffin	Baseball	1st	
	Cindy Brown	Women's Basketball	1st	
	Vicky Bullett	Women's Basketball	1st	
	Cynthia Cooper	Women's Basketball	1st	
	Teresa Edwards	Women's Basketball	1st	
	Jennifer Gillom	Women's Basketball	1st	
	Bridgette Gordon	Women's Basketball	1st	
	Katrina McClain	Women's Basketball	1st	
	Teresa Weatherspoon	Women's Basketball	1st	
	Willie Anderson	Men's Basketball	3rd	
	Stacey Augmon	Men's Basketball	3rd	
	Bimbo Coles	Men's Basketball	3rd	
	Jeff Grayer	Men's Basketball	3rd	
	Hersey Hawkins	Men's Basketball	3rd	
	Danny Manning	Men's Basketball	3rd	
	J.R. Reid	Men's Basketball	3rd	
	Mitch Richmond	Men's Basketball	3rd	
	David Robinson	Men's Basketball	3rd	
	Charles D. Smith	Men's Basketball	3rd	
	Charles E. Smith	Men's Basketball	3rd	
Barcelona, 1992	Dennis Mitchell	100 M Dash	3rd	10.04
	Gail Devers	100 M Dash	1st	10.82
	Mike Marsh	200 M Dash	1st	20.01
	Michael Bates	200 M Dash	3rd	20.38
	Gwen Torrence	200 M Dash	1st	21.81
	Quincy Watts	400 M Run	1st	43.50
	Steve Lewis	400 M Run	2nd	44.21
	Johnny Gray	800 M Run	3rd	1:43.97
	Mike Marsh	400 M Relay	1st	37.40
	Leroy Burrell	400 M Relay	1st	37.40
	Dennis Mitchell	400 M Relay	1st	37.40
	Carl Lewis	400 M Relay	1st	37.40
	Evelyn Ashford	400 M Relay	1st	42.11
	Esther Jones	400 M Relay	1st	42.11
	Carlette Guidry-White	400 M Relay	1st	42.11
	Gwen Torrence	400 M Relay	1st	42.11
	Tony Dees	110 M Hurdles	2nd	13.24
	Kevin Young	400 M Hurdles	1st	46.78
	Sandra Farmer	400 M Hurdles	2nd	53.69
	Janeene Vickers	400 M Hurdles	3rd	54.31
	Andrew Valmon	800 M Relay	1st	2:55.74
	Quincy Watts	800 M Relay	1st	2:55.74
	Michael Johnson	800 M Relay	1st	2:55.74
	Steve Lewis	800 M Relay	1st	2:55.74
	Natasha Kaiser	800 M Relay	2nd	3:20.92
	Gwen Torrence	800 M Relay	2nd	3:20.92
	Jearl Miles	800 M Relay	2nd	3:20.92
	Rochelle Stevens	800 M Relay	2nd	3:20.92
	Hollis Conway	High Jump	3rd	7′ 8″
	Carl Lewis	Long Jump	1st	28′ 5.5″
	Mike Powell	Long Jump	2nd	28′ 4.25″
	Joe Greene	Long Jump	3rd	27′ 4.5″
	Jackie Joyner-Kersee	Long Jump	3rd	23′ 2.5″
	Mike Conley	Triple Jump	1st	59′ 7.5″
	Charlie Simpkins	Triple Jump	2nd	57′ 9″
	Jackie Joyner-Kersee	Heptathlon	1st	7,044 pts.
	Tim Austin	Boxing: Flyweight	3rd	
	Chris Byrd	Boxing: Middleweight	2nd	

Place/Year	Athlete	Event	Place	Time/Distance
	Kevin Jackson	Wrestling: Middleweight	1st	
	Charles Barkley	Men's Basketball	1st	
	Clyde Drexler	Men's Basketball	1st	
	Patrick Ewing	Men's Basketball	1st	
	Magic Johnson	Men's Basketball	1st	
	Michael Jordan	Men's Basketball	1st	
	Karl Malone	Men's Basketball	1st	
	Scottie Pippen	Men's Basketball	1st	
	David Robinson	Men's Basketball	1st	
	Vicky Bullett	Women's Basketball	3rd	
	Daedra Charles	Women's Basketball	3rd	
	Cynthia Cooper	Women's Basketball	3rd	
	Teresa Edwards	Women's Basketball	3rd	
	Carolyn Jones	Women's Basketball	3rd	
	Katrina McClain	Women's Basketball	3rd	
	Vickie Orr	Women's Basketball	3rd	
	Teresa Weatherspoon	Women's Basketball	3rd	
Atlanta, 1996	Dominique Dawes	Gymnastics: Floor Exercise	3rd	
	Dominique Dawes	Gymnastics: Team	1st	
	Michael Johnson	200 M Dash	1st	19.32
	Michael Johnson	400 M Run	1st	43.49
	Allen Johnson	110 M Hurdles	1st	12.95
	Mark Crear	110 M Hurdles	2nd	13.09
	Derrick Adkins	400 M Hurdles	1st	47.54
	Calvin Davis	400 M Hurdles	3rd	47.96
	Tim Harden	400 M Relay	2nd	38.05
	Jon Drummond	400 M Relay	2nd	38.05
	Michael Marsh	400 M Relay	2nd	38.05
	Dennis Mitchell	400 M Relay	2nd	38.05
	LaMont Smith	1600 M Relay	1st	2:55.99
	Alvin Harrison	1600 M Relay	1st	2:55.99
	Derek Mills	1600 M Relay	1st	2:55.99
	Anthuan Maybank	1600 M Relay	1st	2:55.99
	Dan O'Brien	Decathlon	1st	8,824 pts.
	Charles Austin	High Jump	1st	7' 10"
	Carl Lewis	Long Jump	1st	27' 10.75"
	Joe Greene	Long Jump	3rd	27' .50"
	Kenny Harrison	Triple Jump	1st	59' 4"
	Gail Devers	100 M Dash	1st	10.94
	Gwen Torrence	100 M Dash	3rd	10.96
	Kim Batten	400 M Hurdles	2nd	53.08
	Tonja Buford-Bailey	400 M Hurdles	3rd	53.22
	Gail Devers	400 M Relay	1st	41.95
	Chryste Gaines	400 M Relay	1st	41.95
	Gwen Torrence	400 M Relay	1st	41.95
	Inger Miller	400 M Relay	1st	41.95
	Rochelle Stevens	1600 M Relay	1st	3:20.91
	Maicel Malone	1600 M Relay	1st	3:20.91
	Kim Graham	1600 M Relay	1st	3:20.91
	Jearl Miles	1600 M Relay	1st	3:20.91
	Jackie Joyner-Kersee	Long Jump	3rd	22' 11"
	Floyd Mayweather	Boxing: Featherweight	3rd	
	Terrance Cauthen	Boxing: Lightweight	3rd	
	Rhoshii Wells	Boxing: Middleweight	3rd	
	Antonio Tarver	Boxing: Light Heavyweight	3rd	
	Nate Jones	Boxing: Heavyweight	3rd	
	David Reid	Boxing: Light Middleweight	1st	
	Teresa Edwards	Women's Basketball	1st	
	Ruth Bolton	Women's Basketball	1st	
	Lisa Leslie	Women's Basketball	1st	
	Katrina McClain	Women's Basketball	1st	
	Sheryl Swoopes	Women's Basketball	1st	

Place/Year	Athlete	Event	Place	Time/Distance
	Nikki McCray	Women's Basketball	1st	
	Dawn Staley	Women's Basketball	1st	
	Venus Lacey	Women's Basketball	1st	
	Carla McGhee	Women's Basketball	1st	
	Mitch Richmond	Men's Basketball	1st	
	Scottie Pippin	Men's Basketball	1st	
	Gary Payton	Men's Basketball	1st	
	Charles Barkley	Men's Basketball	1st	
	Hakeem Olajuwon	Men's Basketball	1st	
	David Robinson	Men's Basketball	1st	
	Penny Hardaway	Men's Basketball	1st	
	Grant Hill	Men's Basketball	1st	
	Karl Malone	Men's Basketball	1st	
	Reggie Miller	Men's Basketball	1st	
	Jacque Jones	Baseball	3rd	

Index

Personal names, place names, events, organizations, and various subject areas or keywords contained in the *Reference Library of Black America* are listed in this index with corresponding volume and page numbers indicating text references. Page numbers appearing in boldface indicate major treatments of topics, such as biographical profiles and organizational entries. Page numbers appearing in italics refer to photographs, illustrations, and maps found throughout the reference work.

O